BIG BUCKS
&
BLUE PUCKS

Murray Greig

Macmillan Canada
Toronto

Copyright © Murray Greig, 1997

All rights reserved. The use of any part of this publication reproduced, transmitted in any form or by any means, electronic, mechanical, recording or otherwise, or stored in a retrieval system, without the prior consent of the publisher, is an infringement of the copyright law. In the case of photocopying or other reprographic copying of the material, a licence must be obtained from the Canadian Copyright Licensing Agency (CANCOPY) before proceeding.

Canadian Cataloguing in Publication Data

Greig, Murray
Big bucks and blue pucks : from Hull to Gretzky, an anecdotal history of the late, great World Hockey Association

Includes index.
ISBN 0-7715-7423-1

1. World Hockey Association – History. I. Title.
GV847.8.W67M87 1997 796.96264 C97-931146-2

This book is available at special discounts for bulk purchases by your group or organization for sales promotions, premiums, fundraising and seminars. For details, contact: Macmillan Canada, Special Sales Department, 29 Birch Avenue, Toronto, ON M4V 1E2. Tel: 416-963-8830.

Cover and interior design: Dennis Boyes
Typesetting: Archetype

Macmillan Canada
A Division of Canada Publishing Corporation
Toronto, Ontario, Canada

1 2 3 4 5 TRI 01 00 99 98 97

Printed in Canada

CONTENTS

ACKNOWLEDGEMENTS *v*

WARM-UP *1*

Part 1 **THE GAME OF THEIR LIVES** *5*

Part 2 **SUPERSTARS & PLUGGERS** *29*

Part 3 **POSTGAME INTERVIEWS** *59*

Part 4 **OVERTIME** *147*

Part 5 **MINUTIAE FROM THE WHA** *219*

ACKNOWLEDGEMENTS

This project would not have been possible without the patience and cooperation of the dozens of former WHA players and executives I interviewed. To a man, they were helpful and encouraging. Special thanks to: Ralph Backstrom, Ken Brown, Wayne Carleton, Joe Daley, Val Fonteyne, Derek Haas, Al Hamilton, Jim Harrison, Gordie Howe, Frank Hughes, Bill Hunter, Andre Lacroix, Mike Laughton, Danny Lawson, Larry Lund, Dennis Murphy, Rusty Patenaude, Gerry Pinder, Pat Price, Garth Rizzuto, Paul Shmyr, Pat Stapleton, Ron Ward and Bobby Whitlock. Also a hearty thanks to the many journalists who covered the WHA for publications such as *The Hockey News* and *Hockey Spectator,* and to Joe Altomare of Penticton, B.C., for providing access to his impressive collection of back issues of *The Hockey News*.

Permission to use information for the all-time WHA player registry was graciously granted by Scott Adam Surgent, author and publisher of the superb *Complete Historical and Statistical Reference to the World Hockey Association* (c. 1995, Xaler Press, Tempe, Arizona). Permission to reproduce photographs of the author's collection of WHA bubblegum cards was graciously granted by the O-Pee-Chee Company Limited of London, Ontario. All logos portrayed remain the property of their respective rights holders.

I would also like to thank the Canada Council for supporting this project, and Nicole de Montbrun at Macmillan Canada who was a constant source of encouragement and editorial expertise. Finally, thanks to my wife, Judy, and son, Danny, for putting up with all the cigar smoke while it was being written.

WARM-UP

They laughed at the red and blue pucks. Chortled about the championship trophy being named for a finance company. And guffawed at the motley collection of players perceived as grossly inferior to their own.

Indeed, whenever the National Hockey League deigned to acknowledge the birth of the World Hockey Association in 1972, it was with a patronizing smugness. After all, the NHL had enjoyed a monopoly on major league hockey for more than six decades and was about to embark on an ambitious expansion program unrivalled in the annals of professional sports. How could this new venture—cooked up by a couple of *Californians,* no less—be anything more than a mere annoyance?

They were about to find out.

From 1972 to 1979 the renegade league that started off as a mere annoyance grew into a Zamboni-sized thorn in the NHL's side. Besides routinely raiding the rival league's rosters, the WHA clubs trolled the minor league backwaters for untapped talent and made a practice of offering ludicrously high contracts to untried prospects culled from Canada's vast junior hockey system. The result was a war of attrition that triggered a 400 percent rise in the average hockey salary and left both major leagues reeling on the brink of insolvency.

Derek Sanderson became the poster boy of the high-priced lunacy. Signed to a $2.35 million contract by the Philadelphia Blazers, Sanderson decided he'd had enough of the WHA after only eight games. The Blazers then gave him a $1 million settlement to return to the NHL's Boston Bruins.

In 1972 the WHA clubs banded together to lure superstar Bobby Hull from the Chicago Black Hawks. A year later the Houston Aeros coaxed the immortal Gordie Howe out of a two-year retirement to play alongside his teenaged sons. Players like Andre Lacroix, Danny Lawson and Ron Ward—no more than talented journeymen in their NHL days—suddenly emerged as high-scoring superstars, piling up points for colourfully named teams such as the New York Golden Blades, Calgary Cowboys and Cleveland Crusaders.

A losing series against the Soviet Nationals in 1974 did nearly as much to enhance the WHA's credibility as the Winnipeg Jets' theft of Hull from Chicago. Sure, the WHA's version of Team Canada lost to the big, bad Bolsheviks, but how could we not love a team that included a 46-year-old grandfather (Howe) and a back-up goaltender (Gilles Gratton) who blamed recurring abdominal pain on a lance wound he said he had suffered in a previous life during the Spanish Inquisition?

Through its seven-year existence the WHA attracted an amazing cast of colourful characters, both on and off the ice. There was Gary Davidson, the league's first president, who conceived the brilliant idea of using fluorescent red pucks "so they would show up better on television." The league later switched to bright blue pucks, with equally laughable results. There was Wild Bill Hunter, who drafted six Russians for the original Alberta Oilers "because you have to figure that sooner or later the whole damn national team might defect." Then there was Johnny Bassett, flamboyant owner of the Toronto Toros and the Birmingham Bulls, who once toyed with the idea of signing motorcycle daredevil Evel Knievel to a five-game tryout contract.

The superstars—Hull, Howe, Gerry Cheevers, J.C. Tremblay—were all household names by the time they jumped to the WHA, but the league created many more of its own. Robbie Ftorek, Dennis Sobchuk, Real Cloutier and a kid by the name of Wayne Gretzky were some of the young guns who

Jeff Carlson (left), Dave Hanson and Steve Carlson all saw action in the World Hockey Association after starring as the overly rambunctious Hanson Brothers in the movie *Slap Shot*. Hanson and Carlson later played in the National Hockey League. For more on the WHA's connection to *Slap Shot*, see Part 5. (AUTHOR'S COLLECTION)

made their professional debuts playing for the Phoenix Roadrunners, Cincinnati Stingers, Quebec Nordiques and Indianapolis Racers.

Others earned headlines for more unorthodox reasons. Frank (Seldom) Beaton of the Birmingham Bulls was arrested on an outstanding warrant in Cincinnati after he tried to avoid the cops by sneaking off the ice with the hometown Stingers. Steve and Jeff Carlson, a brother act from the Minnesota Fighting Saints, hooked up with future Birmingham bad guy Dave Hanson to portray the brawling Hanson Brothers alongside Paul Newman in the movie *Slap Shot*. And what devoted WHA fan can forget the scowling visage of Andy Brown, major league hockey's last maskless goaltender? Brown played a total of 86 games for the Indianapolis Racers and set the league's single-season record for penalty minutes by a goalie, with 75.

This book is the product of a 25-year fascination with the World Hockey Association and the pioneers who started it all. Like almost everything else from that era—fuzzy dice, the Village People, pet rocks—it's become popular to dismiss the WHA as an aberration that had no impact beyond its mere existence. I didn't believe that 25 years ago when I bought my Frank Mahovlich replica Toronto Toros jersey, and I don't believe it today.

The WHA represents a significant slice of hockey history from the past quarter century, and on the following pages, scattered among the statistics and trivia, several of the men who helped launch the league recall their hopes and fears in pioneering a new era in professional sports. I hope you enjoy their stories as much as I did.

MURRAY GREIG
March 1997
Trail, B.C.

Part 1
THE GAME OF THEIR LIVES
Bill Hunter, Dennis Murphy and Red-Letter Dates in WHA History

Jim Harrison (left) and Paul Shmyr of the Cleveland Crusaders put the crunch on Rick Cunningham of the Toronto Toros. (CANADA WIDE PHOTOS)

According to the history records, the World Hockey Association (WHA) was officially created when Articles of Incorporation were filed in a Delaware courthouse on June 10, 1971. But in actual fact, the seed that eventually blossomed into professional hockey's second major league — and by far the most serious threat ever to the National Hockey League's monopoly — was planted back in 1917, when the NHL's founding fathers made the perpetual "reserve clause" part of the standard player contract.

The clause essentially bound a player to his team for life by allowing the club to renew the contract (upon expiry) without the player's permission. In one form or another the reserve clause had been used by professional baseball since the 1880s, and it would continue to be a fixture in player contracts for baseball, hockey, basketball and football for decades.

The effect of the reserve clause was twofold. Since the movement of players between teams was completely at the discretion of management, average salaries could be rigidly controlled. Once a player was signed, teams could also invoke the clause at any time during future contract talks, making it impossible for a player to ever gain "free agent" status. In standard NHL contracts, the reserve clause also stipulated that the league president would be the sole arbitrator of any salary disputes between the player and management. Since the league president was an employee of the club owners, it wasn't hard to guess which side could usually count on his support.

It took two Californians, Dennis Murphy and Gary Davidson, to exploit the first crack in the seemingly invincible reserve clause when they formed the American Basketball Association (ABA) in 1967. By banning the clause from standard ABA contracts, Murphy and Davidson created a competitive market for pro basketball talent. Players in the established National Basketball Association suddenly had some negotiating leverage. If they weren't happy with what their NBA club was offering, they could jump to the ABA for better money.

For an idea so deceptively simple, it had a devastating impact. Within two years of the founding of the ABA, basketball players went from being among the lowest-paid professional athletes to being the highest-paid. The NBA had no choice but to more than triple its average base salary, and a short time later it dropped the reserve clause altogether. The ABA soldiered on for a few more seasons before the rebel league's most successful franchises were absorbed into the NBA.

Murphy and Davidson were convinced they could pull off the same trick with hockey, even though neither of them knew anything about the game. Davidson, a graduate of the school of law at the University of California at

Los Angeles, was a number cruncher who loved sports almost as much as he loved a good legal fight. He'd lettered in baseball, football, basketball and track in high school, and as co-founder of the ABA had become well versed in the nuances of sports law. Murphy, an affable Irishman, was the salesman. Once mayor of Buena Park, California (population 70,000), he had a born-promoter's instincts for knowing which buttons to push when putting the squeeze on potential investors.

W.D. "Wild Bill" Hunter, founder of the Western Canada Junior Hockey League, was the man behind bringing the World Hockey Association to Edmonton in 1972. Originally known as the Alberta Oilers, the club was one of four former WHA teams to merge with the National Hockey League in 1979. (PHOTO CREDIT: PROVINCIAL ARCHIVES OF ALBERTA)

"I'd followed some of what the National Hockey League had been doing as far as limiting its expansion to certain preferred markets and keeping its doors closed to people who wanted to get involved," Murphy recalled in 1997. "Some of the people who had been rebuffed by the NHL were old acquaintances from our basketball days. It looked like the timing was right to try something new. I called Gary up one day in early 1971 and told him I thought the NHL had been living in its own little world for too long. It was time to shake 'em up. Being a lawyer, he wanted to know more details, but I didn't really have any. I just figured it was time to take on the NHL. We'd worry about the details later.

"The first problem we had was that neither Gary nor I knew the first thing about hockey. But a Canadian friend of mine named Walt Marlow, a sportswriter in Los Angeles, said he could put us in touch with a fellow named Bill Hunter up in Alberta. Gary and I were bright enough to realize it would take some Canadians to get our idea off the ground, so I asked Walt to make the call."

W.D. "Wild Bill" Hunter was a genuine Canadian sports legend in the spring of 1971. Born in Saskatoon, Saskatchewan, he'd been an air force pilot, a sporting goods dealer, a magazine publisher and a radio broadcaster prior to launching a long and lucrative career in hockey management. He was a former general manager (GM) and coach of the Saskatoon Quakers in the old Western Hockey League (WHL) and had owned both the Regina Capitals (senior) and the Medicine Hat Tigers (junior) before founding the Western Canada Major Junior Hockey League (now the WHL), the largest amateur loop on the planet. Hunter was owner, president and general manager of that league's Edmonton Oil Kings when Marlow first contacted him on behalf of Murphy and Davidson, and he immediately recognized the WHA's long-term potential.

"I'd known Walt for several years, and though I'd never heard of the WHA I was excited about it because Walt seemed to be," Hunter recalled in 1996. "Within a few days I flew down to Anaheim, and Murphy picked Walt and me up at the airport and drove us to Davidson's place, where we sat around the pool and discussed their ideas for a new league. It didn't take very long before I realized these guys didn't know a damn thing about hockey. It was ludicrous. I arranged to take Murphy, Davidson and Don Regan, who was Davidson's partner, to a Los Angeles Kings game that night. When the referee went to drop the puck for the opening faceoff, Davidson turned to me with a puzzled look on its face and said, 'What are they doing?' I knew at that moment we had a lot of work ahead of us."

Hunter returned to Edmonton intrigued enough by the concept that he contacted long-time cronies Ben Hatskin in Winnipeg and Bob Brownridge in Calgary. Hatskin, a former centre with the Winnipeg Blue Bombers in the Canadian Football League, had built a vast business empire and was president and owner of the Winnipeg entry in the old WHL. Brownridge, a self-made oil magnate, had played hockey for the 1945–46 Allan Cup champion Calgary Stampeders and cofounded, along with Scotty Munro, the Calgary Centennials junior team. Hatskin and Brownridge agreed to accompany Hunter to an organizational meeting in Los Angeles in late September 1971.

"It was a total joke," recalled Hunter. "It was supposed to be a meeting of potential franchise owners, but it turned out to be a bunch of Murphy's old political pals and hangers-on whom Dennis and Gary had known from the ABA. I almost had to wrestle Ben and Bob into staying down there for the weekend, but by the time it was over we'd weeded out most of the phonies. Then Ben gave everybody who was left an ultimatum. He said that unless I was put in charge of putting together the league, he was gone. Well, everybody in the room knew what kind of businessman Benny Hatskin was, and they respected both his bank account and his confidence in me. That's how I got the green light to start building the WHA."

In the early stages there was more bull than building. Hunter and Murphy hit the road for the better part of 11 months, dangling the WHA carrot in front of potential investors and cajoling prospective owners with promises of major league exposure.

"It was a pretty simple formula," chuckled Murphy. "We appealed to the small-town, big-money egomaniacs... men who simply couldn't resist owning their own professional sports teams. Our original franchise fee was only $25,000, and back then there were lots of guys who had become millionaires by making widgets in Omaha, but nobody knew about 'em except their bankers and their pals down at the country club. But with a sports franchise they would have their names in the paper in L.A. and Chicago and New York.

"Bill and I would hit these smaller cities and then phone up a lawyer or an accountant and ask if he knew anybody in town who might be interested in buying a team. Within a day or two we'd have a half-dozen meetings set up, and then I'd make our pitch. I'd ask 'em: 'Would you rather be known as a guy who owns a hockey team in Detroit, or a guy who manufacturers brassieres in Muskegon?' It was a pretty good line, and they took the bait just about every time."

While Murphy and Hunter were beating the bushes looking for cash, Davidson was putting his legal expertise to work. No doubt recalling the headlines he and Murphy had garnered when they struck the reserve clause from the standard contract in the ABA, on October 20, 1971, he sat down in his California office and wrote the following news release:

The World Hockey Association plans to operate without a reserve clause or any substitute for the reserve clause, such as an option clause, in its players' contracts. This innovative decision, which the WHA feels should and will revolutionize professional sports, is based on the conclusion that the reserve clause as used today will not long withstand the scrutiny focused on it by players, players' associations, the United

States Congress, the public and the Supreme Court. By abolishing the reserve clause altogether, the WHA is setting a trend that all of professional sports must inevitably follow.

The reserve clause is a particular provision in a player contract that binds that player to sign with the same team year after year after year, with only the salary being negotiable. In theory, this clause was designed to serve as an equalizer among teams in a professional league and to prevent the best-financed franchise from cornering most of the top talent and thereby dominating the league. In practice, however, the reserve clause has not achieved this result. Instead, because it is in direct opposition to the principle of freedom of choice, it has served more as an obvious affront to individual rights and dignity than as a credit to professional sports.

A highly competitive and well-balanced league, which is sadly lacking in major professional hockey today, can be achieved without the use of the reserve clause. Thus, the WHA will soon conduct a universal draft among professional, semiprofessional, college, junior, amateur and European hockey players. In the event that a player chosen is unable to reach agreement on a contract with the team drafting him, he has the right to take his dispute to arbitration. The arbitration process will operate uniformly and fairly, and, in the event of a final impasse, will result in placing the player involved into a special draft pool which will enable him to play for another team in the league.

Response was immediate. NHL president Clarence Campbell said: "We don't have to worry about that because in the unlikely event the WHA gets off the ground it won't last until Christmas." The media were equally skeptical. A columnist for a major Canadian daily labelled the WHA's bold move "asinine in the extreme," while another went so far as to predict: "Without the reserve clause the WHA will die a merciful death long before it ever ices any teams."

Two weeks after Davidson's announcement, the WHA unveiled its ten charter franchises at a gala news conference in Manhattan.

"We didn't have 12 teams to announce, which was our goal, but we'd gotten to the point where I thought we should really make a public splash," said Hunter. "Dennis and I had criss-crossed North America from one side to the other, and there were all kinds of rumours flying around about what the league was planning or if it would even get off the ground. It was time to set the record straight.

"We had a media conference at the Americana Hotel in New York, and it broke every record for attendance. Every major television network from both the U.S. and Canada was there, along with reporters and columnists from all over the continent. I was serving as the league spokesman, and when it came time to announce our ten charter franchises, you could've cut the tension in that room with a knife. This was only a couple of weeks after Davidson had announced our league would operate without a reserve clause, and most people realized that meant the dawn of a new era in pro hockey. Everybody was really anxious to know where the teams would be located.

"Well, we had only three Canadian teams at that point—Edmonton, Calgary and Winnipeg—but I knew the Ontario group was close to getting financing and Quebec was interested, too. As it turned out, when Quebec got the San Francisco franchise a few months later, I personally guaranteed the franchise fee. In Western Canada we really wanted Quebec City to be part of the WHA from the start.

"The next big step, after announcing the teams, was to hold our first player draft. That happened in February 1972, and by that time we'd hired former NHL referee Vern Buffey. He was going to head up the WHA officials, but before that we put him to work organizing the draft in Anaheim. It turned out to be the biggest draft in the history of pro sports—more than a thousand players were selected over two days. To speed things along, Buffey set up a basketball clock with a 30-second timer. That's how long each team had to pick a player. That no doubt explains some of the "talent" we had in that first season!"

At the draft the Winnipeg Jets made Chicago Black Hawks' superstar Bobby Hull one of their four "priority picks." Jets' owner Ben Hatskin had already held preliminary talks with Hull and his financial adviser, Harvey Wineberg. Word had leaked out that the negotiations were "starting" at $1 million, which promoted a lot of smirks from those who doubted the WHA would ever see the light of day.

Hull and Wineberg, however, were not among the doubters. According to Hunter, the NHL's charismatic "Golden Jet" had already indicated his willingness to jump to the rebel league.

"Benny Hatskin was absolutely certain Bobby would come over," said Hunter. "They had had a secret meeting at the Hotel Vancouver when the Black Hawks were in town to play the Canucks, and Benny had offered him $1 million for five years. That's a figure that always got a lot of attention... especially in 1972. By the time the draft rolled around, they were talking $2 million. Benny was on the hook for $1 million in cash as a signing bonus, but he needed some help with the rest of the deal. Hull's contract with the Winnipeg Jets marked the first time in the history of pro sports that every member of a league chipped in to sign one player."

The historic event took place on June 27, 1972—a week after *Sports Illustrated* ran a cover photo of Hull in his Black Hawks' uniform under a headline reading: "The Man They Want to Steal!"

Too late, the Hawks realized the WHA was for real and offered Hull $1 million for five years. But by then Hatskin had written up a 40-page contract that included a signing bonus of $1 million cash and $250,000 per year for five years as a player or player-coach, followed by $100,000 per year for five years as a team executive. The other 11 WHA teams had each anted up more than $100,000 to pool with Hatskin's cash, and it was enough loot for the fledgling league to do the unthinkable.

"I have no regrets about leaving Chicago," Hull said at the time. "The whole thing has just made me wonder what the hell the Black Hawks were thinking. They must have thought I was bluffing, or they must have been gambling that the Jets' offer would fall through."

Hull's signing sent shock waves through the hockey establishment. Within weeks, dozens of NHLers followed. The New York Rangers reacted by signing their entire team to long-term contracts—the first salvo in a long war of attrition over salaries.

"Bobby Hull was the best player in the National Hockey League when he jumped to the Jets," said Hunter. "He might not have been the fastest or the strongest, but his enormous skills, combined with his charisma, made him by far the most desirable player for us to lure over. I remember the meeting in Chicago when it came time for the other teams to cough up the cash. Some of the American owners still didn't want to do it, so Benny and I filibustered for more than 12 hours to wear down their resolve. I told them, 'We don't want any cheques from you bastards, either; it's gotta be cash!' They couldn't believe that two guys from Winnipeg and Edmonton were talking to them like that, but after Bobby joined our league and they saw what a huge impact he had on gate receipts and the popularity of our product, these same guys were congratulating us."

There were other celebrated signings. The Philadelphia Blazers enticed flamboyant Derek Sanderson to leave the Boston Bruins for an estimated $2.35 million. The Blazers had started their WHA life as the Miami Screaming Eagles and made a big splash by signing Toronto Maple Leafs' goaltender Bernie Parent, but when the franchise was moved back to Philadelphia a few months later, a newspaper headline quipped, "Screaming Eagles Won't Fly!"

Parent wasn't the only goalie to defect. Gerry Cheevers, who backstopped the Bruins to the Stanley Cup in 1970 and 1972, bolted from Beantown and signed a million-dollar deal with the Cleveland Crusaders. Johnny McKenzie, another key member of Boston's Stanley Cup teams, followed Sanderson to the Blazers.

It was the beginning of a player exodus unprecedented in the annals of professional sport. Between July 1 and October 1, 1972, more than 100 players jumped from the NHL or from minor league teams that were owned by the NHL clubs. Lawsuits and countersuits became the order of the day as the WHA fought an uphill battle for players' rights. The Black Hawks got an injunction to prevent Hull from even practising with the Jets until the validity of the NHL's reserve clause could be tested in a court of law. On November 8 Judge Leon Higginbotham of the U.S. District Court for Eastern Pennsylvania issued a temporary retraining order barring the NHL from using the reserve clause to block players from jumping to the WHA. While it was not a ruling on the legality of the clause, Higginbotham's action served notice to the NHL that the reserve clause would probably be flushed down the legal toilet if it ever went to trial.

"Judge Higginbotham basically ruled that the days of slavery in pro sports were over; the WHA won a clear and decisive victory," said Hunter. "By ruling that Bobby could suit up for Winnipeg, Higginbotham had effectively struck down the reserve clause and proclaimed that, from that day forth, professional athletes had won their freedom. This move sent a message to the owners in every league to start treating their players with respect. In the WHA we looked at the ruling as the start of a partnership. We told our players, 'We'll pay you what you're worth, but each one of you has to be a salesman for the league.' It worked magnificently. All of our players were deeply involved . . . and that, too, is a credit to Bobby Hull."

Added Dennis Murphy: "The future of the WHA was sealed in that courtroom. Bobby *was* our league. We knew it, he knew it and the NHL knew it. When the court permitted him to play for the Jets, the NHL lost a very, very big battle in what was shaping up to be a long and bitter war. Bobby did more to make the World Hockey Association a success than anyone can imagine. In all my years in sports I've never met or been associated within a greater ambassador or a finer gentleman."

Hull's presence guaranteed the WHA's survival through that first tumultuous season, and when former NHL legend Gordie Howe came out of retirement to sign with the Houston Aeros in 1973–74, the league could boast of having the two greatest scorers in the history of major league hockey. The fact that Howe was also the first pro athlete to play on the same team as his sons made it even sweeter. The WHA scored another coup in February 1974, when it agreed to an out-of-court settlement of its $50 million restraint-of-trade lawsuit against the NHL. In what turned out to be the final nail in the coffin of pro hockey's reserve clause, the NHL agreed to pay the upstart league $1.7 million, plus legal costs, to drop the action.

In the fall of 1974 a team of WHA all-stars squared off against the Soviet Nationals in an eight-game series that attracted record television audiences

The Howes of Houston: Marty, Gordie and Mark.

in Canada. The WHA managed just one win and three ties, but the series proved to fans on both sides of the Atlantic that big-league hockey wasn't limited to the NHL.

"Being manager of Team Canada and taking part in the selection of the players and the organization of the training camp was the all-time highlight of my career in hockey," says Hunter. "And to this day I believe that team was the most talented to ever represent Canada in international competition. We had three of the greatest of all time in Hull, Howe and Frank Mahovlich. Our own version of the 'French Connection' with Serge Bernier, Marc Tardif and Rejean Houle, was one of the most potent units in the game. In goal we had the great Gerry Cheevers and on defense we had guys like Pat Stapleton, J.C. Tremblay and Rick Ley . . . all superstars in their own right."

For the next five seasons the WHA soldiered on, through franchise shifts, legal battles and media indifference. There were sporadic merger talks with the NHL, but neither side wanted to make the first concession. The

WHA went from a high of fourteen teams in 1974–75 to just six at the end of the 1978–79 season, when an agreement was finally hammered out for the Edmonton Oilers, Winnipeg Jets, Quebec Nordiques and Hartford Whalers to join the NHL.

In its final season the WHA introduced hockey fans to a skinny 17-year-old named Wayne Gretzky, who signed his first professional contract with the Indianapolis Racers. Less than a month into the season, with the club facing horrendous financial losses, Racers' owner Nelson Skalbania sold Gretzky, Peter Driscoll and Eddy Mio to the Oilers for $850,000. The Cincinnati Stingers unveiled a couple of promising teenagers in Mark Messier and Mike Gartner, while the Birmingham Bulls had Rick Vaive, Michel Goulet and Craig Hartsburg.

By the time the merger was finalized, Gary Davidson, the WHA's first president, was long gone. Dennis Murphy, who succeeded Davidson as league president in 1973, and Bill Hunter, the driving force behind the WHA's Canadian connection, were also on the outside looking in. But for Hunter, at least, there are no lingering regrets.

"I'm very proud to have been associated with the WHA and to have played a role in creating it," he says today. "We were behind the eight ball right from Day One but we persevered and we survived. It took the WHA to open up the game of hockey and give it back to the players and fans...that's something the NHL hadn't done in the 60 years before we came along.

"Even with all the problems and all the headaches, the WHA was still a tremendously successful enterprise. The fact that our league introduced young players like Wayne Gretzky, Mark Messier and Mike Gartner to major league hockey while prolonging the careers of all-time greats like Bobby Hull and Gordie Howe is something I think deserves to be remembered and applauded. And beyond what the World Hockey Association accomplished on the ice and in the record books, I think it's important to remember what it did in the courtroom, too. When Bobby Hull challenged the NHL's reserve clause and won his freedom to play in our league, it broke decades of one-sided control in all pro sports.

"We who were part of the WHA will always owe Bobby a great deal for what he did, and players everywhere should feel indebted to our league for having the courage to challenge the hockey establishment in 1972. Professional sports hasn't been the same since."

Through the Years: Red-Letter Dates in the Late, Great WHA

JANUARY 1971:
- Dennis A. Murphy, co-founder of the American Basketball Association in 1967, conceives the idea for a second major professional hockey league.

APRIL 1971:
- Murphy and Gary L. Davidson, his co-founder in the ABA, formulate plans for the World Hockey Association (WHA).

JUNE 10, 1971:
- Formal Articles of Incorporation for the WHA are filed in Delaware.

JULY 1971:
- Bylaws for the WHA are approved by the League's first Board of Trustees, above the signatures of Gary Davidson (president), Dennis Murphy and Donald J. Regan.
- Los Angeles sportswriter Walt Marlow, a transplanted Albertan, first tips off veteran Edmonton hockey magnate W.D. (Bill) Hunter about rumours of a proposed second major hockey league. Marlow sets up a meeting between Hunter, Murphy and Davidson in Los Angeles.

SEPTEMBER 23-24, 1971:
- First formal meeting of the WHA is held in Los Angeles.

OCTOBER 20, 1971:
- The WHA revolutionizes professional hockey by announcing in Chicago that the league will operate without the standard reserve/option clause in player contracts.

NOVEMBER 1, 1971:
- The original ten WHA franchises are awarded in New York. They are: Alberta Oilers, Calgary Broncos, Chicago Cougars, Dayton Arrows, Los Angeles Sharks, Miami Screaming Eagles, New York Raiders, St. Paul Fighting Saints, San Francisco (no team name) and Winnipeg Jets.

NOVEMBER 21, 1971:
- Two more franchises announced: Ontario (no team name) and the New England Whalers.

JANUARY 7, 1972:
- The Los Angeles Sharks announce the signing of Terry Slater as the WHA's first coach. Within a week, coaches Jack Kelley, from the University of Boston, and Glen Sonmor, from the University of Minnesota, sign to coach the New England Whalers and the (renamed) Minnesota Fighting Saints.
- Long-time National Hockey League referee Vern Buffey becomes the first NHL defector to sign a contract with the WHA.

FEBRUARY 11, 1972:
- San Francisco franchise is purchased by a group headed by Quebec City businessman Paul Racine. Franchise transferred to Quebec City and named "Nordiques."

FEBRUARY 12–13, 1972:
- In his new capacity as referee-in-chief, Buffey oversees the WHA's first general player draft in Anaheim, California. A total of 1,081 amateur, professional and retired players are drafted from all over the world.
- The New England franchise, headed by Howard Baldwin, announces it will be based in Boston. The Ontario franchise, headed by Doug Michel, announces it will be based in Ottawa and nicknamed "Nationals."
- Steve Sutherland, a "priority selection" of the Los Angeles Sharks, is the first player signed to a standard WHA contract.

FEBRUARY 21, 1972:
- The Miami Screaming Eagles announce the signing of Toronto Maple Leafs' goaltender Bernie Parent to a long-term contract for a reported $750,000.

MARCH 1972:
- The Dayton franchise, headed by Paul Deneau, transfers to Houston, Texas and is renamed "Aeros."
- U.S. Olympic team goaltender Mike Curran signs to play for the Minnesota Fighting Saints.

APRIL 14, 1972:
- Ten of the 12 WHA franchises post $100,000 performance bonds at a league meeting in Chicago.

APRIL 28, 1972
- The Miami Screaming Eagles and Calgary Broncos are suspended for failure to post their performance bonds.

MAY 1972:
- James W. Browitt is appointed league administrator and executive vice-president, succeeding Dennis Murphy. Murphy takes over operation of the Los Angeles Sharks.

JUNE 21, 1972:
- Miami franchise is transferred to a group headed by New Jersey businessmen James L. Cooper and Bernard Brown. Team is relocated to Philadelphia and renamed "Blazers." New owners agree to take over Bernie Parent's contract.
- Nick Mileti, owner of professional baseball and basketball franchises in Cleveland, is awarded the WHA's 12th franchise. The team is nicknamed "Crusaders."

JUNE 27, 1972:
- With huge fanfare and world-wide media coverage, the Winnipeg Jets announce the signing of former NHL superstar Bobby Hull to a ten-year, $2.75 million contract. The deal includes a $1 million cash signing bonus.

JULY 1972:
- Hull's signing triggers a flood of NHL defections to the WHA, including such "name" players as J.C. Tremblay (Quebec Nordiques), Gerry Cheevers (Cleveland Crusaders) and Ted Green (New England Whalers).

AUGUST 4, 1972:
- Flamboyant star Derek Sanderson leaves the NHL's Boston Bruins to sign a ten-year contract with the Philadelphia Blazers worth an estimated $2.35 million.
- The WHA announces it has more than 300 players under contract for the 1972–73 season. The league is divided into two divisions of six teams each, with the Cleveland Crusaders, New York Raiders, New England Whalers, Ottawa Nationals, Philadelphia Blazers and Quebec Nordiques in the East, and the Alberta Oilers, Chicago Cougars, Houston Aeros, Los Angeles Sharks, Minnesota Fighting Saints and Winnipeg Jets in the West.

SEPTEMBER 10, 1972:
- Philadelphia Blazers, minus several players whose NHL contracts don't expire until October 1, are the first WHA team to open training camp.

SEPTEMBER 23, 1972:
- Rookie squads play the WHA's first exhibition games.

OCTOBER 1, 1972:
- Professional players report to training camp. WHA president Gary Davidson announces experimental program for use of a coloured puck. Bright red and blue pucks are tried, but player protests result in a return to the conventional black. A tie-breaking "shootout" is used during exhibition games but dropped before the opening of the 78-game regular season schedule.
- A court order prevents former NHL superstar Bobby Hull from suiting up with the Winnipeg Jets.

OCTOBER 11, 1972:
- The WHA's first regular season opens with the Quebec Nordiques in Cleveland to face the Crusaders and the Alberta Oilers playing the Nationals in Ottawa. Ron Anderson of the Oilers scores the very first WHA regular-season goal.

NOVEMBER 8, 1972:
- In a landmark legal ruling by Judge A. Leon Higginbotham in the U.S. District Court for the Eastern Section of Pennsylvania, Bobby Hull is cleared to play in the WHA after missing the Jets' first 14 games. The same night, Hull makes his official WHA debut, assisting on the winning goal in Winnipeg's 3–2 victory over Quebec.

DECEMBER 1972:
- WHA president Gary Davidson announces that a scheduled exhibition series between the WHA All-Stars and the Czechoslovakian National Team has been cancelled because the Czechs were unable to obtain proper sanctioning from the Canadian Amateur Hockey Association.
- WHA general counsel Donald J. Regan reiterates the league's offer for an out-of-court settlement with the National Hockey League in the WHA's challenge to the reserve clause, and predicts that cases currently on file will be resolved in the WHA's favour.

JANUARY 6, 1973:
- The WHA's first all-star game is held in Quebec City. East Division defeats West Division 6–2, with Wayne Carleton of the Ottawa Nationals named MVP. During the all-star break, the WHA Players Association is officially organized.

JANUARY 7, 1973:
- In the first WHA game televised on the full CBS network, the Minnesota Fighting Saints drop a 6–2 decision to the visiting Winnipeg Jets, in front of 13,426 fans.

JANUARY 17, 1973:
- After playing just eight games and scoring six points, Derek Sanderson has his contract bought out by the Philadelphia Blazers for a reported $1 million settlement and returns to the National Hockey League.

JANUARY 30, 1973:
- Jim Harrison of the Alberta Oilers becomes the first major league player in the modern era to record ten points in a single game. Harrison scores three goals and adds seven assists in Alberta's 11–3 victory over the New York Raiders.

FEBRUARY 19, 1973:
- Active only since November 8, Bobby Hull finally cracks the WHA's top-ten scorers by counting 17 points in his last six games.

FEBRUARY 22, 1973:
- Philadelphia's Danny Lawson becomes the first WHA player to reach the 50-goal plateau as the visiting Blazers nip the Ottawa Nationals 6–5.

MARCH 11, 1973:
- On a rainy Sunday in Los Angeles, 12,804 fans show up at the Sports Arena for an 11 a.m. game against the Ottawa Nationals.

APRIL 1973:
- The WHA concludes its first regular season with New England (East) and Winnipeg (West) as divisional champions. A one-game tie-breaker between Minnesota and Alberta is held in Calgary on April 4 to determine the final West division playoff spot (Minnesota wins 4–2).
- Representatives of the WHA and NHL meet secretly in New York to discuss a possible merger. WHA president Gary Davidson later announces the WHA has rejected further talks, adding: "We believe the National Hockey League's reserve clause is wrong and it would be impossible for us to consider any formal association with the NHL so long as they retain it."
- After playing one playoff game for the Philadelphia Blazers, goaltender Bernie Parent leaves the team over a contract dispute. He eventually returns to the NHL.

MAY 1973:
- The New England Whalers capture the WHA's first Avco World Trophy Championship, defeating the Winnipeg Jets 4–1 in the best-of-seven final series.
- Ownership of the New York Raiders is transferred to a 14-man group headed by public relations executive Ralph Brent. The team is renamed "Golden Blades."
- Ownership of the Ottawa Nationals is transferred to a Toronto group headed by John F. Bassett Jr. The team is renamed "Toros."
- Philadelphia Blazers are sold to Vancouver businessman Jim Pattison, who transfers the club to Vancouver and retains the "Blazers" nickname.
- Expansion franchise is granted to a Cincinnati group headed by Brian Heekin III and William O. Dewitt Jr. The team will begin play in the 1975–76 season.

JUNE 1973:
- Gordie Howe, owner of more records than any player in hockey history, ends 21 months of retirement to sign with the Houston Aeros. The Aeros also sign Howe's teenage sons Mark and Marty in a historic "family contract."

JULY 1973:
- Pat Stapleton, formerly of the NHL's Chicago Black Hawks, agrees to terms as playing coach of the Chicago Cougars.

SEPTEMBER 1, 1973:
- League membership increases to 15 with the awarding of the expansion franchises to Indianapolis (Racers) and Phoenix (Roadrunners) for the 1974–75 season.

SEPTEMBER 25, 1973:
- The legendary Gordie Howe, making his first professional appearance with sons Mark and Marty, scores 21 seconds into the Houston Aeros' first exhibition game, against the New England Whalers. Mark Howe earns an assist on the historic goal.

OCTOBER 6, 1973:
- The WHA's second season opens with a 2–2 draw between the New York Golden Blades and Cleveland Crusaders at Madison Square Garden.

OCTOBER 18, 1973:
- The New York Golden Blades franchise is dissolved and all players become property of the league when the WHA guarantees team payroll.

OCTOBER 29, 1973:
- Citing his involvement in outside business interests, Gary Davidson resigns as WHA president at a meeting of the board of trustees in Chicago. A five-man committee, consisting of Davidson, Howard Baldwin, John Bassett Jr., Tif Trimble and Nick Mileti, is delegated to screen candidates for the league presidency.

NOVEMBER 18, 1973:
- The first professional goal involving all three members of the Howe family is scored by Mark on assists from father Gordie and brother Marty during the Houston Aeros' 8–3 loss to the Nordiques in Quebec City.

NOVEMBER 20, 1973:
- Former members of the New York Golden Blades are relocated to Cherry Hill, New Jersey, to form the New Jersey Knights.

NOVEMBER 23, 1973:
- Dennis A. Murphy, co-founder of the league, resigns as president and general manager of the Los Angeles Sharks to assume the role of interim president of the WHA.

JANUARY 3, 1974:
- New Jersey Knights are purchased from the WHA by Baltimore real estate developer Joseph Schwartz.
- All-star game in Minneapolis attracts a crowd of 13,196 to watch the East Division whip the West Division 8–4. Mike Walton of the Minnesota Fighting Saints is named most valuable player (MVP).

JANUARY 17, 1974:
- Gordie Howe scores his 800th major league goal in the Houston Aeros' 7–4 victory over the visiting Vancouver Blazers.

FEBRUARY 19, 1974:
- The 57-year-old NHL and the two-year-old WHA reach an out-of-court settlement in their $50-million court case when representatives of both leagues sign an agreement before U.S. District Court Judge A. Leon Higginbotham in Philadelphia. The landmark ruling strikes down the NHL's reserve clause and also stipulates that the NHL must reimburse the WHA for legal expenses totalling $1.7 million. "Elimination of what was a perpetual reserve clause, without having to go to trial, represents a total victory for the WHA," says president Dennis Murphy.

FEBRUARY 23, 1974:
- The New England Whalers announce that the team will permanently relocate from Boston to Hartford in the 1974–75 season.
- Cincinnati expansion team announces it will be nicknamed "Stingers."

APRIL 11, 1974:
- Detroit industrialists Peter Shagena and Charles Nolton announce their purchase of the Los Angeles Sharks franchise, which they move to Detroit under the new name "Michigan Stags."

APRIL 28, 1974:
- The fourth game of the Houston–Minnesota semi-final playoff series attracts the largest crowd in the WHA's brief history: 17,211 in St. Paul.
- The WHA announces plans for an eight-game series in September against the Soviet National Team. Team Canada will be under the guidance of Bill Hunter (general manager) and Billy Harris (coach).

APRIL 30, 1974:
- The New Jersey Knights franchise is transferred to San Diego and renamed "Mariners."

MAY 1974:
- The Houston Aeros capture the Avco World Trophy by defeating Minnesota (4–2), Winnipeg (4–0) and Chicago (4–0).
- More than 200 junior prospects are selected in the WHA amateur draft in Toronto.

JUNE 1974:
- The WHA announces divisional realignment for the 1974–75 season, with three divisions: Canadian (Vancouver, Edmonton, Winnipeg, Toronto and Quebec); East (Chicago, Cleveland, Indianapolis and New England); and West (Houston, Michigan, Minnesota, Phoenix and San Diego).

JUNE 19, 1974:
- Toronto Toros announce the signing of former NHL superstar Frank Mahovlich.

SEPTEMBER 1974:
- In the eight-game series against the Soviet Union, the WHA version of Team Canada wins one game, loses four and ties three.

SEPTEMBER 26, 1974:
- In the first exhibition game ever played between a WHA team and an opponent from the NHL, rookie Don Larway scores twice to lead the Houston Aeros to a 5–3 victory over the St. Louis Blues.

OCTOBER 15, 1974:
- The WHA's third season of play opens with new arenas in Cleveland, Edmonton and Indianapolis. The Toronto Toros debut Czechoslovakian stars Vaclav Nedomansky and Richard Farda.

NOVEMBER 10, 1974:
- A regular season attendance record is established when the Edmonton Oilers attract 15,326 fans to their first home game in the new Northlands Coliseum. The Oilers defeat the Cleveland Crusaders 4–1.

DECEMBER 5, 1974:
- Paul Deneau, one of the original owners of the Houston Aeros, purchases the Indianapolis Racers.

DECEMBER 27, 1974:
- A major league sports first is realized when a group of Chicago Cougars' players, headed by Pat Stapleton, purchases the team.

JANUARY 11, 1975:
- The New England Whalers attract a sellout crowd of 10,570 for their debut in the new Hartford Civic Center. The Whalers defeat the San Diego Mariners 4–3 in overtime.

JANUARY 18, 1975:
- The Michigan Stags franchise suspends operations.

JANUARY 20, 1975:
- Dennis Murphy announces his resignation as president of the WHA, effective June 1.

JANUARY 21, 1975:
- A capacity crowd of 15,326 is on hand at Edmonton's Northlands Coliseum for the third annual WHA All-Star Game. The West Division defeats the East Division 6–4 and Rejean Houle of the Quebec Nordiques is named MVP.

JANUARY 23, 1975:
- The Baltimore Blades debut in Hartford, losing 4–3 to the New England Whalers.

FEBRUARY 14, 1975:
- Winnipeg's Bobby Hull scores three goals in a 5–3 victory over the Houston Aeros to tie Maurice (Rocket) Richard's major league record of 50 goals in 50 games.

APRIL 4, 1975:
- All-time WHA regular season attendance record set when 17,312 fans in St. Paul watch the Fighting Saints lose 2–1 to the Phoenix Roadrunners.

APRIL 6, 1975:
- Bobby Hull becomes major league hockey's most prolific single-season scorer by netting his 77th goal in a season-ending 5–5 tie against the San Diego Mariners.

APRIL 1975:
- Chicago Cougars franchise suspends operations.

MAY 1975:
- The Houston Aeros repeat as Avco World Trophy champions, with goaltender Ron Grahame named the first recipient of the playoff MVP award.

MAY 7, 1975:
- Baltimore Blades franchise suspends operations.
- Vancouver Blazers franchise is transferred to Calgary and renamed "Cowboys."

MAY 19, 1975:
- Expansion franchise is granted to Denver businessman Ivan L. Mullenix. Team adopts "Spurs" nickname.

JUNE 1975:
- Houston Aeros franchise is purchased by a group headed by Houston realtor George Bolin. Gordie Howe is named "playing president" of the Aeros.

JUNE 19, 1975:
- First WHA intraleague draft held in Toronto.

JULY 1, 1975:
- League office is relocated from California to Toronto.

SEPTEMBER 1975:
- The Toronto Toros and Winnipeg Jets become the first major league teams to hold full training camps in Europe: Toronto in Sweden and Winnipeg in Finland.

OCTOBER 10, 1975:
- The Denver Spurs open the new McNichols Sports Arena with a 7–1 loss to the Indianapolis Racers.

OCTOBER 12, 1975:
- The Calgary Cowboys make their WHA debut at home with a 2–0 loss to the Minnesota Fighting Saints.

OCTOBER 23, 1975:
- In the first WHA game is played at the new Riverfront Coliseum in Cincinnati, the expansion Stingers defeat the Edmonton Oilers 6–4.

NOVEMBER 5, 1975:
- The Houston Aeros open their new arena, The Summit, with a 6–4 victory over the Minnesota Fighting Saints.

DECEMBER 14, 1975:
- Winnipeg's Bobby Hull becomes the first player to score 200 WHA goals as the visiting Jets defeat the Edmonton Oilers 3–1.

JANUARY 2, 1976:
- Denver Spurs franchise transferred to Ottawa and renamed "Civics."

JANUARY 7, 1976:
- In their first home appearance, the Ottawa Civics drop a 4–3 decision to the New England Whalers.

JANUARY 13, 1976:
- Canada defeats the U.S. 6–1 in the fourth annual WHA all-star game in Cleveland. The game is televised nationally in the U.S. on the PBS network. MVPs are Paul Shmyr (Cleveland) and Real Cloutier (Quebec).

JANUARY 15, 1976:
- The Ottawa Civics play their last game in the WHA, a 5–4 overtime loss to Houston in Ottawa.

JANUARY 17, 1976:
- The Ottawa Civics suspend operations.

FEBRUARY 12, 1976:
- Houston's Gordie Howe records his 1,200th major league assist in the Aeros' 4–1 win over Phoenix.

FEBRUARY 28, 1976:
- The Minnesota Fighting Saints suspend operations.

APRIL 1976:
- WHA season attendance of 4,123,121 sets an all-time league record.
- Mark Tardif of the Quebec Nordiques sets a new league scoring record by finishing the regular season with 71 goals and 77 assists.

MAY 1976:
- Winnipeg Jets become the first Canadian-based team to win the Avco World Trophy. Jets' center Ulf Nilsson named MVP of the playoffs.

JUNE 1976:
- Toronto Toros franchise is transferred to Birmingham, Alabama, and renamed "Bulls."
- WHA realigned into two divisions, Eastern and Western.
- League adopts international third period rule, with teams changing ends at midway mark of the final period.
- More than 30 players, coaches and officials from the WHA are invited to participate in the inaugural Canada Cup tournament, including players Bobby Hull (Winnipeg), Gerry Cheevers and Paul Shmyr (Cleveland) and Marc Tardif (Quebec), who are invited to play for Team Canada.

AUGUST 1976:
- San Diego Mariners franchise purchased by fast-food restaurant magnate Ray Kroc.
- WHA approves transfer of Cleveland Crusaders franchise to St. Paul, Minnesota, as a new incarnation of the Fighting Saints.

DECEMBER 1976:
- The Avco World Trophy champion Winnipeg Jets become the first North American team to compete in the prestigious Izvestia Cup tournament in Moscow. The Jets manage just one win in the four-game round robin tournament against club teams from the Soviet Union, Czechoslovakia, Sweden and Finland.

JANUARY 1977:
- The "new" Minnesota Fighting Saints suspend operations.

FEBRUARY 6, 1977:
- Winnipeg's Anders Hedberg scores goals No. 49, 50 and 51 of the season, in the Jets' 6–4 victory over Calgary, to become the first player in major league history to net 50 goals in less than 50 games. The historic hat trick comes in Winnipeg's 49th game of the season, and Hedberg's 47th.

MARCH 1, 1977:
- Gordie Howe notches his 900th career goal (regular season and playoffs) in Houston's 8–3 trouncing of the Phoenix Roadrunners.

APRIL 1977:
- Phoenix Roadrunners suspend operations.

APRIL 9, 1977:
- Gene Peacosh scores the winning goal at 48:40 of overtime to end the longest playoff game in WHA history and lift the Indianapolis Racers to a 4–3 triumph over the Cincinnati Stingers in the opening game of their best-of-seven Eastern Division semifinal.

MAY 1977:
- Calgary Cowboys suspend operation.

MAY 11, 1977:
- The WHA's first all-Canadian final opens in Quebec City between the Nordiques and the Winnipeg Jets.

MAY 26, 1977:
- Quebec Nordiques capture the Avco World Trophy by defeating the Jets 8–2 in the seventh and deciding game of the playoff final in Quebec City.

JUNE 1977:
- Free agents Gordie, Mark and Marty Howe sign multi-year contracts with the New England Whalers.
- Robbie Ftorek, who scored 117 points for the last-place Phoenix Roadrunners, becomes the first American-born player to win MVP honours in major league hockey. In a vote by media representatives, Ftorek edges Winnipeg's Anders Hedberg by 168–167.
- Ignoring the league's "gentleman's agreement" against signing underage juniors, Birmingham Bulls' owner John Bassett Jr. inks 18-year-old Ken Linseman of the Kingston Canadians to a professional contract.

JULY 1977:
- San Diego Mariners suspend operations.

SEPTEMBER 1977:
- Needing just five votes to reject the merger overtures from the WHA, the NHL board of governors gets thumbs down from the Toronto Maple Leafs, Vancouver Canucks, Boston Bruins, Los Angeles Kings, Minnesota North Stars and New York Islanders.

SEPTEMBER 25, 1977:
- Gordie, Mark and Marty Howe play their first exhibition game for the New England Whalers, a 2–2 tie against the NHL's Chicago Black Hawks. In a moving pre-game ceremony, the Whaler's pay tribute to Chicago's Bobby Orr.

NOVEMBER 1977:
- A landmark decision by U.S. District Court Judge T. Emmett Clarke forces the WHA to honour the contract that underaged Ken Linseman signed with the Birmingham Bulls. Judge Clarke rules that a WHA regulation prohibiting the signing of the underage players is a violation of U.S. antitrust laws.

DECEMBER 7, 1977:
- Gordie Howe notches the 1,000th goal (regular season and playoffs) of his major league career, beating Bulls' goaltender John Garrett during the Whalers' 6–3 victory in Birmingham.

DECEMBER 22, 1977:
- In the first major WHA-NHL trade, the Birmingham Bulls swap Vaclav Nedomansky and Tim Sheehy to the Detroit Red Wings for Steve Durbano, Dave Hanson and future considerations.

JANUARY 17, 1978:
- MVP Marc Tardif scores a goal and adds four assists to lead the Nordiques to a 5–4 victory over the WHA All-Stars in the league's sixth annual all-star game in Quebec City. Robbie Ftorek of the Cincinnati Stingers is hit in the face by an errant shot during the game and requires 70 stitches to close the wound.

MARCH 11, 1978:
- Winnipeg's Bobby Hull notches his 44th goal of the season and Number 1,000 (regular season and playoffs) of his major league career in the Jets' 7–4 win over the Quebec Nordiques.

APRIL 1978:
- Quebec's Marc Tardif establishes a new major league record for points in a season with 154 (65 goals, 89 assists), topping the old mark of 152 set by Phil Esposito of the NHL's Boston Bruins in 1970–71.

MAY 22, 1978:
- The Winnipeg Jets complete a four-game sweep of the New England Whalers to win the Avco World Trophy. The Jets' final goal of the series is scored by Anders Hedberg with two seconds left. Two weeks later, Hedberg and linemate Ulf Nilsson sign multiyear contracts with the NHL's New York Rangers.

JULY 11, 1978:
- Seventeen-year-old scoring wizard Wayne Gretzky, of the Sault Ste. Marie Greyhounds, inks a five-year "personal services" contract with Indianapolis Racers' owner Nelson Skalbania for a reported $1.6 million. Within weeks, Gretzky's deal triggers a flood of junior signings, including the "Baby Bulls" package that sees Birmingham owner John Bassett ink teenagers Rob Ramage, Craig Hartsburg, Gaston Gingras and Rick Vaive.

JULY 1978:
- Houston Aeros suspend operations.

OCTOBER 3, 1978:
- Gordie Howe is greeted with a seven-minute standing ovation when the New England Whalers invade the Detroit Olympia for a pre-season exhibition game against the NHL Red Wings. When Howe scores a third-period goal (assisted by sons Mark and Marty), the crowd of 14,000 responds with another six-minute standing ovation.

OCTOBER 16, 1978:
- Wayne Gretzky notches his first professional regular season point by assisting on a goal by Rich Leduc at 16:14 of the second period in the Racers' 4–0 victory over the Quebec Nordiques.

OCTOBER 20, 1978:
- Wayne Gretzky scores his first professional goals in regular season play at 6:02 and 6:41 of the second period in the Racers' 4–3 loss to the Edmonton Oilers. The first goal is assisted by Kevin Morrison, the second by Peter Driscoll and Don Larway.

NOVEMBER 2, 1978:
- Wayne Gretzky, Peter Driscoll and goaltender Eddie Mio are sold by Indianapolis Racers' owner Nelson Skalbania to the Edmonton Oilers for $850,000.

NOVEMBER 3, 1978:
- Wearing jersey Number 20 rather than his familiar Number 99 for the only time in his professional career, Gretzky scores his first goal as an Edmonton Oiler at 00:14 of the second period in Edmonton's 4–3 victory over the Winnipeg Jets.

NOVEMBER 1978:
- Bobby Hull stuns the hockey world by announcing his retirement. In 411 WHA games, Hull has recorded 303 goals, 335 assists and 638 points.

DECEMBER 15, 1978:
- The Indianapolis Racers suspend operations.

MARCH 22, 1979:
- A merger agreement with the NHL is formally announced. The Edmonton Oilers, Winnipeg Jets, Quebec Nordiques and New England Whalers will be accepted into the NHL as "expansion" teams for the 1979–80 season. The Birmingham Bulls and Cincinnati Stingers will suspend operations as WHA franchises at the conclusion of the current season.

MAY 20, 1979:
- The Winnipeg Jets win the WHA's last Avco World Trophy by defeating the Edmonton Oilers 7–3 in the sixth game of their playoff final. The final WHA goal is scored by Edmonton's Dave Semenko (assisted by Ron Chipperfield and Risto Siltanen) at 19:48 of the third period. Edmonton's Wayne Gretzky and Winnipeg's Willy Lindstrom share the playoff goal scoring title with 10 each, while Gretzky tops the point parade with 20. Rich Preston of the Jets is named MVP of the playoffs.

JUNE 1979:
- The World Hockey Association suspends operations.

Part 2

SUPERSTARS & PLUGGERS

50 of the WHA's finest

- Bobby Hull
- Ulf Nilsson
- Anders Hedberg
- Pierre Guite
- Wayne Rivers
- Michel Dion
- J.C. Tremblay
- Gavin Kirk
- Rich Leduc
- Frank Mahvolich
- Ab McDonald
- Steve Sutherland
- Bill Hicke
- Mike Walton
- Don McLeod
- Gerry Cheevers
- Vaclav Nedomansky
- Terry Ruskowski
- Gary Kurt
- Rick Jodzio
- Marc Tardif
- Rosaire Paiement
- Marty Howe
- Mark Howe
- Paul Henderson
- Tom Webster
- Andy Brown
- Gilles Gratton
- Johnny McKenzie
- Larry Pleau
- Bob Woytowich
- Robbie Ftorek
- Les Binkley
- Barry Long
- Glen Sather
- Reg Fleming
- Ted Green
- Wayne Connelly
- Wayne Rutledge
- John Garrett
- Real Cloutier
- Ron Chipperfield
- Chris Bordeleau
- Claude St. Sauveur
- Tom Simpson
- Gerry Odrowski
- Serge Bernier
- Dave Keon
- Mike Amodeo
- Bryan Campbell

BOBBY HULL: It's no stretch to suggest that the initials WHA really stood for "When Hull Arrived." Professional hockey changed forever on June 27, 1972, when the Golden Jet signed his ten-year, $2.75 million contract with Winnipeg—not so much because the signing triggered a massive talent drain on the National Hockey League, but because it forced the NHL to change the way it conducted business. Hawks' owner William Wirtz once estimated that increased spending for player salaries and minor league development, com-

bined with huge legal bills and reduced attendance revenues cost the NHL roughly $1 billion over the lifetime of the WHA. Since the rebel league would never have survived without Hull, the message was clear.

The Black Hawks took Hull's defection very personally, making him persona non grata by deleting all his stats from the official team record and then assigning his famous Number Nine to Dale Tallon, of all people. To his credit, Tallon gave up the number after one week, declaring it "sacrilege" for anyone other than Hull to don it.

There are arguments about hockey's all-time greatest player at every position except left wing, yet Hull's magnificent career was about much more than on-ice excellence. He was, quite simply, the greatest ambassador the game has ever known—and it's high time the NHL welcomed him back.

ULF NILSSON: Pound for pound Ulf Nilsson was probably the toughest Swede ever to play major league hockey in North America. As a youth he was an exceptional soccer player, but knee surgery forced him to give up the game and concentrate on hockey. Nilsson was a member of the Swedish national junior team from 1967–70 and the National team from 1970–74. In the fall of '74 he joined long-time linemate Anders Hedberg as the first Europeans to sign with the Winnipeg Jets, and when the two were paired with Bobby Hull the result was pure magic.

Beginning with his very first WHA game, the five-foot-eleven 175-pound Nilsson was relentlessly targeted by opposition goons, but his willingness to drop the gloves and defend himself went a long way towards exploding the myth of the "chicken Swedes." Nilsson established WHA records for assists (94) and points (120) by a rookie in 1974–75, and though not a great skater or shooter he earned a well-deserved reputation as an adroit stick handler and one of the slickest passers in the business.

After the Jets won the Avco World Trophy in 1977–78, Nilsson and Hedberg joined the New York Rangers in a package deal reportedly worth $3 million. In 170 games over four NHL seasons Nilsson scored 57 goals and 169 points — but without Hull on the left side the two Swedes weren't nearly as sweet.

ANDERS HEDBERG: Had he launched his professional career in New York or Los Angeles, Anders Hedberg might well have become the media darling and endorsement machine that compatriot Bjorn Borg turned into after conquering the pro tennis circuit. But Hedberg, nicknamed "The Swedish Express," performed his best magic in the relative backwater of Winnipeg, and it was hockey's loss that he was unable to showcase his enormous talents in a major market until he jumped to the New York Rangers in 1978–79.

During Hedberg's heyday with the Jets more than a few knowledgeable observers favourably compared his electrifying speed and explosive scoring ability to that of Guy Lafleur of the Montreal Canadiens. And, like Lafleur, Hedberg performed with a peerless sense of *élan* in both ends of the rink. He was the first player in major league history to score more than 50 goals in less than 50 games (51 in 47, 1976–77), then just for good measure he scored number 60 in his 57th game and added number 70 in his 68th.

Hedberg potted 53 goals and 100 points en route to winning the Lou Kaplan Trophy as the WHA's rookie of the year in 1974–75, and over the next three seasons scoring goals in bunches became his trademark. He tallied 236 goals and 458 points in just 286 WHA games, then took his act to Broadway where he notched 397 points in 465 games with the Rangers.

PIERRE GUITE: Pierre (Van Gogh) Guite is on record as being the only WHA player known to have received a tetanus shot because his ear was nearly bitten off in a fight.

The historic event took place February 7, 1976, in Indianapolis, when Guite and Racers' tough guy Kim Clackson squared off for round three in a series of fights that had started two months earlier in Cincinnati. The first fight was close. The second was a clear decision for Guite. The third time they dropped their gloves, Guite again appeared to have the upper hand when Clackson suddenly decided to turn Guite's ear lobe into an *hors d'oeuvre*.

"That's not my opinion of fighting," Guite said afterwards. "If he wants to drop his gloves and slug it out that's fine with me, but I had to get a tetanus shot and now I'm on penicillin for a week."

Stingers' coach Terry Slater, no stranger to hockey violence himself, opined: "Guite is probably one of the top two or three toughest guys in the WHA, but Clackson seems to be looking for punishment by continually agitating him. I'll bet it wasn't a wisdom tooth he bit Pierre with!"

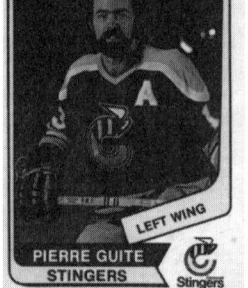

Besides being handy with his fists, Guite could also put the puck in the net. A powerful skater with a great shot, he was an original member of the Quebec Nordiques, who traded him to the Michigan Stags in 1974 as part of the package deal for Marc Tardif. Guite finished his career as an Edmonton Oiler.

WAYNE RIVERS: Wayne Rivers was one of the few players in history to be traded for his coach.

The unlikely scenario unfolded in the summer of 1968 when the New York Rangers traded Rivers, along with Don Caley, to the St. Louis Blues for Camille (The Eel) Henry, Billy Plager and Robbie Irons. When Rivers joined the WHA as an original New York Raider four years later, his coach was none other than Camille Henry!

Wayne's first taste of the big leagues came in 1962 when the Detroit Red Wings promoted him from the American Hockey League's Hershey Bears for a two-game tryout. He was selected by Boston in the NHL intraleague draft two years later and notched 23 points in 58 games for the last-place Bruins in 1964–65. Another long stint in the minors followed, but then the WHA came along to offer the 33-year-old one last shot at the majors. Rivers responded by sniping 37 goals and 77 points for the Raiders the first year and adding 30 goals and 57 points for the New York Golden Blades-New Jersey Knights in the 1973–74 campaign.

With the San Diego Mariners in 1975–76 Rivers fired a career high of 54 goals (tied for second in the WHA), but he slumped to 18 the following season before moving on to the San Francisco Shamrocks in the newly formed Pacific Hockey League, which comprised mostly ex-WHA players.

MICHEL DION: Bo Jackson had nothing on Michel Dion. Sure, being a two-sport athlete in baseball and football was quite an accomplishment for ol' Bo, but how about combining pro baseball with a career as a major league goalie? Dion opted for hockey after one season as a highly touted catcher for the Montreal Expos' affiliate in West Palm Beach, Florida, but there must have been times during his rookie year with the Indianapolis Racers when Dion thought he'd taken the wrong fork in the road.

Dion joined Indianapolis in 1975–76 after a long season of riding buses and stopping pucks for the Mohawk Valley Comets in the North American Hockey League. Despite having a losing record with the Racers (14–15–1), he posted a league-leading 2.74 goals-against average and won the Ben Hatskin Trophy as the WHA's top goaltender. He was almost as sharp the next year in posting a 17–19–3 mark (3.36) for the third-place Racers, but prior to the 1977–78 campaign he was traded to Cincinnati, where he went 31–31–2 with a 3.35 average through the WHA's final two seasons.

Dion was claimed by the Quebec Nordiques in the 1979 dispersal draft of players who were under contract to Cincinnati, and after the merger he played six seasons in the NHL with Quebec, Winnipeg and Pittsburgh. His combined major league record over nine seasons was 122–184–39 with six shutouts.

J.C. TREMBLAY: The Nordiques scored a major coup when they lured "J.C. Superstar" away from the Montreal Canadiens in the spring of 1972. En route to becoming a fixture on the Canadiens' blue line for a dozen years, Tremblay had perfected the art of checking opposing forwards while rarely making bodily contact. He was also a master at scoring goals on the long, blooping flip shots he routinely lofted from his own side of centre ice.

Tremblay broke into pro hockey with the Rochester Americans in 1958 and had two abbreviated tryouts with the Canadiens before finally becoming a regular in the 1961–62 season. Twice an NHL all-star, he was at his best when the money was on the line—as evidenced by his five Stanley Cup championships and 65 points in 108 playoff games.

The Nords named Tremblay their first captain in the WHA, and he responded by leading the club in points (14 goals, 75 assists) and setting five team scoring records in 1972–73. He played in every WHA all-star game from 1973–77 and won the Dennis Murphy Trophy as the league's top defenseman in 1972–73 and 1974–75. Tremblay's total of 358 WHA assists put him second behind Andre Lacroix on the all-time list, and with 424 regular season points he was the highest scoring defenseman in the league's seven-year history.

Tremblay died in 1996 following a lengthy illness.

GAVIN KIRK: Gavin Kirk was the central figure in the "corniest" episode in the mercifully short history of the Ottawa Nationals.

Selected by Quebec in the original WHA draft, Kirk was traded to Ottawa in July 1972 and finished that first season as the Nats' second highest scorer behind Wayne Carleton. But it was the strange sequence of events that began on February 25, 1973 that forever etched his name in the memory of Ottawa fans. On that fateful evening, prior to a game against the Alberta Oilers, the Nats' trainer happened across a half-eaten cob of corn outside the Ottawa dressing room. He picked it up and tossed it to the first player he saw, joking that the cob was a good luck charm. That player was Kirk, who in turn stuffed the cob into a spare glove. Ottawa won the game 2–1 on a flukey goal, and that was enough to convince the Nats of the cob's "mystic power."

For the next three weeks Kirk stored the rapidly decaying cob in his glove. Before each game it became the focus of a solemn ceremony during which he'd bring it out and have six players rub it for luck. The last player to do so would then extract a single kernel of corn and throw it at goaltender Ken Stephenson. It worked. The Nats won 12 of their last 13 games and clinched a playoff spot in their final game of the regular season—a 5–2 triumph over New England. Fittingly enough, Kirk scored Ottawa's first three goals that night.

RICH LEDUC: On October 18, 1978, Rich Leduc scored a goal for the Indianapolis Racers late in the second period of a 4–0 victory over the Quebec Nordiques. Scoring goals was nothing new for Leduc, a flashy centre from Ile Perrot, Quebec. He'd potted 52 for the Cincinnati Stingers in 1976–77 and averaged just over 40 per season through his four-year WHA career. What made this particular scoring shot special was that it came off a pass delivered by a frail-looking 17-year-old from Brantford, Ontario, named Wayne Gretzky. The assist was Gretzky's very first professional point in regular season play, and Leduc helped the kid celebrate by retrieving the puck.

A third-round draft pick of the NHL's California Golden Seals in 1971, Leduc turned pro with the Cleveland Barons in the American Hockey League. Sold to Boston prior to the 1971 season, he had brief tryouts with the Bruins over the next two years then jumped to the WHA's Cleveland Crusaders in May 1974.

Leduc led Cleveland in goals (35) and points (66) in his rookie season and followed up with 36 goals and 58 points in his sophomore year. After the Crusaders folded in 1976 he became a bona fide star with the Stingers, finishing the 1976–77 season with a team-high 107 points. In 1978 he was traded, along with Claude Larose, to Indianapolis for Darryl Maggs and Reg Thomas. Nine months later the Racers sold him to Quebec.

FRANK MAHOVLICH: The Big M could do it all: skate, stickhandle, shoot and, especially, score goals. Few players before or since could match Mahovlich's lethal combination of speed and raw power, and when he was at the top of his game there was no more terrifying sight for opposition goaltenders than big Number 27 swooping in from the left side, ready to unleash his murderous eye-high slapshot.

After a starry junior career at St. Michael's College, Mahovlich broke into the NHL with the Toronto Maple Leafs in 1957–58. He scored 20 goals and edged out a brawny Black Hawk named Bobby Hull for rookie of the year honours, but what should have blossomed into a fairy tale career with the Leafs quickly became a nightmare. In 1960–61 Mahovlich sniped a team record 48 goals but was often booed by Leaf fans who felt he was capable of scoring even more. He won four Stanley Cups in Toronto and two more as a Montreal Canadien during a brilliant 18-year NHL career, then returned to Toronto as captain of the WHA's Toros in 1974–75.

In his very first game after switching leagues Mahovlich notched a hat trick in a 6–2 victory over the New England Whalers, and he went on to record 89 goals and 232 points in 237 games with the Toros and Birmingham Bulls before a knee injury ended his career early in the 1978–79 season.

AB McDONALD: Winnipeg-born "Old McDonald" was expected to see only spot duty when he was signed by the Jets almost as an afterthought in the summer of 1972, but somebody forgot to tell the feisty 36-year-old who had toiled for six different NHL teams after debuting with the Montreal Canadiens in 1958. McDonald not only made the club, he was named captain and became a key penalty killer while contributing 17 goals.

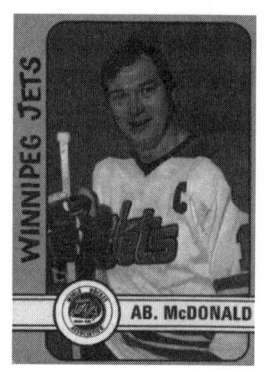

A smooth skater with good instincts around the net, McDonald's best years were with the Chicago Black Hawks from 1960–64 when he patrolled the port side on the original "Scooter Line" with Kenny Wharram and Stan Mikita. He won two Stanley Cups with Montreal and one with the Hawks, and following the first NHL expansion in 1967 he emerged as one of the scoring stars on the original Pittsburgh Penguins by bagging 22 goals and 43 points.

McDonald's savvy helped take some of the load off playing-coach Bobby Hull during the Jets' inaugural season, and his maturity and leadership—both on and off the ice—was a steadying influence on young colts like Garth Rizzuto, Dunc Rousseau and Joe Zanussi. McDonald scored the first regular season goal in franchise history and missed only eight games in two full seasons with Winnipeg before drawing the curtain on a stellar major league career that saw him score 211 goals and an even 500 points in 910 games.

STEVE SUTHERLAND: Somebody always has to be first, and for the World Hockey Association that somebody was tough guy Steve Sutherland. A priority selection of the Los Angeles Sharks in the league's original general player draft, in February of 1972 he became the very first player to sign a standard WHA contract.

Once described by Sharks' GM Dennis Murphy as "a Tasmanian Devil on skates," Sutherland was a rugged left winger who had kicked around the low minors for a number of years before he got his big break. In 1971–72 he scored 44 points and posted 219 penalty minutes in just 52 games for the Port Huron Flags of the International Hockey League, and his willingness to hit (and hurt) anything that moved made him one of the most feared leaders of the Sharks' ultra-intimidating "goon squad" in the WHA's first season. Unlike most enforcers, however, Sutherland could also put the puck in the net. He scored 11 goals in just 43 games in 1972–73, including the first regular season goal in franchise history.

Sutherland moved to Michigan when the Sharks became the Stags, but just before Christmas 1974 he was traded along with Marc Tardif to the Quebec Nordiques for Pierre Guite, Michel Rouleau and Alain (Boom Boom) Caron. He tallied 97 goals and 173 points in 379 WHA games and ranks eighth on the league's all-time list of penalty leaders with 805 minutes.

BILL HICKE: After a phenomenally successful junior career, right winger Bill Hicke was designated as heir apparent to the great Maurice (Rocket) Richard when the latter retired from the Montreal Canadiens in 1960. Alas, living up to that billing proved far too much for the fleet-footed little hustler from Saskatchewan, and Hicke ended up playing five mediocre seasons for the Habs before he was dispatched to the New York Rangers in 1965. His other NHL stops included the Oakland Seals and Pittsburgh Penguins, and he was seri-  ously contemplating retirement after the 1971–72 season when the Alberta Oilers came calling.

Lining up with centre Eddie Joyal and left winger Val Fonteyne on what the Edmonton media quickly dubbed the "Geritol Line," the 35-year-old Hicke showed occasional flashes of the form that had netted him 168 goals and 402 points in 729 NHL games. He scored twice in the Oilers' opening game (including the WHA's first penalty shot, against Les Binkley of the Ottawa Nationals) and finished the season with a respectable 14 goals and 38 points after being relegated to part-time duty. He also served as the first president of the WHA Players Association. In the summer of 1973 Hicke purchased a sporting goods store in Regina and quit hockey to devote his full attention to building up the business and indulging in his hobby of restoring antique cars.

MIKE WALTON: Mike Walton was voted rookie of the year in both the Central Professional Hockey League (with Tulsa) and the American Hockey League (with Rochester) before he got his name engraved on the Stanley Cup with the Toronto Maple Leafs in 1966–67. The following year he fired 30 goals for a brutally inept Leafs team, but in 1971 he was traded twice in one day—first from Toronto to Philadelphia for future considerations, then from the Flyers to the Boston Bruins for Rick MacLeish and Dan Schock.

During some horseplay with his Bruin teammates at a St. Louis hotel in 1973, Walton fell through a plate glass door and nearly bled to death when he was cut and required more than 200 stitches. Six months later he signed with the Minnesota Fighting Saints, and in his first WHA season he won the league scoring title with 57 goals and 117 points. In the Saints' last 25 regular season games he scored 37 times and added 23 assists, including an incredible three-game stretch in which he sandwiched a hat trick between a pair of four-goal games!

"To really appreciate Mike Walton you have to observe him over an extended period of time," Saints' coach Harry Neale commented in 1974. "Some nights I watch him and wonder how the hell he could be the league's leading scorer. Other nights I wonder why he doesn't score 100 goals a season. When his head's screwed on right he's the most complete player in the game."

DON McLEOD: Don (Smokey) McLeod was born in Trail, British Columbia, a smelter town famous for producing smoke, slag and two other talented big-league goaltenders: Seth Martin and Cesare Maniago. Trail is also the only city on the planet to produce two world amateur championship teams, both of which were called "Smoke Eaters." McLeod's nickname wasn't in honour of his hometown team, however, but for his habit of chain smoking. In fact, during Don's glory days with the Houston Aeros the organist would often salute particularly brilliant saves by pounding out the opening bars of *On Top Of Old Smokey.*

McLeod was born with a club foot and wore a cast for the first six years of his life. That was followed by two more years on braces and several operations, but by the time he was a teenager Don excelled in golf and softball and had blossomed into one of the finest young goaltenders in Western Canada. He turned professional in the Detroit Red Wings' system and was later dealt to Philadelphia, but spent most of his first six pro seasons in the minors.

Don signed with Houston in 1972–73 and the following year backstopped the Aeros to their first Avco Trophy title by posting a dazzling 12–2 playoff record with a 2.49 goals-against average. Twice during his career McLeod stopped two penalty shots in the same game and, thanks in part to his revolutionary use of a curved goalie stick, he was credited with a record 43 career assists.

GERRY CHEEVERS: Gerry Cheevers was best known for two things: a face mask with stitches painted on it to represent the cuts he would have sustained without the protection, and an international reputation for being one of the toughest goalies in history to beat one-on-one.

Originally signed by the Toronto Maple Leafs in 1961, "Cheesy" was selected by Boston in the 1965 intraleague draft and spent the next two seasons shuttling between the Bruins and their Central Hockey League affiliate in Oklahoma City. From 1967–68 until his defection to the WHA's Cleveland Crusaders in the summer of 1972, Cheevers was one of the NHL's top goalies, backstopping the Bruins to the Stanley Cup in 1970 and 1972. During that five-year stretch his goals-against average never climbed above 2.83, and in the 1971–72 season he set a modern-day record by going 32 consecutive games without a loss (26 wins, five ties).

After jumping to the Crusaders for a reported $1.4 million, Cheevers became a perennial all-star and earned national accolades for his stalwart play against the Soviets in 1974. Two years later, when his WHA honeymoon ended in a bitter public quarrel with Cleveland GM Jack Vivian, Cheevers got his release from the long-term contract and rejoined the Bruins, for whom he performed admirably until his retirement following the 1979–80 season.

VACLAV NEDOMANSKY: It required a cloak-and-dagger scenario involving bogus travel documents and foreign agents before Toronto Toros' owner Johnny Bassett could successfully smuggle Vaclav Nedomansky and Richard Farda out of Europe in the summer of 1974, but the effort proved well worth the aggravation—at least for a while. Nedomansky, nicknamed "The Big N," was captain of the Czech national team and arguably one of the top ten players on the planet when he jumped to the WHA. A former national junior tennis champ and National League soccer star in his homeland, he was voted MVP at the 1973 world hockey championships and was Europe's all-time leading scorer.

While Farda turned out to be pretty much a bust, Nedomansky didn't disappoint the Toros. For most of the 1974–75 season he was flanked by Frank Mahovlich and Tony Featherstone on Toronto's top line and he responded by scoring 41 goals and 81 points. The following season he sniped 56 goals (third best in the league) and 98 points, but when the Toros became the Birmingham Bulls in 1977–78, Nedomansky's awesome talents suddenly deserted him. In one of the first major NHL-WHA trades he was swapped to the Detroit Red Wings along with Tim Sheehy for Dave Hanson and Steve Durbano. In six NHL seasons with Detroit, St. Louis and the New York Rangers "The Big N" notched 123 goals and 279 points.

TERRY RUSKOWSKI: Early in Terry Ruskowski's rookie season his teammates tagged him with the nickname "Jackhammer" after he went toe-to-toe with rugged San Diego defenseman Kevin Morrison. At five foot nine and 165 pounds Ruskowski was barely a middleweight, but he knew how to throw punches in bunches. Centering Houston's "Kid Line" between Rich Preston and Don Larway, he careened around the rink like a rabid pit bull, and his tenacity and willingness to get physical quickly made him a fan favorite.

"I've always been a fighter; most small guys are because we have to compensate for our lack of size," Ruskowski told *The Hockey News* in 1978. "My father was a boxer and when I was a little kid we used to put on mittens and box each other. My dad would get on his knees and kind of slap me around to get me mad." Terry once cracked a knuckle on his right hand after punching Cleveland's Richie Leduc in the head, and early in the 1975–76 playoffs he re-fractured the hand but didn't miss a game.

In 369 WHA outings Ruskowski racked up 761 penalty minutes. After the Aeros folded he was purchased by the Winnipeg Jets and then reclaimed by the Chicago Black Hawks following the NHL-WHA merger. In 10 NHL seasons with Chicago, Los Angeles, Pittsburgh and Minnesota, Terry notched 426 points and 1,354 penalty minutes.

GARY KURT: Gary Kurt was big. Big body, big hands, big gloves. And even though the six-foot-three, 210-pound former California Golden Seal rarely enjoyed the luxury of playing behind a solid defense, he had a knack for coming up with the big save when a game was on the line.

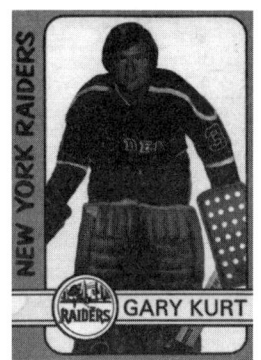

Kurt turned pro in the New York Rangers' organization and was claimed by the American Hockey League's Cleveland Barons in the 1969 "reverse draft." In 1970–71 he was voted to the AHL's second all-star team and won the Hap Holmes Memorial Trophy as the league's top goalie, posting a sparkling 2.67 goals-against average (GAA) and three shutouts. The following season saw him promoted to California in the NHL, where he appeared in 16 games and ballooned to a 4.29 GAA. Behind the Swiss cheese defense of the New York Raiders, in 1972–73 Kurt surrendered 150 goals and posted a 4.78 average, but he remained with the club through its subsequent incarnations as the New York Golden Blades, New Jersey Knights and San Diego Mariners before finally finding some stability with the Phoenix Roadrunners.

Kurt's career record of 72 wins, 86 losses, three shutouts and a 4.17 GAA is modest at best, but on the night of January 20, 1977, he set a single-game mark that was never matched by another WHA goaltender: three assists in the Roadrunners' 9–4 victory over the Cincinnati Stingers.

RICK JODZIO: "In 20 years of hockey I've never seen anything like it. The guy should be banned for life."

That was the reaction of Quebec Nordiques' coach Jean-Guy Gendron on the night of April 11, 1976, after Calgary Cowboys' forward Rick Jodzio triggered the worst bench-clearing brawl in WHA history with an unprovoked attack on Nordiques' superstar Marc Tardif. According to eyewitness accounts Jodzio came off the Calgary bench early in the opening period of the second quarter-final playoff game and raced 80 feet across the ice to cross-check Tardif in the face. He then dropped his gloves and unleashed a flurry of punches to the head of the fallen Nordique, who had to be carried from the ice on a stretcher. At one point the fighting was so heavy that 20 Quebec City police officers were on the ice trying to restore order. Tardif was subsequently diagnosed with a severe brain contusion and missed the remainder of the season.

For Jodzio it was the beginning of the end. He was suspended indefinitely by the WHA and the Quebec attorney-general's office charged him with assault with intent to injure. Several months later he pleaded guilty to a reduced charge of assault causing bodily harm and was fined $3,000. His defense attorney said Jodzio "was not a violent man or a savage... he never wanted to injure Tardif. The incident took place in the heat of action."

MARC TARDIF: Marc Tardif was never the same kind of hockey player after Rick Jodzio nearly decapitated him during a 1976 playoff game (see above). In addition to a severe brain contusion, Tardif had several broken teeth and numerous lacerations. Eyewitnesses said he appeared to be already unconscious when Jodzio started throwing punches, which perhaps explains why the mild-mannered Nords' star had no recollection of the attack for months afterwards.

"It's difficult for me to say exactly what took place because I didn't see it happen. I never saw him. I didn't even know he was coming at me. In fact, I didn't even know Jodzio was on the ice," Tardif told the *Montreal Gazette*. "All I remember is that there was a faceoff in our end and we won it. Then I turned around to try and reach the puck. The next thing I knew I came to in the hospital. They told me I was unconscious for about 30 minutes."

Lingering effects from his injuries cost Tardif the opportunity to represent his country after he was selected to play for the inaugural Canada Cup squad. He was coming off a record-setting year that saw him score 71 goals and 148 points, but in later interviews he spoke wistfully about having to change his style of play as a result of his nightmare encounter with Jodzio.

Tardif was the all-time WHA leader in goals (316) and ranked second in points (666). He remained with the Nords after the merger and retired in 1983.

ROSAIRE PAIEMENT: Rosaire Paiement became the first genuine star on the Vancouver Canucks when they joined the NHL in 1970–71, scoring 34 goals in 78 games after notching only four in three previous big-league tryouts with the Philadelphia Flyers. At one point during the following season, when Paiement struggled to pot just 10 goals in 69 games, the Canucks hired a professional hypnotist to attempt to convince him that he could score like Maurice Richard. It didn't work. Paiement became a free agent, signed a multi-year contract with the WHA's Chicago Cougars on June 23, 1972, and ended up leading the last-place Cougars with 33 goals while playing with Bobby Sicinski and Jan Popiel on what became known as the "Power Line."

Paiement signed with New England after the Cougars folded and counted 83 points in 93 games with the Whalers before he was dealt to the Indianapolis Racers in exchange for Gary MacGregor. While he was with Indy, Paiement's WHA "ironman" streak came to an end at 439 consecutive games when he was punched in the eye by Edmonton's Dave Semenko. Paiement never completely recovered from the injury and called it quits after the 1977–78 season.

Upon retirement Paiement moved to Florida and purchased a hotel and sports bar—appropriately called The Penalty Box Lounge.

MARTY HOWE: One afternoon in the mid-1960s the telephone rang at the Howe residence in suburban Detroit.

"Is your father home?" the caller asked 11-year-old Marty.

"Nope."

"Do you know when he'll be back?"

"Nope."

"Is he at work right now?"

"Nope," Marty replied. "My dad doesn't work. He's a hockey player."

Relating that story 25 years later on a bus carrying him to a sportscard show in rural Alberta, Marty Howe sighed the sigh of a grown man who could still relate to that naive kid.

"Who knew?" he said. "As far as my brother and me were concerned, Gordie was just out there playing with the Red Wings, having fun and going on trips. But in the WHA we learned pretty quickly that hockey is a lot of hard work."

Overshadowed by his father and brother, Marty was nonetheless a superbly talented defenseman—especially considering he didn't begin playing serious hockey until high school. A member of Team Canada '74, he had 184 points in 449 WHA games with the Aeros and Whalers, followed by six seasons in the post-merger NHL with the Hartford Whalers and Boston Bruins.

MARK HOWE: All of the Howes took part in writing their unprecedented chapter in hockey history, but it was Mark who left the most indelible impression. The "old man," as Gordie liked to refer to himself, was still dangerous and at times played like a young colt while Marty was steady, if unspectacular. Mark, on the other hand, did everything with flair, whether it was scoring goals, making plays or using his deceptive speed to open up the ice for his linemates.

On November 5, 1975, Mark scored the 1,000th goal in Aeros' history en route to a hat trick in front of the 12,053 fans who witnessed the first game ever played in the $18-million Summit Arena. Just for good measure, Gordie fired a goal and two assists that night and Marty contributed a pair of helpers. The game was the first for Mark after being hospitalized for four days for treatment of a black widow spider bite. "It was quite a night," former teammate Frank Hughes recalled. "We were all asking Mark afterwards if he knew where the rest of us could find some more spiders."

Mark won the Lou Kaplan Trophy as rookie of the year in 1973–74 and was a co-winner (with Marc Tardif) of the MVP award in the 1978 all-star game. Claimed as a priority selection of the Hartford Whalers in the 1979 NHL expansion draft, he later starred for Philadelphia and Detroit in a 16-year NHL career that saw him chalk up 742 points in 929 games.

PAUL HENDERSON: Paul Henderson scored the most celebrated goal in hockey history on September 28, 1972, when he slammed his own rebound past Vladislav Tretiak with 34 seconds left in the deciding game of the historic Summit Series between the NHL and the Soviet Nationals. That final shot, which today represents almost the same kind of generational freeze-

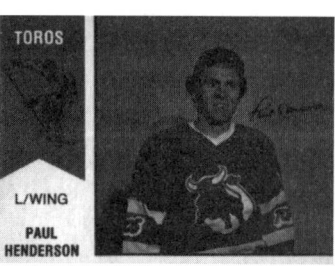

frame for Canadians that John Kennedy's assassination does for Americans, capped an incredible series for the soft-spoken Henderson, who also scored the winning goals in games six and seven. How popular was he? Suffice to say that had 1972 been an election year, Henderson could have been elected prime minister. Easily.

Henderson left the NHL for the Toronto Toros in 1974 and had 283 points in 360 WHA games. After the merger he returned to the NHL for a brief swan song with the Atlanta Flames.

TOM WEBSTER: Tom Webster was nicknamed "Hawkeye" not because of his shot (which was terrific) or his affinity for *M*A*S*H* reruns on TV. He picked up the handle when he started wearing contact lenses to correct his legally blind vision.

Originally owned by the Boston Bruins, Webster became a Buffalo Sabre in the 1970 NHL Expansion Draft, but the Sabres promptly swapped him to the Detroit Red Wings for Roger Crozier. Despite scoring 30 goals for the Wings in 1970–71, he was traded to the California Golden Seals for Ron Stackhouse then jumped from the Seals to the WHA's New England Whalers in the summer of 1972.

Always a proficient scorer, Webster fired 220 goals and 425 points in 352 WHA games. He later returned to the NHL as a coach, most notably with the L.A. Kings from 1989–92.

ANDY BROWN: The Browns were a tough family. Andy's father Adam played 391 NHL games for Detroit, Boston and Chicago and served 333 penalty minutes. Andy did his best to keep up the family tradition, racking up 75 minutes (a record for WHA goalies) in his first year with the Indianapolis Racers after three NHL seasons with the Detroit Red Wings and Pittsburgh Penguins.

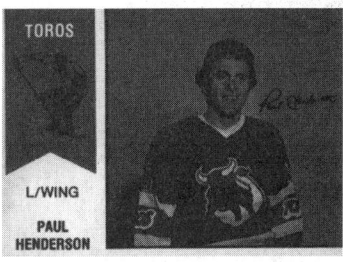

But what really established Brown's reputation for toughness was his utter disdain for facial protection. He threw away his mask for good while still with the Penguins, and on March 31, 1973, he became the last NHL goalie to appear maskless in Pittsburgh's 7–2 loss to the St. Louis Blues.

Besides Brown, who never donned a mask in 86 games with Indy, the only other bare-faced WHA goalies were Winnipeg's Joe Daley and L.A.'s Bob Perreault, both in 1972–73.

GILLES GRATTON: Gilles Gratton was strange, even by a goaltender's standards. He once explained his recurring abdominal pains by claiming he was a reincarnated soldier from the Spanish Inquisition. "I've seen it in my mind," he told *The Hockey News* in 1977. "Was I a knight? No, just a simple soldier. But I was killed when I was run through with a lance."

With the Toronto Toros Gratton once "streaked" a practice, appearing on the ice wearing only his mask and skates. He jumped from the WHA to the NHL and back twice, then briefly quit the game because he felt he was getting hit in the arms too often. "In biblical days I stoned people to death, so now I am stoned by pucks as punishment," he said. "I must quit before I am killed." But for all his weirdness, Gilles could play. He was picked for Team Canada '74 and had a record of 81–66–7 in the WHA with a fine 3.69 average.

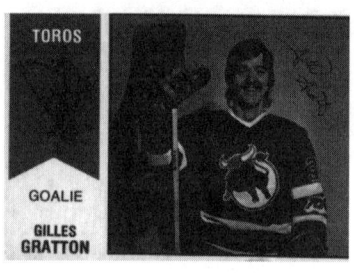

JOHNNY McKENZIE: Johnny McKenzie was one of the first "name" stars from the National Hockey League to defect to the WHA, and as player-coach of the Philadelphia Blazers he scored the first goal in franchise history in a 3–1 exhibition victory over the Ottawa Nationals. In the Blazers' next exhibition outing against Quebec, McKenzie broke his arm in a collision with a goal post and was sidelined for two months. A tireless skater and fierce checker, he broke into the NHL with Chicago in 1958–59 then was traded to Detroit along with Len Lunde for Doug Barkley. He later played for the New York Rangers, who in turn swapped him to the Boston Bruins for Reggie Fleming in 1966. It was as a member of the "Big Bad Bruins" that McKenzie gained his greatest notoriety, playing a key role on Boston's Stanley Cup-winning teams in 1970 and 1972.

Nicknamed "Pie" for his round face, McKenzie for years spent the off-season as a rodeo cowboy until the Bruins put a clause in his contract forbidding the activity. McKenzie was selected for Team Canada '74, and after moving with the Blazers to Vancouver for two seasons, he joined the Minnesota Fighting Saints. When Minnesota folded for the first time he signed as a free agent with the Cincinnati Stingers, then rejoined the "new" Saints before winding up his WHA career with New England. When the Whalers joined the NHL they honoured McKenzie's contribution to the WHA by retiring his number 19.

LARRY PLEAU: For Larry Pleau, being first came naturally.

The Boston-born centre was the first U.S. high school player to graduate to the Montreal Junior Canadiens, and the first to go from the Junior Habs to the U.S. Olympic team. He won rookie of the year honours with the Jersey Devils in the Eastern Hockey League in 1968–69, despite missing part of the season to fulfill his obligation to the U.S. Army.

Pleau played 94 NHL games with Montreal, then on April 19, 1972, he became the first player to sign a contract with the New England Whalers. Six months later Pleau scored the winning goal in the Whalers' home opener, a 4–3 victory over Derek Sanderson, Johnny McKenzie and the rest of the Philadelphia Blazers in front of 14,500 fans at Boston Garden. The following May Pleau sniped the winning goal and the Whalers' first playoff hat trick in a 9–6 victory over the Winnipeg Jets that clinched the inaugural WHA championship.

In a strange twist a few weeks after Pleau became the first Whaler signed to a contract, the Montreal Canadiens traded his NHL rights to the Toronto Maple Leafs in return for defenseman Brad Selwood. Selwood later joined Pleau in New England, and he and Rick Ley would become the only players to remain with the Whalers through the entire seven-year history of the WHA.

BOB WOYTOWICH: A common sight at Pittsburgh's Civic Arena from 1968 to 1971 was a huge banner high up in the stands that read "Bob Woytowich's Polish Army." Penguin fans adored the rangy defenseman they nicknamed "Our Kolbassi Kid," even though he was a Ukrainian-Canadian from Winnipeg.

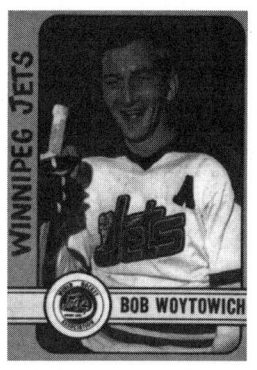

"I was very fortunate to break into pro hockey in the old six-team NHL," Bob recalled after signing with his hometown Jets in 1972. "There were plenty of guys down below waiting for a chance to come up. I was lucky in that I was drafted by the Boston Bruins in 1964. If it had been any other team I might still be waiting, but the Bruins gave me a chance that first season to show that I could play." In 1967 Woytowich was selected by the Minnesota North Stars in the original Expansion Draft, then spent three seasons in Pittsburgh before closing out his NHL career with the Los Angeles Kings in 1971–72.

Like Jets' playing-coach Bobby Hull, legal hassles over his NHL status kept Bob out of the Winnipeg lineup for the first few weeks of the WHA's premiere season, but after being cleared to play his experience and big-league savvy helped settle down the Jets' young blue line corps and he played a key role in propelling the club to the Western Division championship.

Woytowich retired after the 1975–76 season with 60 points in 242 WHA games with Winnipeg and Indianapolis.

ROBBIE FTOREK: Robbie Ftorek went from being a fourth-line centre behind Marcel Dionne, Red Berenson and Guy Charron on the Detroit Red Wings (1972–74) to becoming the first American-born big leaguer to win MVP honours. The fact that he was also the first player in history to score 100 points and get 100 penalty minutes in the same season, and the second to win an MVP award while toiling for a last-place team, only underlined how much he meant to the WHA in general and the Phoenix Roadrunners in particular. Ironically,  the only other player to be an MVP with a last-place club was Ftorek's coach in Phoenix, Al Rollins, who won the Hart Trophy with the Chicago Black Hawks in 1953–54.

After the Roadrunners folded Ftorek joined the Cincinnati Stingers where, in a hockey first, he and teammate Claude Larose received special permission from the league to *both* wear sweater number eight. Larose was the Stingers' top draft choice in 1975 and had already become a star wearing his favorite number, but the Boston-born Ftorek had worn number eight through his entire pro career as a tribute to ex-Bruin great Fleming Mackell.

"When I was a kid I met Mr. Mackell one day at Boston Garden," recalled Ftorek. "He took me into the Bruins' dressing room, cut down a stick to my size and took me around to shake hands with all the players. His kindness left a lasting impression on me, and that's why I've always worn his old number."

LES BINKLEY: After watching the Ottawa Nationals' veteran goaltender block 48 shots one night, a Philadelphia newspaper columnist wrote: "Les Binkley looks somewhat like he sounds, meaning he could pass for a near-sighted, narrow-chested bird watcher."

Maybe so, but looks can be deceiving. Binkley's hockey résumé looked like a travel brochure when the Nats signed the 37-year-old from the NHL's Pittsburgh Penguins in the fall of 1972. He'd played for the Kitchener Dutchmen, Fort Wayne Komets, Baltimore

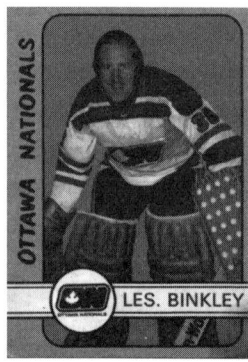

Clippers, Toledo Mercurys, Cleveland Barons and San Diego Gulls over a 12-year minor league career before the Penguins selected him in the 1967 Expansion Draft. At one point in Cleveland, Binkley had actually retired as a player and was serving as the Barons' trainer when an injury to the regular goalie forced him back into the crease. Such is the stuff of legends!

The Nationals had originally hoped to sign Doug Favell from the Philadelphia Flyers as their number one goalie, but when he couldn't be lured to the WHA they settled for Binkley, who signed a five-year no-cut contract for a reported $60,000 per season. He was injured early in the season and won only 10 of 30 games for the Nats, but rebounded to post a 14–9–1 mark with two shutouts and two playoff victories for the Toronto Toros in 1973–74.

Binkley retired after the 1975–76 season and later became a scout for Pittsburgh.

BARRY LONG: "I'm not flashy, but I get the job done."

That's the way big (six foot two, 210 pounds) Barry Long described his style of play after he was named to the Canadian contingent for the WHA's fourth annual All-Star Game in Cleveland. Long turned pro in the Chicago Black Hawks' organization and spent three years with their Central Hockey League affiliate in Dallas before moving on to the Portland Buckaroos in the Western League.

"Portland is where I really started to come on," he said. "Because of my size I had been expected to just run everybody out of the rink. I'm good at taking the body, but I'm not an animal. In Portland I got a chance to develop other skills, like carrying the puck out of my own end. It really paid off, because the next year I was in the NHL with the Los Angeles Kings."

Barry jumped to the Oilers in the spring of 1974 and in his first season with Edmonton he potted 20 goals and 60 points. He was traded to the Winnipeg Jets for future considerations in October 1976 and became an integral part of the Jets' back-to-back Avco Trophy championship teams in 1978 and 1979.

"My first year in Winnipeg I spent adjusting to the Jets' European style of play... hanging onto the puck and playing a control type of game as opposed to a dump-and-chase," Long later recalled. "It was kind of revolutionary back then, but everybody wants to play that way today. We were ahead of our time."

GLEN SATHER: Glen (Slats) Sather is living proof that you don't have to be a great player to become a great coach. Indeed, Sather was a clumsy skater who came up short in almost every other skill category, but he more than made up for his modest talents with grit, savvy and quick fists. Only five foot ten and 180 pounds, he never backed down from a fight and rarely lost one.

Following an unspectacular junior career with the Edmonton Oil Kings, Sather broke into the NHL with the Boston Bruins in 1966–67. From Boston he went to Pittsburgh, the New York Rangers, St. Louis, Montreal and Minnesota. His forte was defensive play and penalty killing, and his best NHL season was 1973–74 when he chalked up 44 points (15–29) in 69 games for St. Louis. He jumped to the Edmonton Oilers in 1976–77 and had the finest statistical season of his career with 19 goals and 53 points. More significantly, he was also asked to replace Bep Guidolin as coach for the last 18 games and responded by guiding the slumping Oilers into the final playoff spot.

Sather's fate was sealed. He remained with the Oilers after the merger and went on to add the titles of general manager and president to his duties as head coach. He was behind the bench for four of Edmonton's five Stanley Cup championships in the 1980s and helped mastermind three Canada Cup titles. Not too shabby for a clumsy penalty killer.

REG FLEMING: Reg Fleming was an established NHL tough guy when the Chicago Cougars came calling in 1972, but he surprised a lot of people by blossoming into a goal scorer in the WHA's first season.

Fleming made his NHL debut in a three-game trial with the Montreal Canadiens in 1959–60, but later that year he was part of an eight-player trade that also saw Ab McDonald move from the Habs to the Chicago Black Hawks. The Hawks dealt Fleming and McDonald to the Boston Bruins for Doug Mohns in 1964, and the Bruins subsequently swapped him to New York for Johnny McKenzie in 1966.

While Fleming gained his greatest fame as a fighter (1,468 penalty minutes in 749 NHL games), he could also put the puck in the net when he got the opportunity. With the first-year Cougars he scored 23 goals and 68 points in 74 games, but the following season, slowed by injuries, he slumped to just 14 points in 45 games. Released by the Cougars, he failed a tryout with the Quebec Nordiques in the fall of 1974 and then drew the curtain on a 20-year career that saw him score 322 points while racking up 1,610 penalty minutes in 869 major league games.

Following his retirement Fleming became a sales rep for a Chicago brewery and later launched his own business, specializing in promotional items.

TED GREEN: "How's your head?"

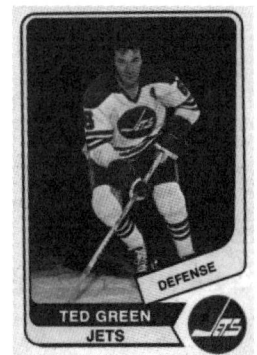

Even though Ted Green played 20 years of major league hockey, won six Stanley Cups (one as a player in Boston and five as an assistant coach in Edmonton) and three Avco World Trophies, and was an All-Star in both the NHL and WHA, he's invariably asked about the plate in his head.

Green and Wayne Maki of the St. Louis Blues were involved in a vicious stick-swing duel in an exhibition game prior to the 1969–70 NHL season. Green sustained serious brain injuries that resulted in the left side of his body being paralyzed. Three major operations were necessary to restore the full use of his body, including one that required the insertion of a steel plate in his skull. After missing an entire season Green made a miraculous comeback which he later chronicled in a book entitled *High Stick!*

Green played an important role in the Bruins' 1972 Stanley Cup triumph, then joined the New England Whalers and captained them to the WHA's first Avco Trophy championship. He was traded from the Whalers to Winnipeg three years later and was a key member of the Jets' Avco Trophy teams in 1976 and 1978.

In an tragically ironic twist, Wayne Maki, the player who nearly cost Ted Green his life, died of a brain tumor a few years after their near-fatal skirmish.

WAYNE CONNELLY: In the first year of the WHA every team seemed to have a player who became known simply as "The Franchise." In Winnipeg, obviously, it was Bobby Hull. In Edmonton it was Jim Harrison. In Ottawa it was Wayne Carleton. And for the Minnesota Fighting Saints it was Wayne Connelly, a hard-shooting right winger who five years earlier had been named player of the year in the NHL's West Division by leading the expansion Minnesota North Stars with 35 goals and 56 points in 74 games.

Connelly's first taste of the big leagues came in a three-game trial with the Montreal Canadiens during the 1960–61 season. Traded to Boston the following year, Wayne spent the next six seasons shuttling back and forth between the Bruins and the San Francisco Seals of the Western Hockey League. Claimed by the North Stars in the 1967 expansion draft, he later played for Detroit, St. Louis and Vancouver before becoming the first National Hockey League player to sign a WHA contract in the spring of 1972.

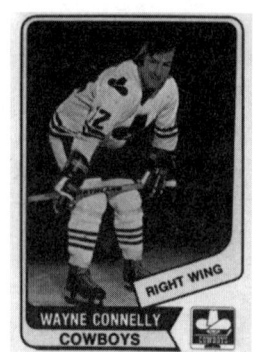

Connelly led the Fighting Saints in scoring with 40 goals and 70 points in their debut season and followed up with 42 goals and 95 points in 1973–74. When the Saints folded their tent in 1976 he signed with the Cleveland Crusaders for half a season and then split his final campaign between the Calgary Cowboys and Edmonton Oilers.

WAYNE RUTLEDGE: Lanky Wayne Rutledge logged a lot of miles on minor league bus trips before finally cracking the NHL as an original draft choice of the Los Angeles Kings. He played junior with the Niagara Falls Flyers before embarking on a five-year minor league career that included stops in Windsor, Kingston, Clinton, St. Paul, Omaha and Springfield. With the expansion Kings the six-foot-two, 200-pound Rutledge was supposed to be the understudy for legendary Terry Sawchuk, but for most of the 1967–68 season he out-

played the taciturn Sawchuk, appearing in 45 games and posting a brilliant 2.87 goals-against average. The saddest scene in the Stanley Cup playoffs that year was a crowd of 12,000 in Los Angeles chanting "We want Rutledge!" while pelting Sawchuk with popcorn boxes, programs and other debris after he allowed four second-period goals in a 9–4 loss to Minnesota. It wasn't something Rutledge soon forgot.

"Terry taught me a lot that one season we were together, and I remember being very angry and feeling very sorry for him the night the North Stars eliminated us," Wayne recalled years later. "It wasn't Terry's fault. A goalie doesn't win or lose a game all by himself."

Rutledge became a genuine star in Houston, spending his entire WHA career with the Aeros. He had a 93–72–7 regular season record and was the league's all-time leader in playoff goals-against average with a sparkling 2.88.

JOHN GARRETT: John Garrett the TV star has always had the good sense to make John Garrett the goaltender sound a lot worse than he was. In fact, Garrett was one of the finest young goaltenders in the seven-year history of the WHA, and he proved it by starring in the NHL for another six seasons after the merger.

Today most fans know Garrett as a quick-witted colour analyst on *Hockey Night in Canada* telecasts, but his self-effacing humour belies a competitive streak honed over six seasons of playing behind porous defenses on the Minnesota Fighting Saints, Toronto Toros, Birmingham Bulls and New England Whalers. He ranks among the WHA's all-time top five goalies in regular season wins (148), playoff wins (15), shutouts (14) and minutes played (18,919) and he appeared in three all-star games. In the NHL he toiled for Hartford, Quebec and Vancouver, posting 68 wins in 207 appearances.

Once while working as a colourman on a telecast in Edmonton, Garrett came close to launching a "comeback" after the Oilers' starting netminder was injured in the warm-up. The team needed a back-up to sit on the bench and general manager Glen Sather remembered that Garrett was up in the press box.

"I signed the first 'multi-minute' contract in history and was actually on my way down to the dressing room when they found out the other guy was okay," chuckled Garrett. "I was ready, but I don't know if the Oilers were."

REAL CLOUTIER: Real (Buddy) Cloutier could skate like Bobby Hull, stickhandle like Bobby Orr and score goals like Guy Lafleur. From the blue line to the crease he seemed to explode off his right wing position, effortlessly coralling passes in full flight and whipping high hard wrist shots past startled goalies, all in one motion. As the first successful teenage pheenom in the WHA, it looked like his biggest problem would be finding a vault large enough to store all his bonus money.

Like Lafleur, Cloutier played his junior hockey for the Quebec Ramparts, scoring an astounding 93 goals and 216 points as 17-year-old in 1973–74. The following season he signed with the Nordiques, but after he potted just 26 goals and 53 points in 67 games his critics smugly concluded Cloutier was just a high-priced underage flash, destined for mediocrity. They were dead wrong.

In 1975–76 the 19-year-old Cloutier became the youngest player in history to score 60 major league goals in a single season and he was named to the second all-star team. The following year he fired a WHA record eight hat tricks en route to 66 goals, 141 points and the league scoring title. He repeated as scoring champ in the WHA's final season, sniping 75 goals and 129 points.

In 235 games with Quebec in the NHL, Cloutier had 122 goals and 284 points. In 1983 he was traded to the Buffalo Sabres for Tony McKegney, Andre Savard and Jean-Francois Sauve. He retired after the 1984–85 season.

RON CHIPPERFIELD: In the words of one Calgary newspaper columnist, Ron Chipperfield "had a talent for making the game look pretty." He wasn't a particularly good skater and his shot was only average at best, but on his good nights "Chipper" played like he owned the puck—setting up his wingers with brilliant passes, snapping shots from the top of the slot, and generally creating havoc every time he crossed the enemy's blue line.

After putting up phenomenal numbers in a four-year junior career with the Brandon Wheat Kings he turned professional with the Vancouver Blazers in 1974–75, scoring 19 goals and 39 points. Ron more than doubled his production the following season (42–41–83), but when the Blazers moved to Calgary and became the Cowboys he came under fire from coach Joe Crozier, who thought the 5-foot-11, 185-pound Chipperfield should be more aggressive. "Everybody has to check—including Ron," said Crozier. "I know some people think that asking him to run around and bump into people is like asking Picasso to paint the back fence, but there has to be a happy medium."

After the Cowboys folded Chipperfield signed with Edmonton. Teamed with Wayne Gretzky and Blair MacDonald, he helped lead the Oilers into the WHA's last Avco Trophy final against Winnipeg. He remained with the team after the merger and served as the Oilers' first captain in the NHL.

CHRIS BORDELEAU: The Winnipeg Jets landed a good one when they lured Christian (Pepe) Bordeleau away from the Chicago Black Hawks in 1972. After all, they had a pretty good left winger named Hull, so it only made sense to reel in a centre who'd had some experience feeding the puck to Number Nine.

Bordeleau was groomed in the Montreal Canadiens' system. He spent four years with the Junior Habs in the Ontario Hockey Association, followed by a two-year apprenticeship with the Houston Apollos in the Central League. He saw action in 61 games with the Montreal from 1968–70, but with an abundance of talented centres the Canadiens sold him to the St. Louis Blues in 1970. Traded to Chicago prior to the 1971–72 season, he saw regular duty between Hull and Chico Maki and responded with 14 goals and 31 points.

Perhaps Bordeleau's greatest asset was his adaptability. He was a throwback to the days of "two-way, all-the-way" hockey and was equally effective killing penalties or shadowing the other team's big scorer as he was at creating offense. In 1972 Bordeleau, Hull and Norm Beaudin became the first line in major league history to have each member record at least 100 points, and Chris notched a career-high 47 goals.

In the fall of 1974 Bordeleau was traded to Quebec for Alain Beaule. He retired from the Nordiques in 1979 with 504 points in 412 WHA games.

CLAUDE ST. SAUVEUR: In the late 1960s a popular TV series called *The Saint* featured a young Roger Moore as a handsome, dashing master thief. Vancouver Blazers' centre Claude St. Sauveur was likewise dubbed "The Saint" after his teammates first witnessed the rookie's deft stickhandling and uncanny ability to steal the puck from opposing players.

Claude's 55 goals and 107 points with the Eastern League's Roanoke Valley Rebels in 1972–73 earned him a spot on the Blazers roster the following season, and he didn't disappoint. With 38 goals and 68 points he finished second to Mark Howe in the rookie of the year vote and was one of the few bright spots on a decidedly dismal Vancouver team.

St. Sauveur jumped to the NHL's Atlanta Flames in 1975–76 for one season, then returned to the WHA with Calgary. He later saw action with Indianapolis, Edmonton and Cincinnati.

TOM SIMPSON: Tom (Shotgun) Simpson became the first professional player in Toronto hockey history to score 50 goals in a single season when he notched 52 for the Toros in 1974–75. Three years later he was out of hockey.

A talented lacrosse player in the off-season, Simpson had a howitzer slapshot that he liked to unleash from the top of the slot as he cut in from his right wing position. He was equally deadly from the point on the Toros' potent power play, which also routinely featured Frank Mahovlich, Wayne Dillon, Vaclav Nedomansky and Jim Dorey.

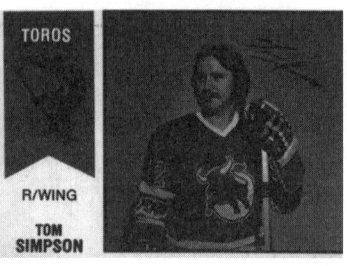

Simpson slumped to just 20 goals the year following his record season, and shortly after the Toros relocated to Birmingham he was traded, along with Gavin Kirk, to the Edmonton Oilers for Tim Sheehy.

He retired in 1977 with 125 goals in 313 WHA games.

GERRY ODROWSKI: Gerry Odrowski's career was a testament to perseverance. He played two full NHL seasons with the Detroit Red Wings from 1960–62, then spent the next five years bouncing around the minors before getting another shot at the big time with the Oakland Seals from 1967–69. Another long exile to the minors followed before Odrowski played his last NHL season with St. Louis (1971–72), and then the WHA came along and he became an original Los Angeles Shark. Odrowski's solid play earned him an invitation to the WHA's first all-star game, and he promptly scored the first goal in the East Division's 6–2 victory over the West.

"Joining the WHA was the best move I made; I finally found a home," Odrowski said after succeeding Bill Hicke as head of the Players Association in 1973. "Hockey is fun again."

SERGE BERNIER: For a guy who never put on skates until he was 13 and didn't play hockey until he was 15, Serge Bernier was a quick learner.

Drafted from the junior Sorel Eperviers by Philadelphia in 1967, he spent two years with Quebec in the American Hockey League before becoming a Flyers' regular in 1970. Bernier tallied 23 goals as a rookie but in 1971 he was dealt to Los Angeles, where he starred for two years before jumping to the WHA. He was one of Team

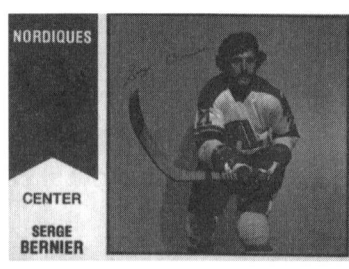

Canada's best forwards in the 1974 series against the Soviet Union, and in the 1974–75 season he scored a career-high 54 goals and 122 points and was named to the second all-star team. He led the Nordiques to the 1977 Avco Trophy championship with 36 points en route to being voted the MVP of the playoffs.

DAVE KEON: Dave Keon, a lightning-quick leprechaun from Noranda, Quebec, was every coach's dream. A tireless worker, effortless skater and creative playmaker, he was 35 years old when he abandoned a 14-year career with the Toronto Maple Leafs to join the Minnesota Fighting Saints in 1975. But even at that advanced age, Saints' coach Harry Neale couldn't have been more pleased.

"Very few WHA teams ever get an opportunity to sign a player of Dave's talents and character; he brings a lot more to the club than just goals and assists," Neale said. "Dave Keon is one of the truly great people in hockey."

Keon played on four Stanley Cup winners in Toronto and was the Leafs' all-time scoring leader when he left the NHL. In Minnesota, working on a line with Johnny McKenzie and Mike Antonovich, he scored 30 points in his first 38 games. After the Saints folded for the first time, Keon finished the season with the Indianapolis Racers then briefly returned to Minnesota for the Saints' last hurrah. Declared a free agent in January 1977, he was reunited with McKenzie when they were both purchased by the New England Whalers.

One of the most memorable sights in the last two years of the WHA was Keon, McKenzie and Gordie Howe turning back the clock and going all out on the Whalers' power play. Keon remained with the Whalers after the merger and played two more seasons in the NHL to round out a fabulous 20-year career.

MIKE AMODEO: When the Winnipeg Jets lost the services of Swedish defenseman Thommie Bergman in 1978, they looked to Bergman's homeland for a replacement and found one in ex-Ottawa National Mike Amodeo.

"I basically went to Sweden to get a job; I played three years with Ottawa and the Toronto Toros, but when the opportunities in the WHA seemed to dry up I went to Europe," Amodeo told a Winnipeg reporter. "I was with a club team in Orebro for two years and it was quite an experience.

The hockey was pretty much what I expected, but there were a lot of surprises with everyday life. It's a completely different society and I had to make some adjustments. Coming back, the hockey seems slower than I remember it, except the small things happen a lot quicker on the ice here than they do in Europe. Overall, the game pace is slower in the WHA, but things like positioning and the transition from defense to offense seem to happen a bit faster."

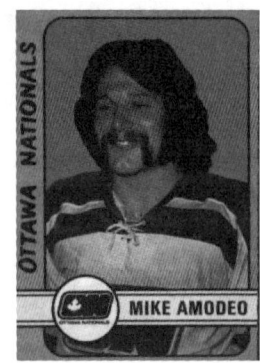

Amodeo played his junior hockey for the Toronto Marlboros and Niagara Falls Flyers and was one of the first players to sign with Ottawa in 1972. He scored just two goals in the first 201 games of his WHA career, but after joining the high-flying Jets late in the 1977–78 season he contributed two goals and four assists in 10 games.

Amodeo remained with the Jets after the merger, but retired after appearing in just 19 games during the 1979–80 NHL season.

BRYAN CAMPBELL: After breaking into the NHL with the Los Angeles Kings, Bryan (Soupy) Campbell had been another on the long list of centres acquired by the Chicago Black Hawks to fill the spot between Bobby Hull and Chico Maki. When the experiment didn't pan out Campbell jumped to the Philadelphia Blazers and for four years he was arguably the most unappreciated forward in the WHA, racking up 73, 89, 62 and 72 points before nagging injuries and unrealistic expectations began to catch up with him.

Campbell's style was to let the puck do the work. He was a master at hitting his wingers with long breakout passes and then trailing the play into the offensive zone, ready to pounce on a rebound or loose puck. Like Frank Mahovlich, Campbell also had a knack for piling up a lot of points while seeming to do very little on the ice. It was an unfair rap (as it was for Mahovlich) that dogged him through six WHA seasons.

Bryan followed the Blazers to Vancouver, but when the franchise moved to Calgary he was traded to the Cincinnati Stingers, who in turn swapped him to the Indianapolis Racers before the 1976–77 season. He played only eight games with Indy before being traded to Edmonton for Gene Peacosh, but over the final two seasons of Campbell's career injuries took their toll, limiting him to just 119 games and 74 points.

Part 3

POSTGAME INTERVIEWS

Twenty Pioneers Recall the Good, the Bad and the Ugly about the Early Days of the WHA

Ralph Backstrom
Ken Brown
Wayne Carleton
Joe Daley
Val Fonteyne
Al Hamilton
Jim Harrison
Gordie Howe
Frank Hughes
Andre Lacroix
Mike Laughton
Danny Lawson
Larry Lund
Rusty Patenaude
Gerry Pinder
Garth Rizzuto
Paul Shmyr
Pat Stapleton
Ron Ward
Bobby Whitlock

RALPH BACKSTROM

Centre ... Born in Kirkland Lake, Ont., Sept. 18, 1937 ... Played left wing and defense during starry junior career with Montreal Junior Canadiens ... Enjoyed 15-year NHL career with Montreal, Los Angeles and Chicago ... Won six Stanley Cups with the Canadiens and appeared in six NHL all-star games ... Won the Calder Memorial Trophy as NHL rookie of the year after scoring 18 goals and 40 points in 64 games with the Canadiens, 1958–59 ... Traded from Montreal to the Los Angeles Kings for Ray Fortin and Gord Labossiere, Jan. 1971 ... Traded by the Kings to the Chicago Black Hawks for Dan Maloney, Feb. 1973 ... Signed multi-year contract with the WHA's Chicago Cougars on Aug. 7, 1973 ... Scored eight game-winning goals for the Cougars in 1973–74, won the Paul Deneau Trophy as the WHA's most gentlemanly player and was named to Team Canada '74 ... Also played for the Denver Spurs, Ottawa Civics and New England Whalers ... **Major league totals**: (Regular season) **NHL** - 1,032 games, 278 goals, 361 assists, 639 points, 386 penalty minutes. **WHA** - 304 games, 100 goals, 153 assists, 253 points, 104 penalty minutes. (Playoffs) **NHL** - 116 games, 27 goals, 32 assists, 59 points, 68 penalty minutes. **WHA** - 38 games, 10 goals, 18 assists, 28 points, 12 penalty minutes.

"I was playing for the Los Angeles Kings when the WHA was formed. One day I got a call from Larry Regan, our general manager, who asked me to meet with him and the owner, Jack Kent Cooke. It turned out they wanted to extend my contract. I was in a battle with Juha Widing for the Kings' scoring title, so I told them I thought I'd be in a little better negotiating position if I finished as the team's top scorer. Right away they wanted to know if I was jumping to the WHA, and I told them no. I hadn't even considered it at that point.

"Cooke calmed down after that and said he would write up two contracts: one for if I finished as the top scorer and one for less money if I finished second. I said, 'Thanks but no thanks,' and the meeting was over. This was on a Friday afternoon. On Sunday Regan called me at home and said, 'We just traded you to Chicago.'

"I went to the Black Hawks for 16 games, and we ended up going all the way to the Stanley Cup finals against Montreal. That was a big thrill for me, since I'd played all those years in Montreal.

"What really started to convince me to jump to the WHA was the time the Black Hawks handed out the first-place bonus money. The Hawks had traded for me because Stan Mikita was hurt and they were in a dogfight with Philadelphia for first place. They wanted a seasoned guy who could help them down the stretch to finish in first, and I did that. But when it came time to hand out the first-place money, all they gave me was 16/80 of a share because I'd been picked up with 16 games left. That sort of triggered it for me. After all those years in the National Hockey League, I was being treated like that.

"After the playoffs I was the only guy on the Black Hawks whose contract was up, and of course the Chicago Cougars were across town and they'd already signed Pat Stapleton as player-coach. The Cougars contacted me with a nice offer, so, keeping in mind that 16/80 bonus share, I decided it was time to try something different. That's how I joined the WHA.

"I was pleasantly surprised at how strong the league was when I went over there. It was very, very competitive. It was a hard sell initially, not because of the quality of play, but because a lot of people were convinced it couldn't last. I think there were only 14 teams in the National Hockey League at that time, and most fans thought that anything that wasn't the NHL had to be an inferior league, but I didn't see it that way. The WHA didn't have a large talent base because it was a new league, but it [the league] had a lot more parity than the NHL, and because of the WHA a lot of hockey jobs opened up all over the place—not just for players, but for coaches, scouts, trainers, radio announcers and a lot of other people.

"What used to really irk me was when I'd run into NHL players who were always bad-mouthing the WHA for being weaker. They seemed to forget that it was because of our league that their salaries had more than doubled in just a few years. At my age I felt that by going to the WHA I was helping, in a small way, to do something for the welfare of future players. That gave me a lot of gratification, especially early on, when some of the teams were having trouble surviving. I played for four different teams in four years in that league, and I was never traded or sold, so you can imagine what it was like. And having come up through the six-team NHL, I knew that what the WHA was trying to accomplish would have a long-term impact on professional hockey.

"To this day I think back to the team we had in Chicago with a lot of fond memories...and the amazing thing is that most of the other WHA teams were built the same way. We had a good mix of veterans and young guys just starting out, and there was a real sense of commitment to what we were doing. The whole league was like that. There were the established superstars like Bobby Hull, Gordie Howe, Frank Mahovlich and Gerry Cheevers, who were the old guard, and then later on, when kids like Wayne Gretzky, Mark Messier and Mike Gartner came along, it really became obvious that the WHA was accomplishing something important.

"I sometimes think it would have been better for my career if I had stayed in the NHL and put in another three or four years, but if I hadn't switched leagues, I would have missed out on the opportunity to play with and against a great bunch of guys...many of whom I still consider close friends. And it wasn't just the players. Men like Dennis Murphy, Bill Hunter and Benny Hatskin—the characters who created the league and built it into what it eventually became—those guys deserve to go down in the annals of hockey history as legends. It was a thrill for me to be involved with people like that.

"The series against the Russians was another great thrill. It gave me an opportunity to prove myself a little bit, I think. I'd played basically my whole career in Montreal as a centreman behind Jean Beliveau and Henri Richard, so I never really got a chance to show what I was capable of until I was picked for Team Canada. I think my record in the NHL would have been a lot better if I'd played elsewhere, but on the other hand I probably wouldn't have won six Stanley Cups.

"With Team Canada I played as a first-line centre between Gordie and Mark Howe, and even though I was at a pretty advanced age for a hockey player (37), I got to prove what I was capable of doing when I got a lot of ice time—something I never felt I got in Montreal. I'm not questioning Toe Blake's coaching, but even in the year that I led the Canadiens in scoring I never got the opportunity to be on the power play. With Team Canada it was a real treat to line up with the Howes and play with Hull and Mahovlich and all those other stars. I had good success in that series because I was surrounded by great players and I got plenty of ice time. It was one of the highlights of my career.

"Another high point, and probably the one I'm most proud of, was going to the Avco World Trophy finals in my first year with the Cougars. We had a very, very close team, but nobody expected us to go very far. It came down to believing in ourselves. We were just a ragtag team of renegades, but we beat the defending champion New England Whalers in the East Division semifinal and then the Toronto Toros in the divisional final before finally losing to Houston. New England had a very strong hockey club, and for us to knock them off in seven games was really something—especially since they'd finished the regular season in first place and we'd finished in fourth.

"For me, the legacy of the WHA is that, to this day, it represents the turning point that enabled hockey players to receive the compensation they deserve. Without the WHA, that compensation would have been put on the back burner for a long, long time. Salaries got better. Benefits got better. Pensions got better. All of that was a direct result of the World Hockey Association.

"It bothers me that the WHA has never gotten the recognition it deserves because by today's standards almost all of the teams in that league would have been very competitive in the NHL. I know there was a lot of animosity when the WHA was formed, but considering what it accomplished in terms of opening up the game, creating jobs and making hockey more popular, I hope that someday the NHL does the right thing and acknowledges those contributions. Same with the records. It's ridiculous that some of the records of Gordie Howe and Bobby Hull and a lot of other players aren't recognized because they were set in the WHA. Look at what Anders Hedberg, Ulf Nilsson and Lars-Erik Sjoberg accomplished by going to the Winnipeg Jets and really opening up professional hockey for European players. All of that was a big part of hockey history, and it started in the WHA.

"I retired after one season with the Whalers (1976–77), but I've been involved with hockey in one way or another since I quit playing. I coached in the pro ranks for three years and at the collegiate level (Denver) for twelve.

"I also got involved in in-line skating in a big way. Back when I was still playing for the Kings, a fella from Montreal named Maury Silver approached me with an idea about off-season conditioning and dryland training. He'd been working on a prototype, which basically was four wheels in a line. We attached the wheels to a pair of my old L.A. Kings skates, and I started experimenting with them on the streets. We worked at perfecting the design, and in 1975 we got a patent on it. We made and sold maybe three thousand pairs of in-line skates during the 1970s, but all the big manufacturers we approached declined because they were convinced nothing would ever replace the traditional roller skate.

"I used to skate up and down the hills in Brentwood, which is a suburb of L.A. I'd take a hockey stick and a pair of gloves along while I was skating, and believe me, I got my share of funny looks! One time I was doing 40 or 50 miles per hour down a long hill when a car suddenly backed out of a garage and onto the road. I barely managed to get around it without breaking my neck, and after I slowed down enough to stop, I reached down and touched the wheels. They were so hot they nearly burned my fingers!

"I knew we were onto something, though. The in-line blade was a great training tool, but I never dreamed it would turn into a billion-dollar industry. I got traded to the Black Hawks shortly afterwards, and Maury kept working on the skates, but eventually the idea was more or less copied by other manufacturers. For a while we thought about hiring some attorneys to see if we had a legitimate case of patent infringement, but it would have been a long and expensive court fight. It was definitely a learning experience, though. We learned that our product was about ten years ahead of its time.

"Later on I became a co-founder of Roller Hockey International, and today I serve as commissioner of the league. My old friend Maury Silver is involved too; he owns the Anaheim Bullfrogs franchise in the league. It's been a very enjoyable experience. Ice hockey is still my first love, but roller hockey is a lot of fun and it's been great watching the sport grow so big at the grass-roots level. What I'm particularly proud of is the fact that roller hockey is helping to promote ice hockey in areas where hockey has never been prominent.

"I've got no complaints. I plan to keep active and stay involved one way or another for at least ten more years. Whether hockey is played on in-line or ice skates, it's still the best game in the world, and it's given me a very good life. I'm grateful that I've had the opportunity to give something back."

KEN BROWN

Goaltender . . . Born in Port Arthur, Ont., Dec. 19, 1948 . . . Played junior hockey with the Estevan Bruins and Moose Jaw Canucks, 1965–68 . . . Spent four years in the Chicago Black Hawks' organization with Dallas in the Central Professional Hockey League, 1968–69 to 1971–72 . . . Selected as most valuable player (MVP) of the 1971–72 CPHL playoffs, winning 8 of 11 starts and leading Dallas to the championship . . . An original Alberta Oiler, Brown had 20 starts in the WHA's premier season and posted one shutout while surrendering 63 goals . . . Platooned with Jacques Plante and Chris Worthy in 1974–75 . . . Retired in 1975 . . . **Major league totals:** (Regular season) **NHL** - 1 period with the Chicago Black Hawks in 1970–71; allowed one goal against. **WHA** - 52 appearances, 20 wins, 19 losses, 3 shutouts, 138 goals against, 1 assist, 4 penalty minutes. No playoff appearances. Career goals-against average: 3.55.

"One of the best lines I heard when rumours about the WHA started drifting down to Dallas was from an old teammate named Billy Young. 'Jesus Christ,' he said, 'Every time I go to retire, somebody starts another goddamned league!' But that's how it was for a lot of players in the minors. Unless the NHL club that owned your rights traded you, the chances of making it to the big show were pretty slim. You were always looking for a new place to play.

"The first contact I had was during the 1971–72 season, when Scotty Munro came down to Dallas and invited my wife and me out for dinner. He was the guy behind the Calgary Broncos WHA franchise, and he was in the middle of trying to put it all together. Calgary had selected me in the WHA draft a few months earlier, so Scotty outlined what the plans were and said he'd keep in touch. I was still under contract to Chicago at the time, so we had to be discreet. But I remember being pretty excited about the possibility of being part of a new league.

"The decision to jump wasn't really too difficult, even though the Hawks went on to win the championship in Dallas that year and I had a really good season. The Calgary franchise never got off the ground, and the Alberta Oilers acquired my rights. Having grown up in Edmonton, I found the possibility of playing back home very attractive—especially since it didn't look like I was going anywhere with Chicago. The Hawks had Tony Esposito and Gerry Desjardins at the time, and the club hadn't talked about moving me, so suddenly the WHA option was very appealing.

"Of course, when Bobby Hull made his move to the WHA, that's when the canoe tipped. He gave the league instant credibility all by himself. Guys like [Gerry] Cheevers and [Johnny] McKenzie and Bernie Parent, too. But what always impressed me was the number of highly skilled players at the next level, the guys who weren't established stars but who really came into their own in the WHA. Guys like Serge Bernier, Francois Lacombe, Ron Ward, Danny Lawson. Very talented hockey players who only needed a chance to show what they could do.

"It was unbelievably exciting that first year because the good hockey minds in the league hadn't yet had time to take advantage of the bad hockey minds, so all the teams were pretty even. Every game, especially over the last two months in the season, was a war. The playoff picture changed from one night to the next, and there were no easy games.

"A lot of wacky stuff went on in that first year, too. Our GM, Bill Hunter, wouldn't pay the hotel rates in New York. Too expensive, he said. So we'd stay in some god-awful little place in another state, fly into New York City to play the Raiders, then fly out again right after the game. Once, we got caught in a snowstorm on a runway someplace in Ohio, and there's ol' Bill, walking up and down the aisle telling us, 'Don't worry boys, we'll take off in about ten minutes.' Then it was, 'Don't worry boys, we'll take off in about an hour.' Hell, we didn't arrive in New York until after 7:00 p.m. The crowd was already in [Madison Square] Garden, waiting for the puck to be dropped, and we were still on the bloody airplane!

"Another time we went to play the New England Whalers at Boston Garden, where they had these big guard dogs patrolling the corridors down by the dressing rooms. We left our stuff in the room and went to the hotel. When we came back a few hours later to get dressed for the game, I saw that one of the damned dogs had shit all over my goal pads. The way I was playing, maybe he was trying to tell me something...

"But even with all that stuff going on I never had second thoughts about jumping leagues, and I don't think any of the other guys on that first Oiler team did either. It was so much fun and such an adventure that we just got used to the occasional little inconveniences that cropped up. One of the really smart things that some of the original WHA teams did was to try to match players to their geographic roots. Most of the guys on the first-year

Oilers had played minor or junior hockey in and around Edmonton, so a lot of us had known each other since we were kids. Quebec and New England did the same thing. It made for a really fun atmosphere.

"One of my favourite memories from that first season was going into New York for a Sunday afternoon game against the Raiders. The Chicago Black Hawks were in town to play the Rangers that night, so a lot of the Hawks came down to watch our game. I stood on my head in the first period; I think we were outshot by something like 21–3, but the score was only 2–1 for the Raiders after 20 minutes. As I was walking down the runway to the dressing room, I looked up and saw Tony Esposito, the Black Hawks' goalie I'd idolized for years, waiting for me. He put his arm around my shoulder and told me that I was playing great and that he enjoyed watching me. It gave me goosebumps.

"We were making history in those days, sure, but I don't think too many of us realized what the long-term impact of the WHA would be. I recall that near the end of that first season I read Curt Flood's book about challenging the baseball reserve clause and about everything he'd sacrificed in his fight for free agency. A lot of what Curt Flood stood for and a lot of what evolved from his fight had a bearing on professional hockey. I was so impressed with his story that I sat down and wrote him a letter, thanking him for being the first pro athlete to challenge the old system. It made me aware of how important the WHA would be to the future of hockey.

"The feeling I always had, even after three years in the league, was that we were pioneers. The WHA threw away the old book on how to do things in pro hockey and wrote a whole new book. On the ice our league was the first to really showcase the European influence, and off the ice everything from travel arrangements to the relationship between players and management was radically different from anything that had come before. Our owners were actually nice to us; they treated us like human beings. They'd come down to the dressing room or show up at practice instead of just sitting up in the clouds and passing judgement. It says something about the way the WHA and the Oilers conducted business that I'm still friends with [original owner] Zane Feldman 25 years later.

"The two things I miss most about playing are the camaraderie and the competition. I hated to practise, hated the warm-ups, but God I loved to play the games. There's no feeling like it.

"I worked as a colourman on the Oiler radio broadcasts for several years after I retired from playing, and that was terrific. Watching Wayne Gretzky and Mark Messier and the rest of those great young players mature into all-time superstars was very, very special. And being there for four Stanley Cup victories was absolutely wild. Later I started a second career in advertising management at the *Edmonton Sun*, and today I've got about 40 people on my staff at the paper fighting a different kind of battle against the competition every day. I'm enjoying it a lot.

"I feel very fortunate to have been part of an era in hockey history when we were fighting for a cause and building a league almost from scratch. I played with and against some of the best players of all time, and it was a genuine thrill to go out every night and give the fans their money's worth. I wouldn't trade those experiences for anything."

WAYNE "SWOOP" CARLETON

Centre . . . Born in Sudbury, Ont., Aug. 4, 1946 . . . Touted as one of the greatest prospects in Canadian junior hockey history, Carleton turned pro as a teenager with the Toronto Maple Leafs . . . Traded to the Boston Bruins for Jim Harrison, he was part of the Bruins' 1969–70 Stanley Cup championship team, skating on a line with Eddie Westfall and Derek Sanderson . . . Drafted by the California Golden Seals in 1971, he played one season on the West Coast before jumping to the WHA as one of the first "name" players to join the Ottawa Nationals . . . Nicknamed "Swoop" for his habit of circling back into his own zone to build up speed . . . Chosen MVP in the first WHA all-star game . . . Also played for the Toronto Toros, New England Whalers, Edmonton Oilers and Birmingham Bulls . . . Traded from the Toros to the Whalers for Jim Dorey, Sept. 1974 . . . Traded from the Whalers to the Oilers for Mike Rogers, Jan. 1976 . . . **Major league totals:** (Regular season) **NHL** - 278 games, 55 goals, 73 assists, 128 points, 172 penalty minutes. **WHA** - 290 games, 132 goals, 180 assists, 312 points, 135 penalty minutes. (Playoffs) **NHL** - 18 games, 2 goals, 4 assists, 6 points, 14 penalty minutes. **WHA** - 25 games, 8 goals, 21 assists, 29 points, 24 penalty minutes.

"I was a big kid and a strong skater until my knees got buggered up. When I was still a kid, both the Montreal Canadiens and the Toronto Maple Leafs wanted me. Scotty Bowman and "Boom Boom" Geoffrion came to see me and my parents on behalf of the Canadiens. If I'd gone with Montreal, had their guidance, there's no question my career would have turned out differently. But my parents and I went with Toronto because it was close to home and we didn't know any better.

"If I had to do it all over again it sure wouldn't be a tough decision to make, knowing what I know today. Montreal would have made me a much better player just by being patient and developing me properly. With the Canadiens I would have learned more about the game and about myself. Years later Scotty Bowman told a mutual acquaintance that the three best junior prospects he ever scouted were Guy Lafleur, Gilbert Perreault and me. That's not bad company.

"I went through so much knee surgery in my junior days—I played only 12 games in two years when I was 17 and 18 years old. I had damaged joints like Bobby Orr, but it happened to me at a younger age so I had more of a chance to heal. Basically the injuries really cut down on my mobility. If the Leafs had left me with the Marlies when I was recovering from the surgeries and let me play out my remaining year or two of junior rather than turning me pro in the Central Hockey League, things might have been different. I played only 12 games in my last year of junior, and then Toronto turned me pro and sent me to Tulsa, Oklahoma. The Central Hockey League was a pretty good league, but then, that same year, I went to Rochester in the American Hockey League. That's when I really started to come on.

"I went back to the Leafs after that, and I don't have to tell you what kind of an organization they run. They're going through the same thing now with the young kids in that hockey club. They take your confidence away. Punch [Imlach] was great at doing that...he either liked you or he didn't. He and I didn't see eye to eye on a lot of things. I was an independent sort and could make my own decisions, and a lot of the guys he liked didn't do that. He was used to controlling people.

"As far as I'm concerned, I spent too much time in the Leafs' organization. They finally traded me to Boston for Jimmy Harrison, and that's when I really started to come around as a player. Looking back, I was a little immature, no question. Here I was, a big strong kid from the country, who'd left home at 16, and I'd already spent a lot of time in hospitals with my knee operations. Those things take a piece out of your career. But in those days they wanted you to play, no matter what. Nowadays it's a different world, with legal beagles and agents.

"In the old days, you had to be a lot tougher, characterwise. Either you stood up for yourself or you lost. That's the difference between today's game and the old days. Now they throw piles of money at these kids, and if you've got a hangnail they don't want you to play. Money was part of it in our day, too, but we didn't think of hockey as a business. That's why we got shafted. It was every kid's dream...being part of Saturday night hockey on CBC. Money wasn't the real issue. How you got there wasn't an issue. If you had talent and you worked hard, you made it...and you did whatever you were told.

"I was playing for Oakland when I first heard that a new league was getting off the ground. Like anything else, it was only rumours at first, but I was definitely interested. I wasn't very happy in Oakland with Charlie Finley and the white skates, even though we had a pretty good team. The year before, we had missed the playoffs by losing on our last road trip. But by late '71 the WHA looked like it was going to start, and a lot of guys—I think it was ten or eleven in Oakland—decided to jump. It was only a hot rumour to start with, but as the season wore on things seemed as if they were really coming to fruition with the new league. And a lot of guys were looking for an opportunity to make a move.

"What really ticked me off was that after I'd won a Stanley Cup in Boston and gone to Oakland as the first overall pick in the draft, I still had to go to salary arbitration, which I lost. So my displeasure started before that last season. Basically I was so disenchanted with the Seals after the arbitration hearing that I was anxious to get out. We probably should have been looking forward to building a contender because we had a lot of talent on that club, but I was sick of the bullshit in the National Hockey League. Players were just pawns back then, and not too many of us thought about the business aspects.

"Hindsight is always twenty-twenty, and looking back on it today, I probably would have played longer and definitely had a better pension if I hadn't jumped to the WHA, but I don't regret those things. You make decisions in life, and you live with them. If they don't work out and if you're lucky, you're still young enough to do something else.

"Besides the money, my main consideration in deciding to go to the WHA was that it would get me out of California. At the end of that year my wife went back to Ontario to have our first child, and I wasn't interested in flying back and forth across the continent all the time to see my family. California just didn't appeal to me. And leaving a Stanley Cup team to go to a team that not only struggles but is in a totally different climate wasn't my idea of a smart move. I'd always played on winning teams, and I wanted to continue doing that. The WHA gave me that chance. Buck Houle did, too. I'd played for him in junior and having him as GM of the Ottawa Nationals definitely helped make up my mind.

"The fun thing in that first year with the Nationals was the mixture of talent. A lot of tough guys were coming out of the Eastern League. The idea was to try and sell the game in the United States. We had a young team in Ottawa, and some of those games were a real test of character. The best thing about it for me was being able to play so close to home.

"That first year wasn't easy, but it was comforting to talk to guys on the other teams who were going through the same experience. We were a bunch of renegades who really felt strongly about what was happening...we were doing something for the benefit of *all* hockey players, whether they want to admit it today or not. The WHA opened up many jobs in the National Hockey League and gave a lot of guys who might not have made it otherwise the opportunity to play.

"There were some pitfalls, sure. We moved from Ottawa to Toronto in a real hurry...we had to pack our bags right before the playoffs. But once that first year was under my belt I never had any doubts the league would survive. Obviously the NHL owners felt that way, too, because they finally had to step up to the plate and pay players what they were worth.

"With the Toros in 1973–74 I had some problems. I was going for the scoring championship, and because of the bonuses the team would have had to pay me if I won it, the owner, Johnny Bassett, told the coach not to play me. Billy Harris was coaching, and he ended up being the head man for Team Canada for the series against the Russians that fall. It was very frustrating for me, and I lost my cool and said more than I should have. That was enough for Harris to bypass me when they were picking players for Team Canada.

"The WHA represented the first time the owners were challenged, and it really showed how much they controlled the game—from Czar [Alan] Eagleson and the Players Association right down the line. They all hated the WHA —but guess what? We made it! That's why even today nobody in the NHL wants to talk about the league or the players' points and records. But I'll tell you something: [longtime NHL referee] Bill Friday said the WHA was the toughest league he ever officiated in. It was a battle every night. We didn't have the most talented players in the game, but we had more guys with character and heart who would stick their nose in anytime, anywhere, and that's what brought us all together.

"It was a great experience, and I think the WHA deserves to be remembered in hockey history as being a lot bigger and better than it was ever given credit for during its lifetime. Even today everybody who moved over to the WHA has an admiration for the guys who first took up the gauntlet by jumping in '72.

"A client of mine recently gave me a clipping and photograph from the *Toronto Star* of the [1974] all-star game. It's a photo of me with Bobby Hull and Gordie Howe. Pretty decent company, eh? Gerry Cheevers was in goal, and I think we won it 8–4. Back then that moment probably didn't mean much to me, but as the years passed and you see the stature that guys like Hull and Howe still hold in the history of the game, you say 'Gee whiz, I played with those guys and against those guys.' It was a really special time.

"The other thing that made the WHA special was that there was a cause. We might have been on different teams, but we became friends because we were all battling for the same thing—to get paid what we were worth. Who would have dreamed back then that in 25 years one guy's contract would be worth more money than all the WHA contracts combined?

"I went from the Toros to the New England Whalers in 1974. It was disappointing because I was on the third line behind [Tom] Webster and [Larry] Pleau, even though I was one of the leading goal scorers. I wasn't getting any power-play time, and I could see the writing on the wall. I got dealt to Edmonton and then played a few games for Birmingham before I packed it in. I probably quit too soon, at age 29, but I felt it was time. Emile Francis wanted me to come back to the NHL with the Rangers, but I wasn't interested in moving my family again. I purchased a lot of real estate around Collingwood, Ontario, during my playing career, and after I quit, I moved back and raised and trained horses. For the past several years I've been a financial consultant with the Investors Group.

"Looking back, I remember how much fun it was. There are many good people I never would have met without the WHA. My only real regret about my hockey career is that after I got my amateur status back and played in the Allan Cup finals for Barrie, we lost 2–1 in the seventh game against Brantford. I'd have loved to have won the Allan Cup to go along with the Memorial Cup I won with the Marlies and the Stanley Cup I won in Boston. That's how I'd like to be remembered, as a winner. I had a lot of athleticism before I wrecked my knees and lost most of my mobility, but I was a late developer as far as mental maturity goes. My main focus was always on winning as a team, no matter where I played.

"For me, the WHA was a league full of winners. The guys I played with and against in that league did what they had to do to make a go of it, and they deserve a lot of thanks from today's players. It's sad and ironic that the WHA's contribution to hockey history has been ignored because the influence from that league is still being felt. Everybody always says Eagleson changed the game, but it wasn't him. It was the World Hockey Association.

"Hockey's a game, but it made me a better person. I've got a great family, I was able to go to school, and the game made me a better, stronger human being. My parents taught me to work hard and enjoy life, and the WHA gave me the chance. It changed hockey forever, and I feel fortunate to have been a part of it."

JOE DALEY

Goaltender... Born in East Kildonan, Man., Feb. 20, 1943... selected as rookie of the year and MVP with Weyburn in the Saskatchewan Junior Hockey League, 1961–62, posting a 3.34 goals-against average and two shutouts... Turned pro with Johnstown in the Eastern Hockey League, 1963–64... Also played for Pittsburgh and Baltimore in the American Hockey League, Cincinnati and Memphis in the Central Professional Hockey League and San Francisco in the Western Hockey League before debuting in the NHL with the Pittsburgh Penguins in 1968–69... Claimed by the Buffalo Sabres in 1970 expansion draft... Traded by Buffalo to the Detroit Red Wings for Don Luce and Mike Robitaille, June 1971... Joined the WHA as an original Winnipeg Jet in 1972 and remained with the Jets until his retirement after the 1978–79 season... All-time WHA goaltending leader in victories (both regular season and playoffs)... Third all-time in shutouts... Seventh all-time in goals-against average... **Major league totals:** (Regular season) **NHL** - 105 games, 34 wins, 44 losses, 19 ties, 3 shutouts, 3.35 goals-against average. **WHA** - 308 games, 167 wins, 113 losses, 13 ties, 12 shutouts, 3.37 goals-against average, 10 assists, 45 penalty minutes. (Playoffs) **WHA** - 49 games, 30 wins, 15 losses, 2 shutouts, 3.30 goals-against average. Three Avco World Trophy championships.

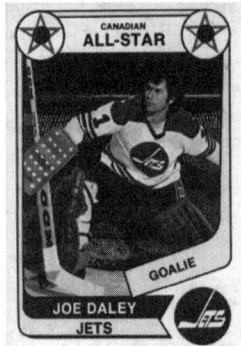

"I was playing in Detroit in the 1971–72 season, and I think it was shortly after New Year's that we started to get wind of rumours about a new league. A fella came to town and invited me and some other players to an informal meeting, but it was all 'backdoor' because we were under contract to the Red Wings, and obviously the WHA wouldn't be welcomed with open arms in the NHL cities.

"The Winnipeg Jets called a month or two later to see if I was interested, and I didn't even have to think about it. I'd fallen into disfavour with the Detroit management and then had a couple of injuries. I wasn't getting the ice time I thought I deserved after I recovered, and we had a war of words at the time. At one point in February or March I told them I wouldn't play another game in a Detroit uniform, so by the time the Jets called, my decision was made. Winnipeg was offering about twice as much money as the Wings as well as the opportunity to play in my hometown, so the decision was basically a no-brainer. After that season, when the Wings wanted to sit down and talk about a contract for the following year, I told them to take a hike. I didn't even consider their offer.

"I was still pretty young, so I didn't really think about whether or not the WHA was going to last. I signed a three-year deal with the Jets, and all the money was put in escrow before the season started, so the security was there. At first I was concerned that I might be blackballed if the league folded, but the chance to play in my hometown cancelled that out.

"Ironically, my career came full circle when I signed with the Jets. I played minor hockey in Winnipeg and then left to play junior in Weyburn, Saskatchewan, where the junior 'A' club was a Detroit farm team. I was in the Red Wings' organization until Pittsburgh took me in the first expansion draft, and then I went to the Buffalo Sabres before I got traded back to Detroit. The funny thing is that I was really looking forward to playing for the Red Wings because I had always respected the way they ran their organization. But it just didn't work out. If things had gone smoothly for me in Detroit, I never would have jumped to the WHA.

"It was almost like an insurance policy for me when the Jets were able to get Bobby Hull under contract. I felt that if a man of his stature was willing to jump leagues there must be some credibility to the whole WHA package. Another smart thing the Jets did was sign up players who were from Manitoba or who had played junior there. A lot of us had known each other or played against each other since we were kids. As more and more guys were signed, it became almost like a reunion. Then when Bobby signed, we all heaved a sigh of relief because it meant the league was for real. I always looked up to Bobby for having the courage to do what he did, especially with all the litigation that was stirred up. When Gordie Howe joined the WHA the next season, those two players became the main reason the league had the longevity that it did.

"It was tough during that first year to ignore the problems that kept popping up around the rest of the league, but I tried to stay focused on what the Winnipeg Jets were trying to accomplish. Compared to most of the other WHA teams, we had a very stable, very professional organization. Looking back, I think the major problem was that some of the owners were probably very wealthy individuals on paper, but they didn't have or couldn't generate the cash flow to sustain a major league franchise. But even the bad owners showed a lot of courage in taking a run at the NHL. The timing was right, but, unfortunately, many of them simply didn't have access to the cash they needed to pull it off.

"We had such a great bunch of guys that first season that I don't think any of us questioned our decision to switch leagues. It was like a great big extended family, a real love affair that included the fans, the management, the players...even the wives and kids. It was incredible how well we all came together. Bobby was one of the all-time greats, and we had proven NHL veterans in guys like Ab McDonald, Billy Sutherland and Wally Boyer. Ernie Wakely and I had shown that we could play in the NHL, and then we had a bunch of young guys and minor leaguers who fit right into the mix. I've never seen anything like it.

"That situation changed a little when the Jets became the first team to sign several European players. There was quite a bit of resentment, at first. After all, these guys were taking jobs away from players who had been there from the start—guys who had become close friends. For Ernie and me, it was especially difficult when Curt Larsson arrived because we could see that he was going to cost one of us a job. Ernie and I had become very good friends, so we decided to be like Don Drysdale and Sandy Koufax and go to management in tandem to make sure we weren't split up. But word got to [owner] Benny Hatskin about what we were planning, so he met with us and said he couldn't afford to pay both our salaries. The only solution was to trade one of us. Since Ernie had his green card to work in the States, he said he'd go. He didn't want to leave, but it was the only thing to do. I felt bad about the whole situation, but I didn't blame Larsson. Other teammates lost their jobs to Swedish players too, and then to top it off we didn't even make the playoffs. It wasn't a happy situation. But the next year we went all the way and won the Avco Trophy, and by that time the Swedes had become good friends and great teammates.

"Bobby was a major factor in Anders Hedberg and Ulf Nilsson developing their skills, but he also showed them how to gut it out in the WHA. Those two guys went through hell, believe me. Every team we faced tried to run them back to Sweden on a flatbed, and early on, it was disheartening for them. You could see by their faces some nights that they were sick and tired of being run through a meat grinder. But Bobby showed them how to handle the bullshit and how to give it back. They had to fight to prove it, but all the Swedes were talented players and they turned out to be great team guys.

"At one time we had seven or eight Swedes and a couple of Finns in our lineup, and I remember being grateful that I had to face them only in practice. They could really fly. But as great as Hedberg and Ulfie Nilsson were, I always thought Kent Nilsson had the most pure talent. He was just too laid back. If Kent had had the same temperament as Ulfie and Anders, he would have put up astronomical numbers.

"Winning three Avco Trophies was a real highlight for me because championships are what you play for. It takes 20 guys to be the best team, and when you win a championship, the 20th guy on the roster can take as much pride in it and feel as much a part of it as a Hull or a Hedberg. As for a single game, I think the night we became the first North American club team to beat the Russian national team was one of my all-time thrills. Not only did I have some rewarding moments and gain a lot of satisfaction out of winning, but to watch our Swedes and Finns get so much joy out of it was something I'll never forget. Those guys had taken it on the chin for so many years in Europe, and for them to finally be on the winning side was special. I remember Anders in the dressing room afterwards shouting, 'Guys, do you have any idea what we've just done?'

"Even though it was only an exhibition game, beating the Russians put the Jets up on a pedestal with some of the great teams in hockey history. We'll never know how good that Winnipeg team was, even with three championships, but for that one night we were right up there with the best. I don't think anybody who was at that game will ever forget it.

"For me, the legacy of the World Hockey Association is that it proved that major league hockey didn't necessarily mean the NHL. Millions of fans in places like Winnipeg, Birmingham, Cincinnati and Houston were exposed to some of the greatest players in the history of the game. The WHA built a foundation for everything that's happened since. I think that's one reason why to this day the NHL has such a hostile attitude toward the WHA; our league opened up new frontiers in the game, to the Europeans and to non-traditional hockey markets in North America and even in places like Japan.

"Having been with the team from the start, I was disappointed when the Jets left Winnipeg. Not for the players, but for the fans…for my own sons and grandchildren, because the team meant something to a new generation. It was the end of a tradition that had been built over 23 years. We had great, great hockey fans here, and as a native Winnipegger I was always proud of that.

"Even though the league lasted only seven seasons, I felt very strongly that the Jets had established the same kind of pride in the uniform that the Montreal Canadiens have always had. It was a special feeling to wear that uniform and be a part of history. When the Jets left Winnipeg and the Nordiques left Quebec, I got the impression the NHL was pretty smug… as if they were saying, 'See, we told you those WHA cities couldn't cut it.' Of course, the NHL never talks about failing in Oakland or Cleveland or Kansas City.

"After I retired in 1979, I kicked around Winnipeg for another year and then moved to Penticton, British Columbia, for four years. We went back to Winnipeg in 1984, and a couple of years later my son and I opened a sports card and memorabilia store. I've been a jockstrap all my life, so running this business has been a fun way to stay in tune with all sports. I get a kick out of talking about the old days with people who come in for a chat. I like the personal contact.

"People sometimes ask me how I want to be remembered, and I always laugh and say, 'I just want to be remembered.' For me, a winning team meant we were all winners. That's the best way to be remembered—as part of team that gave all it had, game in and game out.

"Whatever personal success I had in the WHA was a direct result of being part of dedicated team, with every player doing his job to the best of his abilities. Knowing that I was part of that group, with a burning desire to win every game, is very satisfying."

VAL FONTEYNE

Left wing ... Born in Wetaskiwin, Alta., Dec. 2, 1933 ... Played for the Medicine Hat Tigers in the Western Canada Junior Hockey League and the Kelowna Packers in the Okanagan Senior League before embarking on an 18-year pro career that started with the New Westminster Royals in the Western Hockey League ... Broke into the NHL with the Detroit Red Wings in 1959–60 and played four complete seasons in Detroit before being selected by the New York Rangers in the 1963 intraleague draft ... Sold back to Detroit two years later, then claimed by the Pittsburgh Penguins in the 1967 expansion draft ... Tallied 102 points in four seasons with the Penguins ... Joined the WHA as an original Alberta Oiler in 1972 and was used primarily as a penalty killer ... Although exceptionally strong and extremely fast, Fonteyne was the cleanest player in professional hockey history, averaging just two penalty minutes per year in a career that spanned 13 NHL seasons and two more in the WHA ... Val once went an amazing 185 consecutive games with Detroit and Pittsburgh without drawing a single penalty, and in 20 professional seasons he had 0 penalty minutes on five different occasions ... In 969 major league games, Fonteyne served a grand total of 30 minutes in the sin bin and was never assessed a major penalty. The only time in his pro career he was nailed for five minutes was with the Seattle Americans in 1957–58 ... **Major league totals:** (Regular season) **NHL** - 820 games, 75 goals, 155 assists, 230 points, 26 penalty minutes. **WHA** - 149 games, 16 goals, 45 assists, 61 points, 4 penalty minutes. (Playoffs) **NHL** - 59 games, 3 goals, 10 assists, 13 points, 8 penalty minutes. **WHA** - 5 games, 1 goal, 0 assists, 1 point, 0 penalty minutes.

"There was some talk about a new league being formed as early as 1971, but for a guy like me who was getting towards the end of his career, it didn't seem exciting at the time. Then one day we found out that a big draft had been held, and just about everybody who was playing pro hockey got picked. A lot of the guys in Pittsburgh started talking about maybe making a move, but at the time I figured I'd probably just finish my career there and go on to something else.

"I went back to Alberta that summer and was

working at a hockey school when I got a call from Bill Hunter, asking if I'd meet with him in Edmonton. I thought I should at least hear what he had to say. We got talking, and Bill told me the Oilers were definitely going to play the next season and they wanted me on the team. He made me a nice offer, but I didn't take it right away. I wanted to think it over because it meant leaving the NHL for good. I'd had a pretty good year in Pittsburgh, and I enjoyed playing there, so it seemed like a good idea to wait and see what the Penguins were prepared to do.

"I talked to Jack Riley, who was our GM in Pittsburgh, and he said the Penguins wanted me to play for at least one more year and then they would give me a job in the organization. That sounded pretty good because I was 39 years old at the time and I had to start thinking about what I was going to do when my playing days were over. Well, the next time I talked to Bill Hunter he offered me a lot more money than Riley did—darned near double. Then he sweetened the pot by saying the Oilers would give me a new car so I could drive back and forth to my home in Wetaskiwin, which is about 40 miles from Edmonton. That swung it for me because my wife was expecting our youngest child at the time, and if I went with the Oilers she wouldn't have to be alone or travel very far in those last few months.

"Our first training camp in Edmonton was different from what I was used to in the NHL because there was such a mix of players. I was the old guy on the team, and I'd played with or against a handful of the other fellas, but for the most part they were raw kids who were fighting to get noticed. Most of the teams were like that in the first year of the WHA—a mix of old warhorses, young kids and minor leaguers. But it sure made for a competitive league. The team that impressed me early on was Philadelphia, with Bernie Parent, Derek Sanderson, Johnny McKenzie and Andre Lacroix. There was an awful lot of talent on that team. And, of course, Bobby Hull and the Jets in Winnipeg. The Jets didn't really take off until the second half of the season, but Bobby was basically the guy they built the whole league around.

"I have to admit that up to about Christmastime in that first season I thought I'd made a huge mistake by switching leagues. There was never a problem getting paid or anything like that, but I felt the WHA wasn't catching on like the organizers had thought it would. Maybe it was because I'd been in the NHL for so long, but everything was so new and so different that playing in the WHA didn't feel like big-league hockey, at first.

"Things settled down and got a lot better in the second half of the season, and the next year, which was my last one, the league improved a lot more. The experience ended up being very positive for me. One of the nice things in that second year was getting the chance to play against Gordie Howe again. We'd been teammates in Detroit, and we knew each other well. The first time the Oilers went down to Houston, I had a chance to visit Gordie and his boys before the game, which was nice, but on the ice, of course, he turned into a different person. All those Gordie Howe stories are true! Friendship went right out the window if you were playing against him, but I still enjoyed it.

"The great thing about Howe and Hull was that they played their whole careers in the NHL and the WHA with checkers all over them, all the time, but you never saw them cry about it like the guys do today. I know the game has changed a lot and there's more clutch-and-grab stuff now, but I also think the players were a little tougher back then. For a little guy like me who was basically a penalty killer and a checker, going up against a Howe or a Hull was almost an honour because they played the game so hard. All they needed was one stride to beat you.

"I never even knew about my record as the so-called cleanest player in history until a couple of guys who were doing a story for the *Hockey News* phoned me about it. I can't explain it, except to say that I always tried to use my skating ability to get into position to check an opponent without having to hook or hold him. I wasn't big in stature, but I didn't shy away from going into the corners. I just relied on my one real talent, which was skating, to get the job done. I wasn't a goal scorer, and I wasn't big enough to be a threat with body checks, so I learned how to use my stick to check and position myself so that I wouldn't have to trip or hold to get the job done.

"The only major penalty I ever got was when I was with Seattle in the Western Hockey League. I had a fight one night with a guy in Vancouver. Well, it wasn't much of a fight, really, but we both dropped our gloves. It was like a couple of bantamweights swinging at each other, but I actually remember it. One fight in 20 years! I guess I wouldn't be on Don Cherry's list of favourite hockey players, eh?

"Looking back, I feel very fortunate to be a hockey player in the first place. And to have had the opportunity to play in the NHL and the WHA is something I'll always be grateful for. When I was with Seattle, they didn't even have an affiliation with an NHL club. I thought I would be a career minor leaguer, so everything after that was a bonus. I thought a lot of guys I played with in the Western League, fellas like Guyle Fielder, had much more talent than I did, so I always felt fortunate to play as long as I did.

"Life after hockey has been good, too. I spent 19 years as a truck driver for Canada Post until I retired a few years ago. With my pensions from the

NHL and the post office, we're quite comfortable. But when I think back to the money they were paying us in the NHL way back when, it's no wonder the World Hockey Association came along when it did. I think when I broke in with Detroit I made $7,500, and at the end of my NHL career in Pittsburgh I was making $25,000.

"The WHA came along and paid us all a lot more money, but what was even more important was that it created so many new jobs for hockey players and gave them some leverage in negotiating. Today's players should thank the WHA for making it possible for them to earn the big money they're getting. Without that league, hockey would have been stuck in the dark ages for a long time."

AL HAMILTON

Defense ... Born in Flin Flon, Man., Aug. 20, 1946 ... Outstanding junior career with the Flin Flon Bombers and Edmonton Oil Kings, capped by Edmonton's Memorial Cup triumph over the Oshawa Generals in 1966 ... Played three pro games with the St. Paul Rangers of the Central Professional Hockey League in 1964–65 ... Broke into the NHL with a four-game stint for the New York Rangers in 1965–66 ... Also played for the Omaha Knights in the CPHL and the Buffalo Bisons in the American Hockey League before joining the Rangers on a full-time basis during the 1969–70 season ... Drafted by the Buffalo Sabres in the 1970 expansion draft ... Scored 68 points in two seasons with the Sabres before joining the WHA as an original Alberta Oiler ... Named captain of the Oilers and scored 60 points in 1972–73 ... Played in three WHA all-star games and named to Team Canada '74 ... Hamilton is the Oilers' all-time leader in WHA assists (258) and WHA points (311) ... Briefly returned to the NHL with Edmonton in 1979–80 ... Honoured as the first player in Oilers history to have his number (3) retired ... **Major league totals:** (Regular season) **NHL** - 257 games, 10 goals, 78 assists, 88 points, 258 penalty minutes. **WHA** - 455 games, 53 goals, 258 assists, 311 points, 492 penalty minutes. (Playoffs) **NHL** - 7 games, 0 goals, 0 assists, 0 points, 0 penalty minutes. **WHA** - 26 games, 5 goals, 11 assists, 16 points, 29 penalty minutes.

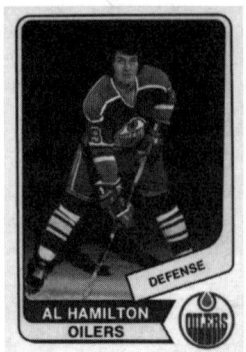

"Bill Hunter had been trying to get hold of me while I was in Buffalo, but I had an unlisted telephone number and, naturally, he didn't want to go through the Sabres' office. We'd heard rumblings about a new league getting off the ground, but at that point I don't think too many NHL players attached much credence to them. Eventually Hunter contacted me. His junior team was in Ottawa for the Memorial Cup, so I went up there just to hear him out. I came away from that meeting quite impressed. After what we'd been through—playing for almost nothing for all those years—what the WHA was offering made us think we'd struck gold.

"I didn't sign right away. I had an agent who probably would have sold me out for a lot less than what I eventually got, so I gassed him and then made my own deal. It was a five-year guaranteed contract for considerably more than I would have made in the other league. The fact I had a history in Edmonton and had played all those years with the junior Oil Kings made it that much better.

"I was pretty concerned about what might happen if the league went under, so the guarantee on the contract was a big factor in my signing. I don't think I would have changed leagues without it. To tell you the truth, even after the WHA got up and running I had some serious doubts about my decision to jump. I think my first game in the WHA was an exhibition against the Los Angeles Sharks. It took about eight hours to play, and there were about three hundred fights. I thought, 'My God, what have I done?' That first training camp was quite a sight, too. We had some guys who hadn't played for a few years...and quite a few who *shouldn't* have played for a few years. There were guys from the Eastern League who could barely skate. Eventually the worst got weeded out, but we didn't have an overabundance of talent on the Oilers through those first couple of seasons. We were always solid on the blue line, though. My forte was getting the puck out of my own end. I averaged around 40 points per year in the years I wasn't hurt, but I wasn't looked on as a real offensive threat. I was a good skater, and I looked after my own end of the rink pretty well.

"The other teams were basically in the same boat when it came to the mix of talent on their rosters, but once Bobby Hull got cleared to play for Winnipeg, there was a feeling that things were going to improve throughout the league. When Bobby made his move, it sent a message to good players in the other league that they could jump, too.

"I don't know if any of us thought we were making history in those early years, but we all knew that we'd jumped ship together, and there was a prevailing sense that either we had to make the thing work or we'd all go down together. We didn't want to screw up because we were so happy to finally be making a decent salary. That was a big factor. And after Hull jumped, some pretty darn good hockey players followed him—players who might never have had a chance to show what they could do in the NHL.

"The talent level in the WHA took a giant leap when the European players started to come over. They brought to the game a dimension that had largely been ignored. Without our league to showcase them, that might never have happened. The Swedes and the Finns changed the way the rest of us played the game, and the contribution they made to the Winnipeg Jets eventually became the blueprint for Edmonton's run of Stanley Cups in the NHL.

"I got a real appreciation for the European system when I played for Team Canada. We had a good crack at winning that series until we got a couple of raw deals in Russia. Of course, we lost a few games in Canada that we should have won, too, so it all evened out. But Team Canada was a darn good hockey club...much better than it's ever been given credit for. It was a great bunch of guys, too, and we really had a hoot together. I think that series also started to open people's eyes to the fact that the WHA wasn't watered-down hockey. By the third or fourth year, I think we could have been very competitive against all but the top two or three NHL clubs.

"Being part of Team Canada was definitely a career highlight for me, as were a lot of the games we played against the Winnipeg Jets over the last couple of seasons. We built up quite a rivalry with the Jets, and those games were always a lot of fun to play—wide open and end-to-end. At the other end of the scale was going into Minnesota to play the Fighting Saints and knowing that the safest thing on the ice was the puck. They had about ten goons whose only talent was trying to run over everybody and everything that got in the way. It was the same in Birmingham. The only saving grace about going down to play the Bulls was that there were always a lot of good-looking girls in the stands. That team was a real rogue's gallery, with 'Bad News' Bilodeau, Frankie Beaton, Steve Durbano. It was always an adventure going in there because you didn't know if you'd come out alive. We were lucky towards the end, though, because by then we had Dave Semenko in our lineup. Not too many opponents were stupid enough to mess with him...not even in Birmingham.

"The thing you have to remember about the WHA is that it never would have gotten off the ground without the arrogance and the ignorance of the

National Hockey League. Nobody in the NHL believed it would happen, and when it did, they still didn't believe anybody would jump. The reality was that the player market, which had been enslaved for so long, was finally ripe for the picking. Once the WHA broke the reserve clause, it opened the floodgate, but the lid never completely blew off...even after the merger. The WHA guys got sold out when the leagues were merged. We basically got sold a bill of goods by the [NHL] Players Association. I mean, with two rival leagues competing for talent, what better situation could a player ask for? Obviously the owners of the teams that were admitted to the NHL thought it was their pot of gold, but the players from the WHA ended up getting hosed because the pension monies weren't matched. It became a real nightmare. We weren't well represented at the merger talks probably because by that time a lot of the WHA players were anxious to get back into the other league.

"I don't spend a hell of a lot of time thinking about the past or about why the WHA has never been given any credit. But for people to say that nothing mattered in Edmonton or Winnipeg or Quebec City or Hartford until those teams got into the NHL is nonsense. How else would major league hockey have arrived in a place like Edmonton, with a market of only 700,000 people? The NHL wouldn't have gone there on its own in a million years. The WHA is responsible for that. The WHA is responsible for getting some great arenas built and introducing millions of fans to a game that they'd never seen before.

"I look back on the WHA with a lot of fondness. In retrospect, I don't regret making the move at all. It was good for me at the time, and it certainly proved to be good for me after hockey. After I retired as a player, I stayed in Edmonton and got involved in real estate and golf course development. Now I have my own marketing company, and I contract my services out to a wide variety of clients.

"Edmonton has been very good to me. I made a lot of contacts over the years here in both junior and pro hockey, and I can't imagine being anyplace else at this point in my life. That's just one more thing I have to thank the World Hockey Association for."

JIM HARRISON

Centre ... Born in Glendon, Alta., July 9, 1947 ... Began an outstanding four-year junior with the Estevan Bruins as a 15-year-old in 1964 ... Loaned to the Edmonton Oil Kings for the 1966 playoffs, Harrison played a key role in the Kings' Memorial Cup victory ... Won the Murray Balfour Memorial Award as MVP in the Western Canada Major Junior Hockey League in 1967–68, and was the leading playoff scorer with 13 goals and 22 assists ... Once scored three goals in 23 seconds during the final minute of regulation time to lift Estevan to a come-from-behind win over Regina ... Turned pro with the Okahoma City Blazers in the Central Professional Hockey League in 1968–69 and scored 26 points in 40 games before being promoted to the parent Boston Bruins ... Traded to the Toronto Maple Leafs for Wayne Carleton in Dec. 1969 ... Scored 39 goals and 47 assists in 175 games with the Leafs ... Drafted by the Calgary Broncos in the WHA's 1972 general player draft, but joined the league as an original Alberta Oiler when the Calgary franchise folded ... Was the Oilers' top scorer in 1972–73, sniping 39 goals and 87 points despite missing 14 games with a shattered kneecap ... On Jan. 30, 1973, Harrison became the first major league player in the modern era to score ten points in a single game, firing three goals and seven assists in Alberta's 11–2 romp over the New York Raiders. Had another seven-assist game two years later with the Cleveland Crusaders ... Selected for Team Canada '74, but injuries limited him to just three starts in the eight-game series ... Traded by the Oilers to Cleveland for Ron Buchanan, Oct. 1974 ... One of three unanimous selections (along with Bobby Hull and Gordie Howe) for the 1974 all-star game ... When the Crusaders folded in 1976, Harrison returned to the NHL with the Chicago Black Hawks ... Retired following a three-game comeback attempt with the Edmonton Oilers in 1979–80 ... **Major league totals:** (Regular season) **NHL** - 324 games, 67 goals, 86 assists, 153 points, 435 penalty minutes. **WHA** - 132 games, 117 goals, 152 assists, 269 points, 360 penalty minutes. (Playoffs) **NHL** - 13 games, 1 goal, 1 assist, 2 points, 43 penalty minutes. **WHA** - 8 games, 1 goal, 3 assists, 4 points, 13 penalty minutes.

"We were all owned by NHL clubs when the first rumours about the WHA started circulating, so the league initially got in touch only with guys who were in the last year of their contracts. I think Bernie Parent and I were the first two Toronto Maple Leafs who were called. These calls came before the big draft, just to see if we'd be interested. I told 'em I was interested, and I ended up being drafted by the Calgary Broncos and Scotty Munro, whom I'd played for in junior.

"When Calgary ran into some problems, I told them I'd be interested in going to Edmonton if there was an opportunity to do that, so the Broncos dealt my rights to the Oilers. Bill Hunter came to see me during the NHL season and said he would guarantee my contract, with the money deposited up front. I was pretty good friends with Parent, and I knew he'd gotten a guaranteed deal from the Miami Screaming Eagles, so it was all starting to sound pretty good. By that time [Leafs' owner] Harold Ballard had heard the rumours, but I'd made a promise to him that I wouldn't sign with the WHA if I got the raise I felt I deserved in Toronto.

"It didn't happen. I was making $12,000 in Toronto, and they offered me $13,000. I wanted $13,500. It sounds like a joke when you look at the money guys are making today, but that $500 was really important to me. I had four or five meetings with Ballard, but he wouldn't budge. He always tried to bully his players. He told me the WHA would never get off the ground because they didn't have any money. Well, I knew [Oilers' co-owner] Dr. [Charles] Allard from my junior days, and I knew he had lots of money. Ballard didn't know what I knew.

"I left it at that and decided to go home to Alberta to think and do some fishing. When the Oilers found out I was on my way home, they met me at the airport and offered me a really good deal. I signed right there. I got a $75,000 signing bonus and a long-term contract that was guaranteed, no matter what happened. That's a long way from a $500 raise, eh?

"Bobby Hull was the saviour of the WHA, no question about that. The fact that all 12 teams chipped in to bring him over underlined what he meant to the credibility of the league. There were four or five other big-name guys who could have made the move before Bobby did, but nobody wanted to be first. He took a big chance and showed a lot of guts by doing it.

"The first couple of years with the Oilers were pretty good compared to what was happening with other teams in the league. Going into New Jersey to play the Knights was a real experience. You'd go to pick up the [complimentary] tickets for your friends or family, and they'd hand you this little tag that said 'Admit one only.' The ice was tilted, and there was no shower for the visiting team. We got dressed in our equipment at the hotel and then took a bus to the back door of the rink. It was like being back in peewee hockey. After I went to Cleveland, it got even funnier. For a while we had to take our skates with us because the club was worried the equipment would get repossessed. There were times when the team couldn't afford to pay us meal money, or we'd go to board a plane and the airline wouldn't let us on because old bills hadn't been paid. Somebody from the club would have to run around and try to book another flight. Some teams' locker rooms were broken into, and sheriffs seized all the equipment, so the players had to go to the local sporting goods store and buy new stuff to play a game that night.

"It was wild, but it was a lot of fun. You never knew what the next day would bring. Unfortunately, those first couple of seasons in the WHA were my better years, and I would have liked to have had those good years in Toronto. I was coming off a 19-goal season in the NHL in 1971–72, and that was considered a big year back then. It would have been nice if I could have stayed in Toronto and played as well as I did in Edmonton. The NHL was still the NHL, and it was the ultimate. My last year with the Leafs I was centring Darryl Sittler and Brian Spencer, and I think we would have become a really good line if we'd stayed together.

"But I don't regret jumping. The money we were being paid in Toronto was an absolute joke. I used to have to get a job every summer just to make ends meet for my family. We never owned a house or decent furniture. The WHA gave me the opportunity to do all that. I had four years guaranteed, with the money in the bank, and if the league folded, I still would have been paid. We were able to buy a house, and I built a fishing lodge in the Northwest Territories. None of that would have happened if the WHA hadn't have come along.

"My ten-point game against New York rates as one of the best moments of my career, for sure. The ironic thing was that I should have had about 15. I missed on three or four breakaways that night, and a couple of other times I set up guys who were wide open, but they shot wide. Playing for Team Canada was another big moment, even though I was coming off a back injury and played only a few games. But to pull on that maple leaf sweater and play for your country is something special. The Russians were unbelievably dirty. They'd spit in you face, spear, butt-end... you name it.

"If I had been in shape and without injuries, I probably would have played more against the Russians. That's one regret I have. We had some awesome talent on Team Canada, and it was a thrill for me to even be practising with guys like Hull and Howe. I wish now that I had had some pictures taken with those guys, but you never think about stuff like that when you're playing. Gordie and Bobby and I were unanimous picks for the all-star game that year, and I wish now that I had a nice picture of us together ...something to show the kids, eh?

"Nobody can believe I made it in those days because I was such a terrible skater. I got there just by being tough and working hard. I couldn't even stop very well, so I'd just run into anybody who got in my way. I can't explain what drove me to play that way; it was something that started when I was a kid. I wanted to see it through. I come from a hardworking family. We were poor, but I always had a lot of support from my family to go out and make it. When I was 14 or 15 and had to leave home to go to Estevan, it was awful, but something made me get on the train and stay there, even though I was terribly homesick. I cried and I wanted to turn back, but I didn't. Other guys went home, but I figured I'd see it through. I honestly think that's something we produce in Canada, especially in the west, that other countries don't have. It's intangible...but maybe it's why these little towns on the Prairies produce so many tough hockey players.

"The WHA was always fighting an uphill battle with the media, and that's one reason why you don't hear much about it...even to this day. We always got great coverage in Edmonton, and I'm sure it was the same in Winnipeg and Quebec, too, but I remember the Vancouver Blazers barely got a mention in the press because they were competing with the NHL Canucks. The NHL basically dictated to the media to only cover their games in the cities where the NHL and the WHA went head-to-head. That mentality is still there. When was the last time you saw a WHA record mentioned in print or on TV? My son was going to write to TSN one night when they announced that Sittler was the only player to score ten points in a game. I did it three years before Darryl and my name is even in the *Guiness Book of World Records,* but because I did it in the WHA I guess it doesn't count.

"When I went back to the NHL, [Alan] Eagleson was representing me. He was trying to stack Chicago with Bobby Orr and Battleship Kelly and a few other guys who were his clients, so naturally that's where I was going. I came back too soon from my third back operation, and right away I had problems with [coach Bob] Pulford. He wanted me to fight in practise to stir the guys up. It was just crap. He thought I was faking my injuries, so he tried to send me to the minors—you can't do that to an injured player. It was unbelievable the crap they put me through, and then Eagleson told me [NHL president John] Ziegler ruled that I had to go down. Later I found out that Ziegler did no such thing. That's what started my long fight for compensation.

"I've had three back operations, and today I have no feeling in my right leg. For 17 years I thought I was fighting all by myself, but then it turned out there were dozens of other players going through the same thing, trying to get what is rightfully theirs. Now there's some light at the end of the tunnel, but the fight's far from over."

GORDIE HOWE

Right wing ... Born in Floral, Sask., Mar. 31, 1928 ... Learned to play hockey on outdoor rinks in Saskatoon ... Attended the New York Rangers' training camp in Winnipeg as a 15-year-old but, lonely and homesick, Howe returned to Saskatoon a few days later ... Attended the Detroit Red Wings camp in Windsor the following season and signed a contract to play for the Wings' junior team in Galt, Ont. ... Because of a Canadian Amateur Hockey Association ruling, Howe was barred from regular season games with the junior club but suited up for practices and exhibitions ... Turned pro with the Omaha Knights in the United States Hockey League in 1945, scoring 48 points in 51 games ... Permanently promoted to the Red Wings the following season ... Scored a goal in his first NHL game, Oct. 16, 1946 ... Brother of Vic Howe, who played 33 NHL games for the Rangers, 1950–55 ... En route to rewriting the NHL record book over the next 25 seasons, Howe won the Hart Trophy as league MVP six times, the Art Ross Trophy as leading scorer six times, and the Lester Patrick Trophy for outstanding service to hockey in the United States (1967) ... Suffered severe head injury during 1950 Stanley Cup playoffs and briefly wore a helmet upon his return to action ... Played on four Stanley Cup championship teams in Detroit ... Named to the NHL's first all-star team 12 times and the second team nine times ... Retired in 1971 as the NHL's all-time leader in virtually every offensive category ... Named to the Order of Canada (Canada's highest civilian honour) in 1972 ... Unanimously elected to the Hockey Hall of Fame in 1972 ... After a two-year layoff he returned to major league hockey with the WHA's Houston Aeros in 1973, becoming the first professional athlete in history to play with his sons ... Scored on his first WHA shot, 21 seconds into Houston's exhibition victory over New England at Madison Square Garden, Sept. 25, 1973 ... Won the Gary Davidson Trophy as the WHA's most valuable player in the 1973–74 season, and two years later the award was renamed the Gordie Howe Trophy ... At age 46 Howe starred for Team Canada '74 against the Soviet Nationals, notching three goals and four assists in seven games ... Played on two Avco World Trophy championship teams in Houston and achieved another first in pro sports when he was named "playing president" of the Aeros in 1975–76 ... In 1975 Michigan sports fans selected Howe as their all-time greatest athlete, over such luminaries as Ty Cobb, Joe Louis and Bobby Layne ... Signed as a free agent by the New England Whalers in June 1977, along with sons Mark and Marty ... Became the first major league player to score 1,000 goals (regular season and playoffs) when he beat Birmingham's John Garrett on Dec. 7, 1977 ... Played on a line with Mark Howe and Wayne Gretzky for the WHA All-Stars in a three-game series against the Soviets, 1979 ... Remained with the Hartford Whalers after the merger and at age 52 played one final season in the NHL, 1979–80 ... Coauthor (with wife, Colleen) of several best-selling books and host of an instructional video series ... Recognized worldwide as "Mr. Hockey" and regarded by many experts as the greatest all-around player in history ... **Major league totals:** (Regular season) **NHL** - 1,767 games, 801 goals, 1,049 assists, 1,850 points, 1,685 penalty minutes. **WHA** - 419 games, 174 goals, 334 assists, 508 points, 399 penalty minutes. (Playoffs) **NHL** - 157 games, 68 goals, 92 assists, 160 points, 220 penalty minutes. **WHA** - 78 games, 28 goals, 43 assists, 71 points, 115 penalty minutes.

Once you get past the awe, the first thing you learn from hanging out with Mr. Hockey is to always be on guard—even in the most innocuous situations. You can be walking down the street, relaxing in a hotel lobby or getting on an elevator when—*whack!*—he playfully nails you with one of those famous elbows or throws a sneaky hip check.

The second thing you discover is that Gordie Howe is a warm, extraordinarily honest man who, despite his venerated status, hasn't lost the common touch that's made him the idol of three generations of hockey fans.

In 1991 I had the singular privilege of accompanying Gordie, Colleen and Marty Howe on a week-long card show tour through British Columbia and Alberta, and judging by the huge lineups and endless photo requests, it was obvious that Number Nine was still Numero Uno—even among fans with only secondhand knowledge of his greatness.

"You can't call it charisma...it goes way beyond that," a fortysomething legal secretary told me after she had stood in line for three hours to get Howe's autograph in Vancouver. "My God, I thought he was old when I was a kid, but my dad was always a Detroit fan, so I started watching Gordie." At that point the woman pulled a dog-eared Eaton's catalogue from her purse. The cover, featuring a colour portrait of Howe representing Trueline Sporting Goods, was dated 1966. "Gordie did a tour for Eaton's that year, and my dad and I went to Victoria just to get an autograph... look, it's right here in the corner. Gordie was wonderful; he posed for a picture with us and told me I had a nice smile. I almost died. Ever since that day he has been my all-time idol. I must have filled ten scrapbooks with his clippings... "

That was a common theme throughout the tour. At every stop, adults, teenagers and little kids fell all over themselves to bask—however briefly—in Howe's aura.

From personal observation, I think the real secret of the legend of Gordie Howe is the man's intuitive ability to make each fan feel a part of his success. The game has changed, many of his records have fallen, but, like Muhammad Ali, Gordie's love affair with his fans transcends time itself.

At a roadside restaurant in the tiny town of Revelstoke, British Columbia, the magic surfaced again. No sooner had our party of eight been seated in a semiprivate booth when a gaggle of middle-aged women from a cosmetics convention descended on us like locusts.

"Mr. Howe—can I call you Gordie, please?—my husband would flip if I could get a picture with you," said the first invader.

"No problem," he answered, "but you better ask him, too—that's Rocket Richard!" Howe joked, pointing to our bus driver. When a very pregnant young lady shyly asked for a signature, Howe winked and said: "Would you like me to sign twice?"

One of the funniest moments on the trip came a few hours later, when Gordie spied a Dairy Queen on the outskirts of Golden and asked the driver to pull over.

"I'm buyin' the cones," Howe announced, then jogged ahead of us through the crisp mountain air. When he entered the restaurant, none of the young staff recognized Gordie, but as he turned to leave, four middle-aged men in business suits did an abrupt double-take. "Great day for a chocolate dip," Howe said, leaving the quartet gasping in open-mouthed amazement.

Howe's generosity of spirit—at least as legendary as his on-ice exploits—is the cornerstone of his appeal. He seldom seems happier than when signing autographs or engaging in small talk...even when he's heard the same story a thousand times.

"That's one record of mine that Wayne Gretzky will never get: putting a million people in the rink at once," he joked after several fans in Kelowna told him they'd attended his final all-star game (1980 in Hartford). "They all have a story; the all-star game comes up a lot. Or they saw me score my five hundredth goal, or they were there when I broke the Rocket's record, or they went to school with one of my kids. One time a guy told me he saw me play with Eddie Shore. I said 'Geez, if I'd played with Eddie Shore I'd be 100 years old!' He said, 'No way, Gordie, I saw you!' I just said, 'Oh yeah...I forgot.'"

Asked if he ever wearies of the endless autographs and photo requests, Howe has a ready answer: "I worked too hard for the privilege...and it *is* a privilege. It means a lot to me that people still want my signature or a picture, and I try to accommodate everyone. The only thing I don't like is rudeness, like when somebody shoves something at me and just says—or demands—'Sign here!' When that happens, I smile and write 'H-E-R-E.'

"Once in awhile somebody will say it's demeaning or improper for athletes to be paid to sign at card shows or formal autograph sessions, but my answer to them is 'Where were you when I was making $6,000 a season?' It sounds amazing, but I can earn more money now just by travelling around the country doing card shows and autograph signings than I did in my tenth season in the National Hockey League. I sign for free when people recognize me in public, but if I'm doing a formal signing at a show, then fees are involved. That's the business end of it.

"Still, I don't like the way some guys handle these things, particularly now that autographs and sports collectibles have become a real industry. You know, I read that a famous baseball player said he didn't think professional athletes should have to shoulder the responsibility of being role models for the public. I can't understand that. Maybe he forgot who's paying his salary."

Howe is also a master storyteller. On the long bus ride across southern Alberta he regaled us with the oft-told legend of his first signing bonus.

"When I came out of junior in Galt, the Red Wings promised me a team jacket, but I never got it. Then I signed for $2,300 a year and went to Omaha. It was a pretty big city for a kid from Saskatchewan, and I felt kind of lost. On top of that, the Wings had again promised I'd get a team jacket as a bonus, but they didn't gave it to me then, either.

"The next year I went to Detroit for $4,500...and this time I was determined to get the damn jacket. I was pretty pleased with the money, but I wasn't leaving until I got the jacket. I hung around for a long time at the Olympia before one of the office people noticed me and asked what I was waiting for. I said [Wings' GM] Jack Adams promised me a jacket as a signing bonus, and I wasn't going home without one. Well, I finally got the thing ...but it was like pulling teeth."

Then Howe recalled his first trip to the Big Apple.

"We were getting $3.50 per day in meal money. Can you imagine trying to eat on that in New York? Ted [Lindsay] and I were amazed by the city. We went into a bar and had a beer each, and the bill was something like $4! All we could afford after that was to split a sandwich from the deli and go back to the hotel."

Howe credits the WHA in general and the Houston Aeros in particular with "bringing back my love of the game. Getting the opportunity to play alongside Mark and Marty was a dream come true...something I'll always be grateful for. After I retired from the NHL in 1971 the Red Wings gave me an office with my name on the door, but I just got the mushroom treatment. I was kept in the dark about all the major decisions, and every once in awhile somebody would open the door and throw in some bullshit.

"The birth of the WHA was a real godsend, and when Colleen put together the deal that brought us to Houston, it was an unbelievable feeling. I made more money in four seasons with the Aeros than I did in my last 20 years in Detroit.

"It doesn't really bother me when my WHA totals aren't included in some of the record books; that's the result of the NHL doing all it could for a number of years to downplay the WHA as not being major league. It's kind of silly, considering that Bobby Hull and Wayne Gretzky and a lot of other great players were there. What bothers me more is that after all the years of calling us second-rate, the NHL wouldn't allow Wayne to win rookie of the year because he got started in the WHA. That's a joke.

"Nobody can tell me the WHA wasn't major league hockey. In Houston we won most of our exhibition games against NHL clubs. One year we challenged Detroit, but they wouldn't play us. And if you look back at the NHL scoring leaders in the first year after the merger, four of the top ten scorers came from the WHA. It was damn good hockey. The Winnipeg Jets, with Bobby and the two Swedes [Anders Hedberg and Ulf Nilsson] was one of the best teams I ever saw. If that team had been left intact after the merger, I think they would've challenged for the Stanley Cup."

Howe realized a lifelong ambition when he was named to Team Canada '74 for the series against the Soviets, and he responded with an awesome performance, even if his memories of the experience aren't particularly fond.

"In a word, it was awful," he says. "We had a great bunch of guys on that team, but the experience in Russia just killed it for me. Bobby and I took some steaks with us, but when we gave them to a Russian cook to prepare, the guy boiled 'em! Can you believe it? The food was terrible. We couldn't wait to get home."

Ironically, one of the special memories from Howe's legendary career came nearly 20 years later, when he returned to Moscow at the invitation of the Soviet Hockey Federation.

"Colleen and I were there with some of our grandchildren," he says. "One day we were out for a walk, and I spotted this old painter on the street, working on some pictures. I went over to take a closer look, and as soon as he saw me he put down his brush and pointed his finger. In English he said, 'Original six!' and then he rattled off the names of the six original NHL teams. Then he grinned and added, 'Houston and Hartford!' Well, you could've shot me right between the eyes.

"It was a smart move on the old guy's part, though. I think we ended up buying eight of his paintings…"

A legend, indeed.

FRANK HUGHES

Right wing ... Born in Fernie, B.C., Oct. 1, 1949 ... Played junior for the Edmonton Oil Kings ... Originally drafted by the Toronto Maple Leafs ... Turned pro with the Phoenix Roadrunners in the Western Hockey League ... A member of the Roadrunners' famed "Go Go Line" with future Houston teammates Andre Hinse and Larry Lund, 1969–72 ... Drafted from Toronto by the California Golden Seals in 1971, Hughes played five games for the Seals in the 1971–72 season ... Left unprotected by California, he was selected by the Atlanta Flames in the 1972 NHL expansion draft and by the Dayton Arrows in the WHA general player draft ... After the Dayton franchise transferred to Texas, Hughes joined the WHA as an original Houston Aero in 1972 ... Led the Aeros with 42 goals in 1973–74 and again in 1974–75, when he notched 48 ... Eight of his goals in 1974–75 were scored against Cleveland's Gerry Cheevers, and 15 came on the power play ... Had six hat tricks in his first three WHA seasons ... Played on Houston's two Avco World Trophy championship teams and was selected to play in the 1975 all-star game ... Traded to Phoenix in Dec. 1976, along with Andre Hinse, for Al McLeod and John Gray ... Reacquired by the Aeros prior to the 1977–78 season, then transferred to the Pacific Hockey League, where he won the scoring championship with 74 points in 42 games for Phoenix ... Retired following one more season in the PHL in which he led the Tucson Rustlers in scoring and finished second overall in the league ... **Major league totals:** (Regular season) **NHL** - 5 games, 0 goals, 0 assists, 0 points, 0 penalty minutes. **WHA** - 392 games, 173 goals, 180 assists, 353 points, 173 penalty minutes. (Playoffs) **WHA** - 54 games, 24 goals, 16 assists, 40 points, 33 penalty minutes.

"I had been with Phoenix in the old Western League for three years when I got called up to the NHL by the California Golden Seals in 1972. I was originally owned by Toronto, but California took me in the 1971 draft. I was brought up by the Seals for a handful of games, but I basically sat on the bench. In the middle of everything else, right after I got there, the club made a coaching change. They got rid of Freddy Glover and brought in Vic Stasiuk, who didn't like anybody who wasn't big and stupid like him. Stasiuk was a real dinosaur, one of those guys who thought you couldn't possibly be a hockey player unless you were built like a brick outhouse. I could see the writing on the wall, so I ended up asking to be sent back down to Phoenix just to get some ice time.

"As it turned out, the Seals didn't protect me in the 1972 expansion draft and I was picked by the Atlanta Flames. The WHA had already had its big draft, and I was picked by Dayton. Billy Dineen, who had already signed to coach the WHA club, contacted me about what they were trying to do, and it sounded good. But the Flames looked interesting, too. They were starting from scratch, like the WHA, and I really wanted to show the California Seals that they'd made a mistake by leaving me unprotected. It was a tough choice because Atlanta and Dayton were both offering me the same money—about $40,000. What decided it for me was that I was so pissed off with the NHL's attitude. In both Toronto and California they'd told me I was too small to play big-league hockey, and I had a feeling it would probably be the same old bullshit in Atlanta. That's why I chose the WHA.

"There were no guarantees the league would survive, even after [Bobby] Hull and those guys came over. Everyone was jumpy about it, but we had a great coach in Dineen and he had really done his homework when he put together that first Houston team. Billy didn't try to get any big-name NHL players to jump during the first year. Instead he concentrated on signing good, character-type guys who he'd seen or played against in the minors and who for one reason or another never got much of a shot in the NHL. You have to remember that in those days, if you were brought up from the American Hockey League or the Western League, you had only two or three games to show something. If you didn't, you were sent right back to the minors.

"Billy understood that. He knew there were top-quality players on the farm teams who only needed a chance. He signed guys like Gord Labossiere, who was a proven goal scorer. Then he got veteran leaders like Murray Hall and Teddy Taylor, and our tough guy, John Schella. Dineen had a blueprint for building the Houston Aeros, and he stuck to it.

"We had pretty good success the first year, but the next season, when the Howes were added to the mix, our team went from being pretty good to being great. Even at that, though, we had trouble drawing crowds at home. We always outdrew the Rockets basketball team, but for a city the size of Houston we weren't marketed well enough to fill the building. When the Howes were in Houston, I don't think we played a single road game in Canada that wasn't a sellout, but we could average only around eight thousand fans a night at home.

"The thing I'll always remember about those early Aero teams was how close we were. It was a group commitment, and everybody had an important role to play. There was some concern, when Gordie and his sons arrived, that there might be some jealousy over the money they were getting, but that never happened. We all realized that the Howes made us a much better team, and that meant more money for everyone.

"The other thing that stands out in my mind is how much fun we had. We had our own plane, an old DC-3, and every time we got on it, I said a silent prayer. The engines routinely caught fire, we'd make emergency landings all over the place, and half the time the thing wouldn't even start. We'd be up there bouncing around, smoke billowing out…but it never seemed to disrupt our card games! Doug Harvey, one of the greatest hockey players of all time, was our assistant coach. He'd crack open the beer, start telling stories…it was great. I couldn't put a price tag on the fun we had.

"For me, playing with Gordie was the ultimate thrill, no doubt about it. He knew I idolized him. We were both right wingers, and I used to study him out on the ice. On the road he'd invite me out for a beer or to have dinner with him. He was a super guy. But on the ice he could be scary. One night in Minnesota we had a bench-clearing brawl. I was pinned against the boards, and there was big scrum about ten feet in front of me. Somebody had knocked Marty [Howe] down and was on top of him, getting ready to throw a punch. All of a sudden I see this big mitt come out of nowhere. It's Gordie. Quick as a flash he hooks two fingers into the guy's nostrils and yanks him off Marty. I thought Gordie was gonna tear the poor bastard's nose right off his face, but that time he showed a little mercy.

"Another night we were in Edmonton. Gordie always used one particular brand of stick with thick, custom-made shafts because his hands were so damn big. Well, this particular night he was trying out a different brand of stick because the company had given him an endorsement deal.

"The Oilers had brought some kid up from the minors who stuck to Howe like glue all night. We were up something like 6–1, and I could see it coming. Gordie wasn't happy about this kid shadowing him, and on every shift the stick and the elbows were getting a little higher. Finally, with about five minutes left in the game, Gordie just shish-kebabed the kid right at centre ice. He reefed him so hard that the stick splintered into about four pieces. I thought the kid was dead.

"Gordie got kicked out of the game for it, but he didn't miss a beat. He skated over to our bench, tossed the trainer the little hunk of stick that he was still holding and said, 'I never want to see another one of these pieces of shit again; they're no good for nothin!' The rest of us just about pissed ourselves, we laughed so hard. After my 48-goal year the Atlanta Flames made me a good offer to go back to the NHL, but I wouldn't even consider it while I had a chance to play with Gordie. That's how much I respected the guy.

"Those championship teams in Houston were two of the best I ever saw. In fact, we challenged the Montreal Canadiens to a one-game, winner-take-all showdown in 1975, but they didn't want anything to do with us. It's always bothered me that the NHL had such a patronizing attitude toward the WHA, especially when you look at the talent that came up through our league. Besides Mark and Marty Howe, the Aeros developed players like John Tonelli, Terry Ruskowski and Rich Preston...all of whom became stars in the NHL. I remember going into Birmingham and facing a starting lineup that had Kenny Linseman at centre between Rick Vaive and Mark Napier. Steve Durbano was on defense, and John Garrett was in goal. All those guys became big names in the National Hockey League. It bugs me that to this day a lot of people still think the WHA was second-rate because that's bull. If our league was so bad, how did one of our teams [Edmonton] manage to win the Stanley Cup just four years after the merger?

"By the time I went to the Pacific Hockey League, I was looking to pack it in. I had two good years in Phoenix and Tucson and then retired. It was a great arrangement in Phoenix because by that time I was partners in a masonry business with my former brother-in-law. I only played the games; I didn't have to practise. It was just senior-calibre hockey, but it was fun.

"After I retired from playing, I stayed with the masonry business for a few years, then got divorced and moved back home to British Columbia. I worked in the mines for awhile, then became a golf pro for several years. Now I'm in real estate, and I'm enjoying it.

"I don't play at all anymore. We had an Aeros reunion in 1996, and we beat the 1980 U.S. Olympic Team in an exhibition game that was shown on TV. It was great. That was the last time I was on skates. I figured it was a good way to go out. How many guys can say the last game they played was against Olympic gold medallists?"

ANDRE LACROIX

Centre . . . Born in Lauzon, Que., June 5, 1945 . . . Played junior with Montreal and Peterborough in the Ontario Hockey Association . . . two-time winner of the Red Tilson Memorial Trophy as MVP in the OHA (1964–65, 1965–66), beating out Bobby Orr . . . Played two seasons with the Quebec Aces in the American Hockey League before being drafted by the Philadelphia Flyers in the original NHL expansion draft (1967) . . . Scored 72 goals and 160 points in just over three seasons with the Flyers, then was traded to the Chicago Black Hawks for Rick Foley (October 1971) . . . Briefly centred Bobby Hull and Chico Maki with the Hawks . . . Selected by the Quebec Nordiques in the WHA's 1972 general player draft . . . Rights transferred to the Miami Screaming Eagles, Mar. 1972 . . . Signed by the Philadelphia Blazers, May 1972 . . . First WHA scoring champion, with 50 goals and 124 points in 78 games . . . When the Blazers moved to Vancouver in 1973, Lacroix refused to move, suiting up instead with the New York Golden Blades. Stayed with the team through franchise incarnations as the New Jersey Knights and San Diego Mariners . . . Collected record 106 assists with the Mariners in 1974–75 . . . Claimed by Houston in dispersal draft after San Diego franchise folded . . . Although his rights were purchased by the Winnipeg Jets after the Houston franchise was dissolved, Lacroix never played in Winnipeg, and his rights were dealt to the New England Whalers, where he finished his WHA career in 1978–79 . . . Played 29 games for Hartford after the merger, then retired . . . Played in every WHA all-star game and was voted to the first all-star team three times . . . Named to Team Canada '74 and notched seven points in eight-game series against the Soviet Union . . . All-time WHA leader in games played (551), assists (547), and points (798); fourth in goals (251) . . . **Major league totals:** (Regular season) **NHL** - 325 games, 79 goals, 119 assists, 198 points, 44 penalty minutes. **WHA** - 551 games, 251 goals, 547 assists, 798 points, 412 penalty minutes. (Playoffs) **NHL** - 16 games, 2 goals, 5 assists, 7 points, 0 penalty minutes. **WHA** - 48 games, 14 goals, 29 assists, 43 points, 30 penalty minutes.

"I was picked by Quebec in the original WHA draft, but about a thousand players were selected, so nobody gave it much thought until several months later. The Miami Screaming Eagles, who never played a game, acquired my playing rights from Quebec while I was still in the NHL. Bernie Parent got a lot of publicity for the WHA when he signed a contract with Miami during the NHL season, and that made people realize that the WHA was for real. I really got interested when the Miami franchise relocated to Philadelphia because I loved playing there with the Flyers.

"Money was a big part of it, sure. I negotiated all my contracts, and the Blazers, without even knowing what I was making in Chicago, said they'd double my salary and give me a five-year deal. It was amazing because Philadelphia was where I really wanted to go. I had been treated very well by the Flyers during my time there, and it was a very good hockey town. The fans were terrific. The only problem I had with the Flyers was playing for Vic Stasiuk. He wasn't good at bringing the team together and he was terrible at communicating with the guys.

"One of the things that really bothered me about Stasiuk was when he ordered me, Serge Bernier, Bernie Parent, Jean Guy Gendron and Simon Nolet not to speak French around him or the team or else he would fine us. Can you imagine a coach doing that today? It happened at a Thursday afternoon practice in Philly. Stasiuk was in a bad mood for some reason anyway, and after we got off the ice, he called all the French-speaking guys together and laid down the rule: no French anywhere around the team, or we'd be fined. And he really spelled it out. We couldn't speak French on the ice, in the dressing room, on planes or buses or at hotels. If we did, it would cost us money. We were shocked. This was our native language, and some of these guys could hardly speak English.

"The fireworks came two days later, when we flew to Montreal for a game against the Canadiens. It was a front-page story in the Montreal papers —not in the sports section, but on the front page—'Flyers Can't Speak French.' Stasiuk was booed like hell by the fans, and then [league president] Clarence Campbell got involved. He wanted an explanation, so he called Marcel Pelletier, who was the Flyers' director of personnel. Campbell then talked to Stasiuk, who denied everything, saying the players had made it up. Then the incident was just swept under the carpet and forgotten. But it really hurt me and the rest of the guys, too, I think. That was just one of the things

Stasiuk did that made me see he wasn't much of a coach, but I still enjoyed my time with the Flyers. They're a great organization.

"I was traded to the Black Hawks for Rick Foley in 1971, but nothing good happened for me in Chicago because they had no idea how to use me. Bobby Hull and Chico Maki would always play together, no matter what, so the Hawks went through about a dozen guys trying to find the right centre for them.

"Returning to play in Philadelphia with the Blazers was a dream come true because I had never wanted to leave the Flyers. We had built a pretty good team in Philly since the expansion year [1967], and I felt I was an important part of it. Those were the days when 20 goals was considered a very good plateau, and I scored 24, 22 and 20 in my three years with the Flyers, averaging around 55 points per season. I'd heard some rumours about the WHA, but nothing serious until I got a phone call about going to the Blazers. I talked to Bobby Hull because he'd already made up his mind to jump to Winnipeg, and then when guys like Derek [Sanderson] and Johnny [McKenzie] made the move, I knew it was for real.

"Being one of the pioneers of the WHA was exciting for me because I had also been part of the original NHL expansion. The WHA was another new beginning, and it sure opened up a lot of doors for hockey players in both leagues. The decision to jump wasn't very difficult because I had always been a player who made up his own mind about things; I didn't let other people's opinions influence me too much. Even back in junior, when I was playing in the OHA for the Montreal Junior Canadiens [1964], I refused to sign the C form, which everybody else was signing, so they sent me to the Peterborough team as punishment. But I turned a negative situation into something positive; it became one of the best things that ever happened to me because I learned to speak English and to get along on my own. It was tough for a young kid, but I made it. I won the Red Tilson Memorial Trophy as the league MVP two years in a row in Peterborough, beating out Bobby Orr. That's one of my proudest accomplishments in hockey.

"It was the same situation at the start of the WHA—a lot of criticism from guys in the NHL, a lot of bad-mouthing the league. But we turned it into a positive. We stuck to it and made it work, and within a few years we were on a par with the NHL. For the Flyers especially, the WHA came along at a good time. So many guys jumped from Philly and the Flyers' farm team in Quebec that players like Dave Schultz and Don Saleski came up a lot sooner than they would have without the WHA. I don't think the Flyers would have won their two Stanley Cups if the WHA hadn't come along.

"I was one of the few guys who were in the WHA from beginning to end, and let me tell you, it was a very, very enjoyable experience. It was fun hockey, but it was tough, too. And there were always some problems with the league, of course. The worst thing was that they gave franchises to anybody who wanted one, and many of those people had no idea how to run a professional organization. It led to some problems, and each season a few incidents made us wonder whether the league could survive. But the WHA went to great lengths to promote itself, too.

"One time, early on, I got a call from the club owner when we were in New York. He said to come up and see him. My wife was with me, and she was pregnant at the time, but we went up to the executive office to see what the guy wanted. Well, we walk in, and the first thing I see is these two gorgeous girls. They'd both been *Penthouse* centrefolds, and they said they wanted to take me out for lunch and talk over some business. My wife didn't object, so off I went with these two beautiful women. It turned out they wanted me to pose for a photo shoot for a women's magazine. They said it would be very tasteful, and they'd use shadows and dark lighting, that kind of thing. They wanted to shoot me in the shower and the locker room. They said it would be good publicity for the WHA to show one of the top scorers 'out of uniform.' I guess I should have taken it as a compliment, but I was embarrassed. I have a brother who is a priest, and I was thinking of my parents, too. I would never do something like that. I told them Derek [Sanderson] would probably do it in a minute, but I was the wrong guy for the job.

"I saw a lot of bizarre things because I was on teams that kept folding or moving—but it's not true that I was traded. The only time in my hockey career that I was traded was in the NHL, when I went from the Flyers to the Black Hawks. In the WHA, when the Blazers moved from Philly to Vancouver, I refused to go because the Blazers and the league owed me about $20,000 in bonuses. I wanted my money, and I told them if I didn't get it, I wasn't moving with the team. At about the same time the New York Raiders' franchise was basically dead, but the league wanted to keep a team in New York, so they formed the New York Golden Blades. By the way, I still say today that the Golden Blades' uniform was the best-looking one I ever wore! Anyway, since I'd won the scoring title, the league thought it would be good if I was in New York to help sell the WHA there. They also knew I refused to move to Vancouver, so the league made a secret deal with the New York owner. They sent him the $20,000 in bonus money I was owed, and right afterward the Golden Blades announced that they had 'traded' Ron Ward and a goaltender, Peter Donnelly, to Vancouver for me, Don Herriman and the rights to Bernie Parent. That whole story was orchestrated by the league.

"As it turned out, I didn't get my bonus money when I reported to New York—the owner had already spent it! I was pretty mad. A couple of weeks later, to showcase the WHA and the new Golden Blades, the league had scheduled a preseason extravaganza at Madison Square Garden with us, Winnipeg, Houston and New England playing each other in minigames. It was, I think, Gordie Howe's first road appearance with the Aeros, and with Bobby and the Winnipeg Jets also there it was going to get a lot of publicity. But I told the club I wouldn't dress unless I got my money. A few hours before the exhibition was supposed to start, the league office flew a guy to New York to give me the $20,000 in person.

"The Golden Blades had great uniforms, and New York was a fun place to play, but there were all kinds of problems. After about a month [director of personnel] Jerry De Lise told us there was no money to cover our paycheques. The team was already broke. They had until midnight to pay us, or we would all become free agents. At 11:45 that night there was a knock on my door, and there was Jerry, hand-delivering an envelope with my pay in it. Another 15 minutes and I could've signed with anybody I liked!

"Not long after that the Golden Blades folded, and the league took over the operation of the team. We became the Jersey Knights. We found out about it when we walked into our dressing room at the [Madison Square] Garden and everything was gone. Uniforms, equipment, signs, everything. We went from playing in one of the best rinks in the world to playing in one of the worst, in Cherry Hill, New Jersey. It was tiny and dark, and there was no dressing room for the other team. They had to put on all their equipment at the hotel and then bus over, skates and all. It was embarrassing. We were professional hockey players, and I thought the WHA was doing a pretty good job of projecting a good image, but that whole experience with the Knights was something else. It was laughable. We finished dead last, and hardly anybody came to see us play—although the fans who did show up were very good.

"The team moved again after the 1973–74 season, this time to San Diego. It was great. We had good management, and it finally looked like we were going to stay in one place long enough to become part of the community and win the fans over to WHA hockey. I started the season in great shape because I'd played for Team Canada against the Russians in September 1974. That was great, playing alongside Howe and Hull and the rest of those guys, but I was disappointed with the way the series turned out, especially after we'd started so well. There were all kinds of problems after we got to Moscow, and the officiating was awful. That year was also special for me because it was the year I was named the most outstanding French Canadian athlete, beating out Guy Lafleur and Marcel Dionne in a vote by the press.

"The first season with the Mariners went very well for the team and for me. We finished second in the West, and we had pretty good crowds and a good mix of players. Wayne Rivers scored 54 goals, and Gene Peacosh and Rick Sentes both scored over 40. I broke the 100-assist mark and finished with 106. That was very satisfying because to me 100 assists is like a baseball player hitting .380 or .400—it's very difficult to do. Assists were more satisfying to me than goals, and even though I was a centre and had always been a good goal scorer, I took a lot more pride in being known as a guy who could set up his wingers for scoring chances.

"Another thing I appreciated about playing in San Diego was that the fans were so knowledgeable about hockey. There was a Western Hockey League team there for years, and the fans loved the game. We had a pretty high profile, too, considering it was California and hockey wasn't nearly as popular in that part of the country as it is now. Even when the owner defaulted in early 1976 and the team wouldn't be getting regular paycheques, the players voted to continue the season.

"One time we flew all the way to Baltimore, a whole plane load of professional hockey players, and we didn't get a meal because the club had downgraded our tickets to the cheapest seats. That's a long flight with nothing to eat. Guys were walking up and down the aisles, asking if anyone had a spare bun. When [San Diego Padres' owner] Ray Kroc bought the club [1976–77], we all expected things to turn around, but we were barely a .500 club, and attendance started to fall off quickly. Kroc sold us to a group that said the team was going to be relocated to Florida, but that plan fell apart, and once again I changed uniforms, this time as a free agent. There was a dispersal draft after the Mariners folded, and I signed with the Houston Aeros.

"It was basically the same story in Houston. The Aeros had been the class of the league for a few years when the Howes were there, and the club had always been a good draw both at home and on the road. But by 1977–78 everybody could see that the end of the WHA was coming and that whatever teams were left would probably join the NHL. It was too bad Houston didn't make it because I think they would support an NHL club today. The year I was with the Aeros, there were financial problems. One time we were picked up in motor homes because the team couldn't afford to pay for a bus! It was funny because by the last year our league was the equal of the NHL. The

Houston club folded, and even though Winnipeg bought the rights to most of the Houston players, I ended up going to Hartford. The next year, after the merger, four of the top ten NHL scorers came from the WHA, so people who say the WHA wasn't major league hockey don't know what they're talking about. It was strange being back in the NHL for a couple of months with the Whalers, but I still say the WHA was just as good as the NHL at the end.

"I retired in December 1979 with no regrets about having jumped leagues. For me, the WHA was a very gratifying experience, and I'm proud that I was part of history. It bothers me quite a bit that there's still an attitude that the WHA wasn't big-league hockey, but what can you do? I think it's terrible that none of the goals and points scored in the WHA are counted in hockey records—especially when it comes to the Hall of Fame.

"My only regret today is that for all those years I never had an agent— not to get me more money, but to make the contacts that might have kept me in hockey after my playing days ended. I did some TV and radio colour in Hartford, and for a while I worked with the Whalers' front office, but there wasn't anything for me there. I asked them to create a position for me to help prepare players for life after hockey, but they turned me down. I had a construction company in Hartford, but then the economy went sour, and I got out of that business and became an arena consultant. Today I'm part owner of two rinks in Oakland, California, and I'm involved with the planning and operation of some others, but I really miss hockey.

"I'd love to get back in the game with a coaching position in junior or college hockey, but nobody is willing to give me a chance. That's all I ask— just an opportunity to show what I can do. I love to teach, and I think I'm a good communicator. A few years ago I applied for the coaching job at Colgate University. All I wanted was an interview, a chance to tell them what I could bring to the job. They wouldn't even interview me because I don't have a college education. It's absurd. I played professional hockey for 15 years, and I got 996 big-league points, but nobody wants to give me a chance to teach. That's my only regret—that I haven't had the opportunity to pass along some of what I've learned to kids. I've been a student of hockey all my life. Even when I was playing, I studied other players to see how they handled different situations. I learned a lot from all my coaches, and I filed it all away. When I was a kid, I idolized and studied Jean Beliveau and Henri Richard. That helped make me a better player, and now I'd like to be able to pass that knowledge down. Not just the on-ice part of hockey, either. I want kids to be able to say 'Andre taught me a lot about hockey, but he taught me more about life.'

"I just need somebody to believe in me…to give me the chance. Unfortunately, there's a lot of politics in hockey today, and I'm on the outside looking in."

MIKE LAUGHTON

Centre … Born in Nelson, B.C., Feb. 21, 1944 … Following a stellar amateur career with his hometown Nelson Maple Leafs in the Western International Hockey League, Laughton got his first taste of the professional game with the Victoria Maple Leafs and Vancouver Canucks in the Western League … Became one of the first B.C.-bred players to make the NHL when he was claimed by Oakland in the original expansion draft and debuted with the Seals in the 1967–68 season … Played 189 games for Oakland and the California Golden Seals over the next four seasons before being dealt to the Montreal Canadiens prior to the 1971–72 season … Unable to crack the Canadiens' formidable lineup, Laughton was sent to the Nova Scotia Voyageurs in the American Hockey League, where he was promptly named captain and led the team to the AHL championship … Claimed by the New York Raiders in the WHA's 1972 general player draft, he signed with the Raiders that summer … Remained with the club through its subsequent incarnations as the New York Golden Blades, New Jersey Knights and San Diego Mariners … Claimed by the Calgary Cowboys from San Diego in the 1975 intraleague draft … Retired from the WHA when he couldn't come to terms with the Cowboys … Returned to Nelson as player-coach of the senior "A" Maple Leafs in the WIHL … **Major league totals:** (Regular season) **NHL** - 189 games, 39 goals, 48 assists, 87 points, 101 penalty minutes. **WHA** - 203 games, 43 goals, 47 assists, 90 points, 100 penalty minutes. (Playoffs) **NHL** - 11 games, 2 goals, 4 assists, 6 points, 0 penalty minutes. **WHA** - 10 games, 4 goals, 1 assist, 5 points, 0 penalty minutes.

"I considered myself very fortunate to have had the opportunity to play with so many outstanding veteran hockey players on my way up the ladder to the NHL, so I tried to pass a bit of that along when I joined the New York Raiders in the WHA.

"When I first came out of senior hockey in Nelson, Toronto sent me to Victoria to play with their farm club in the Western Hockey League. In those days the WHL was only a step below the National league, so it was a little intimidating at first. Most of the guys around the league had some experience in the NHL or the American Hockey League, and here I was, coming from a senior team in the boonies. I'll never forget how guys like Andy Hebenton and Lou Jankowski took me under their wing and guided me through my first pro season. They were great teachers, both on and off the ice. Hebenton held the NHL ironman streak for years, and he was still one of the most talented guys in the game when we were playing together in Victoria. It was a real treat to be able to watch and learn from him. He'd spend extra time with me after practice, working on faceoffs or giving me pointers about different guys around the league. It was terrific.

"The Western Hockey League is where I saw the business side of the game for the first time, so when I got to the NHL with Oakland, my feet were already wet, more or less. That first year with the Seals was a really wonderful experience. NHL expansion was brand new, and we were introducing the game to fans in cities that had never seen big-league hockey before. Another neat thing was that Whitey Ford, the great Yankees pitcher, was part of the original ownership group in Oakland. For any kid who grew up as a baseball fan in the 1950s, it was a tremendous thrill to meet him and just shoot the breeze. In that first season Whitey was sort of the communicator between management and the players, so he often used to come down to the dressing room just to hang around and get to know us.

"I was really disappointed when the Seals were sold and [Charlie] Finley and his group took over. He wasn't a hockey fan, he didn't really understand the game, and I don't think he ever took the time to appreciate it. He had a screwy way of doing things, and money was always the bottom line. For example, I started a tradition with the Seals. After our home games, win or lose, I'd go out on the ice with a bucket of 20 or 30 pucks and flip 'em up into the stands. The fans loved it! Kids would yell and scream…there'd be five hundred so people at one end of the rink waiting for me to flick them the pucks. Freddy Glover came up to me one night and told me to cut it out or he'd deduct the price of the pucks from my paycheque! That was Finley's way: worry about the cost of pucks but treat the players like crap.

"After the Seals dealt me to Montreal, it was a real eye-opener. Hockey was like a religion with the Canadiens, and I saw that right from the first day of training camp. The camp was divided into teams, and we played real games against each other. It was very intense, and you had some great, great hockey players fighting each other for position, day in and day out.

"Then I got sent to Nova Scotia, which was no surprise, considering the Canadiens had guys like Henri Richard, Jacques Lemaire and Pete Mahovlich at centre. Plus I was still having some problems with my knee. I tore the ligaments and had surgery in 1970, and it wasn't 100 percent.

"Nova Scotia was a great place to play. [GM and coach] Al MacNeil named me the captain, and I got to learn the Canadiens' system and get an appreciation for how they built their hockey clubs. We had a terrific team, with players like Larry Robinson, Yvon Lambert and Tony Featherstone. Michel Deguise and Michel Plasse were our goaltenders. Al was a real results-oriented guy, and he used to go over the opposing team's roster with me and ask for suggestions about how to handle certain guys—stuff like that. He taught me a lot.

"Halifax was a great learning experience and I was really looking forward to staying in the Canadiens organization, but then I found out they were going to loan me to the New York Islanders for the 1972–73 season. It was supposedly going to be temporary, on the understanding that there would be something for me in the Montreal organization down the road. Still, I wasn't thrilled about it. By that time the WHA had held its draft, and I was selected by the Raiders. They invited me down to New York for a weekend to talk about a contract, and I ended up signing with them right away. They gave me a three-year guaranteed deal for a lot more than I was earning in Halifax, and even though it meant leaving the Canadiens' organization, I was looking forward to the challenge of helping to build a new league.

"We had quite a mix of players at the first Raiders' camp, but everybody was rating us right up there with Bobby and the Winnipeg Jets as one of the WHA's showcase teams. We were all hand-picked draft choices who had been successful in other leagues, but we had problems right away with playing at Madison Square Garden, where we were fourth in the pecking order behind the Rangers, the Knicks basketball team and, if you can believe it, the circus! The rent at the Garden was huge, and almost immediately we could see that WHA hockey was going to be a tough sell. One night we'd have a decent crowd, and the next game it looked like there were more ushers than fans in the stands.

"Being in the WHA was disheartening at times, but the fun we had on the ice and travelling around the league helped take our minds off what was happening in the front office. We had a really funny trainer named Fraser Gleeson. He was one of the first in the business to try to get hockey players interested in dryland training, and he developed complicated programs and exercise routines for us. It was hilarious watching him try to explain it. And in those days, who knew? A lot of what Fraser tried to do made good sense, but it was so new and so weird that we didn't take it seriously.

"Fraser was always riding two of our defensemen, Jean Gauthier and Kent Douglas, about their weight. They were both very talented players who had spent a lot of time in the National Hockey League. Douglas had even been rookie of the year way back when with the Toronto Maple Leafs. But they had both packed on a lot of extra pounds playing in the minors, and now they had to shed the weight. Douglas was the first guy I ever saw use cellophane wrap. He'd spend half an hour before practice wrapping cellophane around his body before he put on his equipment. It made him sweat a lot, he said. But 20 minutes into the workout he'd be as red as a beet, huffing and puffing, with his eyes bugging out because the bloody cellophane was nearly choking him to death! It was priceless. Gauthier was just a big, fun-loving guy who never took anything too seriously. He'd forgotten more about playing defense than a lot of guys in the WHA ever learned, but for some reason he was in [coach Camille] Henry's doghouse a lot.

"Henry was an old-style coach, but I always admired the fact that he wasn't afraid to try new ideas. He was probably the first coach to use walkie-talkies with a guy up in the press box. He'd have Kent or Jean or one of our other veterans up there during the game, and they'd talk back and forth about matching lines or setting plays. It was really something to watch.

"The Raiders became the New York Golden Blades in the second season, and then the Jersey Knights. That gold-and-purple Blades uniform is one of the nicest I ever saw in all my years in hockey; in fact, I still have the whole thing: jersey, pants, socks...even the white skates. Beautiful! When we moved to Jersey, we started to wonder where it would end. We had to take buses from the city to Cherry Hill Arena, and because the place seated fewer than five thousand fans, it was like playing in a little hick town. There were no players' benches...at least not normal ones. Instead of one long bench, there were three rows of five seats. Somebody said the two teams looked like choirs when we were sitting down. There was a big dip in the ice, too. In fact, the ice was sloped enough that it looked like the visiting team was skating uphill for two periods of every game. Once, one of our defensemen, Ted Scharf, was waiting for a pass when the puck skipped out of the dip and hit him right between the eyes. It was awful.

"After the New Jersey experience, moving to San Diego was a treat. We had a great facility, good fans and solid ownership. It was a joy to play there, and the team started to come around. In that first year on the coast Andre Lacroix had 106 assists, Wayne Rivers had 54 goals and we were one of the highest-scoring teams in the league. We beat Toronto in the opening round of the playoffs but then lost out to Houston, which was disappointing. I had more knee problems through the regular season, but I bounced back and had a really good playoff, with four goals in ten games.

"The Calgary Cowboys drafted me from San Diego in the 1975 intra-league draft, but by that time my knee was acting up again. I was 32 years old, and I could still play, but I wanted to be paid what I thought I was worth. Calgary was giving big contracts to kids right out of junior and guys who hadn't been around nearly as long as I had, but when I went looking for the same kind of deal, they balked. Maybe it was because of my age or because of the injuries, but we just couldn't strike a deal. I went back home, back to senior hockey as a player-coach for a couple of years, then called it a day.

"For me, the WHA was a wonderful experience. I wouldn't have traded it for anything. After having gone to the NHL as part of the first expansion, I could see that hockey was on the brink of taking off in the U.S. I think the WHA gave the game the final push it needed. I was proud to be an original New York Raider, and even with all the problems the franchise went through before we moved to San Diego, it was always a hell of a lot of fun. To me, that was the main thing. I took the game very seriously on the ice, but it was always important that everything else was fun.

"The WHA provided that. It was great watching teammates like Ronnie Ward and Lacroix develop into superstar-type players, and it was a thrill to be one of the veterans on the club and to always be handed the responsibility of checking the other team's big line. Going head-to-head against Gordie Howe's line in Houston or Bobby and the Swedes in Winnipeg is something I'll never forget.

"One regret I have is that I didn't keep more souvenirs from those days. I've got my Golden Blades uniform, and I made a point of getting a few crested pucks in every city we played, but when you're playing, you never think about getting mementos for later years.

"I feel very fortunate to have been a part of hockey history, and the WHA gave me the means to have a very enjoyable life after I quit playing. I owned a sporting goods store, and I built a nice house for my family on a beautiful piece of lakefront property. Today we're very comfortable. I owe a lot of that to the World Hockey Association."

DANNY LAWSON

Right wing . . . Born in Toronto, Ont., Oct. 30, 1947 . . . Capped a brilliant junior career with the Hamilton Red Wings by scoring 52 goals and 90 points in 54 games, 1967–68 . . . Turned pro with the Fort Worth Wings in the Central Hockey League the following season and scored nine points in eight games to earn a promotion to Detroit . . . Traded by the Red Wings, along with Brian Conacher, to the Minnesota North Stars for Wayne Connelly in Feb. 1969 . . . Split 1969–70 season between Minnesota and the Iowa Stars of the CHL . . . Split 1970–71 between the North Stars and the Cleveland Barons of the American Hockey League . . . Drafted by the Buffalo Sabres in the 1971 intraleague draft . . . Played one full season with the Sabres before joining the WHA as an original Philadelphia Blazer . . . Among the league's top five scorers from the first week of the season, on Feb. 22, 1973, Lawson became the first WHA player to score 50 goals . . . Led the Blazers in hat tricks and recorded a five-goal game en route to finishing the season with a league-high 61 goals . . . Notched 50 goals and 88 points for the Vancouver Blazers in 1973–74 . . . Played 144 games with the Calgary Cowboys before being traded, along with Mike Ford, to the Winnipeg Jets for Ron Ward and Veli Pekka Ketola, Mar. 1977 . . . Lawson is the all-time Blazers-Cowboys franchise leader in goals (212), assists (197) and points (409) . . . **Major league totals:** (Regular season) **NHL** - 219 games, 28 goals, 29 assists, 57 points, 61 penalty minutes. **WHA** - 392 games, 218 goals, 204 assists, 422 points, 142 penalty minutes. (Playoffs) **NHL** - 16 games, 0 goals, 1 assist, 1 point, 2 penalty minutes. **WHA** - 26 games, 6 goals, 9 assists, 15 points, 25 penalty minutes.

"I was with the Buffalo Sabres when I first heard about the WHA. I was spending the summer in Orangeville, Ontario, when I got a phone call from Donny Luce, who was a teammate with the Sabres. He told me a meeting was going to be held in Toronto regarding this new league and I should come down and hear more about it. I figured, 'What the hell, why not?' When I got to the Skyline Hotel, I saw quite a few familiar faces from around the National Hockey League—guys I guess the new league figured they might have a shot at recruiting. The meeting was run by a couple of agents who were obviously looking to land new clients.

"I listened to their pitch, then told them I'd be interested in finding out more about it. Eventually I was contacted again, and then everything spiralled. I was intrigued because the WHA people indicated I'd be used differently if I made the move. They felt my style should be offensive-minded, and I'd never been used that way in the NHL. It sounded good. They basically coaxed me with a carrot by saying that in their league I could be the kind of player I'd been in junior. The fact they offered me twice as much money as the Sabres wasn't so hard to take either, but for me the appeal of the WHA was that I'd be able to play the type of hockey I always knew I was capable of.

"I made a commitment to jump leagues even before I knew that guys like Hull and [J.C.] Tremblay and [Derek] Sanderson were going to move. I knew there would probably be a few 'name' NHL guys going over, but I thought it would mostly be players like me, who were looking for a second chance.

"In Buffalo the year before I'd been one of the top scorers through the exhibition schedule, playing on the French Connection line with Gil Perreault and Rick Martin. We were together until early in the season, when we came home from a tough three-game road trip. None of us had played well, so [coach Punch] Imlach thought he would shake things up by moving me to the checking line. That's where I stayed. It was frustrating because I'd always been a scorer in junior and I knew I could be one in the NHL, but I wasn't being used properly.

"The chance to change all that was a big factor in my jumping to the Philadelphia Blazers. I was looking for something that would give my career a kick-start, and the WHA turned out to be it. The funny thing is that I didn't get the old feeling back until we were 15 or 20 games into the season. That's when I hit my stride, and I ended up scoring 61 goals. A big part of that success was that I had one of the most incredible centres who ever played the game: Andre Lacroix.

"Andy was a genuine superstar, but he never got the recognition he deserved. With him at centre and Donny Herriman on the left side, our line just took off. We knew each other so well, and on the nights when everything was clicking, we flat-out dominated. One of the worst things of my career was when Andy and I split up, after the first season. I went to Vancouver with the Blazers, and he went to New York. If you ask me, the chemistry that Lacroix and I had happens to a hockey player just once in his career, if he's lucky.

"There were a lot of eye-openers during the first year in Philly, not the least of which was the amount of money floating around in those big contracts for Sanderson, Pie McKenzie and Bernie Parent. We couldn't believe the dollars those guys were getting. Sanderson's signing the big contract and then playing only a few games before being bought out for a million bucks didn't cause as much of a distraction as you might think. In my case, it took the heat off what I was trying to bring to the team. Derek and I knew each other from our junior days. We'd had our share of battles both there and in the NHL, but we were always able to patch things up. I liked the guy. I also felt sorry for him, knowing how tough things had been for him at a young age. The bizarre thing was that, after he got all that money, he fell in with a bad group of people who were just leeches. He had to start living up to his media image, and that wasn't really him. It was sad because he had incredible talent.

"We started off the season using coloured pucks, which was a joke because nobody could see them. At our first home game the Zamboni got stuck and the ice started breaking up into big chunks, so the game was cancelled. That almost started a riot because the fans started throwing the free pucks they had been given as souvenirs.

"We opened the season with seven straight losses, which shocked everybody, considering we had some of the biggest stars in the league. We won only four of our first 20 games, and by December we were buried in last place. Things didn't start to turn around until just after Christmas. We won a game in Minnesota, and then on the way to L.A. for a New Year's Eve game against the Sharks, we stopped in Las Vegas for a couple of days. For 48 hours nobody slept; it was around-the-clock partying. Well, we crawled into L.A. and beat the Sharks 3–1. Right after the game we flew back to play an afternoon game in New York the next day. Bernie stood on his head, and we blanked the Raiders 3–0. Over the second half of the season we were one of the hottest teams in the league, and we ended up coming from way behind to make the playoffs.

"The off-ice stuff was just as wild. One night after a game in New York the team stopped off at a little bar in Blackwood, New Jersey. It turned out that a gang of bikers used this particular bar as one of their favourite hangouts, and they showed up just after we got there. They started mouthing off, and one of them threw a shot glass at our table and hit [back-up goalie] Marcel Paille in the side of the head.

"That did it. A big tough defenseman named Dave Hutchison ran over and grabbed the biggest biker and was getting ready to plow his face through the window when the guy reached up with a choke wire and tried to get it around Dave's neck. Hutch flipped the guy over in a reverse choke hold, and the wire ended up going around the biker's neck, so Dave dragged him outside like a side of beef and proceeded to beat the shit out of him. By this time everybody else was fighting and throwing bottles and glasses, and a couple of minutes later a whole squad of cops showed up.

"It was pretty messy. Guys were cut up, and there was blood all over the place. But it sure brought our team closer together. Bernie ended up getting a broken finger in the fight, and he missed some games because of it, but word never leaked out about how it happened. The club did some fancy talking, and none of us faced serious charges. It was all covered up.

"Probably the proudest moment of my WHA career came in February of that season, when I became the first player in the league to score 50 goals. It was an unreal feeling because I'd never imagined doing that as a pro hockey player. Hitting 60 was special, too. I'll never forget that—the club put on this big testimonial dinner at one of the nicest hotels in Philadelphia and brought in my family and friends to celebrate. Andre was there, along with most of my teammates, and there were huge blown-up photos of me shooting and scoring. I couldn't believe they would do all of that for me.

"The move from Philly to Vancouver was especially difficult for me because Andre didn't come with us. We phoned each other all the time because he was going through the same thing in New York. Without each other to play with, neither of us was as effective as we'd been in Philly. I salvaged what was basically a rotten season by scoring 50 goals, but it just wasn't the same.

"By the next season I could feel the pressure mounting, but we didn't have the horses. Soupy Campbell, Claude St. Sauveur and I were doing most of the scoring. At one point I even asked [coach] Andy Bathgate if he would consider playing again, just to take some of the heat off the three of us. Then there was the hoopla over the Blazers' signing an 18-year-old named Pat Price to a huge contract. We called him 'Pat the Brat' because he showed up with a real attitude problem. Soupy and I ended up baby-sitting him for most of the year. Price was pretty hard to take at first, and I know some of the guys came close to punching him out, but after he settled down and matured a bit, he turned out to be pretty valuable.

"I was devastated when I wasn't picked for Team Canada '74. I remember really looking forward to the selections because I'd been one of the highest scorers in the league since it started and because a series against the Russians would suit a guy like me, who could skate fast. I worked hard that summer to get in the best shape of my life, but in the end I got screwed by [Team Canada coach] Billy Harris. It was a slap in the face when I wasn't even invited to camp...it hurts to this day.

"I figured I'd be a natural pick for Team Canada because of my speed. That was my biggest weapon, and I was proud of it. And I'd proven I could score, too...especially from close range. Inside 20 feet I was deadly. The biggest drawback to my game was that I didn't have a broad scope of what was happening away from me when I didn't have the puck. Maybe I was too focused on scoring goals or too naive to realize I could be an effective player without the puck, but that was definitely my weakest point. It became obvious once I stopped playing with Andre. With a guy like him at centre, all I had to do was go to the net and the puck would be there, right on my stick. He could do that with his eyes closed. But even considering all that, I should have been part of Team Canada. Later that year the *New York Times* ran a big feature and rated me as the best right winger in the world, including the Russians. I still don't understand how they could have put me ahead of Yvan Cournoyer, but the article got people wondering why I wasn't picked for Team Canada. I still get asked about it. Not being part of that team was the biggest disappointment of my career, no question.

"When the Blazers moved to Calgary and became the Cowboys I went along, but I was already thinking about quitting hockey. I was having problems with some of my off-ice businesses, and it was getting harder to concentrate on playing. The Cowboys ended up trading me to Winnipeg, and for a while I got back into it, even though I played 21 games for the Jets with a cracked ankle and a broken hand. It was great to play on the same team as Hull and the Swedes. I really wanted a chance to play with Hedberg and Nilsson, just to compare it to playing with Lacroix, but it never happened.

"After finishing the season with the Jets, I knew I wanted to get out. I was still young enough, but the desire to continue wasn't there anymore. I had a lot of business interests at the time, and for the next few years that's what I concentrated on. When I was almost 40 years old, I got myself back into great shape and went to the Edmonton Oilers NHL training camp, but it was too far to come back. I joined the Canadian National team and then played and coached in Germany for a couple of years. At first the Germans were worried that I might not be able to skate well enough, but I ended up winning the scoring title in my first season.

"When I returned from Europe, I went back to Calgary and built a few companies. I was in real estate for a while, and now I'm a special projects consultant for clients all over the world. I'm active with the Calgary Flames Alumni team, and I play in a young men's league with other former pros, so hockey is still a big part of my life."

LARRY LUND

Centre . . . Born in Penticton, B.C., Sept. 9, 1940 . . . Played junior with the Edmonton Oil Kings, followed by two seasons with the Muskegon Zephyrs in the International Hockey League (1961–63) . . . Joined the Western Hockey League's San Francisco Seals in 1963–64, followed by a brief stint with the Minneapolis Bruins in the Central Professional Hockey League . . . Lund's rights were acquired by the Toronto Maple Leafs, but he didn't play a single game in the NHL . . . Played four seasons with the Seattle Totems in the WHL (1965–69) and joined the Quebec Aces in the AHL for nine games in the 1968–69 season before returning to the WHL with the Phoenix Roadrunners (1969–72) . . . Centred the "Go Go Line," one of the WHL's highest-scoring trios, with wingers Frank Hughes and Andre Hinse . . . Drafted by Dayton as a priority selection in the WHA's 1972 general player draft, Lund became an original Houston Aero later that summer . . . Scored the first regular-season goal in franchise history, Oct. 12, 1972 . . . Superb faceoff man . . . Played his entire WHA career in Houston, finishing as the all-time franchise leader in goals (149), assists (277) and points (426) . . . Ranks number ten among WHA's all-time scoring leaders . . . **Major league totals:** (Regular season) **WHA** - 459 games, 149 goals, 277 assists, 426 points, 419 penalty minutes. (Playoffs) **WHA** - 59 games, 20 goals, 45 assists, 65 points, 116 penalty minutes.

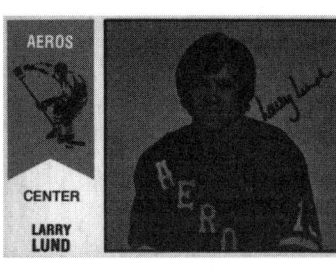

"I was one of Dayton's four priority selections in the original WHA draft. Frankie Hughes, Andre Hinse and I had been playing together for three years in Phoenix, and the Dayton club, which became the Houston Aeros, drafted all three of us. We didn't hear about the draft at the time it took place; we were contacted afterward by Bill Dineen, whom I'd played with and against in the minors for many years. I had a lot of respect for Bill, and when he said the WHA was going to make it, that was good enough for me.

"The idea of a new league was appealing to me from the start, but I didn't jump at it immediately. We were affiliated with the Toronto Maple Leafs in Phoenix, and they were pretty deep down the middle with Davey Keon, Norm Ullman, Darryl Sittler and Jimmy Harrison. I didn't think I had much of a chance of going to Toronto, but I thought the Leafs might deal me to another NHL club. I wanted to keep my options open. I'd been in the minors for a long time, and the NHL was still the ultimate. For anyone who grew up listening to Foster Hewitt calling games on the radio, it would be a dream come true to play at Maple Leaf Gardens or the Montreal Forum.

"In the summer of 1972 my agent, a fellow named Don Harris, came to Penticton to meet with Dineen, who wanted to negotiate a contract for me to play in Houston. They were staying at the same hotel, and the talks were going pretty well. One day when Don was out, the hotel desk paged him for a telephone call. Dineen heard the page and thought he'd do Donny a favour by taking the call for him. It turned out to be Jim Gregory, the GM of the Leafs, on the line. I don't know if Bill pretended to be my agent or not, but my stock went up quite a bit after that.

"Toronto ended up offering me more money than Houston did, so it was a difficult decision to make. I thought about it a lot, but in the end I went with the WHA because I respected the fact that they were going out on a limb, trying to make the idea work. I admired their philosophy, I think. Plus, I was a little ticked off that it took an offer from another team to make the Leafs sit up and take notice of me. Frankie, Andre and I had all put up big numbers in Phoenix, but the Leafs seemed content to leave us in limbo down there. The fact that the Aeros had made me one of their priority picks and had gone to a lot of trouble to sign me meant a lot, too.

"After I signed with the Aeros, I became really interested in watching the WHA take shape. When Bobby Hull jumped, I knew we'd make it. His mere presence gave the league instant credibility and knocked down the final barrier for other players who were watching and waiting to make the move.

"The Houston club concentrated on signing guys who had proven themselves in the minors for years, rather than going after big-name NHL stars. That turned out to be a real plus because, when Gordie Howe and his sons joined us the next year, they fit into the mix perfectly. I honestly think Bill Dineen was planning that months before it happened, because as much as the Howes improved the Houston Aeros, I don't know if the three of them would have had the same effect on other WHA teams. We had such a great mix of talent and personalities that Gordie and Mark and Marty meshed with us instantly.

"One of the fondest memories from my WHA career was our first exhibition game with the Howes, at Madison Square Garden. The league put on a big extravaganza with us, the New England Whalers, the New York Golden Blades and the Winnipeg Jets playing a mini tournament. Twenty-one seconds into our first game, Gordie took a pass from Mark and whipped a shot past the New England goalie. The place went nuts. I vividly recall turning to Dineen on the bench and telling him, 'There's the Avco Trophy, right there.' I knew at that moment that we were going to be the team to beat that season.

"That prediction turned out to be true, and winning our first Avco Trophy was one of the big thrills of my career. To be part of such a well-rounded club and to see the way the city of Houston took us into their hearts was very special. I felt so happy for Gordie, too. He was the ultimate team player. There were times during the season when he was so sore he could barely reach down to tie his skates, but he went out there game after game because it was so important for the team and for the league.

"My proudest moment didn't even happen on the ice. It was at a banquet during a big youth hockey tournament in Houston. The Aeros were there, along with hundreds of kids, parents and coaches. Gordie was at the head table, sitting beside Eugene Cernan, who was the last astronaut to walk on the moon. Of course, with Houston being the centre for the U.S. space program, all the astronauts were well known and very popular. When it came time for the speakers, Cernan spoke very well, very professionally, and got a nice warm ovation. Then Gordie was introduced. He stood up, walked over to the microphone, and for the next ten or fifteen minutes he gave an unrehearsed speech in that down-home way of his that had the entire room completely mesmerized. He talked about being a kid in Saskatchewan and about the importance of being a team player and having fun. Nothing too deep, but straight from the heart. I remember watching him and thinking that this shy, poorly educated hockey player from a little place like Floral was standing up there next to a man who had walked on the moon, and he was stealing the show.

"Well, when Gordie finished the whole place erupted in a standing ovation that lasted for a couple of minutes. I felt very, very proud to be a Canadian and a hockey player at that moment. It was the off-ice Gordie Howe at his greatest, and I'll never forget it.

"Even though it took a lot of players to start the league and make a go of it, I think it was because of Howe and Bobby Hull and guys like J.C. Tremblay in Quebec that the WHA made it through those first few seasons. It was important for us to have a big-league image and to be able to sustain it over the long haul, but only a handful of players could carry the league all by themselves. Bobby was a one-man publicity machine for the WHA, both on and off the ice, and it must have been a terrible burden at times. When Gordie and the boys were in Houston, it was the same thing. On the road they were constantly being asked to do interviews or make public appearances for the league.

"I think it's ironic that today most of what the WHA accomplished is swept under the carpet by the National Hockey League, but it's not surprising because the WHA never got much exposure throughout its existence. For those seven years the two leagues were basically at war with each other at a cost of millions of dollars, but it seemed like the only time the WHA got major media exposure was for bench-clearing brawls or when franchises folded. I think the lack of a television contract really hurt us. Some teams had local TV deals, but our games were almost never shown in other parts of the country. Many newspapers never even reported the league standings and statistics. That hurt us a lot, both from a revenue and an exposure point of view.

"I was proud to be a Houston Aero from Day One of the first season to the day the franchise folded. It was a great experience for me, both as a hockey player and as a person. To have had the opportunity to play with the Howes, Frankie Hughes, Andre Hinse and so many other great teammates and to win two Avco Trophies is something I'll remember for the rest of my life.

"I retired after the Aeros folded and went back to Penticton to run my business. I started the Okanagan Hockey School in 1963, and today it's the longest-running one in the world. We've had some pretty illustrious graduates, including Andy Moog, Kevin Dineen and Cam Neely. It keeps me busy year-round, and it's a great way to stay involved in the game."

EDGAR "RUSTY" PATENAUDE

Right wing ... Born in Williams Lake, B.C., Oct. 17, 1949 ... Had a brilliant junior career with the Moose Jaw Canucks and Calgary Centennials, scoring 212 points in 163 games ... Selected by the Pittsburgh Penguins in the 1969 amateur draft, but never played in the NHL ... Played one game with the Baltimore Clippers in the American Hockey League, then spent the 1970–71 season with the Amarillo Wranglers in the Central Hockey League, notching 37 points in 72 games ... Moved to the Fort Wayne Comets of the International Hockey League the following season and scored 35 goals and 77 points ... Selected by the Alberta Oilers in the WHA's 1972 general player draft ... Named Oilers' rookie of the year in 1972–73 after scoring 29 goals and 57 points in his debut season ... Oilers' all-time leading goal scorer in the WHA with 136 ... Acquired by the Indianapolis Racers prior to the 1977–78 season, Patenaude retired after scoring 23 goals and 42 points in 73 games for Indy ... **Major league totals:** (Regular season) **WHA** - 431 games, 159 goals, 131 assists, 290 points, 368 penalty minutes. (Playoffs) **WHA** - 10 games, 1 goal, 6 assists, 7 points, 22 penalty minutes.

"After I led the Fort Wayne Comets in scoring, I expected to get called up to the Pittsburgh Penguins, but I never heard a word from them. It was pretty disappointing, because both the club and I had had a good season, and I thought I could have added something to the Pittsburgh lineup. When I got home that summer, there were two letters waiting for me: one from Bill Hunter and the Alberta Oilers, inviting me to their WHA camp, and one from a club in Vienna, Austria. The Austrians even sent a contract; all I had to do was sign it and send it back. It was a pretty good offer too, about $25,000 plus a car and an apartment for a 40- or 45-game schedule.

"We'd been hearing rumours about the WHA for about a year, and I knew that I'd been picked by the Oilers in the big draft, but that letter from Hunter was the first contact I had with them. It wasn't a difficult decision to make. It was pretty obvious by that time that I didn't fit into Pittsburgh's plans, and I figured if I couldn't make it in the WHA I could still go overseas.

"When I signed my contract with Alberta, I probably didn't get as much money as I could have, but that wasn't my main priority at that point. It was an opportunity to play close to home, and I was just happy to have the chance to play big-league hockey. As far as I was concerned, the WHA was big league. There were some growing pains that first season, but by Christmastime I knew the league was going to survive. The guys who had come over from the NHL, especially big-name stars like Bobby Hull and Gerry Cheevers, did a lot to bring a big-league image to the WHA and really helped put us on the map. With the Oilers, we had guys like Al Hamilton and Val Fonteyne, who had been in the NHL for a long time. They weren't the big-name stars, but they added a lot of class and experience to our hockey club. Fonteyne was one of the all-time great people in the game, and I learned a lot just by watching and listening to him.

"It's funny now when I think back on it, but even early on in my WHA career I didn't think there was a chance in hell that the league would merge with the NHL. There was a real attitude that we were rebels fighting for our identity, and that was the same thing with the owners. If anything, I thought the NHL would continue to be so pissed off with our league that they would eventually just crush us. But by the time we had superstars like Hull, Gordie Howe, Rejean Houle, Marc Tardif and Frank Mahovlich playing in our league, I guess the NHL had no choice but to try to figure out a way to end the raiding of players. The NHL was so powerful that I didn't think a merger would ever happen.

"I had my share of big moments, for sure. I'd like to be remembered as a guy who gave everything he had on every shift. I wasn't the most talented player in the world, but I was quick and I could score goals. Playing in the all-star game with Howe and Hull was a big thrill, even though I hated Gordie in a lot of ways. He was just so damn dirty. He'd hack you and slash you like he was swinging an axe. Off the ice he was very nice, though. Hull was a classy guy—period. As a right winger I often ended up playing against him, and I was always amazed at how strong and talented he was. He could carry two guys on his back and still score a goal, but he never resorted to cheap shots or using his stick.

"The games we played against the Russians were memorable too, but probably my greatest thrill was playing on a line with Norm Ullman when he scored his 500th career goal. Normie was a real gentleman and a great guy. We were roommates on the road and became very good friends. He was old enough to be my dad, but he could skate like the wind. After he got number 500, the Oilers threw a big dinner for him. He gave some recognition to me and Kenny Baird for being good linemates, and I can remember how proud I felt to have been part of such a milestone event. Normie lived with his parents when he was in Edmonton because his wife and family were still back in Toronto. He used to visit me and my wife in the evenings, and we'd kill a few beers and talk about the game until three or four o'clock in the morning. Those were special times.

"By the time I went to Indianapolis with Barry Wilkins for my last season [1977–78], I'd pretty well made up my mind to pack it in. I'd always played the game with the goal of getting something out of it, and by that time I was close to accomplishing what I wanted, which was to pay for my house and my ranch and move back home to Williams Lake. I'd had some back problems and knee problems, but by the end of that season everything was paid for, so it was the right time to quit.

"I went to a wedding in Banff the following summer, and Glen Sather asked me to come back to the Oilers. He offered me a two-year contract if I made the team, but I declined. It's ironic because Blair MacDonald, who played behind me in Edmonton, ended up being the right winger on Wayne Gretzky's line. If I'd made the team, I might have gotten that spot. But hindsight is always twenty-twenty, eh?

"To my mind, the WHA made just as big an impact on the game of hockey as the Russians or the European players. I think our league opened up a lot of doors by giving so-called journeymen players the chance to show what they could do, and because of that, new markets were developed for hockey, especially in the United States.

"I don't put on the skates much anymore. I play a couple of benefit games with the Oilers Alumni every year, but that's it. I don't miss playing the games, but I miss the camaraderie with the guys. In those first couple of seasons we built some great friendships that have lasted to this day.

"It amazes me that people still send me hockey cards and pictures from the WHA to autograph. Where do they find this stuff? But I appreciate it, I really do. It's always nice to be remembered."

GERRY PINDER

Left wing . . . Born in Saskatoon, Sask., Sept. 15, 1948 . . . Never played a game in the minor leagues . . . After a sensational final junior season with Saskatoon that saw him score 78 goals and 140 points in 55 games, Pinder played two seasons with the Canadian Olympic team before debuting with the NHL's Chicago Black Hawks in 1969–70 . . . Played two seasons in Chicago before being traded to the California Golden Seals, along with Gerry Desjardins and Kerry Bond, for Gary Smith in Sept. 1971 . . . Led the Golden Seals in scoring with 23 goals and 54 points in 1971–72 . . . Selected by the Calgary Broncos in the WHA's 1972 general player draft . . . Joined the WHA as an original Cleveland Crusader in 1972 . . . After the Crusaders folded, Pinder signed for one season with the San Diego Mariners before wrapping up his career with five games with the Edmonton Oilers in 1977–78 . . . **Major league totals:** (Regular season) **NHL** - 223 games, 55 goals, 69 assists, 124 points, 135 penalty minutes. **WHA** - 356 games, 93 goals, 141 assists, 234 points, 436 penalty minutes. (Playoffs) **NHL** - 17 games, 0 goals, 4 assists, 4 points, 6 penalty minutes. **WHA** - 18 games, 5 goals, 10 assists, 15 points, 40 penalty minutes.

"We first heard and read about the World Hockey Association about halfway through the season when I was with the California Golden Seals. Many of us were interested right away because of the way [owner] Charlie Finley treated us. He was a very nice man, charming and genuinely likable, but he was a real tightwad when it came to paying his players.

"The first few newspaper stories I read mentioned only Gary Davidson and Dennis Murphy, but when Bill Hunter's name started to crop up, I began to take the rumours about the WHA a little more seriously. I'd known Bill since my junior days, when we used to have some real wars with his Oil Kings in Edmonton, and I knew he was a pretty shrewd hockey man.

"I was initially contacted by the Cleveland Crusaders either late in the NHL season or shortly after it ended—I can't recall exactly. Nick Mileti, who was the owner of the Crusaders, made it clear that he wanted to have some serious contract talks. Later that spring I was flown down to Cleveland with Skip Krake, a very good hockey player who had played in the NHL for Boston and L.A. and Buffalo. We were both pretty excited about the opportunity. I loved to play in the NHL, but the added adventure of going to a new league was really appealing. After a few years in the NHL you come to realize that it isn't the be-all and end-all, so I was intrigued about what the WHA might become.

"When we got down to Cleveland, we were treated very well. Mileti also owned the Indians baseball team, and we did some negotiating in one of the private boxes at the ball park. I was impressed with the whole set-up, and when it came time to talk about dollars, the Crusaders were very accommodating. I had a financial adviser in Chicago named Harvey Wineberg who would go over the fine print, but I did my own negotiating. Almost everything was wrapped up on that weekend. At the end of the two days the Crusaders were offering me roughly three times the salary I was making with California, with one-third of it in cash that would be deposited in my bank account as soon as I signed. I think I was making $28,000 with the Seals, and I knew damn well that Finley wasn't going to come close to Cleveland's money, but I didn't sign right away. I left the details up to Harvey and went back to Saskatoon.

"I was playing in a golf tournament a week or so later and had just finished my putt on the 18th green when a guy came running out of the clubhouse and said there was a phone call for me. It was Finley. He said 'I'll give you a $500 raise over last year. Not only that, but we'll pay all your legal bills to get out of that contract with the WHA.' He had no clue what I'd been offered. And when I told him, I don't think he believed me. He told me to wait a day or two, and he'd call again. When he did, it was the same thing. He just didn't believe the WHA was going to get off the ground, and he never, ever believed that any of his players were serious about jumping.

"What Finley didn't know was that my financial adviser was also advising Paul Shmyr and Bobby Hull. Paul and I both knew a bit about Bobby's negotiations, and we had a pretty good idea that he was going to jump to the Winnipeg Jets well before it happened. Hull would instantly give the WHA credibility, so I had no doubts whatsoever about going to Cleveland.

"Even more than the money, it was the adventure of doing something new and challenging that prompted me to switch leagues. It was all about fun. The NHL was pretty much a closed shop in those days, and the owners could treat you as badly as they wanted. I looked at the new league as an opportunity to participate as more than just a spear-carrier, and that's exactly how it turned out. I wasn't a star player by any means, but I'd been in the NHL for a few years and spent some time with the Olympic team. When the management and scouts in Cleveland began asking my opinion on whether to sign certain guys or how to play certain teams, it really made me feel good. That kind of cooperation between players and management was unheard of in the National Hockey League.

"I had joined the Canadian Olympic team in the fall of 1967, and I've always considered the two years I spent there as being the equivalent of playing in the NHL with a weaker team or playing in the minor leagues at an extremely high calibre. We played against the Russians, Swedes, Czechs and Finns all the time, so I wasn't the least bit surprised when the European players made such an impact in the WHA. In fact, I remember being interviewed by reporters just before the 1972 Summit Series between the NHL and the Russians, and I predicted that the NHL would be lucky to win three of the eight games. That didn't get much mention because it wasn't what the reporters wanted to hear. They thought I was nuts. Nobody was happier than I was when the NHL came back to win that series, but at the same time it showed everyone on this side of the pond that in some ways European hockey was better than North American hockey.

"The WHA learned a lesson from that series long before the National Hockey League did. When Lars-Erik Sjoberg and Anders Hedberg and Ulf Nilsson were signed by the Winnipeg Jets, they proved right away that they could play big-league hockey in North America. So did Vaclav Nedomansky, when he joined the Toronto Toros. Big Ned had always given us fits when I was with the Olympic team. It was impossible to knock him off his skates, and he had one of the best wrist shots I ever saw. We might never have seen any of these guys playing in North America if it hadn't have been for the WHA.

"Opening up the game to the Europeans was one of the league's greatest contributions, but the flip side was that the WHA also created more jobs in both leagues for guys who didn't have the talent to play major league hockey but who got there for the simple reason that they were goons. That was probably the league's biggest problem. We were trying to sell the game in the United States, but there was a watering-down effect on the talent level. Intimidation became a big part of the game, both in our league and in the NHL. Fights and brawls happened all the time, and it was very frustrating for a guy like me, who excelled at offensive hockey. It got to the point where teams like the Los Angeles Sharks and the Birmingham Bulls had six or eight guys on the roster who were basically thugs. That was counterproductive to what we were trying to accomplish as a league. And there was a similar effect on the officials. A lot of the referees the WHA hired weren't ready for prime time, and that hurt the league's image.

"My proudest moment was probably the first Crusaders game. To be standing out there for the anthem on opening night, knowing that everything was new and that a whole season of adventure was ahead of us was very exciting. I also had the honour of playing in the first couple of all-star games, and that's something I'll never forget. To meet the guys I'd been banging heads with all season and get to know them as people was very enlightening. It made me realize that we were all united for a common cause, even though we wore different uniforms.

"A defining moment in my career was the first minute of our first playoff game against Toronto in 1974. I caught a stick right in the eye. I played the next four seasons basically blind on one side. You think you're indestructible when you're 24 or 25 years old, but that was the beginning of the end for me. When I came back from the injury, I couldn't play as well as I could before, and playing got more and more frustrating. My injury wasn't highly publicized at the time, and I always downplayed it because if you're going to continue playing pro hockey you don't want the coaches to know you can't see. If it hadn't happened, I probably would have played a lot better and at least a few years more. As it was, I hung around for four more seasons, but my game really suffered.

"The long-term effect of that injury was that it made me a different kind of player than I'd always been. I had lots of ability for a guy who didn't skate as well as he should have, but I had a bad problem with my temper. After I came back from the injury, my temper was even worse. I always felt it was against the law for opponents to hit me or slash me, so I used to retaliate. For a little guy like me to take 120 or 130 penalty minutes every season was just plain dumb because it hurt the team. And at my size I wasn't going to win many battles anyway.

"I ended up having three operations on my eye, but the damage had been done. After the Crusaders folded, I went to the San Diego Mariners for one season, but I didn't play very well. It was a screwy environment on that team, but I enjoyed the city very much. I went to Edmonton for a few games at the end of my career, but by that point I knew it was over.

"After I quit playing, I went back to university and graduated with a business degree. I've been in real estate and development ever since. It wasn't a tough adjustment because I'd planned for it. Once you get used to the fact that your life has to become more structured and you can't take those long lunches every day, life after hockey isn't too tough.

"I honestly don't care that the WHA hasn't received more recognition. I keep in touch with a lot of the guys I played with in Cleveland, and I still play a few games with the Calgary Flames Alumni. As players, we know what we did and what it meant. To me that's more important than record books or accolades.

"I think back on the courage shown by Bobby Hull when he jumped from Chicago. He had the run of that city, and he was one of the biggest names in the NHL when he jumped. The rest of us just followed his lead, but it was Bobby alone who redefined the salary structure in pro hockey for all time. Most of the guys earning millions of dollars in the NHL today weren't even born when the WHA was formed, so that tells you something about the long-term effect of that league.'

GARTH RIZZUTO

Right wing ... Born in Trail, B.C., Sept. 11, 1947 ... Signed his first professional contract with the Chicago Black Hawks after starring in major junior with Moose Jaw ... Spent three years with the Dallas Black Hawks in the Central Professional Hockey League before being claimed by the Vancouver Canucks in the 1970 expansion draft ... Split the 1970–71 season between the Canucks and the Rochester Americans in the American Hockey League ... Also saw action with the Seattle Totems in the Western Hockey League before joining the WHA as an original Winnipeg Jet in 1972 ... Superb penalty killer ... Teamed with Danny Johnson on the Jets' top penalty-killing unit to set a WHA record of 27 consecutive games without surrendering a power-play goal, 1972–73 ... **Major league totals**: (Regular season) **NHL** - 37 games, 3 goals, 4 assists, 7 points, 16 penalty minutes. **WHA** - 102 games, 13 goals, 14 assists, 27 points, 40 penalty minutes. (Playoffs) **WHA** - 14 games, 0 goals, 1 assist, 1 point, 14 penalty minutes.

"I was scouted in my hometown of Trail by a gentleman named Art Misisco; I owe him a lot for giving me the push I needed to turn professional. In those days you had to sign what was known as a C form, which pretty much bound you to a club for as long as you played hockey. I signed when I was still in junior, and the Black Hawks turned me pro after I got a three-year suspension in Moose Jaw for a little altercation I had with a timekeeper.

"I became Chicago's property in 1964 while I was still in Kelowna. The junior Buckaroos were a farm club of the Portland Buckaroos in the Western Hockey League, and Portland was owned by Chicago. To make a long story short, the Hawks sent me to Dallas in the Central League, and even though I had a couple of back-to-back 30-goal seasons, Chicago was very deep down the middle. You can imagine what it was like going to camp every year and playing behind guys like Phil Esposito, Stan Mikita, Pit Martin and Red Hay. In the 1970 NHL expansion draft I got picked up by Vancouver, and that turned out to be one of the best things that ever happened to me in hockey.

"I could skate, and I wasn't afraid to stick my nose in and mix it up...I think those are the qualities that won me a spot in the Canucks' lineup. We had a great mix of guys...leaders like Kurt [captain Orland Kurtenbach], slick veterans like Teddy Taylor and Murray Hall, and young guys like Pat Quinn and Dunc Wilson, who became very important pieces of the puzzle.

"I split that season between Vancouver and Rochester in the American Hockey League and had a pretty good year. But when I came to training camp the next fall the Canucks had assigned my number to Jocelyn Guevremont, so I could see the writing on the wall. I went back to Rochester in 1971 and then finished the season with the Seattle Totems. I didn't know what was going to happen—whether the Canucks would trade me or offer me another contract.

"I had a job selling boats during the off-season, and one day at work that summer a friend by the name of Peter Allen saw a story in the newspaper about this new World Hockey Association. I'd heard of it before, of course, but I didn't think it was going to amount to anything. Peter said I should call around to some of the teams, but I thought that was a pretty silly idea. I wouldn't call, so Peter did. The next thing I knew, Annis Stukus, the GM of the Winnipeg Jets, contacted me and asked me to come to Manitoba to meet with him.

"I was making $14,000 with the Canucks, so when Stukus offered me a guaranteed three-year contract for $30,000, $40,000 and $50,000, it didn't take long to decide to go to the WHA. Like any kid growing up, I dreamed of playing in the NHL. That's where you wanna be because it's the pinnacle of the sport. My heart was in the NHL and with the Canucks, but, unfortunately, the money wasn't there.

"The WHA was an eye-opener, no doubt about it. Because we had Bobby Hull, the Jets were the league's biggest draw in that first season, and it was really exciting to be part of it.

"We didn't have the biggest team in the league, and we were far from being the toughest, so we had problems early on. We'd go to places like Minnesota, where they had a player who had done time in prison for manslaughter, or Los Angeles, where the Sharks were literally always out for blood, and every player on the other team would be trying to take runs at Bobby. They were too stupid to realize he was the WHA's bread and butter.

"It wasn't unusual to see three or four bench-clearing brawls in one game in those days. One time when we were playing in Los Angeles, the benches emptied after only about 20 seconds, and there were fights all over the place. I had a freshly stitched gash on my head, so I happened to be wearing a helmet that night. When the fighting started, I paired off with Tommy Serviss, a good friend whom I'd played junior with in Moose Jaw. I figured we'd just hang onto each other's jerseys and make it look good until everything quieted down, but all of a sudden he threw an overhand punch at my head. As I reached up to grab him around the throat, I could hear him screaming in agony. His finger had hooked through one of the holes in my helmet, and the more I struggled the more it was cutting him!

"It must have been a funny sight; I had blood all over my face, but it was from Tommy's finger. He couldn't detach his hand from my helmet, and we just squirmed around until the linesmen arrived. I ended up having to take off my helmet so we could be separated, and poor Tommy had to have it cut off his finger. It was wild.

"My fondest memory of that first year, besides playing with classy guys like Bobby, Ab McDonald and Wally Boyer, was going up against the New England Whalers in the Avco Trophy final. They ended up beating us in five games, but the one game we won was shown on national TV. I was on a makeshift line with Brian Cadle and John Shmyr, and I must have had 20 big hits in that game. It was incredible.

"Another great memory is of killing penalties with Danny Johnson. In the WHA we couldn't ice the puck when we were playing shorthanded, so it was an art to be able to bank a shot off the boards without getting an icing call. Danny and I worked at that all season, and we ended up setting a record by going 27 games without being scored on. It was quite a thrill.

"For me, just getting the chance to play in the WHA meant a lot. Guys like Bobby, Bill Hunter and Benny Hatskin were the real pioneers. They had balls as big as the moon to throw down the gauntlet and take on the National Hockey League. Especially Bobby. I always thought he felt hurt when the NHL brought in the rule to limit stick curvature because it took away an exciting part of his game. In the WHA they threw away that rule, and for a few years there was Bobby Hull—once again the most exciting and dangerous player in the world. It took tremendous guts for him to do what he did, challenging the reserve clause and winning the right for players to finally be paid what they were worth. For that alone, I think every professional playing the game today should kiss Bobby's butt.

"I'm extremely proud to be an original NHL Canuck, and I take the same pride in being able to say that I was an original Winnipeg Jet. My only regret is that I wasn't better prepared for life after hockey. I tore up my knee after my second season in the WHA, and when I returned, I had to make a choice between going back to the American Hockey League or calling it quits. I chose the latter.

"Maybe some of the young guys coming up today don't want to think about it, but when your playing days are over you've got to have something at the other end. Hockey was good to me while it lasted, and being active with the Canucks Alumni for the past 20 years has been my way of giving something back.

"It's funny when I look back on it now—being in the Chicago organization in the old six-team league, then going through the first two NHL expansion drafts and the WHA. I'm the Forrest Gump of hockey, I guess. But I wouldn't trade those experiences for anything."

PAUL SHMYR

Defense ... Born in Cudworth, Sask., Jan. 28, 1946 ... Played junior with the New Westminster Royals and won a league scoring title while playing both defense and centre ... Shmyr's pro rights were originally owned by the New York Rangers, who traded him to Chicago for Camille Henry in Aug. 1967 ... Turned pro with the Dallas Black Hawks in the Central Professional Hockey League in 1967–68 and saw his first NHL action in a three-game trial with the parent Chicago Black Hawks in 1968–69 ... Played 71 games for Chicago over the next two seasons before being traded to the California Golden Seals in Oct. 1971, along with Gilles Meloche, for Gerry Desjardins ... Selected by the Miami Screaming Eagles in the WHA's 1972 general player draft ... WHA rights transferred to Cleveland by the Philadelphia Blazers in July 1972 ... Signed a multi-year contract with the Crusaders, Aug. 1972 ... Elected team captain ... Named to the WHA's first all-star team three times and participated in six all-star games ... Co-winner (with Real Cloutier) of the 1976 all-star game MVP award ... Won the Dennis A. Murphy Trophy as the WHA's top defenseman, 1975–76 ... Named to Team Canada '74 ... One of four WHA players selected to try out for Team Canada '76 ... Played for the WHA All-Stars in the three-game series against the Moscow Dynamo in 1979 ... Joined the San Diego Mariners for one season after the Crusaders folded and finished his WHA career with the Edmonton Oilers ... As captain of the Oilers, Shmyr opted to wear a Soviet-style *K* on his uniform rather than the traditional *C* ... Ranks fourth on the WHA's all-time list for games played (511) and fifth in all-time penalty minutes (860) ... Returned to the NHL with the Minnesota North Stars after the merger ... Released by the North Stars after the 1980–81 season and signed as a free agent with the Hartford Whalers for his final NHL season (1981–82) ... **Major league totals:** (Regular season) **NHL** - 343 games, 13 goals, 72 assists, 85 points, 528 penalty minutes. **WHA** - 511 games, 61 goals, 248 assists, 309 points, 860 penalty minutes. (Playoffs) **NHL** - 34 games, 3 goals, 3 assists, 6 points, 44 penalty minutes. **WHA** - 43 games, 5 goals, 18 assists, 23 points, 107 penalty minutes.

PAUL SHMYR
OILERS Defense

"I was in Oakland with the Golden Seals when I first heard about the WHA. I had originally been drafted by the Miami Screaming Eagles, but by the time we were approached, my WHA rights had been transferred from Miami to Philadelphia and then to the Cleveland Crusaders. My financial adviser, who was in Chicago, contacted me early on and told me not to sign anything with the Seals until he had a chance to talk dollars with the Crusaders. We came to terms almost right away. Cleveland offered more than twice as much as I was making in California, along with a nice bonus. All the money was put in escrow, and the contract was guaranteed, with a no-trade clause.

"I flew into Cleveland, and at the hotel the night before I was going to sign I got a phone call from Charlie Finley, owner of the Golden Seals. A month or two before, they had offered me a two-year deal for half of what the Crusaders were going to pay me, but now Finley said he would match Cleveland's offer, no matter what. I thought it was a nice gesture on his part but he was too late. I'm a man of my word, and I had given the Crusaders my word. That was the end of it.

"I give Charlie Finley credit, though. Before hanging up, he told me that if things didn't work out or if the WHA folded I would be welcomed back to Oakland with open arms. That was a nice thing to do. I never had any problems with Charlie, although I know a lot of other players did. For some reason we got along very well. If my deal with Cleveland had gone sour, I would've gone back to the Seals in a minute because I enjoyed my time in Oakland very much.

"That original Crusaders team was by far the closest team I was ever on. We did everything together. After every practice and every game, no matter where we were or how well or how poorly we played, we made a point of all going out together for a meal or a drink. There was a real bonding that was brought on, I suppose, by the fact that we were all in the same boat. None of us was sure if the league would make it or if the next paycheque would be the last one, so we looked to each other for support. We were in it together, and we understood what we were up against.

"This feeling was totally different than anything I had experienced in the National Hockey League. For so many years the NHL owners treated their players like cattle and got away with it. I remember when I was coming up that the standard practice for NHL teams was to mail their rookies a contract with the dollar amount already filled in. There was no negotiation whatsoever. If the player didn't sign the thing and mail it back, he was banished to the minors. That happened to me in my rookie season with Chicago. I didn't sign the contract, so they exiled me to Dallas for almost three years. That's how dumb we were. All we knew how to do was play hockey, be loyal to the team and keep our mouths shut about how much—or how little—we were getting paid.

"There was none of that crap in the WHA. Sure, there were problems meeting the payroll when teams were changing ownership or whatever, but all things considered the WHA had a much better attitude than what I'd seen in the other league. And I never had any problems with my paycheque. I was one of the lucky ones, I guess, because I got every penny that I signed for. When the team was really struggling a couple of years later, some of the other guys had problems getting paid, but my cheque was always on time and for the right amount.

"I think just being part of such a great organization and having fun during those four seasons in Cleveland were the high points of my career. And winning the trophy as best defenseman was a real thrill. I always wanted to be known as a guy who came to play every shift and who played well on the road, and I think winning that award was a recognition for that.

"Being a team player was also very, very important to me, so being picked for Team Canada '74 was something I was extremely proud of. I still am. That series was a real benchmark for the WHA because it proved our league could compete at the same level as the best in the world. We had a fabulous collection of players, and to this day I think we could have won the series if we'd just had a little more time to prepare.

"Right after we got home from Moscow, my wife and I went on a holiday to Hawaii. We were getting on a crowded bus at a mall, and the Hawaiian bus driver recognized me! He said: 'Do you play hockey? Is your name Paul Shmyr?' You could have knocked me over with a feather. He was all excited, telling us that he'd watched the Soviet series on TV and that now he was going to start following hockey. It was incredible.

"Being selected to try out for the first Canada Cup team in 1976 was quite an experience, too. There were four of us from the WHA—me, Bobby Hull, Gerry Cheevers and Marc Tardif. We figured that it was a set-up and that we'd all be cut, so the NHL could point a finger and show everyone how 'inferior' our league was.

"That's pretty much the way it turned out, too, except for the fact that Bobby was by far the most dominant player at training camp, and there was no way they could cut him. I know this really upset [Alan] Eagleson because he hated our league and the fact that the WHA was able to get Hull in the first place. Bobby and I were roommates during the Team Canada training camp, and he was sure he'd get cut along with me and Cheevers. Tardif was injured, so he didn't even show up. But Bobby busted his ass to make that team, and along with Orr he was easily one of the best players for Canada. I was really proud of him because he stuck it right in Eagleson's face.

"After the Crusaders folded, I went to San Diego and then on to Edmonton, but it was a different feeling than I'd had in Cleveland. Those were four fabulous seasons, watching the team grow together, and I'd been there right from the start. The league was changing, too. It started going after young players like Mike Gartner and Wayne Gretzky and the Baby Bulls in Birmingham. There was still a good mix of older guys, but I could see the WHA was evolving with an eye towards joining the NHL.

"The funny thing, in retrospect, is that the leagues should never have merged. It happened only because Eagleson was in bed with the owners, and he had to find a way to kill the competition. Of course, we didn't know many of the details at the time. It was all behind-closed-doors stuff, and we were told it was for the good of the players, but that turned out to be a crock. I think the WHA could have survived and even thrived on its own by building around guys like Gretzky and Gartner and Mark Messier. That would have attracted more young guys, and within a few years the NHL would've been desperate enough to go to the WHA.

"After the merger I went to the Minnesota North Stars for two seasons, then to Hartford for one more before I retired. I had a lot of investments at the time, but I was looking to do something different. I promoted the last outdoor rock concert ever held at Empire Stadium in Vancouver, and then I owned a night club and restaurant in the city for awhile. I sold them after a few years, and now I own and operate a network marketing company with clients all over North America."

PAT "WHITEY" STAPLETON

Defense . . . Born in Sarnia, Ont., July 4, 1940 . . . Played centre as well as defense in the minors . . . Graduated from the junior St. Catharines Teepees to the Sault Ste. Marie Thunderbirds in the Eastern Professional Hockey League, 1960–61 . . . Drafted by the Boston Bruins from Chicago Black Hawks, June 1961 . . . Played 69 games for the Bruins in 1961–62 before returning to the EPHL's Kingston Frontenacs the following season . . . Joined the Western Hockey League's Portland Buckaroos in 1963–64 . . . Traded by Boston to the Toronto Maple Leafs, along with Orland Kurtenbach and Andy Hebenton for Ron Stewart, 1964 . . . Drafted by Chicago from Toronto, June 1965 . . . Split the 1965–66 season between Chicago and the St. Louis Braves of the Central Professional Hockey League . . . Set NHL record for points in a game by a defenseman (six) on Mar. 30, 1969 . . . Perennial NHL all-star . . . Selected to play for Team Canada '72 in historic Summit Series against the Soviet Nationals . . . Jumped to the WHA's Chicago Cougars as player-coach, July 1973 . . . Won the Dennis A. Murphy Trophy as the league's best defenseman, 1973–74 . . . Selected for Team Canada '74 . . . Became part owner and president of the Chicago Cougars, Dec. 1974 . . . Played in five WHA all-star games . . . Selected by the Indianapolis Racers from the Chicago Cougars in WHA dispersal draft, June 1975 . . . Signed with the Cincinnati Stingers for 1977–78 season . . . Returned to Indianapolis as coach of the Racers (and Wayne Gretzky's first professional coach) 1978–79 . . . **Major league totals:** (Regular season) **NHL** - 635 games, 43 goals, 294 assists, 337 points, 353 penalty minutes. **WHA** - 375 games, 26 goals, 212 assists, 238 points, 187 penalty minutes. (Playoffs) **NHL** - 65 games, 10 goals, 39 assists, 49 points, 38 penalty minutes. **WHA** - 34 games, 2 goals, 21 assists, 23 points, 38 penalty minutes.

"I was still in the NHL with the Chicago Black Hawks when the WHA was formed, but I recall being mildly curious about how the Cougars were doing on the other side of town. There was naturally a lot of interest in the WHA franchise when Bobby made his first appearance with the Jets, and I think I slipped over to the Amphitheatre to watch one or two games myself. I didn't evaluate the quality of the hockey very closely; it was more to satisfy my curiosity about what the other league had to offer. I think most players at the time were looking at the WHA as an opportunity to open up more jobs at the highest professional level, and it certainly did that.

"I don't think the Black Hawks really expected to lose Bobby to the WHA until the moment he signed with Winnipeg, and from what I've read and heard since, I believe Bobby probably gave them every opportunity to extend the olive branch and get him back. I think emotionally he wanted to remain a Black Hawk; he loved Chicago, and Chicago loved him. But in the end it was strictly a financial consideration, and the WHA threw open the vault to get him.

"One of the strangest repercussions after Bobby left was that the Hawks removed his name from the team record books. I didn't think that was warranted; after all, he was only doing what was right for him and his family. No player in his right mind would have said no to what the WHA was offering him. The other thing that upset me was when the Hawks gave Bobby's number [nine] to another player. It was petty, and I thought it was uncalled for. The guy ended up refusing to wear it.

"After I saw all of that and realized that the Hawks were probably going to radically change their lineup the next season, my decision to sign as player-coach with the Cougars wasn't a difficult one. Again, it was strictly financial. There was a huge difference between what the Cougars guaranteed me and what the Hawks were offering. The chance to step into management with the Cougars was a factor, too. Deep down, every hockey player thinks he can coach, and I looked at that as a wonderful opportunity. I also had several business interests in Chicago at the time, and I didn't want to leave the city, so going to the Cougars was a natural move.

"I was actually surprised at the parity of the WHA when I joined. All the teams did a good job of finding and signing young players who were on the verge of breaking into the NHL, and combining that with the steady flow of veteran players from the other league made hockey in the WHA very competitive. It was also a lot of fun to play there.

"Being part of Team Canada '74 was great. Paul Henderson, Frank Mahovlich and I had been part of the '72 team, and the difference in the 1974 team was incredible. We were able to go to school on what we'd learned in the first series, and it really helped in the way we prepared for the Russians. They were not an unknown entity this time; we knew exactly what we were facing. It turned out to be a hell of an exciting series.

"Not much has been written or publicized about the 1974 series, but it was much closer than what you might think by looking at the scores. We should have won the opening game in Quebec City instead of tying. Big Frank beat Tretiak with a shot in the dying seconds, but it just missed the top corner. In Vancouver we had a big lead, but the Russians scored twice in the last few minutes of the third period to get another tie. Then we were robbed of a win in Moscow when Bobby scored late in the third period but the referee ruled that time had run out.

"I was disappointed we didn't do better. Compared to 1972, the Russians were much better prepared, and you could see that they'd picked up on a lot of our strategies and tactics. Even the crowds in Moscow had taken something from our fans. The Russians had big sections of cheerleaders, and they cheered and whistled and tried to drown out the Canadian fans every time we did something on the ice. It was quite exciting.

"The season that followed the Russian series was tough for us in Chicago because the owners bailed out and we had to find a way to keep the team afloat. Ralph Backstrom, Rod Zaine, a fella by the name of Jeff Rosen and I put up our own money to keep the Cougars going. But by that point we'd lost our purpose, so it wasn't a good situation. It was more a matter of finding a way to keep guys in their jobs. A lot of the players had families and kids to take care of, so we did what we could to keep it running for the rest of the season.

"From Chicago I went to Indianapolis just as a player for a couple of seasons, then spent a year with Cincinnati before going back to Indy to coach in 1978–79. It was a treat to coach Wayne Gretzky when he first came up with the Racers. We could all see right away that he was something special. He had that extra sense, and he challenged defensemen like a seasoned veteran. I was also really impressed with his maturity. He was only 17 and he'd just signed a million-dollar contract, but it didn't go to his head. He'd had a certain amount of notoriety for a long time already, but being the centre of attention in Indianapolis didn't faze him one bit. He was always very humble, very polite. I remember thinking that Wayne's parents did a great job in raising him.

"I look back on my six years in the WHA as a really exciting time. The league gave me the opportunity to try new things and learn a lot about myself and my capabilities. I don't really have one 'highlight moment' per se —other than cashing my first paycheque! Some of the best times involved playing against Bobby and the Winnipeg Jets. The Jets were a great, great hockey club and a lot of fun to play against. They challenged you hard at every level. I always looked forward to playing them, especially in Winnipeg.

"For me, the thrill of the game was measured in the entertainment value for the fans. I always wanted to be thought of as a player who tried to give the fans full value for their ticket dollars. I think that was an important philosophy in the WHA, and a lot of it goes back to what Bobby and Gordie Howe and some of the other big stars did to promote the league.

"Even toward the end, when there was quite a bit of violence and intimidation, I felt there was still entertainment value in the WHA. Intimidation doesn't always come in the form of fights and high sticks; it can be speed, team work, goaltending, defensive play. The World Hockey Association gave players a stage for showcasing their talents in all those areas, and the game of hockey is better off for it today.

"After I retired, I got a chance to travel across Canada and really appreciate the different areas of the country when I got involved in a skill development program for young hockey players. I'm still involved in that, along with doing a bit of farming in Ontario and lending a hand with the local junior club. I like to teach, and I think it's important for experienced players to give something back to the game.

"In my era, the guys breaking into the NHL were fortunate to have contact with the fellows who had played before and then turned to coaching. In my case, guys like Harry Watson and Hal Laycoe and Billy Reay played important roles in my development as a hockey player. To a large degree, I think we're missing that continuity in the game today. The trend now is for teams to go with younger coaches. While most of them have the book knowledge, I think a lot of them are lacking in practical experience.

"That's why I like working with kids. I've got some things to pass along that can help them both on and off the ice. If you can get the person right, you'll get the player right. That's what we should be concentrating on with the young kids coming up."

RON "MAGIC" WARD

Centre … Born in Cornwall, Ont., Sept. 12, 1944 … Starred in junior hockey and lacrosse in his hometown … Drafted by the Toronto Maple Leafs and turned pro with the Tulsa Oilers in the Central Professional Hockey League, 1965–66 … Superb checker who was often used as a defenseman … Named to the CPHL all-star team after leading the league with 54 goals and 85 points, 1967–68 … Scored 35 goals and 78 points with the Rochester Americans in 1968–69 and voted the American Hockey League's rookie of the year … Contract purchased by the Western Hockey League's Vancouver Canucks, 1969 … Traded by the Canucks back to Toronto for Brad Selwood and Rene Robert, May 1969 … Played for Phoenix in the WHL, Toronto in the NHL and Tulsa in the CPHL during 1969–70 … Claimed by Vancouver from Toronto in 1970 NHL expansion draft … Played the entire 1970–71 season with Rochester … Dressed for 71 games with the Canucks in 1971–72, scoring two goals and six points … Selected by the New York Raiders in the WHA's 1972 general player draft and signed with the club that summer … Nicknamed "Magic" for his uncanny ability to score goals from close range … Scored the first regular-season goal in Raiders' history … Set a major league record by scoring five goals in 25:55 in the Raiders' 9–4 victory over Ottawa (Jan. 4, 1973) … Had another five-goal game for the Cleveland Crusaders in 1975 … Finished second behind Philadelphia's Andre Lacroix in the 1972–73 WHA scoring race with 51 goals and 118 points … Dealt to the Vancouver Blazers, along with Peter Donnelly, as compensation for the New York Golden Blades' signing of Lacroix and Don Herriman, May 1973 … Traded by Vancouver to the Los Angeles Sharks for George Gardner and Ralph MacSweyn, Oct. 1973 … Traded by Los Angeles to the Cleveland Crusaders for Bill Young and Ted Hodgson, Feb. 1974 … Signed with the "new" Minnesota Fighting Saints after the Cleveland franchise folded, Aug. 1976 … Signed with the Winnipeg Jets after the Minnesota franchise folded … Traded by Winnipeg to the Calgary Cowboys, along with Veli Pekka Ketola, for Mike Ford and Danny Lawson, Mar. 1977 … Retired after scoring five goals and five assists in nine games for the Cowboys … **Major league totals:** (Regular season) **NHL** - 89 games, 2 goals, 5 assists, 7 points, 6 penalty minutes. **WHA** - 359 games, 170 goals, 210 assists, 380 points, 103 penalty minutes. (Playoffs) **WHA** - 13 games, 3 goals, 4 assists, 7 points, 4 penalty minutes.

"My first contact with the WHA was during the Memorial Cup tournament in 1972. Some people from the Raiders called me up and asked if I'd be interested in switching leagues. I didn't know much about the WHA at that point, but it sounded like a good opportunity because I'd just spent a whole season riding the bench in Vancouver. For me, that was like stealing. I wanted to play a regular shift. No hockey player wants to sit on the bench night after night, no matter what he's being paid. When I first went to the Canucks, I figured they were finally going to give me a decent shot, but all I did was kill penalties and take the odd shift up front when a game was hopelessly lost.

"The Raiders ended up making me a very generous offer—$40,000—which was twice as much as I made with Vancouver. As a matter of courtesy I went back to [Canucks' GM] Bud Poile and told him about it. All I wanted was for him to say I had a shot at being their third centre in the upcoming season. The NHL was where I wanted to be, but it didn't make a lot of sense if I wasn't going to get the ice time. Well, Poile basically told me I wasn't even in the Canucks' plans...he was writing me off. So that was it. I was gone.

"When I signed with the Raiders, it was on the understanding that I would play defense. That's where I loved to be. I'd played a lot of defense in junior, and I was a Bobby Orr–style rusher. I liked to carry the puck out of my zone and watch the play develop, then hit the forwards with breakaway passes. To me, being a defenseman was like being a quarterback. You had a chance to control the tempo of the game, and as long as you kept the play in front of you, nothing bad could happen.

"I was really looking forward to being a full-time defenseman on the Raiders because we had three guys on the blue line who were very talented but had major weight problems: Kent Douglas, Billy Speer and Jean Gauthier. Huge talent and huge stomachs! As good as those guys were as hockey players, I knew they weren't in shape, so I figured I'd get lots of extra ice time.

"It didn't quite work out that way. In training camp a couple of our regular centres got hurt, and [coach] Camille Henry remembered that I'd won a scoring title as a centre in Tulsa, so he asked me to fill in up front. He said it would only be for a few games. Ha! One day in practice I asked Camille to put me between Wayne Rivers and Brian Bradley, who I didn't think were being used properly. We clicked right away, and I never played another game on defense in New York.

"When the season opened, Bradley and Rivers and I were getting tons of ice time, and it seemed like everything we did resulted in a goal. Stan Fischler, a hockey writer in New York, named us the Silk Line because we worked so smoothly together. Bradley was the back-checker. He was a tough, strong guy who was great at digging the puck out of the corner and taking a hit to make a pass. Rivers was the shooter. He could really fly on his skates, and his shot was so hard and so accurate that if the goaltender stopped it, there was hardly ever a chance to block the rebound. Me, I skated like a plough horse, and my shot would never be confused with Bobby Hull's, but I had a knack for planting myself in front of the net and getting a little piece of any puck that came within six feet of me.

"I was such a terrible skater that I used to tell Rivers and Bradley not to move their feet if I was lugging the puck out of our zone because there was no way I could keep up to them. Sit down, I'd tell 'em. Take a load off! Sometimes it seemed like it took me five minutes to cross the neutral zone, but I usually made it with the puck still on the end of my stick. The success I had scoring goals in New York was mostly due to those two guys. They'd make all the plays, and I'd get credit for the goal because the puck went into the net off my head or my arm or my butt. The one real talent I had was for tipping shots out of the air past a goaltender. Eye-hand coordination. All those years that I played lacrosse had something to do with it, I think.

"The five-goal game that I had against Ottawa was funny, actually. All night long, any puck that came near me somehow ended up in the net. The guys were giving me a hard time on the bench because none of those goals was what you'd describe as a pretty play. I probably could have had a couple more, too. After I got the fifth one, we ended up with a couple of late power plays, and the coach wanted to send me out, but I didn't want to be greedy. It was quite a turnaround for a guy who had been a benchwarmer the season before.

"When I went to Vancouver in the deal for Andre Lacroix, I didn't know what to expect. I was a bit apprehensive because of what I'd been through with the Canucks. As it turned out, I didn't have too long to think about it because the Blazers traded me to the L.A. Sharks right away, and then a couple of months later I was dealt to the Cleveland Crusaders.

"I really loved playing in Cleveland. It was a good hockey town, and the team had a lot of quality guys. Unfortunately, in my second season there, I got into [GM] Jack Vivian's doghouse, and I was riding the bench again. [Gerry] Cheevers and I would be sitting on the end of the bench, and he'd give me a hard time about making $100,000 to pull splinters out of my butt.

I'd say 'What about you? You're making $200,000!' It wasn't that funny, though; I wanted to play.

"One night against the Toronto Toros we were playing putrid hockey, so the coach tapped me on the shoulder and said 'Can you play right wing?' I told him I could play anywhere, but I couldn't score goals from the bench. He threw together a line with me, Jimmy Harrison and Gerry Pinder—three natural centres.

"Harrison was incredible. That guy was a very special hockey player. The more he played, the better he got. It was easy because all Pinder and I had to do was wait for Jimmy to pick up the puck and carry the three opposing forwards on his back. We'd go to the net, and he'd put the puck on our sticks. Well, after the first period we were down 4–2, and I had scored both our goals. Halfway through the second period we were trailing 8–2, but we ended up coming back and winning the game 10–9! I finished the night with five goals and three assists, and Jimmy and Gerry had big nights, too. But three games later, Harrison and I were benched again. Go figure.

"When the Crusaders moved to Minnesota, I went along, but after the Fighting Saints folded, I was ready to pack it in. I went home for a while, then my agent got a call from the Winnipeg Jets asking me to join them for the rest of the season. I thought that might be my best chance to be on an Avco Trophy champion, so I jumped at it. It was super to get a chance to play with Bobby Hull. Unfortunately, the Jets sent me to the Calgary Cowboys late in the season as part of a trade for Danny Lawson. That really burned me because I could see my playoff money going out the window.

"I finished strong in Calgary—got ten points in nine games—but the next season I couldn't catch on with anybody. I tried to go to the Quebec Nordiques, but they weren't interested. Then I tried to get back into the NHL with the Cleveland Barons. I had been a popular player with the Crusaders, and I felt I could have really helped the Barons at least as a penalty killer or specialty guy, but they didn't want anything to do with me. Was I blackballed? I think so. I was getting up there in years, but to this day I believe I could have helped the Barons be a better hockey club.

"Looking back, I have to say that I honestly loved my time in the WHA. It was an honour to play with and against so many great players, and being able to do it in such a fun atmosphere was a real bonus. I loved having the chance to show that you don't have to be able to skate like a Bobby Hull or a Bobby Orr to make a valuable contribution.

"It's very gratifying when people come up to me today and say they remember me as being a natural goal scorer who was entertaining to watch, but I always had more fun playing the game than the fans did watching me. I was a player with limited skills, but I worked hard, and I like to think that I was able to complement the talent of the guys I played with.

"After I retired, I worked as a salesman for awhile and coached a junior team for one season. Several years ago I opened a catering business in Cleveland, which I still enjoy very much. I coach high school hockey, and that keeps me involved in the game.

"If the opportunity arose, I'd love to get back to coaching a junior 'A' team in Canada. I was always a student of the game; I ate, drank and slept hockey. To be able to pass along some of what I've learned to young players getting ready to step into the pro ranks is something I really want to do. It would be a nice way to round out my career."

BOBBY WHITLOCK

Centre . . . Born in Charlottetown, P.E.I., July 16, 1949 . . . Son of Maritimes senior hockey legend Roy (Buck) Whitlock, who recorded more than 1,000 goals and 1,200 assists in a 20-year career . . . Played junior with the Halifax Canadiens and later moved on to the Edmonton Oil Kings and Kitchener Rangers . . . Never drafted by the NHL . . . Signed as a free agent by the Minnesota North Stars in 1969 and assigned to the Iowa Stars in the Central Professional Hockey League . . . Had a brief NHL tryout with Minnesota in 1970, but recorded no statistics . . . Owner of a hard, accurate slapshot, Whitlock was a gifted scorer, averaging just over 30 goals per year as a pro . . . Spent the 1970–71 season with the Cleveland Barons in the American Hockey League . . . Named the Western Hockey League's rookie of the year in 1971–72 after notching 33 goals and 79 points for the Phoenix Roadrunners . . . Selected by the Los Angeles Sharks in the WHA's 1972 general player draft . . . Traded to Chicago Cougars, Aug. 1972 . . . Traded by Chicago back to L.A. for Don Gordon and Jim Watson, Feb. 1974 . . . Joined the Indianapolis Racers in 1974–75 and led the team in scoring with 31 goals and 57 points in 73 games . . . Retired in 1976 . . . **Major league totals:** (Regular season) **WHA** - 244 games, 81 goals, 98 assists, 179 points, 155 penalty minutes. No playoff appearances.

CENTER
BOBBY WHITLOCK

"I took a roundabout route to big-league hockey because I wasn't drafted until the WHA came along. I had a pretty good junior career, but because of my size nobody wanted me. I'm five foot ten, but in those days I weighed only around 155 pounds, so they didn't think I could take the pounding in the pros.

"The North Stars asked me to come to their tryout camp in 1969, and I played well enough that they offered me a contract to go to their Central League affiliate in Iowa. I had close to 30 goals and more than 50 points in the first 60 or so games, so they called me up to the NHL. By that time I was all the way up to 158 pounds, and I thought I was going to get killed. In my first NHL game I got into a scrap with Dennis Hextall. If Claude Larose hadn't come charging in to bail me out I would've been dead, no doubt about it.

"That was pretty much the extent of my NHL career. I went to Cleveland in the American Hockey League the next season, and then on to Phoenix in the Western League, where we had a really good team. I was fortunate enough to win the Rookie of the Year award, but apparently that didn't impress the North Stars very much. I didn't hear from them at all, and shortly after the season ended, I got a call at home in P.E.I. from the L.A. Sharks of the WHA. They invited me down to California to talk about a contract, and when I got there they gave me a hotel room at Disneyland, handed me a cheque for $20,000 as a signing bonus and told me to have fun!

"Well, you can imagine what was going through my head. Three years earlier the North Stars had grudgingly given me a $2,000 bonus for a $5,000 playing contract. Now the Sharks were dangling $20,000 up front to convince me to sign a three-year deal that started at $60,000! I signed right away and had a terrific week being wined and dined all over Los Angeles. The Sharks told me how much they wanted me on the team and said that I was going to be one of their big stars—the whole nine yards. I was on cloud nine on the long flight back to Prince Edward Island. It was like winning the lottery! But no sooner had I got back home when the phone rang. It was the Sharks, telling me I'd been traded to the Chicago Cougars.

"That was my introduction to what life would be like in the WHA. It was a real adventure because it seemed like something new or unexpected popped up every day. But right from the opening day of training camp I knew I would like it. Every team around the league had gone shopping for three or four core NHL guys and then filled up the roster with whatever talent they could find in the minors or the amateur ranks. The Cougars held two training camps that first year: one for the guys who had never played pro hockey—and there was a pile of them—and one for the guys who were coming out of the high minors and the NHL. That made it easy for me right off the bat because I was in with the big boys.

"We had good veteran players like Rosaire Paiement, Reggie Fleming and Larry Cahan, and those guys did a lot to keep things together in the first season. We had a pretty good hockey club, but we were inconsistent. The neat thing in those first couple of seasons, though, was that there was a lot of parity in the league. Even when we were playing poorly, we'd still beat the better teams often enough to keep the fans interested.

"It didn't take too many games before I realized that the WHA wasn't going to fade into the sunset. Bobby Hull and the rest of the superstars who had jumped from the NHL ensured that we weren't going to be a fly-by-night operation, and as the first season wore on, you could feel the excitement mounting. Whenever we had a free Monday night, the guys would all get together at a popular bar in downtown Chicago to watch football on TV. The Black Hawks used to go there too, so we got to know a lot of them. At first they had this patronizing attitude about our league, but after a few months, once they realized the Cougars weren't going to go away, a lot of the Black Hawks started asking us questions about how much money we were making and what the travel was like.

"One of the smart things the Cougars did in going head-to-head with the Hawks was to promote us as the 'working man's' team. We played in the old International Amphitheatre on the south side of the city, and it could be pretty scary just driving out there. But the fans really took us into their hearts.

"One of my best memories from the first season was when the Winnipeg Jets came to town the first time after Hull won his court case to play in the WHA. The place was jammed to the rafters, and the noise was incredible. The reporters had built up a story about me having one of the hardest shots in the league and this game being a showdown between me and Bobby to see whose shot was harder. It was a little embarrassing, but I went along with it. Sure enough, both of us shattered the plexiglass behind the net that night, and the papers ran a picture of Bobby and me each holding up a piece of the broken glass. That was pretty special.

"If I had to pick one moment as the most memorable, though, it would have to be when we skated out during the introductions in our first home game. For me, that moment meant a hell of a lot. It was vindication for all the years in the minors when everybody told me I was too small to make it to the big leagues. I had wanted to be a pro hockey player all my life, and to finally realize that ambition filled me with pride. I remember thinking about my dad, who had such a great career in senior hockey. He had a chance to go to the Montreal Canadiens once, but he turned them down to stay at home. Skating out there for my first game as a Chicago Cougar, I felt proud for both of us.

"By the time I was traded to Los Angeles in early 1974, you could already see the league was getting much better. The fringe players were being weeded out, and instead of picking up guys from the minors or raiding the NHL, most of the teams were signing the best young kids out of junior hockey. That made a big difference in the overall talent level. I think that's probably when the NHL started to realize the impact of the WHA because of the serious bidding wars for kids like Dennis Sobchuk and Pat Price.

"I played out the season in L.A., but then my contract was up, and I didn't feel like moving to Michigan when the club went there. I ended up going to Indianapolis for a couple of seasons, and then I had a falling out with [coach] Jacques Demers, and I packed it in for good. My first year in Indy I led the Racers in scoring, and the next season I was seventh in the league in points when Demers said he was sending me to the minors because I wasn't scoring enough goals. That pretty much ended it for me. The fun was gone from the game, and I knew Demers was going to be around a lot longer than I would be.

"Like a lot of young guys who signed pretty good contracts, I blew most of my money and was just about broke when I left the game. When we moved to British Columbia, I think I had about $500 to show for my pro hockey career. I went back to senior hockey as a playing coach in Trail for a few seasons and started an insurance business, which I still run.

"I get a kick out of the hockey cards that people still send to me. Or they send photos from the old days that they want autographed. It amazes me that after all these years anybody would have that stuff. But I appreciate it. There's not much mention of the WHA anymore, but I'm proud that I was part of it. I think our league started the process of taking the game away from the owners and giving it back to the players. Maybe that's gone too far the other way now, but you can't change history. For me, that's the legacy of the World Hockey Association."

Part 4

OVERTIME

- **All-Time Regular-Season Player Registry and Statistics**
- **All-Time Regular-Season Goaltender Registry**
- **All-Time Playoff Player Registry and Statistics**
- **All-Time Playoff Goaltender Registry**
- **All-Time WHA Coach Registry**
- **All-Time Career Statistical Leaders (Regular Season)**
- **All-Time Career Statistical Leaders (Playoffs)**
- **All-Time Top Single-Season Individual Performances**
- **All-Time Best and Worst Regular-Season Team Performances**
- **All-Time Playoff Won-Lost Records**
- **Year-by-Year Regular-Season Final Standings**
- **Year-by-Year Playoff Series Results and Statistical Leaders**
- **Year-by-Year Avco World Trophy Championship Rosters**
- **Year-by-Year Regular-Season Top Ten Scorers**
- **Year-by-Year Regular-Season Goaltending Leaders**
- **Year-by-Year Regular-Season Penalty Minute Leaders**
- **Year-by-Year All-Star Teams (As Selected by the Media)**
- **Year-by-Year All-Star Game Rosters and Summaries**
- **The WHA vs. International Competition**
- **All-Time Regular-Season Penalty Shots**
- **Year-by-Year WHA Award Winners**
- **The WHA vs. the NHL: Exhibition Game Results**
- **Priority Picks and Rounds 1–20, 1972 WHA General Player Draft**
- **WHA Intraleague Drafts, 1975–78**
- **WHA Expansion Drafts, 1974 and 1975**
- **WHA Dispersal Drafts, 1975–79**
- **WHA's Top 20 Amateur Draft Picks, 1973–77**
- **1979 NHL-WHA Reclamation Draft**
- **1979 National Hockey League Entry Draft**

1972  1979

KEY TO ABBREVIATIONS

WHA teams
Alb – Alberta Oilers
Bal – Baltimore Blades
Bir – Birmingham Bulls
Cal – Calgary Cowboys
Chi – Chicago Cougars
Cin – Cincinnati Stingers
Cle – Cleveland Crusaders
Den – Denver Spurs
Edm – Edmonton Oilers
Hou – Houston Aeros
Ind – Indianapolis Racers
LA – Los Angeles Sharks
Mia – Miami Screaming Eagles
Mich – Michigan Stags
Min – Minnesota Fighting Saints
NE – New England Whalers
NJ – New Jersey Knights
NY – New York Raiders
Ott – Ottawa Nationals/Civics
Phi – Philadelphia Blazers
Phx – Phoenix Roadrunners
Que – Quebec Nordiques
SD – San Diego Mariners
Tor – Toronto Toros
Van – Vancouver Blazers
Win – Winnipeg Jets

Statistics
A – assists
G – goals
GA – goals against
GAA – goals-against average
GF – goals for
GP – games played
PIM – penalties in minutes
PTS – points
SO – shutouts

ALL-TIME REGULAR-SEASON PLAYER REGISTRY AND STATISTICS

A

	Years	Games	Goals	Assists	Points	Penalty Minutes
Abbey, Bruce	1975–76	17	1	0	1	12
Abgrall, Dennis	1976–78	145	36	50	86	35
Abrahamsson, Christer	1974–77	102	0	2	2	18
Abrahamsson, Thommie	1974–77	203	28	67	95	126
Adair, Jim	1973–74	70	12	17	29	10
Adduono, Ray	1973–78	221	45	152	197	67
Adduono, Rick	1978–79	80	20	33	53	67
Ahearn, Kevin	1972–74	78	20	22	42	18
Aherns, Chris	1977–78	4	0	0	0	15
Alexander, Claire	1978–79	54	8	23	31	16
Allen, Jeff	1977–78	2	0	0	0	0
Alley, Steve	1977–79	105	25	36	61	47
Amodeo, Mike	1972–79	300	11	65	76	273
Anderson, Ron C.	1972–74	91	19	17	36	47
Anderson, Ron F.	1972–75	115	3	35	38	44
Andrascik, Steve	1974–76	97	9	13	22	79
Andrea, Paul	1972–74	135	36	48	84	26
Angotti, Lou	1974–75	26	2	5	7	9
Antonovich, Mike	1972–79	486	182	188	370	183
Arbour, John	1972–77	336	30	164	194	568
Archambault, Michel	1972–73	57	12	25	37	36
Archambault, Yves	1972–74	11	0	1	1	0
Arndt, Danny	1975–78	120	16	23	39	21
Ash, Bob	1972–75	200	6	46	52	88
Ashton, Ron	1974–75	36	1	3	4	66
Asmundson, Duke	1972–76	258	16	54	70	211
Atkinson, Steve	1975–76	42	2	6	8	22
Aubry, Serge	1972–77	142	0	4	4	88

B

	Years	Games	Goals	Assists	Points	Penalty Minutes
Backstrom, Ralph	1973–77	304	100	153	253	104
Bailey, Garnet (Ace)	1978–79	38	5	4	9	22
Baird, Ken	1972–78	333	91	99	190	500
Ball, Terry	1972–77	307	28	134	162	174
Balon, Dave	1973–74	9	0	0	0	2
Baltimore, Bryon	1974–79	331	18	72	90	390
Barber, Ian (Butch)	1972–74	78	4	19	23	41
Barlow, Bob	1974–75	51	6	20	26	8
Barrie, Doug	1972–77	351	37	122	159	620
Bateman, Jamie	1974–76	31	1	3	4	100
Bathgate, Andy	1974–75	11	1	6	7	2
Baxter, Paul	1974–79	270	25	88	113	962
Beaton, Frank (Seldom)	1975–78	153	12	21	33	614
Beaudin, Norm	1972–76	311	97	155	252	69
Beaudoin, Serge (Jethro)	1973–79	332	20	103	123	519
Beaule, Alain	1973–75	154	8	57	65	136
Bennett, John	1972–73	34	4	6	10	18
Bennett, Wendell	1974–75	67	4	15	19	92
Benzelock, Jim (Big Cat)	1972–76	166	18	27	45	72
Bergeron, Yves	1972–73	65	14	19	33	32
Berglund, Bill	1973–75	5	0	0	0	0
Bergman, Thommie	1974–78	234	22	97	119	261
Bernier, Jean	1974–78	260	17	84	101	50
Bernier, Serge	1973–79	417	230	336	566	486
Biggnell, Larry	1975–76	41	5	5	10	43
Bilodeau, Gilles (Bad News)	1975–79	143	9	15	24	570
Bilodeau, Yvon	1975–76	4	0	0	0	2
Binkley, Les	1972–76	80	0	0	0	0
Black, Milt	1972–75	186	28	31	59	55
Blackburn, Don	1973–76	146	40	74	114	34
Blackwood, Bill	1977–78	3	0	0	0	0
Blain, Jacques	1972–73	70	1	10	11	78

B

	Years	Games	Goals	Assists	Points	Penalty Minutes
Blanchet, Bob	1974–76	4	0	0	0	0
Blanchette, Bernie	1972–73	47	7	7	14	10
Block, Ken	1972–79	455	16	187	203	192
Blum, Frank	1972–74	7	0	0	0	0
Boddy, Greg	1976–77	64	2	19	21	60
Boland, Mike	1972–73	41	1	15	16	44
Bolduc, Dan	1975–78	88	15	13	28	51
Bond, Kerry	1974–76	86	24	15	39	32
Bordeleau, Christian	1972–79	412	179	325	504	162
Bordeleau, Paulin	1976–79	234	101	76	177	125
Borgeson, Don	1974–76	145	59	52	111	66
Boucha, Henry	1975–76	36	15	20	35	47
Boudrias, Andre	1976–78	140	22	48	70	34
Boudreau, Bruce	1975–76	30	3	6	9	4
Boudreau, Michel	1972–74	36	8	7	15	4
Bowles, Brian	1975–76	3	0	0	0	0
Bowman, Kirk	1973–74	10	0	2	2	0
Boyd, Bob	1973–75	54	1	14	15	35
Boyd, Jim	1974–77	169	49	80	129	68
Boyer, Wally	1972–73	69	6	28	34	27
Boylan, Dean	1973–75	64	1	5	6	122
Brackenbury, Curt	1973–79	265	41	50	91	753
Bradley, Brian	1972–75	190	41	61	102	38
Bray, Duane	1976–77	46	2	6	8	62
Bredin, Gary	1974–76	144	26	31	57	49
Brewer, Carl	1973–74	77	2	23	25	42
Brindley, Doug	1972–74	103	28	20	48	19
Broderick, Ken	1976–78	73	0	3	3	2
Brodeur, Richard	1972–79	305	0	12	12	19
Bromley, Gary (Bones)	1976–78	67	0	1	1	6
Brown, Andy	1974–77	86	0	2	2	75
Brown, Arnie	1974–75	60	3	5	8	40
Brown, Bob	1972–74	80	7	17	24	46
Brown, Ken	1972–75	52	0	1	1	4
Brubaker, Jeff	1978–79	12	0	0	0	19
Buetow, Brad	1973–74	25	0	0	0	4
Buchanan, Ron (Bucky)	1972–76	205	83	102	185	48
Burchell, Randy	1976–77	5	0	1	1	0
Burgess, Don	1972–78	446	107	122	229	87
Busniuk, Ron	1974–78	286	9	64	73	762
Butters, Bill (Capt. Crunch)	1974–78	217	4	51	55	530
Bye, Brian	1975–76	1	0	0	0	0
Byers, Mike	1972–76	263	83	74	157	40

C

	Years	Games	Goals	Assists	Points	Penalty Minutes
Cadle, Brian	1972–73	56	4	4	8	39
Caffrey, Terry	1972–76	164	59	111	170	30
Cahan, Larry	1972–74	78	1	10	11	46
Callighen, Brett	1976–79	213	66	95	161	280
Campbell, Bryan (Soupy)	1972–78	433	123	253	376	219
Campbell, Colin	1973–74	78	3	20	23	191
Campbell, Scott	1977–79	149	11	44	55	364
Campeau, Richard	1972–74	82	1	18	19	74
Cardiff, Jim	1972–75	200	4	47	51	398
Cardwell, Steve	1973–75	152	32	36	68	22
Carleton, Wayne (Swoop)	1972–77	290	132	180	312	135
Carlin, Brian	1972–74	70	13	22	35	6
Carlson, Jack (Big Bird)	1974–79	272	36	51	87	694
Carlson, Jeff	1975–76	7	0	1	1	14
Carlson, Steve (Zipper)	1975–79	172	33	47	80	132
Carlyle, Steve	1972–76	22	13	59	72	109
Caron, Alain (Boom Boom)	1972–75	193	82	50	132	30

Overtime

C

	Years	Games	Goals	Assists	Points	Penalty Minutes
Caron, Jacques	1975–77	26	0	1	1	0
Carroll, Greg	1976–78	151	30	66	96	116
Cartier, Jean Yves	1972–73	15	0	3	3	8
Cassolato, Tony	1976–79	184	44	44	88	137
Charlebois, Bob	1972–76	188	32	50	82	34
Chartre, Claude	1972–75	18	2	3	5	0
Cheevers, Gerry (Cheesy)	1972–76	191	0	2	2	134
Chernoff, Mike	1973–75	39	11	10	21	4
Chipchase, Jack	1972–73	3	0	0	0	2
Chipperfield, Ron	1974–79	369	153	177	330	187
Christiansen, Keith (Huffer)	1972–74	138	23	55	78	60
Clackson, Kim	1975–79	271	6	39	45	932
Clark, Gordie	1978–79	21	3	3	6	2
Clarke, Jim	1975–76	59	1	9	10	57
Clearwater, Ray	1972–77	214	27	77	104	141
Climie, Ron	1972–77	248	98	106	204	68
Cloutier, Real (Buddy)	1974–79	369	283	283	566	169
Coates, Brian	1973–78	202	42	43	85	86
Colborne, Howie	1973–74	2	0	0	0	0
Cole, Jim	1976–77	2	0	1	1	0
Conacher, Brian	1972–73	69	8	19	27	32
Connelly, Gary	1973–74	4	0	1	1	2
Connelly, Wayne	1972–77	366	167	162	329	93
Connor, Cam	1974–78	274	83	88	171	904
Conroy, Mike	1975–76	4	0	1	1	0
Constantin, Charles	1974–78	190	28	35	63	229
Cormier, Michel	1974–77	182	70	69	139	52
Corsi, Jim	1977–79	63	0	1	1	2
Cote, Alain	1977–79	108	17	18	35	31
Cote, Roger	1972–75	153	3	14	17	104
Cottringer, Tom	1972–73	2	0	0	0	0
Cournoyer, Norm	1973–77	32	4	7	11	14
Coutu, Rich	1973–76	24	0	0	0	0
Crashley, Bart	1972–74	148	22	53	75	26
Critch, Glen	1975–76	3	0	0	0	0
Cross, Jim	1977–78	2	0	0	0	0
Crowder, Keith	1978–79	5	1	0	1	17
Crowley, Paul	1975–76	4	0	0	0	0
Cuddie, Steve	1972–75	222	17	47	64	235
Cunniff, John	1972–76	65	10	10	20	35
Cunningham, Gary	1973–74	2	0	0	0	0
Cunningham, Rick	1972–77	323	23	91	114	458
Curran, Mike (Lefty)	1972–77	130	0	1	1	58
Curtis, Paul	1974–75	76	4	15	19	32

D

	Years	Games	Goals	Assists	Points	Penalty Minutes
Daley, Joe	1972–79	308	0	10	10	45
D'Alvise, Bob	1975–76	59	5	8	13	10
Danby, John	1972–76	150	16	25	41	16
David, Richard	1978–79	14	0	4	4	4
Davidson, Blair	1976–77	2	0	0	0	2
Davis, Billy	1977–79	17	1	2	3	2
Davis, Kelly	1978–79	18	0	1	1	20
Deadmarsh, Butch	1974–78	253	63	66	129	570
Dean, Barry	1975–76	71	9	25	34	110
Debol, Dave	1977–79	68	13	29	42	11
Deguise, Michel	1973–76	50	0	2	2	0
Delorenzi, Ray	1974–76	42	8	12	20	4
Delorme, Ron	1975–76	22	1	3	4	28
DeMarco, Ab	1977–78	47	6	8	14	20
Derksen, Brian	1973–74	1	0	0	0	2

D

	Years	Games	Goals	Assists	Points	Penalty Minutes
Deschamps, Andre	1976–77	9	1	2	3	19
Descoteaux, Norm	1973–75	29	1	7	8	6
Desjardine, Ken	1972–76	154	4	24	28	148
Desjardins, Gerry	1974–75	41	0	1	1	13
Devine, Kevin	1974–79	288	74	81	155	411
Dillabough, Bob	1972–73	72	8	8	16	8
Dillon, Wayne	1973–79	212	71	128	199	78
Dion, Michel	1974–79	149	0	0	0	30
Dobek, Bob	1975–77	72	10	18	28	19
Donaldson, Gary	1976–77	5	0	0	0	6
Donnelly, John	1972–73	15	1	1	2	44
Donnelly, Pat	1975–76	21	5	7	12	4
Donnelly, Peter	1972–76	100	0	1	1	11
Dorey, Jim (Flipper)	1972–79	431	52	232	284	617
Dornseif, Dave	1977–79	4	0	1	1	0
Douglas, Kent	1972–73	60	3	15	18	74
Douglas, Jordy	1978–79	51	6	10	16	15
Doyle, Gary	1973–74	1	0	0	0	0
Driscoll, Peter	1974–79	326	90	101	191	587
Dryden, Dave	1974–79	242	0	14	14	6
Dube, Norm	1976–79	148	33	52	85	29
Dubois, Michel (Plywood)	1975–77	59	2	5	7	117
Dudley, Rick	1975–79	270	131	146	277	516
Dufour, Guy	1972–74	84	30	25	55	32
Dumas, Rich	1974–75	1	0	0	0	0
Dunn, Dave	1976–78	108	9	31	40	208
Dupras, Richard	1973–74	2	0	0	0	0
Durbano, Steve	1977–78	45	6	4	10	284
Dyck, Eddie	1974–75	32	0	0	0	6

E

	Years	Games	Goals	Assists	Points	Penalty Minutes
Earl, Tom	1972–77	347	40	59	99	116
Edur, Tom	1973–76	217	17	79	96	116
Erickson, Grant	1972–76	266	54	78	132	79
Erikkson, Bengt	1978–79	33	5	10	15	2
Evans, Chris	1975–78	204	11	51	62	136
Evo, Bill	1974–76	97	14	18	32	64

F

	Years	Games	Goals	Assists	Points	Penalty Minutes
Falkenberg, Bob	1972–78	376	14	74	88	183
Falkman, Chris	1972–73	45	1	5	6	12
Farda, Richard	1974–77	177	34	86	120	12
Featherstone, Tony	1974–76	108	29	45	74	31
Fedorko, Mike	1976–77	4	0	0	0	0
Ferguson, Norm	1972–78	436	181	184	365	45
Fisher, John	1972–73	40	0	5	5	0
Fitchner, Bob	1973–79	414	68	139	207	501
Fleming, Reggie	1972–74	120	25	57	82	142
Flett, Bill (Cowboy)	1976–79	201	103	84	187	68
Folco, Peter	1975–77	21	1	8	9	15
Foley, Rick	1975–76	11	1	2	3	6
Fontaine, Len	1974–75	21	1	8	9	6
Fonteyne, Val	1972–74	149	16	45	61	4
Forbes, Dave	1978–79	73	6	5	11	83
Ford, Mike	1974–78	233	33	99	132	172
Fortier, Dave	1977–78	54	1	15	16	86
Fortier, Florent	1975–76	4	1	1	2	0
Fortunato, Joe	1976–77	1	0	0	0	0

F

	Years	Games	Goals	Assists	Points	Penalty Minutes
Fotiu, Nick	1974–76	110	5	4	9	238
Fraser, Rick	1974–75	4	0	0	4	2
French, John	1972–78	420	108	192	300	130
Ftorek, Robbie	1974–79	373	216	307	523	365

G

	Years	Games	Goals	Assists	Points	Penalty Minutes
Gallant, Gord	1973–77	273	31	59	90	849
Gambucci, Gary	1974–76	112	29	24	53	33
Gardner, George	1972–74	79	0	1	1	2
Garneau, J.C.	1974–75	17	0	5	5	27
Garrett, John	1973–79	323	0	7	7	75
Gartner, Mike	1978–79	78	27	25	52	123
Garwasiuk, Ron	1973–74	51	6	13	19	100
Gateman, Marty	1975–76	12	0	1	1	6
Gaudette, Andre	1972–75	223	61	105	166	34
Gauthier, Jean	1972–73	31	2	1	3	21
Gellar, Sam	1972–74	28	7	4	11	15
Gendron, Jean Guy	1972–74	127	28	41	69	155
Geoffrion, Danny	1978–79	77	12	14	26	74
George, Wes	1978–79	12	4	2	6	34
Gibbons, Brian	1972–76	217	15	88	103	251
Gibbons, Gerard	1973–76	31	2	4	6	30
Gibson, Jack	1972–76	126	38	22	60	108
Gibson, Johnny	1978–79	9	0	1	1	5
Gilbert, Ed	1978–79	29	3	3	6	40
Gilbert, Jeannot	1973–75	131	24	60	84	32
Gill, Andre (Cannon)	1972–74	46	0	0	0	6
Gilligan, Bill	1977–79	128	27	40	67	113
Gillow, Russ	1972–76	109	0	1	1	12
Gilmore, Tom	1972–75	202	48	60	108	439
Gilmour, Dave	1975–76	1	0	0	0	0
Gingras, Gaston	1978–79	60	13	21	34	35
Giroux, Rejean	1972–74	71	15	18	33	55
Given, David	1974–75	1	0	0	0	0
Glenwright, Brian (Wimpy)	1972–74	65	5	7	12	0
Globensky, Allan	1973–76	42	1	2	3	18
Goldsworthy, Bill (Goldy)	1977–79	49	12	12	24	24
Goldthorpe, Billy	1973–76	33	1	0	1	87
Golembrosky, Frank	1972–73	60	8	12	20	53
Gordon, Don	1973–75	94	18	14	32	43
Gorman, Dave	1974–79	260	56	83	139	187
Gosselin, Rich (Goose)	1978–79	3	0	0	0	0
Goulet, Michel	1978–79	78	28	30	58	65
Grahame, Ron (Reverend)	1973–77	143	0	2	2	28
Gratton, Bill	1975–76	6	0	1	1	2
Gratton, Gilles	1972–75	161	0	9	9	46
Gratton, Jean-Guy	1972–75	188	31	41	72	53
Gravel, John	1972–73	8	1	3	4	0
Gray, John	1974–79	363	146	146	292	458
Green, Ted	1972–79	458	42	138	180	304
Greig, Bruce	1976–79	61	7	9	16	131
Grenier, Richard	1976–77	34	11	9	20	4
Gresdal, Gary	1975–76	2	0	1	1	5
Gretzky, Wayne (Brinks)	1978–79	80	46	64	110	19
Grierson, Don	1972–74	143	33	40	73	128
Grigg, Chris	1975–76	2	0	0	0	0
Gruen, Danny	1974–77	181	56	61	117	185
Guidon, Robert	1972–79	463	112	145	257	156
Guite, Pierre	1972–79	373	92	105	197	585
Gulka, Bud	1974–75	5	1	0	1	10

H

	Years	Games	Goals	Assists	Points	Penalty Minutes
Haas, Derek	1975–76	30	5	9	14	6
Hagman, Matti	1977–78	53	23	31	56	16
Hale, Larry	1972–78	413	11	95	107	216
Hall, Del	1975–78	186	89	88	177	44
Hall, Murray	1972–76	312	96	125	221	155
Hamilton, Al	1972–79	455	53	258	311	492
Hanmer, Craig	1974–75	27	1	0	1	15
Hampson, Ted	1972–76	305	60	143	203	51
Handrahan, Alf	1977–78	14	1	3	4	42
Haney, Merv	1972–73	7	0	1	1	4
Hangsleben, Al	1974–79	334	36	73	109	437
Hanna, John	1972–73	66	6	20	26	68
Hansis, Ron	1976–78	100	17	12	29	57
Hanson, Dave	1976–79	103	13	40	53	497
Harbaruk, Nick	1974–77	181	45	44	89	78
Hardy, Joe (Gypsy)	1972–75	210	46	94	140	201
Hargreaves, Jim	1973–76	175	12	20	32	151
Hargreaves, Ted	1973–74	74	7	12	19	15
Harker, Derek	1972–73	29	0	5	5	46
Harris, Duke	1972–75	193	53	47	100	52
Harris, Hugh	1973–78	336	107	173	280	241
Harrison, Jim (Max)	1972–76	132	117	152	269	360
Hart, Richard	1976–77	4	0	0	0	0
Hartsburg, Craig	1978–79	77	9	40	49	73
Harvey, Mike	1972–73	40	6	13	19	14
Hatoum, Eddie	1972–74	52	4	13	17	10
Heatley, Murray	1973–76	156	48	54	102	86
Heaver, Paul	1975–77	71	1	12	13	83
Hebenton, Clay	1975–77	58	0	0	0	2
Hedberg, Anders	1974–78	286	236	222	458	201
Heggedal, Howie	1972–73	8	2	1	3	0
Heindl, Billy	1973–74	67	4	14	18	4
Heiskala, Earl	1972–74	94	14	23	37	195
Henderson, Paul	1974–79	360	140	143	283	112
Henry, Pierre	1972–73	19	2	3	5	13
Herriman, Don	1972–75	155	36	71	107	143
Hicke, Billy	1972–73	73	14	24	38	20
Hickey, Pat	1973–75	152	61	63	124	102
Hicks, Glenn	1978–79	69	6	10	16	48
Hillman, Larry	1973–76	192	6	49	55	182
Hillman, Wayne	1973–75	126	3	16	19	88
Hinse, Andre	1973–77	256	102	151	253	69
Hislop, Jamie	1976–79	206	61	102	163	68
Hobin, Mike	1975–77	77	18	19	37	16
Hodgson, Ted (Chief)	1972–74	107	18	34	53	121
Hoekstra, Ed	1972–74	97	13	28	41	12
Hoganson, Dale	1973–79	378	30	161	191	186
Hoganson, Paul	1973–78	143	0	2	2	18
Holbrook, Tery	1974–76	93	11	15	26	13
Holden, Bill	1973–74	2	0	0	0	0
Holland, Jerry	1977–78	22	2	1	3	14
Holmgren, Paul	1975–76	51	14	16	30	121
Holmquist, Leif	1975–76	19	0	0	0	2
Hopiavouri, Ralph	1972–75	70	6	15	21	71
Hornung, Larry	1972–78	373	34	121	155	103
Horton, Bill	1972–75	193	4	35	39	131
Houle, Rejean	1973–76	204	118	139	257	115
Howe, Gordie	1973–79	419	174	334	508	399
Howe, Mark	1973–79	426	208	296	504	198
Howe, Marty	1973–79	449	67	117	184	460
Howell, Harry	1973–76	170	7	36	43	58
Huck, Fran	1973–78	228	67	127	194	133
Hughes, Bill	1972–73	3	0	0	0	2

H

	Years	Games	Goals	Assists	Points	Penalty Minutes
Hughes, Brent	1975–79	268	23	79	102	180
Hughes, Frank	1972–78	392	173	180	353	173
Hughes, John	1974–79	372	18	130	148	778
Hull, Bobby (Golden Jet)	1972–78	411	303	335	638	183
Hull, Steve	1975–77	80	11	17	28	6
Humphreys, Ed	1975–77	30	0	1	1	0
Hunter, Dave	1978–79	72	7	25	32	134
Hurley, Paul (The Shot)	1972–77	311	10	76	86	181
Huston, Ron (Spike)	1975–77	159	42	83	125	14
Hutchison, Dave	1972–74	97	0	15	15	185
Hyndman, Mike	1972–74	86	12	22	34	32
Hynes, David	1976–77	22	5	4	9	4

I

	Years	Games	Goals	Assists	Points	Penalty Minutes
Inglis, Lee	1973–75	10	0	2	2	0
Inkpen, Dave	1975–79	293	13	76	89	273
Inness, Gary	1977–79	63	0	0	0	51
Irwin, Glenn	1974–79	233	7	24	31	633
Israelson, Larry	1974–77	105	22	31	53	36

J

	Years	Games	Goals	Assists	Points	Penalty Minutes
Jacques, Jeff	1974–77	199	50	68	118	231
Jacquith, Gary	1975–76	2	0	0	0	0
Jakubo, Mike	1972–73	7	0	0	0	0
Jarrett, Gary	1972–76	298	104	119	223	239
Jarry, Pierre	1977–78	18	4	10	14	4
Jodzio, Rick	1974–77	137	15	16	31	357
Johnson, Bob	1975–76	42	0	1	1	9
Johnson, Danny	1972–75	232	53	58	111	62
Johnson, Jim	1972–75	157	32	71	103	54
Johnston, Larry	1974–75	49	0	9	9	93
Johnstone, Ed	1974–75	23	4	4	8	43
Jones, James H.	1973–75	81	14	9	23	62
Jones, James W.	1973–74	1	0	0	0	0
Jones, Robert	1972–76	161	30	48	78	60
Jordan, Ric	1972–77	183	11	23	34	180
Joyal, Eddie (The Jet)	1972–76	239	57	55	112	26
Junkin, Joe	1973–75	69	0	2	2	9
Justin, Dan	1975–77	23	0	2	2	6

K

	Years	Games	Goals	Assists	Points	Penalty Minutes
Kampurri, Hannu	1978–79	2	0	0	0	0
Kannegiesser, Gordon	1972–75	127	1	34	35	62
Karlander, Al	1973–77	269	63	109	172	107
Kassian, Dennis	1972–73	50	6	7	13	14
Keeler, Mike	1973–74	1	0	0	0	0
Kennedy, Jamie	1972–73	54	4	6	10	11
Kennett, Murray	1974–76	106	8	21	29	39
Keogan, Murray	1974–76	114	42	42	84	91
Keon, Dave	1975–79	291	102	189	291	20
Kerslake, Doug	1974–76	23	5	1	6	14
Ketola, Veli Pekka	1974–77	235	84	99	183	118
Ketter, Kerry	1975–76	48	1	9	10	20
Kiely, John	1975–76	22	0	1	1	6
King, Steve	1972–74	136	32	56	88	54
Kirk, Gavin	1972–79	422	117	243	360	279
Klatt, Billy	1972–74	143	50	28	78	34
Knibbs, Darrell	1972–73	41	3	8	11	0
Kokkola, Keith	1974–77	52	0	5	5	130

	Years	Games	Goals	Assists	Points	Penalty Minutes
K						
Konik, George	1972–73	54	4	12	16	34
Krake, Skip	1972–76	207	52	77	129	318
Krezanski, Reg	1974–75	2	0	0	0	2
Krupicka, Jarda	1972–73	36	2	2	4	6
Kryskow, Dave	1976–78	116	36	38	74	63
Kurt, Gary	1972–77	176	0	10	10	12
Kuzmicz, George	1974–76	35	0	12	12	22
L						
Labossiere, Gord	1972–76	301	102	162	264	144
Labraaten, Dan	1976–78	111	42	43	85	51
Lacombe, Francois	1972–79	439	38	139	177	422
Lacroix, Andre	1972–79	551	251	547	798	412
Laframboise, Pete	1976–77	17	0	5	5	12
Lagace, Jean Guy	1976–77	78	2	25	27	110
Lagace, Pierre	1977–79	38	2	5	7	14
Lahache, Floyd	1977–78	11	0	3	3	13
Laing, Bill	1974–76	97	10	16	26	99
Lalonde, Rick	1975–76	2	0	0	0	0
Landon, Bruce	1972–77	122	0	2	2	36
Langevin, Dave	1976–79	216	19	59	78	260
Langway, Rod	1977–78	52	3	18	21	52
Lapierre, Camille	1972–74	33	5	12	17	2
LaPointe, Norm	1975–78	77	0	1	1	8
Lariviere, Garry	1974–79	289	26	126	152	316
Larose, Claude	1975–79	252	88	114	202	45
Larose, Paul	1973–75	33	1	8	9	9
Larose, Ray	1972–74	86	1	11	12	45
Larsson, Curt	1974–77	68	0	3	3	14
Larway, Don	1974–79	324	94	91	185	318
Laughton, Mike	1972–75	203	43	47	90	100
Lavender, Brian	1975–76	37	5	6	11	7
Lawson, Danny	1972–77	392	218	204	422	142
LeBlanc, J.P.	1972–76	248	56	134	190	232
Leclerc, Rene	1972–79	448	134	177	311	463
Leduc, Bob	1972–75	168	47	66	113	109
Leduc, Rich	1974–79	394	195	195	390	399
Legge, Barry	1974–79	345	26	80	106	341
Legge, Randy	1974–77	192	3	31	34	166
Leiter, Bobby	1975–76	51	17	17	34	8
Lemelin, Jacques	1972–73	9	0	1	1	0
Lemieux, Richard	1976–77	33	6	11	17	9
Leroux, Gerry	1978–79	10	0	3	3	2
Lesuk, Bill	1975–79	318	55	81	136	269
Levasseur, Louis	1975–79	85	0	1	1	6
Ley, Rick	1972–79	478	35	220	255	716
Liddington, Bob	1972–77	346	96	82	178	115
Lilyholm, Len (Wolfman)	1972–73	77	8	13	21	37
Lindh, Mats	1975–77	138	33	32	65	14
Lindskog, Doug	1976–77	2	0	0	0	2
Lindstrom, Willy	1975–79	316	123	138	261	133
Linseman, Kenny	1977–78	71	38	38	76	126
Liut, Mike	1977–79	81	0	3	3	9
Lloyd, Owen	1977–78	3	0	1	1	4
Locas, Jacques	1974–78	187	49	70	119	111
Lockett, Ken	1976–77	45	0	0	0	15
Lodboa, Dan	1972–73	58	15	18	33	16
Lomenda, Mark	1974–77	164	31	61	92	46
Long, Barry	1974–79	386	51	171	222	322
Long, Ted	1976–77	1	0	0	0	0
Lukowich, Bernie	1975–77	21	5	3	8	18
Lukowich, Morris	1976–79	222	132	87	219	317

L

	Years	Games	Goals	Assists	Points	Penalty Minutes
Luska, Chuck	1978–79	78	8	12	20	116
Lund, Larry	1972–78	459	149	277	426	419
Lunde, Len	1973–74	72	26	22	48	8
Lyle, George	1976–78	202	86	75	161	190

M

	Years	Games	Goals	Assists	Points	Penalty Minutes
MacDonald, Blair	1973–79	476	172	165	337	153
MacGregor, Bruce	1974–76	135	37	38	75	23
MacGregor, Gary	1974–79	251	92	70	162	87
MacKenzie, Al	1973–74	2	0	0	0	0
MacKinnon, Paul	1978–79	73	2	15	17	70
MacMillan, Bobby	1972–74	153	27	61	88	129
MacNeil, Bernie	1972–76	119	19	19	38	131
MacSweyn, Ralph	1972–74	151	2	44	46	97
Magee, Dean	1978–79	5	0	1	1	10
Maggs, Darryl	1973–79	402	51	177	228	540
Mahovlich, Frank (Big M)	1974–78	237	89	143	232	75
Mara, Peter	1974–76	97	20	28	48	24
Marotte, Gilles	1977–78	73	3	20	23	76
Marrin, Peter	1973–79	278	81	112	193	127
Marsh, Jim	1976–77	1	0	0	0	0
Marsh, Peter	1976–79	230	91	76	167	270
Martin, Tom	1972–75	214	59	77	136	59
Mattson, Markus	1977–79	71	0	1	1	6
Mavety, Larry	1972–77	248	37	113	150	418
Maxwell, Bryan	1975–78	124	6	23	29	217
Mayer, Jim	1976–79	74	13	12	25	21
Mazur, John	1977–78	1	0	0	0	0
McAneely, Bob	1972–76	163	29	34	63	133
McAneely, Ted	1975–76	79	2	17	19	71
McCallum, Dunc	1972–75	100	9	20	39	136
McCartan, Jack (Dusty)	1972–75	42	0	0	0	19
McCaskill, Ted (Terrible)	1972–74	91	13	13	26	213
McCrimmon, Jim	1973–76	107	3	8	11	158
McCulloch, Don	1974–75	51	1	9	10	42
McDonald, Ab	1972–74	148	29	41	70	24
McDonald, Brian	1972–77	304	89	101	190	268
McDonough, Al	1974–77	200	66	73	139	52
McDuffe, Peter	1977–78	12	0	0	0	0
McGlynn, Dick	1972–73	30	0	0	0	12
McKay, Ray	1974–78	212	14	44	58	134
McKenzie, Brian	1973–75	87	19	20	39	72
McKenzie, Johnny (Pie)	1972–79	477	163	250	413	617
McLeod, Al (Moose)	1974–79	342	15	93	108	311
McLeod, Don (Smokey)	1972–78	332	0	43	43	34
McLeod, Jim	1972–75	97	0	1	1	4
McMahon, Mike	1972–76	266	29	101	130	249
McManama, Bob	1975–76	37	3	10	13	28
McMasters, Jim	1972–74	83	1	7	8	41
McMullen, Dale	1977–78	1	0	0	0	0
McNamara, Mike	1972–73	19	0	0	0	5
McNamee, Pete	1973–77	175	16	31	47	189
Meehan, Gerry	1978–79	2	0	0	0	0
Meloche, Denis	1972–74	45	7	14	21	18
Meloff, Chris	1972–73	28	1	6	7	40
Melrose, Barry	1976–79	178	5	27	32	343
Menard, Paul	1972–73	1	0	0	0	0
Mercredi, Vic	1975–76	3	0	0	0	29
Merrell, Barry	1976–77	10	1	3	4	0
Messier, Mark	1978–79	52	1	10	11	58
Methe, Gerry	1974–75	5	0	1	1	4
Micheletti, Joe	1976–79	142	31	70	101	151

M

	Years	Games	Goals	Assists	Points	Penalty Minutes
Migneault, John	1972–76	258	49	61	110	107
Milani, Tom	1976–77	2	0	0	0	0
Miller, Perry	1974–77	201	31	60	91	309
Miller, Warren	1975–79	238	65	83	148	163
Mio, Eddie	1977–79	44	0	2	2	4
Miszuk, John	1974–77	214	6	66	72	179
Moffatt, Lyle	1975–79	276	53	61	114	244
Mononen, Lauri	1975–77	142	36	50	86	29
Morenz, Brian	1972–76	223	53	57	110	165
Moretto, Angelo	1978–79	18	3	1	4	2
Morgan, Ron	1973–74	4	0	1	1	7
Morin, Wayne	1976–77	13	2	0	2	25
Morris, Bill	1974–75	36	4	8	12	6
Morris, Peter	1975–77	78	7	13	20	36
Morris, Rick (Quick)	1972–78	413	102	90	192	567
Morrison, George	1972–77	361	123	142	265	110
Morrison, Kevin	1973–79	393	125	224	349	462
Morrow, Dave	1978–79	10	2	10	12	29
Mortson, Keke	1972–78	73	13	17	30	102
Mosdell, Wayne	1972–73	9	0	1	1	12
Mott, Darwin	1972–73	1	0	0	0	0
Mott, Morris	1976–77	2	0	1	1	5
Mowat, Bob (Rat)	1974–75	53	9	10	19	34
Muloin, Wayne (Mr. Guts)	1972–76	257	10	43	53	178
Myers, Murray	1972–76	148	37	36	73	44

N

	Years	Games	Goals	Assists	Points	Penalty Minutes
Napier, Mark	1975–78	237	136	118	254	134
Neale, Robbie	1973–75	59	9	14	23	38
Nedomansky, Vaclav	1974–78	252	135	118	253	43
Neeld, Greg	1975–76	17	0	1	1	18
Neilson, Jim	1978–79	35	0	5	5	18
Nesterenko, Eric (Elbows)	1973–74	29	2	5	7	8
Nevin, Bob	1976–77	13	3	2	5	0
Newell, Rick	1974–75	25	0	4	4	39
Newton, Cam (Gambler)	1973–76	102	0	2	2	0
Niekamp, Jim	1972–77	383	16	96	112	484
Nilsson, Kent	1977–79	158	81	135	216	16
Nilsson, Ulf	1974–78	300	140	344	484	341
Nistico, Lou	1973–77	187	44	72	116	375
Noris, Joe	1975–78	198	72	116	188	60
Norris, Jack	1972–76	191	0	9	9	10
Norwich, Craig	1977–79	145	13	74	87	121
Nugent, Kevin	1978–79	25	2	8	10	20

O

	Years	Games	Goals	Assists	Points	Penalty Minutes
O'Connell, Tim	1976–77	16	0	3	3	4
O'Donnell, Fred	1974–76	155	32	26	58	165
O'Donoghue, Dan	1972–76	147	25	35	62	63
Odrowski, Gerry (The Big O)	1972–76	182	16	114	130	230
Olds, Wally	1972–76	89	5	12	17	10
O'Neil, Paul	1978–79	1	0	0	0	0
Orr, Billy	1973–74	44	3	9	12	16
O'Shea, Danny	1974–75	76	16	25	41	47
O'Shea, Kevin	1974–75	68	10	10	20	42
Ouimet, Francois	1975–77	25	1	10	11	12
Ouimet, Ted	1974–75	1	0	0	0	0

Overtime

P

	Years	Games	Goals	Assists	Points	Penalty Minutes
Paiement, Pierre	1972–73	8	1	0	1	18
Paiement, Rosaire	1972–78	455	146	221	367	602
Paille, Marcel	1972–73	15	0	0	0	0
Paradise, Dick	1972–74	144	5	22	27	260
Parent, Bernie	1972–73	63	0	1	1	36
Parizeau, Michel	1972–79	519	142	252	394	318
Park, Jim	1975–78	42	0	2	2	14
Patenaude, Edgar (Rusty)	1972–78	431	159	131	290	368
Patrick, Craig	1976–77	30	6	11	17	6
Patrick, Glenn	1976–77	23	0	4	4	62
Patry, Denis	1974–75	3	1	2	3	2
Patterson, Dennis	1976–77	23	0	2	2	2
Payette, Jean	1972–74	107	19	40	59	52
Peacosh, Gene	1972–77	367	165	165	330	134
Pearson, Mel	1972–73	70	8	12	20	12
Peloffy, Andre	1977–78	10	2	0	2	2
Pelyk, Mike	1974–76	150	24	49	73	238
Pentland, Dwayne	1976–77	29	1	2	3	6
Perkins, Ross	1972–75	225	44	93	137	95
Perreault, Bob	1972–73	1	0	0	0	0
Perry, Brian	1972–75	145	33	31	64	49
Pesut, George	1976–77	17	2	0	2	2
Peters, Garry	1972–74	57	4	12	16	42
Phaneuf, Jean Luc	1975–77	78	10	15	25	6
Pinder, Gerry	1972–78	356	93	141	234	436
Pizunski, Ed	1975–76	1	0	0	0	0
Plante, Jacques	1974–75	31	0	1	1	2
Plante, Michel	1972–74	92	16	14	30	37
Pleau, Larry	1972–79	468	157	215	372	180
Plumb, Ron	1972–79	549	65	262	327	341
Polano, Nick	1972–73	17	0	3	3	24
Popiel, Jan (Pope)	1972–77	296	78	82	160	256
Popiel, Poul	1972–78	467	62	265	327	618
Powis, Lynn	1975–78	153	50	65	115	60
Pratt, Kelly	1973–74	50	4	6	10	50
Prentice, Bill	1972–78	158	8	14	22	265
Preston, Rich	1974–79	388	133	152	285	237
Price, Pat	1974–75	69	5	29	34	54
Primeau, Kevin	1977–78	7	0	1	1	2
Pritchard, Jim	1974–75	2	0	0	0	0
Proceviat, Dick (Goodyear)	1972–77	321	16	90	106	265
Pumple, Rich	1972–75	128	27	30	57	90

R

	Years	Games	Goals	Assists	Points	Penalty Minutes
Raeder, Cap	1975–77	29	0	0	0	2
Ramage, Rob	1978–79	80	12	36	48	165
Rautakallio, Pekka (Rocky)	1975–77	151	15	70	85	16
Reed, Bill	1974–76	40	0	5	5	26
Reichmuth, Craig	1972–75	189	25	25	50	322
Repo, Seppo (The Fox)	1976–77	80	29	31	60	10
Rhiness, Brad	1976–78	70	12	17	29	16
Richardson, Steve	1974–76	72	9	22	31	74
Riggin, Pat	1978–79	46	0	3	3	22
Riihiranta, Heikki	1974–77	187	10	38	48	84
Riley, Ron	1972–73	22	0	5	5	2
Rivers, Wayne	1972–77	357	158	176	334	183
Rizzuto, Garth	1972–74	102	13	14	27	40
Roberto, Phil	1977–78	53	8	20	28	91
Roberts, Doug	1975–77	140	7	31	38	84
Roberts, Gordie	1975–79	311	42	144	186	502
Robertson, Joe	1974–75	29	5	8	13	27
Rochon, Francois	1973–77	255	71	60	131	95

R

	Years	Games	Goals	Assists	Points	Penalty Minutes
Rogers, John	1975–76	44	9	8	17	34
Rogers, Mike	1974–79	396	145	222	367	109
Rollins, Jerry	1975–79	130	9	18	27	378
Rombough, Lorne	1973–74	3	1	2	3	0
Roselle, Bob	1975–76	1	0	0	0	0
Rota, Randy	1976–78	93	17	28	45	20
Rouleau, Michel	1972–75	115	13	35	48	289
Rousseau, Dunc	1972–74	135	26	25	51	114
Roy, Pierre	1972–79	316	22	84	106	864
Ruhnke, Kent	1976–78	72	19	20	39	4
Rupp, Duane	1974–76	114	3	42	45	78
Ruskowski, Terry	1974–79	369	83	254	337	761
Russell, Bob	1975–77	115	20	24	44	60
Rutledge, Wayne	1972–78	175	0	4	4	39
Ryan, Terry	1972–73	76	13	6	19	13
Rycroft, Al	1972–73	7	0	2	2	0
Rydman, Blaine	1972–74	39	0	1	1	90

S

	Years	Games	Goals	Assists	Points	Penalty Minutes
Sacharuk, Larry	1978–79	15	2	9	11	25
St. Sauveur, Claude	1972–79	285	112	112	224	131
Sandbeck, Cal	1977–79	17	1	2	3	41
Sanders, Frank	1972–73	76	8	8	16	94
Sanderson, Derek (Turk)	1972–73	8	3	3	6	69
Sanza, Nick	1975–76	1	0	0	0	0
Sarner, Craig	1975–76	1	0	0	0	0
Sarrazin, Dick	1972–73	68	7	15	22	2
Sather, Glen (Slats)	1976–77	81	19	34	53	77
Scharf, Ted	1972–77	238	16	21	37	343
Schella, John	1972–78	385	39	143	182	844
Schneider, Buzz	1976–77	4	0	0	0	2
Schraefel, Jim	1973–74	33	1	1	2	0
Selby, Brit	1972–75	152	23	51	74	73
Selwood, Brad (Rags)	1972–79	431	42	143	185	556
Semenko, Dave (Sammy)	1977–79	142	16	20	36	298
Sentes, Rick	1972–77	337	137	143	280	233
Serafini, Ron	1975–76	16	0	2	2	15
Serviss, Tom	1972–77	287	38	78	116	101
Shanahan, Sean	1978–79	4	0	0	0	7
Shaw, Jim	1974–76	37	0	0	0	0
Sheehan, Bobby	1972–78	240	75	110	185	45
Sheehy, Tim	1972–78	433	178	173	351	156
Sheridan, John	1974–76	69	18	13	31	20
Sherrit, Jim	1973–76	193	63	72	135	59
Shirton, Glen	1973–74	4	0	0	0	0
Shmyr, John	1972–75	89	2	8	10	58
Shmyr, Paul	1972–79	511	61	248	309	860
Shutt, Byron	1978–79	65	10	7	17	115
Sicinski, Bob	1972–77	353	76	184	260	56
Siltanen, Risto	1978–79	20	3	4	7	4
Simpson, Tom (Shotgun)	1972–77	313	125	84	209	160
Sittler, Gary	1974–75	5	1	1	2	14
Sjoberg, Lars-Erik	1974–78	295	25	169	194	145
Slater, Peter	1972–74	92	13	13	26	89
Sleep, Mike	1975–77	22	4	2	6	6
Sleigher, Louis	1978–79	62	26	12	38	46
Smedsmo, Dale	1975–78	110	10	22	32	291
Smith, Al	1972–79	260	0	10	10	129
Smith, Brian	1972–73	48	7	6	13	19
Smith, Gary (Suitcase)	1978–79	22	0	3	3	0
Smith, Guy	1972–74	39	4	18	12	31
Smith, Rick	1973–76	200	20	89	109	260

S

	Years	Games	Goals	Assists	Points	Penalty Minutes
Smith, Ross	1974–75	15	1	6	7	19
Snell, Ron	1973–75	90	24	25	49	40
Sobchuk, Dennis	1974–79	348	145	186	331	205
Sobchuk, Gene	1974–76	81	24	19	43	37
Speck, Fred	1972–75	123	22	42	64	96
Speer, Bill	1972–74	135	4	26	30	70
Spencer, Irv	1972–74	73	2	28	30	49
Spring, Danny	1973–76	200	39	51	90	38
Spring, Frank	1977–78	13	2	4	6	2
Stanfield, Jack	1972–74	113	9	15	24	10
Stapleton, Pat (Whitey)	1973–78	375	26	212	238	187
Steele, Billy	1975–77	84	11	22	33	21
Stephenson, Bob	1977–79	117	30	30	60	80
Stephenson, Ken	1972–74	106	3	23	26	117
Stevens, Mike	1974–76	76	2	16	18	71
Stewart, John A.	1975–77	95	15	24	39	45
Stewart, John C.	1974–79	271	60	92	152	213
Stewart, Paul	1976–79	65	3	6	9	289
Stoughton, Blaine	1976–79	219	89	90	179	121
Sullivan, Danny	1972–74	2	0	0	0	0
Sullivan, Peter	1975–79	313	125	170	295	107
Sutherland, Bill	1972–74	60	10	21	31	40
Sutherland, Steve	1972–78	379	97	76	173	805
Swain, Garry	1974–77	171	22	33	55	70
Swenson, Cal	1972–74	102	12	25	37	21
Syvret, Dave	1975–77	38	1	11	12	24
Szura, Joe	1972–74	115	21	39	60	29

T

	Years	Games	Goals	Assists	Points	Penalty Minutes
Tajcnar, Rudy	1978–79	2	0	0	0	0
Tamminen, Juhani	1975–77	130	17	43	60	22
Tannahill, Don	1974–77	222	58	76	134	34
Tardif, Marc	1973–79	446	316	350	666	418
Tataryn, Dave	1975–76	23	0	0	0	2
Taylor, Ted	1972–78	421	123	164	287	600
Tebbutt, Greg	1978–79	38	2	5	7	83
Terbenche, Paul	1974–79	277	18	74	92	74
Tetreault, Jean	1974–76	9	1	1	2	0
Thomas, Reg	1973–79	428	121	138	159	199
Tidey, Alex	1975–76	74	16	11	27	46
Titcomb, Gord	1974–75	2	0	1	1	0
Tonelli, John	1975–78	224	64	86	150	278
Topolnisky, Craig	1977–78	10	0	2	2	4
Tremblay, J.C.	1972–79	454	66	358	424	126
Trevelyn, Tom	1974–75	20	0	2	2	4
Trognitz, Willie	1977–78	29	2	1	3	94
Trooien, Jerry	1972–73	2	0	0	0	0
Trottier, Guy	1972–75	174	62	75	137	89
Troy, Jim	1975–78	68	2	0	2	174
Tumlinson, Gord	1972–73	3	0	0	0	0
Turkiewicz, Jim	1974–79	392	25	119	144	234
Turnbull, Frank	1975–78	4	0	0	0	0

U–V

	Years	Games	Goals	Assists	Points	Penalty Minutes
Ullman, Norm	1975–77	144	47	83	130	40
Vaive, Rick	1978–79	75	26	33	59	248
Van Horlick, John	1975–76	2	0	0	0	12
Veneruzzo, Gary	1972–77	348	151	123	274	212
Viau, Pierre	1972–73	4	0	0	0	0
Vien, Mario	1975–76	26	0	0	0	2
Volmar, Doug	1974–75	10	0	1	1	4

W

	Years	Games	Goals	Assists	Points	Penalty Minutes
Wakely, Ernie	1972–79	334	0	7	7	
Walker, Russ	1973–76	214	52	40	92	17
Wall, Bob	1972–76	255	23	89	112	319
Walsh, Brian	1976–77	5	0	2	2	113
Walsh, Ed	1978–79	3	0	0	0	12
Walter, Dave	1973–76	26	2	3	5	0
Walters, Ron	1972–75	166	44	41	85	8
Walton, Mike (Shakey)	1973–76	211	136	145	281	74
Walton, Rob	1973–76	150	40	71	111	148
Ward, Ron (Magic)	1972–77	359	170	210	380	54
Warner, Jim	1978–79	41	6	9	15	103
Warr, Steve	1972–74	72	3	8	11	20
Watson, Bryan (Bugsy)	1978–79	21	0	2	2	79
Watson, Jim	1972–76	231	8	33	41	56
Webster, Tom (Hawkeye)	1972–78	352	220	205	425	228
Weir, Stan	1978–79	68	31	30	61	241
Weir, Wally	1976–79	150	5	24	29	20
West, Steve	1974–79	142	29	50	79	410
Westrum, Pat	1974–78	237	7	45	52	35
Wetzel, Carl	1972–73	1	0	0	0	356
Whidden, Bob	1972–76	98	0	1	1	0
White, Alton	1972–75	145	38	46	84	11
Whitlock, Bobby	1972–76	244	81	98	179	45
Widing, Juha	1977–78	71	18	24	42	155
Wilkie, Ian	1972–74	33	0	0	0	8
Wilkins, Barry	1976–78	130	6	45	51	2
Williams, Butch	1976–77	29	3	10	13	154
Williams, Tommy (Bomber)	1972–74	139	31	58	89	16
Williamson, Gary	1973–74	9	2	6	8	20
Willis, Hal	1972–74	92	4	23	27	0
Winograd, Bob	1972–77	60	1	12	13	183
Wiste, Jim	1972–76	228	64	108	172	23
Wood, Wayne	1974–79	104	0	4	4	80
Worthy, Chris	1973–76	82	0	0	0	32
Woytowich, Bob	1972–76	242	9	51	60	22
Wyrozub, Randy	1975–76	55	11	14	25	140
						8

Y–Z

	Years	Games	Goals	Assists	Points	Penalty Minutes
Yakiwchuk, Dale	1978–79	4	0	0	0	0
Young, Bill	1972–74	142	28	30	58	140
Young, Howie	1974–77	98	17	25	42	109
Zaine, Rod	1972–75	214	11	33	44	58
Zanussi, Joe	1972–74	149	7	43	50	106
Zimmerman, Lynn	1975–78	28	0	1	1	4
Zrymiak, Jerry	1972–77	156	7	40	47	112
Zuk, Wayne	1973–74	2	0	0	0	0
Zuke, Mike	1976–78	86	26	38	64	49

ALL-TIME REGULAR-SEASON GOALTENDER REGISTRY

	Years	GP	MIN	GA	W	L	T	SO	GAA
Abrahamsson, Christer	1974–77	102	5739	342	41	46	7	3	3.58
Archambault, Yves	1972–74	11	523	44	2	7	0	0	5.05
Aubry, Serge	1972–77	142	7511	470	63	55	5	4	3.75
Berglund, Bill	1973–75	5	216	13	2	1	0	0	3.61
Binkley, Les	1972–76	80	4228	261	30	36	2	1	3.72
Blanchet, Bob	1974–76	4	211	11	2	2	0	1	3.13
Blum, Frank	1972–74	7	158	8	1	0	0	0	3.02
Broderick, Ken	1976–78	73	3938	259	29	31	2	4	3.95
Brodeur, Richard	1972–79	305	17101	1037	165	114	12	8	3.64
Bromley, Gary	1976–78	37	3489	203	31	21	3	1	3.49
Brown, Andy	1974–77	86	4777	314	25	50	3	3	3.55
Brown, Ken	1972–75	52	2500	138	20	19	0	3	3.55
Burchell, Randy	1976–77	5	136	8	1	0	0	0	3.53
Caron, Jacques	1975–77	26	1422	69	14	6	3	3	2.91
Cheevers, Gerry	1972–76	191	11352	591	99	78	9	14	3.12
Corsi, Jim	1977–79	63	3380	208	26	27	1	3	3.69
Cottringer, Tom	1972–73	2	122	8	1	1	0	0	3.93
Coutu, Rich	1973–76	24	1416	97	9	13	1	0	4.11
Curran, Mike	1972–77	130	7377	423	63	50	8	7	3.44
Daley, Joe	1972–79	308	17835	1002	167	113	13	12	3.37
Deguise, Michel	1973–76	50	2585	156	18	18	3	1	3.62
Desjardins, Gerry	1974–75	41	2282	162	9	28	1	0	4.26
Dion, Michel	1974–79	149	7750	450	62	66	6	5	3.48
Donnelly, Peter	1972–76	100	5559	344	44	44	2	5	3.71
Doyle, Gary	1973–74	1	60	4	1	0	0	0	4.00
Dryden, Dave	1974–79	242	13820	808	112	113	10	8	3.51
Dumas, Rich	1974–75	1	1	0	0	0	0	0	0.00
Dyck, Ed	1974–75	32	1692	123	3	21	3	0	4.36
Gardner, George	1972–74	79	4423	287	23	45	5	1	3.89
Garrett, John	1973–79	323	18919	1110	148	151	15	14	3.52
Gill, Andre	1972–74	46	2512	164	8	31	2	0	3.92
Gillow, Russ	1972–76	109	5623	333	37	47	6	4	3.50
Grahame, Ron	1973–77	143	8888	425	102	37	3	12	2.99
Gratton, Gilles	1972–75	161	9102	560	81	66	7	4	3.69
Grigg, Chris	1975–76	2	80	13	0	0	0	0	9.75
Hebenton, Clay	1975–77	58	3209	229	17	30	3	0	4.28
Hoganson, Paul	1973–78	143	7244	436	44	71	4	5	4.11
Holden, Bill	1973–74	2	70	4	0	1	0	0	3.43
Holmquist, Leif	1975–76	19	1079	54	6	9	3	0	3.00
Hughes, Bill	1972–73	3	170	11	0	1	1	0	3.88
Humphreys, Ed	1975–77	30	1681	101	14	13	1	1	3.60
Inness, Gary	1977–79	63	3459	251	17	36	4	0	4.35
Johnson, Bob	1975–76	42	2377	144	17	22	1	1	3.63
Junkin, Joe	1973–75	69	3961	234	27	32	4	2	3.68
Kampurri, Hannu	1978–79	2	90	10	0	1	0	0	6.67
Kiely, John	1975–76	22	1087	78	6	8	1	0	4.31
Kurt, Gary	1972–77	176	9932	690	72	86	7	3	4.17
Landon, Bruce	1972–77	122	6695	386	50	50	9	2	3.46
LaPointe, Norm	1975–78	77	4105	280	30	37	3	2	4.09
Larsson, Curt	1974–77	68	3820	265	30	30	2	1	4.16
Lemelin, Jacques	1972–73	9	435	29	3	4	1	0	4.00
Levasseur, Louis	1975–79	85	4916	281	37	36	8	5	3.43
Liut, Mike	1977–79	81	4396	270	31	39	4	3	3.69
Lockett, Ken	1976–77	45	2397	148	18	19	1	1	3.70
Mattson, Markus	1977–79	68	3767	241	30	29	3	0	3.84

	Years	GP	MIN	GA	W	L	T	SO	GAA
McCartan, Jack	1972–75	42	2263	139	16	19	1	1	3.69
McDuffe, Peter	1977–78	12	539	39	1	6	1	0	4.34
McLeod, Don	1972–78	332	18926	1051	157	144	15	11	3.33
McLeod, Jim	1972–75	97	5176	324	32	51	3	2	3.76
Menard, Paul	1972–73	1	45	5	0	1	0	0	6.67
Mio, Eddie	1977–79	44	2210	148	15	20	1	2	4.02
Newton, Cam	1973–76	102	6106	352	48	51	3	2	3.46
Norris, Jack	1972–76	191	11030	582	86	82	12	5	3.16
Ouimet, Ted	1974–75	1	20	3	0	0	0	0	9.00
Paille, Marcel	1972–73	15	611	49	2	8	0	0	4.81
Parent, Bernie	1972–73	63	3653	220	33	28	0	2	3.61
Park, Jim	1975–78	54	2883	178	23	23	4	1	3.70
Perreault, Bob	1972–73	1	60	2	1	0	0	0	2.00
Plante, Jacques	1974–75	31	1592	88	15	14	1	1	3.32
Raeder, Cap	1975–77	29	1428	77	12	11	1	2	3.24
Riggin, Pat	1978–79	46	2511	158	16	22	5	1	3.78
Rutledge, Wayne	1972–78	175	10372	563	93	72	7	6	3.25
Sanza, Nick	1975–76	1	20	5	0	0	0	0	15.00
Shaw, Jim	1974–76	37	1832	133	11	16	2	0	4.36
Smith, Al	1972–79	260	15389	834	141	98	15	10	3.25
Smith, Gary	1978–79	22	1290	92	7	13	1	0	4.28
Sullivan, Danny	1972–74	2	120	10	1	1	0	0	5.00
Tataryn, Dave	1975–76	23	1261	100	7	12	1	0	4.76
Tumlinson, Gord	1972–73	3	106	10	0	2	0	0	5.66
Turnbull, Frank	1975–78	4	166	15	0	2	0	0	5.42
Vien, Mario	1975–76	26	1228	105	4	14	3	0	5.13
Wakely, Ernie	1972–79	334	19331	1064	164	137	21	16	3.30
Walsh, Ed	1978–79	3	144	9	0	2	0	0	3.75
Wetzel, Carl	1972–73	1	60	3	0	1	0	0	3.00
Whidden, Bob	1972–76	98	5725	327	34	51	9	2	3.43
Wilkie, Ian	1972–74	33	1766	118	15	13	1	1	4.01
Wood, Wayne	1974–79	104	5167	285	38	36	3	2	3.88
Worthy, Chris	1973–76	82	4368	199	27	39	4	3	3.97
Zimmerman, Lynn	1975–78	28	1661	115	12	15	1	0	4.15

ALL-TIME PLAYOFF PLAYER REGISTRY AND STATISTICS

A

	GP	G	A	PTS	PIM
Abgrall, Dennis	4	2	0	2	5
Abrahamsson, Chris	3	0	0	0	0
Abrahamsson, Thommie	28	2	7	9	15
Adduono, Ray	28	12	18	30	38
Ahearn, Kevin	14	1	2	3	9
Alley, Steve	5	1	0	1	5
Amodeo, Mike	27	1	7	8	59
Anderson, Ron C.	1	0	0	0	0
Andrea, Paul	14	3	8	11	2
Antonovich, Mike	57	21	20	41	22
Arbour, John	28	3	13	16	63
Archambault, Yves	3	0	0	0	0
Arndt, Danny	8	0	0	0	0
Ash, Bob	17	1	4	5	6
Asmundson, Duke	29	4	5	9	21
Aubry, Serge	3	0	0	0	0

B

	GP	G	A	PTS	PIM
Backstrom, Ralph	38	10	18	28	12
Baird, Ken	16	4	6	10	30
Ball, Blake	2	0	0	0	2
Ball, Terry	28	5	8	13	14
Bailey, Garnet	2	0	0	0	4
Baltimore, Bryon	19	0	1	1	9
Barrie, Doug	12	1	1	2	31
Bateman, Jamie	5	0	0	0	16
Baxter, Paul	30	6	11	17	94
Beaton, Frank	10	12	2	4	31
Beaudin, Norm	31	18	19	37	14
Beaudoin, Serge	10	2	0	2	56
Bennett, Wendell	5	1	2	3	6
Benzelock, Jim	21	2	2	4	36
Bergman, Thommie	13	3	10	13	8
Bernier, Jean	32	4	7	11	4
Bernier, Serge	50	28	46	74	41
Bilodeau, Gilles	6	0	0	0	52
Binkley, Les	10	0	0	0	0
Black, Milt	18	2	4	6	10
Blackburn, Don	12	3	6	9	6
Block, Ken	16	0	6	6	8
Blum, Frank	2	0	0	0	9
Boddy, Greg	4	1	2	3	14
Boland, Mike	1	0	0	0	12
Bolduc, Dan	30	3	10	13	8
Bond, Kerry	7	1	0	1	11
Bordeleau, Christian	53	16	34	50	16
Bordeleau, Paulin	27	16	15	31	14
Borgeson, Don	8	1	2	3	2
Boudreau, Michel	2	0	0	0	0
Boudrias, Andre	28	3	14	17	10
Boyd, Bob	7	0	0	0	4
Boyd, Jim	10	4	3	7	4
Boyer, Wally	14	4	2	6	4
Brackenbury, Curtis	48	5	9	14	160
Bradley, Brian	6	0	1	1	2
Brewer, Carl	12	0	4	4	11
Brindley, Doug	14	0	1	1	8
Broderick, Ken	5	0	0	0	0
Brodeur, Richard	51	0	2	2	4
Bromley, Gary	5	0	0	0	2
Brubaker, Jeff	3	0	0	0	12
Buchanan, Ron	14	7	3	10	2
Burgess, Don	22	4	9	13	4
Busniuk, Ron	39	2	5	7	132
Butters, Bill	34	1	4	5	87
Byers, Mike	25	10	11	21	20

C

	GP	G	A	PTS	PIM
Cadle, Brian	3	0	0	0	0
Caffrey, Terry	8	3	7	10	6
Callighen, Brett	23	9	13	22	38
Campbell, Bryan	8	3	2	5	6
Campbell, Scott	16	1	3	4	33
Campeau, Richard	4	1	0	1	17
Cardiff, Jim	4	0	0	0	11
Cardwell, Steve	15	0	1	1	34
Carleton, Wayne	25	8	21	29	24
Carlson, Jack	28	3	4	7	68
Carlson, Steve	29	3	8	11	23
Carlyle, Steve	5	0	1	1	4
Caron, Jacques	1	0	0	0	0
Carroll, Greg	4	1	2	3	0
Cassolato, Tony	7	0	0	0	8
Charlebois, Bob	16	2	1	3	8
Cheevers, Gerry	19	0	0	0	10
Chipperfield, Ron	28	15	15	30	14
Christiansen, Keith	15	1	1	2	2
Clackson, Kim	33	0	7	7	138
Clearwater, Ray	18	2	3	5	10
Climie, Ron	15	4	0	4	2
Cloutier, Real	48	33	30	63	31
Coates, Brian	21	0	3	3	41
Conacher, Brian	5	1	3	4	4
Connelly, Wayne	36	16	15	31	16
Connor, Cam	23	5	4	9	92
Constantin, Charles	20	0	2	2	19
Cooley, Gaye	1	0	0	0	0
Cormier, Michel	5	1	0	1	2
Corsi, Jim	1	0	0	0	0
Cote, Alain	15	1	2	3	2
Cote, Roger	2	0	0	0	0
Crashley, Bart	6	0	2	2	2
Cuddie, Steve	26	1	9	10	32
Cunniff, John	18	2	2	4	2
Cunningham, Rick	21	1	6	7	33
Curran, Mike	7	0	0	0	10

D

	GP	G	A	PTS	PIM
Daley, Joe	49	0	3	3	30
Danby, John	19	1	1	2	0
Deadmarsh, Butch	8	0	1	1	14
DeMarco, Ab	1	0	0	0	0
Devine, Kevin	18	4	4	8	50
Dillabough, Bob	9	1	0	1	0
Dillon, Wayne	18	9	10	19	13
Dion, Michel	7	0	0	0	0
Dobek, Bob	16	1	2	3	4
Dorey, Jim	51	5	33	38	131
Douglas, Jordy	10	4	0	4	23
Driscoll, Peter	23	3	11	14	49
Dryden, Dave	18	0	0	0	0
Dube, Norm	24	5	14	19	17
Dubois, Michel	2	0	1	1	0
Dudley, Rick	4	0	1	1	7
Dunn, Dave	29	5	6	11	23
Durbano, Steve	4	0	2	2	16

E

	GP	G	A	PTS	PIM
Earl, Tom	46	3	11	14	28
Edur, Tom	13	3	4	7	0
Erickson, Grant	24	2	5	7	2
Erikkson, Bengt	10	1	4	5	0
Evans, Chris	10	5	5	10	4

F

	GP	G	A	PTS	PIM
Falkenberg, Bob	28	1	5	6	24
Farda, Richard	1	0	0	0	0
Featherstone, Tony	6	2	1	3	2
Ferguson, Norm	26	10	9	19	9
Fitchner, Bob	37	6	12	18	34
Fleming, Reggie	12	0	4	4	12
Flett, Bill	15	5	4	9	4
Fonteyne, Val	5	1	0	1	0
Forbes, Dave	3	0	1	1	7
Ford, Mike	34	5	25	30	20
Fortier, Florent	1	0	9	0	0
Fotiu, Nick	20	5	2	7	84
French, John	44	14	25	39	6
Ftorek, Robbie	13	6	10	16	10

G

	GP	G	A	PTS	PIM
Gallant, Gord	14	2	2	4	98
Gambucci, Gary	12	4	0	4	6
Gardner, George	3	0	0	0	0
Garrett, John	32	0	1	1	16
Gartner, Mike	3	0	0	0	2
Gaudette, Andre	9	0	1	1	0
Gellard, Sam	3	0	0	0	0
Geoffrion, Danny	4	1	2	3	2
Gibbons, Brian	22	3	7	10	26
Gibbons, Gerard	1	0	0	0	0
Gibson, Jack	14	2	3	5	16
Gilbert, Jeannot	11	3	6	9	2
Gill, Andre	11	0	0	0	4
Gilligan, Bill	3	1	0	1	0
Gillow, Russ	9	0	0	0	0
Gilmore, Tom	10	2	7	9	17
Globensky, Allan	2	1	0	1	0
Goldsworthy, Bill	4	1	1	2	11
Goldthorpe, Billy	3	0	0	0	25
Gordon, Don	18	4	8	12	4
Gorman, Dave	9	1	3	4	24
Grahame, Ron	36	0	2	2	2
Gratton, Gilles	13	0	0	0	5
Gratton, Jean-Guy	14	1	1	2	4
Gray, John	23	3	8	11	37
Green, Ted	61	2	16	18	59
Gresdal, Gary	1	0	0	0	14
Gretzky, Wayne	13	10	10	20	2
Grierson, Don	17	1	5	6	29
Gruen, Danny	3	2	0	2	0
Guindon, Robert	64	24	19	43	33
Guite, Pierre	33	6	1	7	29
Gustaffson, Bengt	2	1	2	3	0

H

	GP	G	A	PTS	PIM
Haas, Derek	1	0	0	0	0
Hale, Larry	65	4	15	19	22
Hall, Del	5	2	3	5	0
Hall, Murray	54	21	17	38	32
Hamilton, Al	26	5	11	16	29
Hampson, Ted	33	8	14	22	18
Hangsleben, Al	47	4	12	16	97
Hansis, Ron	14	2	2	4	8
Hanson, Dave	6	0	1	1	48
Harbaruk, Nick	13	3	1	4	10
Hardy, Joe	27	4	10	14	13
Hargreaves, Jim	15	1	0	1	8
Hargreaves, Ted	4	0	1	1	10
Harris, Duke	28	7	7	14	6
Harris, Hugh	16	2	9	11	25
Harrison, Jim	8	1	3	4	13
Heatley, Murray	10	1	0	1	2
Hedberg, Anders	42	35	28	63	30
Heggedal, Howie	1	0	0	0	0
Heindl, Billy	5	0	1	1	2
Heiskala, Earl	5	1	1	2	4
Henderson, Paul	5	1	1	2	0
Herriman, Don	4	1	0	1	14
Hickey, Pat	17	3	4	7	16
Hicks, Glenn	7	1	1	2	4
Hillman, Larry	17	1	5	6	40
Hillman, Wayne	10	0	2	2	18
Hinse, Andre	42	15	16	31	28
Hislop, Jamie	7	2	5	7	4
Hodgson, Ted	9	1	3	4	13
Hoekstra, Ed	9	1	2	3	0
Hoganson, Dale	27	2	6	8	15
Hoganson, Paul	5	0	1	1	0
Holbrook, Terry	8	0	1	1	0
Hopiavouri, Ralph	12	0	2	2	6
Hornung, Larry	37	2	12	14	6
Horton, Bill	9	0	1	1	10
Houle, Rejean	20	12	6	18	10
Howe, Gordie	78	28	43	71	115
Howe, Mark	74	41	51	92	48
Howe, Marty	75	9	14	23	85
Howell, Harry	7	1	0	1	12
Huck, Fran	16	3	15	18	14
Hughes, Brent	22	2	9	11	18
Hughes, Frank	54	24	16	40	33
Hughes, John	10	1	1	2	14
Hull, Bobby	60	43	37	80	38
Humphreys, Ed	1	0	0	0	0
Hunter, Dave	13	2	3	5	42
Hurley, Paul	25	0	8	8	18
Huston, Ron	5	1	1	2	0
Hutchison, Dave	3	0	0	0	2
Hyndman, Mike	6	0	3	3	17

I

	GP	G	A	PTS	PIM
Inkpen, Dave	5	0	1	1	4
Irwin, Glenn	18	0	2	2	17
Israelson, Larry	3	0	0	0	0

J

	GP	G	A	PTS	PIM
Jacques, Jeff	6	0	4	4	2
Jarrett, Gary	22	9	8	17	34
Jarry, Pierre	5	1	0	1	4
Jodzio, Rick	2	0	0	0	14
Johnson, Bob	2	0	0	0	0
Johnson, Danny	18	5	1	6	5
Johnson, Jim	16	3	5	8	6
Jordan, Ric	17	0	0	0	14
Joyal, Eddie	5	2	0	2	4

K

	GP	G	A	PTS	PIM
Kannegiesser, Gordon	12	0	3	3	8
Karlander, Al	21	3	7	10	6
Keeler, Mike	1	0	0	0	0
Keogan, Murray	5	0	1	1	0
Keon, Dave	36	12	23	36	8
Ketola, Veli Pekka	13	7	5	12	2
King, Steve	17	0	4	4	18
Kirk, Gavin	38	14	19	33	33
Klatt, Billy	16	4	5	9	23
Krake, Skip	19	2	4	6	66
Kryskow, Dave	9	4	4	8	2
Kurt, Gary	4	0	0	0	0

L

	GP	G	A	PTS	PIM
Labossiere, Gord	50	16	28	44	46
Labraaten, Dan	24	8	18	26	23
Lacombe, Francois	54	5	10	15	36
Lacroix, Andre	48	14	29	43	30
Lagace, Pierre	3	0	1	1	2
Laing, Bill	4	0	1	1	4
Landon, Bruce	8	0	1	1	0
Langevin, Dave	13	0	1	1	25
Langway, Rod	4	0	0	0	9
Lapierre, Camille	4	0	2	2	0
LaPointe, Norm	4	0	0	0	0
Lariviere, Garry	38	3	15	18	18
Larose, Claude	4	2	1	3	0
Larose, Ray	8	0	0	0	2
Larsson, Curt	3	0	0	0	2
Larway, Don	38	12	8	20	33
Laughton, Mike	10	4	1	5	0
Lawson, Danny	26	6	9	15	25
LeBlanc, J.P.	6	0	5	5	2
Leclerc, Rene	34	10	11	21	52
Leduc, Bob	17	4	8	12	46
Leduc, Rich	16	3	8	11	20
Legge, Barry	10	0	5	5	12
Legge, Randy	10	0	0	0	18
Leiter, Bobby	3	2	0	2	0
Lesuk, Bill	50	7	11	18	48
Levasseur, Louis	15	0	1	1	4
Ley, Rick	73	7	33	40	142
Liddington, Bob	18	6	5	11	11
Lilyholm, Len	5	1	0	1	0
Lindh, Mats	33	4	9	13	6
Lindstrom, Willy	51	26	22	48	50
Linseman, Kenny	5	2	2	4	15
Liut, Mike	3	0	2	2	9
Lockett, Ken	5	0	0	0	0
Lomenda, Mark	9	3	1	4	17
Long, Barry	43	3	13	16	20
Lukowich, Bernie	10	3	4	7	8
Lukowich, Morris	27	15	13	28	58
Luksa, Chuck	3	0	0	0	7
Lund, Larry	59	20	45	65	116
Lunde, Len	5	0	1	1	0
Lyle, George	26	6	6	12	42

M

	GP	G	A	PTS	PIM
MacDonald, Blair	43	20	21	41	12
MacGregor, Bruce	4	0	1	1	0
MacGregor, Gary	3	0	0	0	4
MacKinnon, Paul	10	2	5	7	4
MacMillan, Bobby	16	2	6	8	4
MacNeil, Bernie	3	0	0	0	4
MacSweyn, Ralph	6	1	2	3	4
Maggs, Darryl	34	5	9	14	95
Mahovlich, Frank	9	4	1	5	2
Marrin, Peter	14	0	8	8	4
Marsh, Peter	7	3	0	3	0
Martin, Tom	22	8	13	21	4
Mavety, Larry	24	4	11	15	52
Maxwell, Bryan	6	0	1	1	33
McAneely, Bob	7	2	0	2	0
McAneely, Ted	4	0	0	0	0
McCallum, Dunc	10	2	3	5	6
McCartan, Jack	4	0	1	1	0
McCaskill, Ted	6	2	3	5	12
McDonald, Ab	18	2	6	8	4
McDonald, Brian	26	6	5	11	61
McDonough, Al	8	3	1	4	2
McKay, Ray	7	0	1	1	8
McKenzie, Brian	5	0	1	1	0
McKenzie, Johnny	33	14	15	29	42
McLeod, Al	26	2	9	11	19
McLeod, Don	31	0	1	1	6
McMahon, Mike	32	1	14	15	13
McNamee, Pete	18	1	2	3	32
Melrose, Barry	5	0	1	1	10
Methe, Gerry	2	0	0	0	0
Micheletti, Joe	18	0	11	11	6
Migneault, John	8	0	0	0	0
Miller, Perry	20	4	6	10	27
Miller, Warren	34	1	10	11	56
Mio, Eddie	3	0	0	0	0
Miszuk, John	10	0	1	1	10
Moffatt, Lyle	49	13	11	24	46
Mononen, Lauri	5	1	3	4	2
Morenz, Brian	21	2	4	6	19
Morgan, Ron	2	1	0	1	0
Morris, Peter	3	0	1	1	7
Morris, Rick	27	4	5	9	52
Morrison, George	38	14	17	31	14
Morrison, Kevin	28	2	15	17	22
Mortson, Keke	12	0	4	4	16
Mowat, Bob	4	0	0	0	0
Muloin, Wayne	20	2	4	6	18
Myers, Murray	2	0	0	0	0

N

	GP	G	A	PTS	PIM
Napier, Mark	5	0	2	2	14
Neale, Robbie	5	0	0	0	4
Nedomansky, Vaclav	6	3	1	4	9
Newell, Rick	5	0	1	1	2
Newton, Cam	11	0	0	0	0
Niekamp, Jim	16	2	2	4	18
Nilsson, Kent	19	5	19	24	14
Nilsson, Ulf	42	14	53	67	51
Nistico, Lou	6	6	1	7	19
Noris, Joe	18	4	5	9	12
Norris, Jack	10	0	0	0	2
Norwich, Craig	3	0	1	1	4

O

	GP	G	A	PTS	PIM
O'Donnell, Fred	20	2	5	7	35
O'Donoghue, Don	4	0	1	1	0
Odrowski, Gerry	11	1	4	5	6
Olds, Wally	9	0	2	2	4
Orr, Billy	12	1	0	1	6
O'Shea, Danny	11	0	0	0	6
O'Shea, Kevin	1	0	0	0	0

P

	GP	G	A	PTS	PIM
Paiement, Rosaire	44	13	22	35	72
Paille, Marcel	1	0	0	0	0
Paradise, Dick	12	0	1	1	8
Parent, Bernie	1	0	0	0	0
Parizeau, Michel	33	10	14	24	24
Park, Jim	6	0	1	1	0
Patenaude, Edgar	10	1	6	7	22
Patrick, Glenn	2	0	0	0	0
Peacosh, Gene	30	12	9	21	27
Pearson, Mel	5	2	0	2	0
Peloffy, Andre	2	0	0	0	0
Pentland, Dwayne	2	0	0	0	0
Perkins, Ross	5	1	3	4	2
Perry, Brian	6	1	2	3	6
Pinder, Gerry	18	5	10	15	40
Plante, Michel	4	0	0	0	2
Pleau, Larry	66	29	22	51	37
Plumb, Ron	41	5	15	20	48
Popiel, Jan	26	9	6	15	16
Popiel, Poul	71	7	47	54	118
Powis, Lynn	13	7	5	12	9
Prentice, Bill	41	8	17	25	24
Preston, Rich	51	16	22	38	39
Primeau, Kevin	2	0	0	0	2
Proceviat, Dick	20	0	4	4	12
Pumple, Rich	9	3	5	8	11

R

	GP	G	A	PTS	PIM
Raeder, Cap	15	0	1	1	0
Rautakallio, Pekka	5	0	2	2	0
Rhiness, Brad	5	0	1	1	0
Riihiranta, Heikki	4	0	4	4	6
Riley, Ron	2	0	0	0	0
Rivers, Wayne	24	8	6	14	14
Rizzuto, Garth	14	0	1	1	14
Roberto, Phil	4	1	0	1	20
Roberts, Doug	19	1	1	2	8
Roberts, Gordie	46	4	20	24	81
Rochon, Francois	14	2	2	4	0
Rogers, Mike	46	13	21	34	14
Rota, Randy	10	4	3	7	4
Rouleau, Michel	3	0	0	0	4
Rousseau, Dunc	18	3	2	5	2
Roy, Pierre	23	1	12	13	76
Ruhnke, Kent	5	2	0	2	0
Rupp, Duane	7	0	2	2	0
Ruskowski, Terry	52	18	36	54	174
Russell, Bob	5	1	0	1	0
Rutledge, Wayne	16	0	0	0	2
Ryan, Terry	5	0	2	2	0
Rydman, Blaine	1	0	0	0	0

S

	GP	G	A	PTS	PIM
St. Sauveur, Claude	5	1	0	1	0
Sandbeck, Cal	5	0	0	0	10
Sanders, Frank	4	0	1	1	0
Sather, Glen	5	1	1	2	2
Scharf, Ted	14	0	0	0	5
Schella, John	66	4	25	29	143
Schraefel, Jim	5	0	3	3	0
Selby, Brit	23	4	7	11	15
Selwood, Brad	63	6	12	18	81
Semenko, Dave	16	4	2	6	37
Sentes, Rick	41	14	5	22	45
Serviss, Tom	11	0	0	0	0
Shaw, Jim	5	0	0	0	0
Sheehan, Bobby	5	1	3	4	0
Sheehy, Tim	39	16	21	37	26
Sherrit, Jim	27	8	10	18	8
Shmyr, John	3	0	1	1	2
Shmyr, Paul	43	5	18	23	107
Shutt, Byron	3	1	1	2	14
Sicinski, Bob	34	6	11	17	6
Siltanen, Risto	11	0	9	9	4
Simpson, Tom	22	6	2	8	5
Sjoberg, Lars-Erik	52	1	22	23	42
Slater, Peter	6	0	0	0	2
Sleep, Mike	3	0	0	0	0
Smedsmo, Dale	2	0	1	1	0
Smith, Al	35	0	1	1	14
Smith, Brian	10	0	2	2	0
Smith, Gary	10	0	0	0	0
Smith, Guy	11	2	0	2	4
Smith, Rick	23	2	8	10	28
Snell, Ron	4	0	0	0	0
Sobchuk, Dennis	25	11	8	19	12
Sobchuk, Gene	5	0	0	0	0
Speck, Fred	6	3	2	5	2
Spencer, Irv	4	0	0	0	4
Spring, Danny	6	1	2	3	0
Stanfield, Jack	16	1	0	1	2
Stapleton, Pat	34	2	21	23	38
Steele, Billy	2	0	0	0	0
Stephenson, Ken	8	1	3	4	18
Stevens, Mike	5	0	1	1	0
Stewart, John A.	3	0	0	0	0
Stewart, John C.	6	1	1	2	0
Stoughton, Blaine	11	4	6	10	6
Sullivan, Peter	52	21	32	53	8
Sutherland, Bill	18	5	9	14	13
Sutherland, Steve	52	9	6	15	12

S

	GP	G	A	PTS	PIM
Swain, Garry	25	3	5	8	56
Swenson, Cal	15	1	5	6	7
Szura, Joe	12	0	0	0	0

T

Tamminen, Juhani	1	0	0	0	0
Tannahill, Don	20	4	9	13	8
Tardif, Marc	44	27	32	58	35
Taylor, Ted	63	18	21	39	147
Terbenche, Paul	26	2	8	10	10
Thomas, Reg	19	9	10	19	8
Tidey, Alex	11	3	6	9	10
Tonelli, John	34	11	14	25	38
Tremblay, J.C.	34	2	23	25	4
Trottier, Guy	17	6	7	13	4
Troy, Jim	4	0	0	0	29
Turkiewicz, Jim	11	1	3	4	0

U–V

Ullman, Norm	9	1	6	7	2
Veneruzzo, Gary	18	5	0	5	11

W

Wakely, Ernie	31	0	0	0	2
Walker, Russ	13	2	0	2	46
Wall, Bob	26	1	8	9	8
Walton, Mike	23	20	15	35	26
Ward, Ron	13	3	4	7	4
Warner, Jim	1	0	0	0	0
Warr, Steve	4	0	0	0	0
Watson, Bryan	3	0	1	1	2
Watson, Jim	22	2	4	6	20
Webster, Tom	43	28	26	54	19
Weir, Stan	12	2	5	7	2
Weir, Wally	32	2	8	10	67
West, Steve	18	3	3	6	2
Westrum, Pat	9	0	2	2	21
White, Alton	6	1	0	1	0
Widing, Juha	5	0	1	1	0
Wilkie, Ian	1	0	0	0	0
Wilkins, Barry	4	0	1	1	2
Williams, Tommy	19	6	14	20	12
Williamson, Gary	12	0	0	0	0
Wiste, Jim	14	3	9	12	13
Wood, Wayne	1	0	0	0	0
Worthy, Chris	4	0	0	0	0
Woytowich, Bob	18	1	1	2	4

Y–Z

Young, Bill	5	1	1	2	4
Zaine, Rod	18	2	1	3	2
Zanussi, Joe	18	2	5	7	6
Zimmerman, Lynn	4	0	0	0	0
Zrymiak, Jerry	2	1	0	1	2
Zuke, Mike	5	2	3	5	0

ALL-TIME PLAYOFF GOALTENDER REGISTRY

	GP	MIN	GA	W	L	SO	GAA
Abrahamsson, Christer	3	91	5	0	1	0	3.33
Archambault, Yves	3	153	11	0	2	0	4.31
Aubry, Serge	3	18	1	0	0	0	3.33
Binkley, Les	10	464	39	3	6	0	5.17
Blum, Frank	2	120	15	0	2	0	7.50
Broderick, Ken	5	228	12	1	3	0	3.17
Brodeur, Richard	51	2949	177	26	23	3	3.60
Bromley, Gary	5	268	7	4	0	0	1.57
Caron, Jacques	1	14	3	0	1	0	12.86
Cheevers, Gerry	19	1151	63	7	12	0	3.28
Cooley, Gaye	1	1	0	0	0	0	0.00
Corsi, Jim	2	66	7	0	1	0	6.36
Curran, Mike	7	379	23	2	5	0	3.64
Daley, Joe	49	2706	149	30	15	2	3.30
Dion, Michel	7	371	22	2	4	0	3.56
Dryden, Dave	18	958	63	6	11	0	3.95
Gardner, George	3	116	11	1	2	0	5.69
Garrett, John	32	1816	124	15	15	1	4.10
Gill, Andre	11	614	38	6	5	0	3.71
Gillow, Russ	9	346	17	1	2	0	2.95
Grahame, Ron	36	2158	116	22	14	4	3.23
Gratton, Gilles	13	662	37	5	5	0	3.35
Hoganson, Paul	5	348	17	3	2	1	2.93
Humphreys, Ed	1	20	0	0	0	0	0.00
Johnson, Bob	2	120	8	0	2	0	4.00
Kurt, Gary	4	207	12	1	2	0	3.48
Landon, Bruce	8	389	21	4	2	0	3.24
LaPointe, Norm	4	273	16	0	3	0	3.52
Larsson, Curt	3	130	7	2	0	0	3.23
Levasseur, Louis	13	778	39	8	5	1	3.01
Liut, Mike	3	179	10	1	2	0	3.35
Lockett, Ken	5	260	19	1	3	0	4.38
McCartan, Jack	4	213	14	1	2	0	3.94
McLeod, Don	31	1786	96	18	13	1	3.23
Mio, Eddie	3	90	6	0	0	0	4.00
Newton, Cam	11	546	40	2	6	0	4.39
Norris, Jack	10	509	36	2	7	0	4.24
Paille, Marcel	1	26	5	0	1	0	11.54
Parent, Bernie	1	70	3	0	1	0	2.57
Park, Jim	6	294	12	3	2	2	2.45
Raeder, Cap	15	879	38	7	8	2	3.24
Rutledge, Wayne	16	694	42	9	6	0	2.88
Shaw, Jim	5	262	18	2	2	0	4.12
Smith, Al	35	1947	124	18	15	1	3.82
Smith, Gary	10	563	35	8	2	0	3.73
Wakely, Ernie	31	1740	109	15	16	2	3.76
Wilkie, Ian	1	41	4	0	1	0	5.85
Wood, Wayne	1	29	3	0	0	0	6.21
Worthy, Chris	4	206	15	1	2	0	4.37
Zimmerman, Lynn	4	239	21	1	2	0	5.27

ALL-TIME WHA COACH REGISTRY

REGULAR SEASON	W	L	T	PCT
Bathgate, Andy	21	37	1	.364
Baun, Bob	15	35	5	.318
Blackburn, Don	18	23	3	.443
Boileau, Marc	74	64	5	.535
Brophy, John	32	42	6	.438
Crozier, Joe	109	117	13	.483
Demers, Jacques	146	148	22	.497
Dineen, Bill	318	199	28	.609
Drake, Clare	18	28	2	.396
Filion, Maurice	45	46	6	.495
Gendron, Jean-Guy	96	59	4	.616
Goldsworthy, Bill	8	20	1	.293
Guidolin, Bep	25	36	2	.413
Hanna, John	14	18	1	.439
Harris, Billy	99	89	9	.525
Henry, Camille	39	55	4	.418
Hillman, Larry	78	55	8	.582
Howell, Harry	69	61	6	.529
Hucul, Sandy	78	66	14	.538
Hull, Bobby	81	79	9	.506
Hunter, Bill	15	33	4	.327
Ingram, Ron	92	106	14	.467
Kelley, Jack	63	48	5	.565
Kelly, Pat	24	30	3	.447
Kinasewich, Ray	38	37	3	.506
Kromm, Bobby	98	59	4	.621
Leduc, Bob	20	16	1	.554
Leger, Gilles	16	33	1	.330
McCartan, Jack	2	1	0	.667
McCaskill, Ted	20	39	0	.339
McKenzie, John	4	10	0	.286
McVie, Tom	11	8	0	.579
Moore, Gerry	19	61	3	.247
Neale, Harry	208	175	21	.541
Needham, Bill	80	64	12	.551
Pilous, Rudy	34	26	5	.562
Plante, Jacques	38	36	4	.513
Pronovost, Marcel	26	50	2	.346
Richard, Maurice	1	1	0	.500
Rollins, Al	28	48	4	.375
Ryan, Ron	83	59	9	.579
Sather, Glen	95	76	7	.553
Shaw, Brian	68	63	6	.518
Slater, Terry	116	130	12	.473
Smith, Floyd	33	41	6	.450
Sonmor, Glen	83	87	11	.489
Stapleton, Pat	73	100	8	.425
Talbot, Jean-Guy	14	26	1	.354
Vivian, Jack	21	22	2	.489
Watson, Phil	40	43	0	.482
Wilson, John	56	93	9	.383

PLAYOFFS (Ranked by wins)	W	L	PCT
1. Bill Dineen	44	27	.620
2. Harry Neale	33	32	.508
3. Bobby Kromm	23	10	.697
4. Jack Kelley	14	7	.667
5. Marc Boileau	12	5	.706
6. Bobby Hull	9	9	.500
Jean-Guy Gendron	9	11	.450
7. Larry Hillman	8	1	.889
Tom McVie	8	2	.800
Billy Harris	8	9	.471
Ron Ingram	8	10	.444
Pat Stapleton	8	10	.444
Jacques Demers	8	12	.400
Glen Sather	8	15	.348
8. Bill Needham	6	8	.429
9. Don Blackburn	5	5	.500
Joe Crozier	5	5	.500
Maurice Filion	5	6	.455
10. Harry Howell	4	6	.400
11. Ron Ryan	3	4	.429
Sandy Hucul	3	7	.300
12. Bob Leduc	2	4	.333
Terry Slater	2	8	.200
13. Floyd Smith	1	2	.333
Brian Shaw	1	4	.200
Glen Sonmor	1	4	.200
Jack Vivian	1	4	.200
14. Ray Kinasewich	0	1	.000
Bill Hunter	0	4	.000
Phil Watson	0	4	.000
John Wilson	0	4	.000

ALL-TIME COACHING LEADERS:

Regular-season wins:
1. Bill Dineen (318)
2. Harry Neale (208)
3. Jacques Demers (146)

Regular-season losses:
1. Bill Dineen (199)
2. Harry Neale (175)
3. Jacques Demers (148)

Regular-season winning percentage: (Minimum 100 games):
1. Bobby Kromm (.621)
2. Jean-Guy Gendron (.616)
3. Bill Dineen (.609)

Avco World Trophy championships:
Bill Dineen (2), Marc Boileau, Larry Hillman, Jack Kelley, Bobby Kromm, Tom McVie.

ALL-TIME CAREER STATISTICAL LEADERS – REGULAR SEASON

Games played:
1. Andre Lacroix – 551
2. Ron Plumb – 549
3. Michel Parizeau – 519
4. Paul Shmyr – 511
5. Mike Antonovich – 486
6. Rick Ley – 478
7. Johnny McKenzie – 477
8. Blair MacDonald – 476
9. Larry Pleau – 468
10. Poul Popiel – 467

Goals:
1. Marc Tardif – 316
2. Bobby Hull – 303
3. Real Cloutier – 282
4. Andre Lacroix – 251
5. Anders Hedberg – 236
6. Serge Bernier – 230
7. Tom Webster – 220
8. Danny Lawson – 218
9. Robbie Ftorek – 216
10. Mark Howe – 208

Assists:
1. Andre Lacroix – 547
2. J.C. Tremblay – 358
3. Marc Tardif – 350
4. Ulf Nilsson – 344
5. Serge Bernier – 336
6. Bobby Hull – 335
7. Gordie Howe – 334
8. Christian Bordeleau – 325
9. Robbie Ftorek – 307
10. Mark Howe – 296

Total points:
1. Andre Lacroix – 798
2. Marc Tardif – 666
3. Bobby Hull – 638
4. Serge Bernier and Real Cloutier – 566
5. Robbie Ftorek – 523
6. Gordie Howe – 508
7. Christian Bordeleau and Mark Howe – 504
8. Ulf Nilsson – 484
9. Anders Hedberg – 458
10. Larry Lund – 426

Penalty minutes:
1. Paul Baxter – 962
2. Kim Clackson – 932
3. Cam Connor – 904
4. Pierre Roy – 864
5. Paul Shmyr – 860
6. Gord Gallant – 849
7. John Schella – 844
8. Steve Sutherland – 805
9. John Hughes – 778
10. Ron Busniuk – 762

Goaltending victories:
1. Joe Daley – 167
2. Richard Brodeur – 165
3. Ernie Wakely – 164
4. Don McLeod – 157
5. John Garrett – 148
6. Al Smith – 141
7. Dave Dryden – 112
8. Ron Grahame – 102
9. Gerry Cheevers – 99
10. Wayne Rutledge – 93

Goals-against average: (Minimum 50 games)
1. Ron Grahame – 2.99
2. Gerry Cheevers – 3.12
3. Jack Norris – 3.16
4. Wayne Rutledge and Al Smith – 3.25
5. Ernie Wakely – 3.30
6. Don McLeod – 3.33
7. Joe Daley – 3.37
8. Mike Curran – 3.40
9. Louis Levasseur and Bob Whidden – 3.43
10. Bruce Landon and Cam Newton – 3.46

Shutouts
1. Ernie Wakely – 16
2. Gerry Cheevers and John Garrett – 14
3. Joe Daley and Ron Grahame – 13
4. Don McLeod – 11
5. Al Smith – 10
6. Richard Brodeur and Dave Dryden – 8
7. Mike Curran – 7
8. Wayne Rutledge – 6

Goaltending minutes:
1. Ernie Wakely – 19,331
2. Don McLeod – 18,926
3. John Garrett – 18,919
4. Joe Daley – 17,835
5. Richard Brodeur – 17,101
6. Al Smith – 15,389
7. Dave Dryden – 13,820
8. Gerry Cheevers – 11,352
9. Jack Norris – 11,030
10. Wayne Rutledge – 10,372

ALL-TIME CAREER STATISTICAL LEADERS – PLAYOFFS

Games played:
1. Gordie Howe – 78
2. Marty Howe – 75
3. Mark Howe – 74
4. Rick Ley – 73
5. Poul Popiel – 71
6. Larry Pleau and John Schella – 66
7. Larry Hale – 65
8. Bobby Guindon – 64
9. Brad Selwood and Ted Taylor – 63
10. Ted Green – 61

Goals:
1. Bobby Hull – 43
2. Mark Howe – 41
3. Anders Hedberg – 35
4. Real Cloutier – 33
5. Larry Pleau – 29
6. Serge Bernier, Gordie Howe and Tom Webster – 28
7. Marc Tardif – 27
8. Willy Lindstrom – 26
9. Bobby Guindon and Frank Hughes – 24
10. Mike Antonovich, Murray Hall and Peter Sullivan – 21

Assists:
1. Ulf Nilsson – 53
2. Mark Howe – 51
3. Poul Popiel – 47
4. Serge Bernier – 46
5. Larry Lund – 45
6. Gordie Howe – 43
7. Bobby Hull –37
8. Terry Ruskowski – 36
9. Christian Bordeleau – 34
10. Jim Dorey and Rick Ley – 33

Total points:
1. Mark Howe – 92
2. Bobby Hull – 80
3. Serge Bernier – 72
4. Gordie Howe –71
5. Ulf Nilsson – 67
6. Larry Lund – 65
7. Real Cloutier and Anders Hedberg – 63
8. Marc Tardif – 58
9. Poul Popiel, Terry Ruskowski and Tom Webster – 54
10. Peter Sullivan – 53

Penalty minutes:
1. Terry Ruskowski – 174
2. Curt Brackenbury – 160
3. Ted Taylor – 147
4. John Schella – 143
5. Rick Ley – 142
6. Kim Clackson – 138
7. Ron Busniuk – 132
8. Jim Dorey – 131
9. Poul Popiel – 118
10. Larry Lund – 116

Goaltending victories:
1. Joe Daley – 30
2. Richard Brodeur – 26
3. Ron Grahame – 22
4. Don McLeod and Al Smith – 15
5. John Garrett and Ernie Wakely – 15
6. Wayne Rutledge – 9
7. Louis Levasseur and Gary Smith – 8
8. Gerry Cheevers and Cap Raeder – 7
9. Dave Dryden and Andre Gill – 6
10. Gilles Gratton – 5

Goals-against average:
(Minimum 10 games)
1. Wayne Rutledge – 2.88
2. Louis Levasseur – 3.01
3. Ron Grahame and Don McLeod – 3.23
4. Cap Raeder – 3.a24
5. Gerry Cheevers – 3.28
6. Joe Daley – 3.30
7. Gilles Gratton – 3.35
8. Richard Brodeur – 3.60
9. Gary Smith – 3.73
10. Ernie Wakely – 3.76

Shutouts:
1. Ron Grahame – 4
2. Richard Bodeur – 3
3. Joe Daley, Jim Park, Cap Raeder and Ernie Wakely – 2
4. John Garrett, Paul Hoganson, Louis Levasseur, Don McLeod and Al Smith – 1

Goaltending minutes:
1. Richard Brodeur – 2,949
2. Joe Daley – 2,706
3. Ron Grahame – 2,158
4. Al Smith – 1.947
5. John Garrett – 1,816
6. Don McLeod – 1,786
7. Ernie Wakely – 1,740
8. Gerry Cheevers – 1,151
9. Dave Dryden – 958
10. Cap Raeder – 879

ALL-TIME TOP SINGLE-SEASON INDIVIDUAL PERFORMANCES

Goals:
1. 77 Bobby Hull (Win, 1974–75)
2. 75 Real Cloutier (Que, 1978–79)
3. 71 Marc Tardif (Que, 1975–76)
4. 70 Anders Hedberg (Win, 1976–77)
5. 66 Real Cloutier (Que, 1976–77)
6. 65 Marc Tardif (Que, 1977–78)
   Morris Lukowich (Win, 1978–79)
7. 63 Anders Hedberg (Win, 1977–78)
8. 61 Danny Lawson (Phi, 1972–73)
9. 60 Real Cloutier (Que, 1975–76)
   Mark Napier (Bir, 1976–77)
10. 59 Robbie Ftorek (Cin, 1977–78)

Assists:
1. 106 Andre Lacroix (SD, 1974–75)
2. 94 Ulf Nilsson (Win, 1974–75)
3. 89 Ulf Nilsson (Win, 1977–78)
   Marc Tardif (Que, 1977–78)
4. 85 Ulf Nilsson (Win, 1976–77)
5. 82 Andre Lacroix (SD, 1976–77)
6. 80 Andre Lacroix (NY/NJ, 1973–74)
7. 77 J.C. Tremblay (Que, 1975–76)
   Marc Tardif (Que, 1975–76)
   Andre Lacroix (Hou, 1977–78)
   Robbie Ftorek (Cin, 1978–79)
8. 76 Ulf Nilsson (Win, 1975–76)
9. 75 J.C. Tremblay (Que, 1972–73)
   Larry Lund (Hou, 1974–75)
   Chris Bordeleau (Que, 1976–77)
   Real Cloutier (Que, 1976–77)
10. 74 Andre Lacroix (Phi, 1972–73)

Total points:
1. 154 Marc Tardif (Que, 1977–78)
2. 148 Marc Tardif (Que, 1975–76)
3. 147 Andre Lacroix (SD, 1974–75)
4. 142 Bobby Hull (Win, 1974–75)
5. 141 Real Cloutier (Que, 1976–77)
6. 131 Anders Hedberg (Win, 1976–77)
7. 129 Real Cloutier (Que, 1977–78)
8. 126 Ulf Nilsson (Win, 1977–78)
9. 124 Andre Lacroix (Phi, 1972–73)
   Ulf Nilsson (Win, 1976–77)
10. 123 Bobby Hull (Win, 1975–76)

Penalty minutes:
1. 365 Curt Brackenbury (Min-Que, 1975–76)
2. 351 Kim Clackson (Ind, 1975–76)
3. 297 Gord Gallant (Que, 1975–76)
4. 295 Cam Connor (Phx, 1975–76)
5. 284 Steve Durbano (Bir, 1977–78)
6. 279 Frank Beaton (Bir, 1977–78)
7. 274 Frank Beaton (Edm, 1976–77)
8. 258 Pierre Roy (Que, 1975–76)
   Gilles Bilodeau (Bir, 1977–78)
9. 248 Scott Campbell (Win, 1978–79)
   Rick Vaive (Bir, 1978–79)
10. 244 Paul Baxter (Que, 1976–77)

Goaltending victories:
1. 44 Richard Brodeur (Que, 1975–76)
2. 41 Joe Daley (Win, 1975–76)
   Dave Dryden (Edm, 1978–79)
3. 39 Ron Grahame (Hou, 1975–76)
   Joe Daley (Win, 1976–77)
4. 35 Ernie Wakely (SD, 1975–76)
5. 33 Bernie Parent (Phi, 1972–73)
   Don McLeod (Hou, 1973–74)
   Ron Grahame (Hou, 1974–75)
   Don McLeod (Van, 1974–75)
   Al Smith (NE, 1974–75)
6. 32 Gerry Cheevers (Cle, 1972–73)
7. 31 Al Smith (NE, 1972–73)
8. 30 (Six players tied)

Goals against average:
(Minimum 25 games)
1. 2.56 Don McLeod (Hou, 1973–74)
2. 2.74 Michel Dion (Ind, 1975–76)
   Ron Grahame (Hou, 1976–77)
3. 2.84 Gerry Cheevers (Cle, 1972–73)
   Joe Daley (Win, 1975–76)
4. 2.89 Dave Dryden (Edm, 1978–79)
5. 2.90 Joe Daley (Win, 1972–73)
6. 2.91 Russ Gillow (LA, 1972–73)
7. 3.03 Gerry Cheevers (Cle, 1973–74)
   Ron Grahame (Hou, 1974–75)
8. 3.05 Wayne Rutledge (Hou, 1972–73)
9. 3.06 Jack Norris (Alb, 1972–73)
10. 3.08 Al Smith (NE, 1973–74)

Shutouts:

5 – Gerry Cheevers (Cle, 1972–73)
   Joe Daley (Win, 1975–76)

4 – Mike Curran (Min, 1972–73)
   Gerry Cheevers (Cle, 1973–74)
   Gerry Cheevers (Cle, 1974–75)
   Ron Grahame (Hou, 1974–75)
   Ken Broderick (Edm, 1976–77)
   John Garrett (Bir, 1976–77)
   Ron Grahame (Hou, 1976–77)
   Michel Dion (Cin, 1977–78)

3 – Shared by 13 goalies

ALL-TIME BEST AND WORST REGULAR-SEASON TEAM PERFORMANCES

NOTE: Teams that folded prior to the completion of a full season are not counted in the following records.

Most wins:
53 – Houston (1974–75)
     Houston (1975–76)
52 – Winnipeg (1975–76)
50 – Quebec (1975–76)
     Houston (1976–77)
     Winnipeg (1977–78)

Most losses:
57 – Indianapolis (1974–75)
53 – Los Angeles (1973–74)
     Michigan-Baltimore (1974–75)
52 – Toronto (1975–76)
51 – Indianapolis (1977–78)
50 – Chicago (1972–73)
     Vancouver (1973–74)

Most ties:
9 – Cleveland (1973–74)
    New England (1978–79)
8 – Phoenix (1974–75)
    Indianapolis (1976–77)
7 – New England (1975–76)
    Calgary (1976–77)

Most home wins:
33 – Houston (1975–76)
     Quebec (1975–76)
     Houston (1976–77)
30 – New England (1972–73)
     Winnipeg (1976–77)

Most home losses:
26 – Indianapolis (1974–75)
22 – Chicago (1972–73)
     Los Angeles (1973–74)
21 – Michigan-Baltimore (1974–75)
     Indianapolis (1977–78)

Most home ties:
6 – Phoenix (1975–76)
5 – Quebec (1972–73)
    Phoenix (1974–75)
    Birmingham (1978–79)

Most road wins:
25 – Houston (1974–75)
23 – Winnipeg (1975–76)
22 – Winnipeg (1977–78)
20 – Houston (1973–74)
     Houston (1975–76)

Most road losses:
32 – Michigan-Baltimore (1974–75)
     Edmonton (1975–76)
     Toronto (1975–76)
31 – Los Angeles (1973–74)
     Indianapolis (1974–75)
     Birmingham (1976–77)
     Calgary (1976–77)

Most road ties:
9 – New England (1978–79)
5 – Los Angeles (1972–73)
    Cleveland (1973–74)
    New England (1975–76)
    Calgary (1976–77)
    Indianapolis (1976–77)

Most points:
106 – Houston (1974–75)
      Houston (1975–76)
      Houston (1976–77)
      Winnipeg (1976–77)
104 – Quebec (1975–76)
102 – Winnipeg (1977–78)

Fewest wins:
18 – Indianapolis (1974–75)
21 – Michigan-Baltimore (1974–75)
24 – Toronto (1975–76)
     Indianapolis (1977–78)
25 – Los Angeles (1973–74)

Fewest losses:
24 – Houston (1976–77)
25 – Houston (1973–74)
     Houston (1974–75)
27 – Houston (1975–76)
     Quebec (1975–76)
     Winnipeg (1975–76)

Fewest ties:
0 – Philadelphia (1972–73)
    Los Angeles (1973–74)
    Houston (1974–75)
    Quebec (1974–75)
    Houston (1975–76)

Fewest home wins:
13 – Indianapolis (1974–75)
15 – Michigan-Baltimore (1974–75)
16 – Toronto (1975–76)
17 – Chicago (1972–73)
     Los Angeles (1973–74)
     Indianapolis (1977–78)

Fewest home losses:
3 – Houston (1976–77)
7 – Houston (1975–76)
    Quebec (1975–76)
8 – New England (1972–73)
    New England (1974–75)

Fewest home ties:
0 – Shared by 14 teams

Fewest road wins:
5 – Indianapolis (1974–75)
    Calgary (1976–77)
6 – Michigan-Baltimore (1974–75)
7 – Edmonton (1975–76)
    Indianapolis (1977–78)

Fewest road losses:
14 – Houston (1974–75)
15 – Los Angeles (1972–73)
16 – Houston (1973–74)
     Winnipeg (1975–76)
17 – New England (1977–78)
     Winnipeg (1977–78)

Fewest road ties:
0 – Shared by 12 teams

Fewest points:
39 – Indianapolis (1974–75)
46 – Michigan-Baltimore (1974–75)
50 – Los Angeles (1973–74)
53 – Toronto (1975–76)
     Indianapolis (1977–78)

ALL-TIME PLAYOFF WON-LOST RECORDS

NOTE: Teams not listed never qualified for Avco World Trophy playoff competition. The one-game tie breaker between the Minnesota Fighting Saints and Alberta Oilers in 1973 is included in the standings but is not counted as a series.

TEAM	Years	GP	W	L	GF	GA	Series W-L:	Avco Trophy:
Birmingham	1	5	1	4	12	29	0-1	–
Calgary	1	10	5	5	36	37	1-1	–
Chicago	1	18	8	10	67	72	2-1	–
Cincinnati	2	7	1	6	19	29	0-2	–
Cleveland	4	22	7	15	62	78	1-4	–
Edmonton	6	33	9	24	113	141	1-5	–
Houston	6	71	44	27	273	224	10-4	1974 &'75
Indianapolis	2	16	8	8	48	52	1-2	–
Los Angeles	1	6	2	4	16	23	0-1	–
Minnesota	3	29	14	15	103	107	2-3	–
New England	7	74	41	33	272	256	8-6	1973
Ottawa	1	5	1	4	17	24	0-1	–
Philadelphia	1	4	0	4	6	19	0-1	–
Phoenix	2	10	3	7	25	40	0-2	–
Quebec	5	52	26	26	204	198	6-4	1977
San Diego	3	28	12	14	89	111	2-3	–
Toronto	2	18	9	9	72	72	1-2	–
Winnipeg	6	70	48	22	316	238	11-3	1976, '78 & '79

YEAR-BY-YEAR REGULAR-SEASON FINAL STANDINGS

1972–73

EASTERN DIVISION	GP	W	L	T	PTS	GF	GA	PCT
New England Whalers	78	46	30	2	94	318	263	.602
Cleveland Crusaders	78	43	32	3	89	287	239	.570
Philadelphia Blazers	78	38	40	0	76	288	305	.487
Ottawa Nationals	78	35	39	4	74	279	301	.474
Quebec Nordiques	78	33	40	5	71	276	313	.455
New York Raiders	78	33	43	2	68	303	334	.435

WESTERN DIVISION	GP	W	L	T	PTS	GF	GA	PCT
Winnipeg Jets	78	43	31	4	90	285	249	.576
Houston Aeros	78	39	35	4	82	284	269	.525
Los Angeles Sharks	78	37	35	6	80	259	250	.512
Alberta Oilers	78	38	37	3	79	269	256	.506
Minnesota Fighting Saints /	78	38	37	3	79	250	269	.506
Chicago Cougars	78	26	50	2	54	245	295	.346

1973–74

EASTERN DIVISION	GP	W	L	T	PTS	GF	GA	PCT
New England Whalers	78	43	31	4	90	291	260	.576
Toronto Toros	78	41	33	4	86	304	272	.551
Cleveland Crusaders	78	37	32	9	83	266	264	.532
Chicago Cougars	78	38	35	5	81	271	273	.519
Quebec Nordiques	78	38	36	4	80	306	280	.513
New York Golden Blades / New Jersey Knights	78	32	42	4	68	278	313	.436

WESTERN DIVISION	GP	W	L	T	PTS	GF	GA	PCT
Houston Aeros	78	48	25	5	101	318	219	.647
Minnesota Fighting Saints	78	44	32	2	90	332	275	.576
Edmonton Oilers	78	38	37	3	79	268	269	.506
Winnipeg Jets	78	34	39	5	73	264	296	.468
Vancouver Blazers	78	27	50	1	55	278	345	.353
Los Angeles Sharks	78	25	53	0	50	239	339	.321

1974-75

CANADIAN DIVISION	GP	W	L	T	PTS	GF	GA	PCT
Quebec Nordiques	78	46	32	0	92	331	299	.590
Toronto Toros	78	43	33	2	88	349	304	.564
Winnipeg Jets	78	38	35	5	81	322	293	.519
Vancouver Blazers	78	37	39	2	76	256	270	.487
Edmonton Oilers	78	36	38	4	76	279	279	.487

EASTERN DIVISION	GP	W	L	T	PTS	GF	GA	PCT
New England Whalers	78	43	30	5	91	274	279	.583
Cleveland Crusaders	78	35	40	3	73	236	258	.468
Chicago Cougars	78	30	47	1	61	261	312	.391
Indianapolis Racers	78	18	57	3	39	216	338	.250

WESTERN DIVISION	GP	W	L	T	PTS	GF	GA	PCT
Houston Aeros	78	53	25	0	106	369	247	.679
San Diego Mariners	78	43	31	4	90	326	268	.577
Minnesota Fighting Saints	78	42	33	3	87	308	279	.558
Phoenix Roadrunners	78	39	31	8	86	300	265	.551
Michigan Stags / Baltimore Blades	78	21	53	4	46	205	341	.295

1975-76

CANADIAN DIVISION	GP	W	L	T	PTS	GF	GA	PCT
Winnipeg Jets	81	52	27	2	106	345	254	.654
Quebec Nordiques	81	50	27	4	104	371	316	.642
Calgary Cowboys	80	41	35	4	86	307	282	.538
Edmonton Oilers	81	27	49	5	59	268	345	.364
Toronto Toros	81	24	52	5	53	335	398	.327

EASTERN DIVISION	GP	W	L	T	PTS	GF	GA	PCT
Indianapolis Racers	80	35	39	6	76	245	247	.475
Cleveland Crusaders	80	35	40	5	75	273	279	.469
Cincinnati Stingers	80	35	44	1	71	285	340	.444
New England Whalers	80	33	40	7	73	255	290	.460

WESTERN DIVISION	GP	W	L	T	PTS	GF	GA	PCT
Houston Aeros	80	53	27	0	106	341	263	.663
Phoenix Roadrunners	80	39	35	6	84	302	287	.525
San Diego Mariners	80	36	38	6	78	303	290	.488
Minnesota Fighting Saints	59	30	25	4	64	211	212	.542
Denver Spurs - Ottawa Civics	41	14	26	1	29	134	172	.354

1976-77

EASTERN DIVISION	GP	W	L	T	PTS	GF	GA	PCT
Quebec Nordiques	81	47	31	3	97	353	295	.599
Cincinnati Stingers	81	39	37	5	83	354	303	.512
Indianapolis Racers	81	36	37	8	80	276	305	.493
New England Whalers	81	35	40	6	76	275	290	.469
Birmingham Bulls	81	31	46	4	66	289	309	.407
Minnesota Fighting Saints (franchise folded Jan. 17, 1977)	42	19	18	5	43	136	129	.512

WESTERN DIVISION	GP	W	L	T	PTS	GF	GA	PCT
Houston Aeros	80	50	24	6	106	320	241	.663
Winnipeg Jets	80	46	32	2	94	366	291	.588
San Diego Mariners	81	40	37	4	84	284	283	.519
Edmonton Oilers	81	34	43	4	72	243	304	.444
Calgary Cowboys	81	31	43	7	69	252	296	.426
Phoenix Roadrunners	80	28	48	4	60	281	383	.375

1977-78

	GP	W	L	T	PTS	GF	GA	PCT
Winnipeg Jets	80	50	28	2	102	381	270	.638
New England Whalers	80	44	31	5	93	335	269	.581
Houston Aeros	80	42	34	4	88	296	302	.550
Quebec Nordiques	80	40	37	3	83	349	347	.519
Edmonton Oilers	80	38	39	3	79	309	307	.494
Birmingham Bulls	80	36	41	3	75	287	314	.469
Cincinnati Stingers	80	35	42	3	73	298	332	.456
Indianapolis Racers	80	24	51	5	53	267	353	.331
*Soviet All-Stars	8	3	4	1	7	27	36	.438
*Team Czechoslovakia	8	1	6	1	3	21	40	.188

NOTE: The Soviet All-Stars and Team Czechoslovakia played each WHA team once during December 1977 and January 1978, with the results counting in the standings for the WHA teams.

1978-79

	GP	W	L	T	PTS	GF	GA	PCT
Edmonton Oilers	80	48	30	2	98	340	266	.613
Quebec Nordiques	80	41	34	5	87	288	271	.544
Winnipeg Jets	80	39	35	6	84	307	306	.525
New England Whalers	80	37	34	9	83	298	287	.519
Cincinnati Stingers	80	33	41	6	72	274	284	.450
Birmingham Bulls	80	32	42	6	70	286	311	.438
Indianapolis Racers	25	5	18	2	12	78	130	.240
(franchise folded Dec. 15, 1978)								
*Soviet All-Stars	6	4	1	1	9	27	20	.750
*Team Czechoslovakia	6	1	4	1	3	14	33	.250

NOTE: As in 1977-78, each WHA club played the touring Soviets and Czechs once, with the results counting in the standings. The Indianapolis franchise folded prior to the tour.

YEAR-BY-YEAR PLAYOFF SERIES RESULTS AND STATISTICAL LEADERS

1973

Tiebreaker: Minnesota claimed the fourth and final Western Division playoff spot by defeating Alberta 4–2 in a one-game tiebreaker played in Calgary. The teams ended the regular season with identical 38–37–3 records.

Eastern Division semifinal:
Cleveland 3, Philadelphia 2 (OT)
Cleveland 7, Philadelphia 1
Cleveland 3, Philadelphia 1
Cleveland 6, Philadelphia 2
(Cleveland wins series, 4–0)

Eastern Division semifinal:
New England 6, Ottawa 3
New England 4, Ottawa 3 (OT)
Ottawa 4, New England 2
New England 7, Ottawa 3
New England 5, Ottawa 4 (OT)
(New England wins series, 4–1)

Eastern Division final:
New England 3, Cleveland 2
New England 3, Cleveland 2
New England 5, Cleveland 4
Cleveland 5, New England 2
New England 3, Cleveland 1
(New England wins series, 4–1)

Western Division semifinal:
Winnipeg 3, Minnesota 1
Winnipeg 5, Minnesota 2
Minnesota 6, Winnipeg 4
Winnipeg 3, Minnesota 2 (OT)
Winnipeg 8, Minnesota 5
(Winnipeg wins series, 4–1)

Western Division semifinal:
Houston 7, Los Angeles 2
Los Angeles 4, Houston 2
Los Angeles 3, Houston 2
Houston 3, Los Angeles 2 (OT)
Houston 6, Los Angeles 3
Houston 3, Los Angeles 2
(Houston wins series, 4–2)

Western Division final:
Winnipeg 5, Houston 1
Winnipeg 2, Houston 0
Winnipeg 4, Houston 2
Winnipeg 3, Houston 0
(Winnipeg wins series, 4–0)

Avco World Trophy final:
New England 7, Winnipeg 2
New England 7, Winnipeg 4
Winnipeg 4, New England 3
New England 4, Winnipeg 2
New England 9, Winnipeg 6
(New England wins series, 4–1)

STATISTICAL LEADERS:

Goals:
13 – Norm Beaudin, Win
12 – Larry Pleau, NE
    Tom Webster, NE
 9 – Bobby Hull, Win
    Tim Sheehy, NE

Assists:
16 – Jim Dorey, NE
    Bobby Hull, Win
15 – Norm Beaudin, Win
14 – Tim Sheehy, NE
    Tom Webster, NE

Points:
28 – Norm Beaudin, Win
26 – Tom Webster, NE
25 – Bobby Hull, Win

Goaltender wins:
12 – Al Smith, NE
 5 – Gerry Cheevers, Cle
    Joe Daley, Win
 4 – Wayne Rutledge, Hou
    Ernie Wakely, Win

Penalty minutes:
41 – Jim Dorey, NE
30 – Gerry Pinder, Cle
27 – Skip Krake, Cle

Overtime scorers:
Norm Beaudin, Win
Ron Buchanan, Cle
Mike Byers, NE
Murray Hall, Hou
Brit Selby, NE

1974

Eastern Division semifinal:
New England 6, Chicago 4
New England 4, Chicago 3 (OT)
Chicago 8, New England 6
Chicago 2, New England 1 (OT)
Chicago 4, New England 2
New England 2, Chicago 0
Chicago 3, New England 2
(Chicago wins series, 4–3)

Eastern Division semifinal:
Toronto 4, Cleveland 0
Toronto 4, Cleveland 3
Toronto 4, Cleveland 2
Cleveland 3, Toronto 2 (OT)
Toronto 4, Cleveland 1
(Toronto wins series, 4–1)

Eastern Division final:
Toronto 6, Chicago 4
Chicago 4, Toronto 3
Chicago 3, Toronto 2
Toronto 7, Chicago 6
Toronto 5, Chicago 3
Chicago 9, Toronto 2
Chicago 5, Toronto 3
(Chicago wins series, 4–3)

Western Division semifinal:
Houston 5, Winnipeg 2
Houston 3, Winnipeg 2
Houston 10, Winnipeg 1
Houston 5, Winnipeg 4
(Houston wins series, 4–0)

Western Division semifinal:
Minnesota 2, Edmonton 1
Minnesota 8, Edmonton 5
Minnesota 6, Edmonton 2
Edmonton 2, Minnesota 1
Minnesota 5, Edmonton 4
(Minnesota wins series, 4–1)

Western Division final:
Minnesota 5, Houston 4 (OT)
Houston 5, Minnesota 2
Minnesota 4, Houston 1
Houston 4, Minnesota 1
Houston 9, Minnesota 4
Houston 3, Minnesota 1
(Houston wins series, 4–2)

Avco World Trophy final:
Houston 3, Chicago 2
Houston 6, Chicago 1
Houston 7, Chicago 4
Houston 6, Chicago 2
(Houston wins series, 4–0)

STATISTICAL LEADERS:

Goals:
10 – Mike Walton, Min
 9 – Murray Hall, Hou
    Mark Howe, Hou
    Frank Hughes, Hou
    Larry Lund, Hou
    Rosaire Paiement, Chi
 8 – Andre Hinse, Hou
    Jan Popiel, Chi

Assists:
14 – Ralph Backstrom, Chi
    Gordie Howe, Hou
    Larry Lund, Hou
    Poul Popiel, Hou
    13 – Pat Stapleton, Chi
12 – Wayne Carleton, Tor

Points:
23 – Larry Lund, Hou
19 – Ralph Backstrom, ChiMark Howe, Hou
18 – Mike Walton, Min

Goaltender wins:
12 – Don McLeod, Hou
6 – Andre Gill, Chi
5 – Gilles Gratton, Tor

Penalty minutes:
71 – Darryl Maggs, Chi
67 – Gord Gallant, Min
60 – Ted Taylor, Hou

Overtime scorers:
Ralph Backstrom, Chi
John French, NE
Wayne Muloin, Cle
Mike Walton, Min
Penalty shot:
* *Toronto's Wayne Dillon scored on Chicago's Cam Newton in opening game of Eastern Division final.*

1975

Quarter final:
Houston 8, Cleveland 5
Houston 5, Cleveland 3
Cleveland 3, Houston 1
Houston 7, Cleveland 2
Houston 3, Cleveland 1
(Houston wins series, 4–1)

Quarter final:
Minnesota 6, New England 5
New England 3, Minnesota 2 (OT)
Minnesota 8, New England 3
New England 5, Minnesota 2
Minnesota 4, New England 0
Minnesota 6, New England 1
(Minnesota wins series, 4–2)

Quarter final:
Quebec 5, Phoenix 2
Quebec 6, Phoenix 2
Quebec 3, Phoenix 0
Phoenix 6, Quebec 5 (OT)
Quebec 4, Phoenix 2
(Quebec wins series, 4–1)

Quarter final:
San Diego 5, Toronto 3
San Diego 7, Toronto 6
Toronto 5, San Diego 2
Toronto 6, San Diego 5
San Diego 4, Toronto 3
San Diego 6, Toronto 4
(San Diego wins series, 4–2)

Semifinal:
Quebec 4, Minnesota 1
Minnesota 5, Quebec 3
Quebec 6, Minnesota 1
Minnesota 4, Quebec 2
Quebec 6, Minnesota 3
Quebec 4, Minnesota 2
(Quebec wins series, 4–2)

Semifinal:
Houston 4, San Diego 0
Houston 2, San Diego 1
Houston 6, San Diego 0
Houston 5, San Diego 4
(Houston wins series, 4–0)

Avco World Trophy final:
Houston 6, Quebec 2
Houston 5, Quebec 3
Houston 2, Quebec 0
Houston 7, Quebec 2
(Houston wins series, 4–0)

STATISTICAL LEADERS:

Goals:
10 – Rejean Houle, Que
     Mark Howe, Hou
     Marc Tardif, Que
     Mike Walton, Min
8 – Serge Bernier, Que
    Wayne Connelly, Min
    Gordie Howe, Hou

Assists:
13 – Christian Bordeleau, Que
     Fran Huck, Min
     Larry Lund, Hou
12 – Gordie Howe, Hou
     Mark Howe, Hou
11 – Marc Tardif, Que

Points:
22 – Mark Howe, Hou
21 – Marc Tardif, Que
20 – Gordie Howe, Hou

Goaltender wins:
12 – Ron Grahame, Hou
8 – Richard Brodeur, Que
6 – John Garrett, Min

Penalty minutes:
63 – Ron Busniuk, Min
59 – Curt Brackenbury, Min
41 – Jack Carlson, Min
     Rene Leclerc, Que
     Garry Swain, NE

Overtime scorers:
Michel Cormier, Phx
Rick Ley, NE
Jim Sherrit, Hou

1976

Preliminary round:
New England 5, Cleveland 3
New England 6, Cleveland 1
New England 3, Cleveland 2
(New England wins series, 3–0)

Preliminary round:
Phoenix 3, San Diego 2 (OT)
San Diego 4, Phoenix 3
Phoenix 6, San Diego 4
San Diego 5, Phoenix 1
San Diego 2, Phoenix 1
(San Diego wins series, 3–2)

Quarter final:
Winnipeg 7, Edmonton 3
Winnipeg 5, Edmonton 4 (OT)
Winnipeg 3, Edmonton 2
Winnipeg 7, Edmonton 2
(Winnipeg wins series, 4–0)

Quarter final:
Calgary 3, Quebec 1
Calgary 8, Quebec 4
Calgary 3, Quebec 2
Quebec 4, Calgary 3
Calgary 6, Quebec 4
(Calgary wins series, 4–1)

Quarter final:
New England 4, Indianapolis 1
Indianapolis 4, New England 0
New England 3, Indianapolis 0
New England 2, Indianapolis 1
Indianapolis 4, New England 0
Indianapolis 5, New England 3
New England 6, Indianapolis 0
(New England wins series, 4–3)

Quarter final:
Houston 8, San Diego 6
Houston 3, San Diego 1
Houston 8, San Diego 4
San Diego 3, Houston 2
San Diego 3, Houston 2
Houston 3, San Diego 2
(Houston wins series, 4–2)

Semifinal:
Winnipeg 6, Calgary 1
Winnipeg 3, Calgary 2
Winnipeg 6, Calgary 3
Calgary 7, Winnipeg 3
Winnipeg 4, Calgary 0
(Winnipeg wins series, 4–1)

Semifinal:
New England 4, Houston 2
Houston 5, New England 2
New England 4, Houston 1
Houston 4, New England 3
Houston 4, New England 2
New England 6, Houston 1
Houston 2, New England 0
(Houston wins series, 4–3)

Avco World Trophy final:
Winnipeg 4, Houston 3
Winnipeg 5, Houston 4
Winnipeg 6, Houston 3
Winnipeg 9, Houston 1
(Winnipeg wins series, 4–1)

STATISTICAL LEADERS:

Goals:
13 – Anders Hedberg, Win
12 – Bobby Hull, Win
10 – Tom Webster, NE

Assists:
19 – Ulf Nilsson, Win
12 – Mike Ford, Win
11 – Rosaire Paiement, NE

Points:
26 – Ulf Nilsson, Win
20 – Bobby Hull, Win
19 – Anders Hedberg, Win
     Tom Webster, NE

Goaltender wins:
10 – Joe Daley, Win
 7 – Al Smith, NE
 6 – Ron Grahame, Hou

Penalty minutes:
64 – Terry Ruskowski, Hou
57 – Nick Fotiu, NE
51 – Bill Butters, Hou

Overtime scorers:
Del Hall, Phx
Ulf Nilsson, Win

Penalty shots:
 * Houston's Gord Labossiere scored on San Diego's Ernie Wakely in the opening game of quarter-final series.
 * New England's Tom Earl failed to score against Houston's Ron Grahame in the opening game of semifinal series.

1977

Eastern Division semifinal:
Quebec 5, New England 2
Quebec 7, New England 3
Quebec 4, New England 3 (OT)
New England 6, Quebec 4
Quebec 3, New England 0
(Quebec wins series, 4–1)

Eastern Division semi-final:
Indianapolis 4, Cincinnati 3 (3OT)
Indianapolis 7, Cincinnati 2
Indianapolis 5, Cincinnati 3
Indianapolis 3, Cincinnati 1
(Indianapolis wins series, 4–0)

Eastern Division final:
Quebec 3, Indianapolis 1
Quebec 8, Indianapolis 3
Quebec 6, Indianapolis 5 (OT)
Indianapolis 2, Quebec 0
Quebec 8, Indianapolis 3
(Quebec wins series, 4–1)

Western Division semifinal:
Houston 4, Edmonton 3 (OT)
Houston 6, Edmonton 2
Edmonton 7, Houston 2
Houston 4, Edmonton 1
Houston 4, Edmonton 3
(Houston wins series, 4–1)

Western Division semifinal:
Winnipeg 5, San Diego 1
Winnipeg 4, San Diego 1
San Diego 5, Winnipeg 4
San Diego 6, Winnipeg 4
Winnipeg 3, San Diego 0
San Diego 3, Winnipeg 1
Winnipeg 7, San Diego 3
(Winnipeg wins series, 4–3)

Western Division final:
Winnipeg 4, Houston 3 (OT)
Houston 7, Winnipeg 2
Winnipeg 4, Houston 3
Winnipeg 6, Houston 4
Houston 3, Winnipeg 2
Winnipeg 6, Houston 3
(Winnipeg wins series, 4–2)

Avco World Trophy final:
Winnipeg 2, Quebec 1
Quebec 6, Winnipeg 1
Winnipeg 6, Quebec 1
Quebec 4, Winnipeg 2
Quebec 8, Winnipeg 3
Winnipeg 12, Quebec 3
Quebec 8, Winnipeg 2
(Quebec wins series, 4–3)

STATISTICAL LEADERS:

Goals:
14 – Serge Bernier, Que
     Real Cloutier, Que
13 – Anders Hedberg, Win
     Bobby Hull, Win
12 – Paulin Bordeleau, Que

Assists:
22 – Serge Bernier, Que
21 – Ulf Nilsson, Win
17 – Dan Labraaten, Win

Points:
36 – Serge Bernier, Que
29 – Anders Hedberg, Win
27 – Real Cloutier, Que

Goaltender wins:
12 – Richard Brodeur, Que
11 – Joe Daley, Win
 4 – Ron Grahame, Hou

Penalty minutes:
67 – Terry Ruskowski, Hou
51 – Curt Brackenbury, Que
47 – Cam Connor, Hou

Overtime scorers:
Gene Peacosh, Ind
Morris Lukowich, Hou
Paul Baxter, Que
Peter Sullivan, Win
Paulin Bordeleau, Que

1978

Quarter final:
New England 6, Edmonton 4
New England 4, Edmonton 1
Edmonton 2, New England 0
New England 9, Edmonton 1
New England 4, Edmonton 1
(New England wins series, 4–1)

Quarter final:
Houston 4, Quebec 3 (OT)
Quebec 5, Houston 4 (OT)
Quebec 5, Houston 1
Quebec 3, Houston 0
Houston 5, Quebec 2
Quebec 11, Houston 2
(Quebec wins series, 4–2)

Quarter final:
Winnipeg 9, Birmingham 3
Winnipeg 8, Birmingham 3
Birmingham 3, Winnipeg 2
Winnipeg 5, Birmingham 1
Winnipeg 5, Birmingham 2
(Winnipeg wins series, 4–1)

Semifinal:
(Winnipeg awarded a bye)
New England 5, Quebec 1
Quebec 3, England 2
New England 5, Quebec 4
New England 7, Quebec 3
New England 6, Quebec 3
(New England wins series, 4–1)

Avco World Trophy final:
Winnipeg 4, New England 1
Winnipeg 5, New England 2
Winnipeg 10, New England 2
Winnipeg 5, New England 3
(Winnipeg wins series, 4–0)

STATISTICAL LEADERS:

Goals:
10 – Mike Antonovich, NE
9 – Real Cloutier, Que
   Anders Hedberg, Win
8 – Bobby Guindon, Win
   Mark Howe, NE
   Bobby Hull, Win

Assists:
13 – Ulf Nilsson, Win
11 – Dave Keon, NE
10 – Serge Bernier, Que

Points:
17 – Mike Antonovich, NE
16 – Real Cloutier, Que
   Dave Keon, NE
15 – Bobby Guindon, Win
   Anders Hedberg, Win
   Mark Howe, NE
   Marc Tardif, Que

Goaltender wins:
8 – Louis Levasseur, NE
5 – Richard Brodeur, Que
4 – Gary Bromley, Win

Penalty minutes:
61 – Kim Clackson, Win
50 – Wally Weir, Que
48 – Dave Hanson, Bir

Overtime scorers:
Marc Tardif, Que
Ted Taylor, Hou

Penalty shot:
Anders Hedberg of Winnipeg scored against Birmingham's John Garrett in the opening game of quarter-final series.

1979

Quarter final:
New England 5, Cincinnati 3
Cincinnati 6, New England 3
New England 2, Cincinnati 1
(New England wins series, 2–1)

Semifinal:
Edmonton 6, New England 2
Edmonton 9, New England 5
New England 4, Edmonton 1
New England 5, Edmonton 4
Edmonton 5, New England 2
New England 8, Edmonton 4
Edmonton 6, New England 3
(Edmonton wins series, 4–3)

Semifinal:
Winnipeg 6, Quebec 3
Winnipeg 9, Quebec 2
Winnipeg 9, Quebec 5
Winnipeg 6, Quebec 2
(Winnipeg wins series, 4–0)

Avco World Trophy final:
Winnipeg 3, Edmonton 1
Winnipeg 3, Edmonton 2
Edmonton 8, Winnipeg 3
Winnipeg 3, Edmonton 2
Edmonton 10, Winnipeg 2
Winnipeg 7, Edmonton 3
(Winnipeg wins series, 4–2)

STATISTICAL LEADERS:

Goals:
10 – Wayne Gretzky, Edm
   Willy Lindstrom, Win
9 – Ron Chipperfield, Edm
8 – Morris Lukowich, Win
   Blair MacDonald, Edm
   Rich Preston, Win

Assists:
12 – Terry Ruskowski, Win
11 – Kent Nilsson, Win
10 – Brent Callighen, Edm
   Ron Chipperfield, Edm
   Wayne Gretzky, Edm
   Blair MacDonald, Edm

Points:
20 – Wayne Gretzky, Edm
19 – Ron Chipperfield, Edm
18 – Blair MacDonald, Edm

Goaltender wins:
8 – Gary Smith, Win
6 – Dave Dryden, Edm
4 – John Garrett, NE

Penalty minutes:
42 – Dave Hunter, Edm
35 – John Hughes, Edm
29 – Dave Semenko, Edm

YEAR-BY-YEAR AVCO WORLD TROPHY CHAMPIONSHIP ROSTERS

1972–73 NEW ENGLAND WHALERS:

Kevin Ahearn, Mike Byers, Terry Caffery, John Cunniff, John Danby, Jim Dorey, Tom Earl, John French, Ted Green (captain), Paul Hurley, Ric Jordan, Jack Kelley (general manager and coach), Bruce Landon, Rick Ley, Larry Pleau, Brit Selby, Brad Selwood, Tim Sheehy, Al Smith, Guy Smith, Tom Webster, Tommy Williams.

1973–74 HOUSTON AEROS:

Bill Dineen (general manager and coach), Ron Grahame, Don Grierson, Larry Hale, Murray Hall, Andre Hinse, Ed Hoekstra, Gordie Howe, Mark Howe, Marty Howe, Frank Hughes, Gordon Kannegiesser, Gordon Labossiere, Larry Lund, Dunc McCallum, Don McLeod, Poul Popiel, Bill Prentice, Wayne Rutledge, John Schella, Jim Sherrit, Jack Stanfield, Joe Szura, Ted Taylor (captain), Gary Williamson.

1974–75 HOUSTON AEROS:

Bill Dineen (general manager and coach), Ron Grahame, Larry Hale, Murray Hall, Andre Hinse, Gordie Howe, Mark Howe, Marty Howe, Frank Hughes, Glenn Irwin, Gordon Labossiere, Don Larway, Larry Lund, Poul Popiel, Bill Prentice, Rich Preston, Terry Ruskowski, Wayne Rutledge, John Schella, Jim Sherrit, Ted Taylor (captain).

1975–76 WINNIPEG JETS:

Duke Asmundson, Norm Beaudin, Thommie Bergman, Joe Daley, Mike Ford, Ted Green, Bobby Guindon, Anders Hedberg, Larry Hillman, Larry Hornung, Bobby Hull, Veli Pekka Ketola, Bobby Kromm (coach), Curt Larsson, Bill Lesuk, Mats Lindh, Willy Lindstrom, Lyle Moffatt, Ulf Nilsson, Gerry Odrowski, Rudy Pilous (general manager), Heikki Riihiranta, Lars-Erik Sjoberg (captain), Peter Sullivan.

1976–77 QUEBEC NORDIQUES:

Serge Aubry, Paul Baxter, Jean Bernier, Serge Bernier, Marc Boileau (coach), Christian Bordeleau, Paulin Bordeleau, Andre Boudrias, Curt Brackenbury, Richard Brodeur, Real Cloutier, Charles Constantin, Jim Dorey, Norm Dube, Maurice Filion (general manager), Bob Fitchner, Pierre Guite, Ed Humphreys, Francois Lacombe, Garry Lariviere, Steve Sutherland, Marc Tardif (captain), J.C. Tremblay, Wally Weir.

1977–78 WINNIPEG JETS:

Mike Amodeo, Ken Baird, Gary Bromley, Kim Clackson, Joe Daley, Billy Davis, Dave Dunn, Mike Ford, Ted Green, Bobby Guindon, Anders Hedberg, Larry Hillman (coach), Bobby Hull, Dave Kryskow, Dan Labraaten, Bill Lesuk, Willy Lindstrom, Barry Long, Markus Mattsson, Lyle Moffatt, Kent Nilsson, Ulf Nilsson, Rudy Pilous (general manager), Lynn Powis, Kent Ruhnke, Lars-Erik Sjoberg (captain), Peter Sullivan.

1978–79 WINNIPEG JETS:

Scott Campbell, Kim Clackson, Joe Daley, Roland Eriksson, John Ferguson (general manager), John Gray, Bobby Guindon, Glenn Hicks, Bill Lesuk, Willy Lindstrom, Barry Long (co-captain), Morris Lukowich, Paul MacKinnon, Tom McVie (coach), Lyle Moffatt, Kent Nilsson, Rich Preston, Terry Ruskowski, Lars-Erik Sjoberg (co-captain), Gary Smith, Peter Sullivan, Paul Terbenche, Steve West.

YEAR-BY-YEAR REGULAR-SEASON TOP TEN SCORERS

1972-73

Goals:
1. 61 – Danny Lawson (Phil)
2. 53 – Tom Webster (NE)
3. 51 – Bobby Hull (Win)
   Ron Ward (NY)
4. 50 – Andre Lacroix (Phil)
5. 47 – Chris Bordeleau (Win)
6. 43 – Gary Veneruzzo (LA)
7. 42 – Wayne Carleton (Ott)
8. 40 – Wayne Connelly (Min)
   Gary Jarrett (Cle)
9. 39 – Jim Harrison (Alta)
   Terry Caffrey (NE)
10. 38 – Norm Beaudin (Win)

Assists:
1. 75 – J.C. Tremblay (Que)
2. 74 – Andre Lacroix (Phil)
3. 67 – Ron Ward (NY)
4. 65 – Norm Beaudin (Win)
5. 63 – Bob Sicinski (Chi)
6. 61 – Terry Caffrey (NE)
7. 60 – Gord Labossiere (Hou)
8. 56 – Jim Dorey (NE)
9. 54 – Chris Bordeleau (Win)
10. 53 – Ken Block (NY)
    Bobby Sheehan (NY)

Points:
1. 124 – Andre Lacroix (Phil)
2. 118 – Ron Ward (NY)
3. 106 – Danny Lawson (Phil)
4. 103 – Norm Beaudin (Win)
   Bobby Hull (Win)
   Tom Webster (NE)
5. 101 – Chris Bordeleau (Win)
6. 100 – Terry Caffrey (NE)
7. 96 – Gord Labossiere (Hou)
8. 91 – Wayne Carleton (Ott)
9. 89 – J.C. Tremblay (Que)
10. 88 – Bobby Sheehan (NY)
    Bob Sicinski (Chi)

1973-74

Goals:
1. 57 – Mike Walton (Min)
2. 53 – Bobby Hull (Win)
3. 50 – Danny Lawson (Van)
4. 43 – Tom Webster (NE)
5. 42 – Wayne Connelly (Min)
   Frank Hughes (Hou)
6. 40 – George Morrison (Min)
   Marc Tardif (LA)
7. 39 – Gary Veneruzzo (LA)
8. 38 – Ron Climie (Edm)
   Mark Howe (Hou)
   Claude St. Sauveur (Van)
9. 37 – Serge Bernier (Que)
   Wayne Carleton (Tor)
10. 33 – Ralph Backstrom (Chi)
    Larry Lund (Hou)
    Tom Simpson (Tor)
    Ron Ward (Van-LA-Cle)

Assists:
1. 80 – Andre Lacroix (NY-NJ)
2. 69 – Gordie Howe (Hou)
3. 62 – Bryan Campbell (Van)
4. 60 – Mike Walton (Min)
5. 56 – Andre Hinse (Hou)
6. 55 – Wayne Carleton (Tor)
7. 53 – Wayne Connelly (Min)
   Larry Lund (Hou)
8. 52 – Pat Stapleton (Chi)
9. 50 – Ralph Backstrom (Chi)
10. 49 – Serge Bernie (Que)
    Chris Bordeleau (Win)

Points:
1. 117 – Mike Walton (Min)
2. 111 – Andre Lacroix (SD)
3. 100 – Gordie Howe (Hou)
4. 95 – Wayne Connelly (Min)
   Bobby Hull (Win)
5. 92 – Wayne Carleton (Tor)
6. 89 – Bryan Campbell (Van)
7. 88 – Danny Lawson (Van)
8. 86 – Serge Bernier (Que)
   Larry Lund (Hou)
9. 84 – Frank Hughes (Hou)
10. 83 – Ralph Backstrom (Chi)

1974-75

Goals:
1. 77 – Bobby Hull (Win)
2. 54 – Serge Bernie (Que
   Wayne Rivers (SD)
3. 53 – Anders Hedberg (Win)
4. 52 – Tom Simpson (Tor)
5. 50 – Marc Tardif (Mich-Que)
6. 48 – Frank Hughes (Hou)
   Mike Walton (Min)
7. 44 – Gary MacGregor (Chi)
   Dick Sentes (SD)
8. 43 – Gene Peacosh (SD)
9. 41 – Andre Lacroix (SD)
   Vaclav Nedomansky (Tor)
10. 40 – Rejean Houle (Que)
    Tom Webster (NE)

Assists:
1. 06 – Andre Lacroix (SD)
2. 94 – Ulf Nilsson (Win)
3. 75 – Larry Lund (Hou)
4. 68 – Serge Bernier (Que)
5. 66 – Wayne Dillon (Tor)
6. 65 – Gordie Howe (Hou)
   Bobby Hull (Win)
7. 61 – Kevin Morrison (SD)
8. 59 – Ray Adduono (SD)
9. 58 – Gavin Kirk (Tor)
10. 56 – J.C. Tremblay (Que)

Points:
1. 147 – Andre Lacroix (SD)
2. 142 – Bobby Hull (Win)
3. 122 – Serge Bernier (Que)
4. 120 – Ulf Nilsson (Win)
5. 108 – Larry Lund (Hou)
6. 107 – Wayne Rivers (SD)
7. 100 – Anders Hedberg (Win)
8. 99 – Gordie Howe (Hou)
9. 95 – Wayne Dillon (Tor)
10. 93 – Mike Walton (Min)

1975-76

Goals:
1. 71 – Marc Tardif (Que)
2. 60 – Real Cloutier (Que)
3. 56 – Vaclav Nedomansky (Tor)
4. 53 – Bobby Hull (Win)
5. 51 – Rejean Houle (Que)
6. 50 – Anders Hedberg (Win)
7. 47 – Del Hall (Phx)
8. 44 – Danny Lawson (Cal)
9. 43 – Rick Dudley (Cin)
   Mark Napier (Tor)
10. 42 – Ron Chipperfield (Cal)
    Rusty Patenaude (Edm)

Assists:
1. 77 – Marc Tardif (Que)
   J.C. Tremblay (Que)
2. 76 – Ulf Nilsson (Win)
3. 72 – Chris Bordeleau (Que)
   Robbie Ftorek (Phx)
   Andre Lacroix (SD)
4. 70 – Gordie Howe (Hou)
   Bobby Hull (Win)
5. 68 – Serge Bernier (Que)
6. 67 – Ray Adduono (SD)
7. 56 – Norm Ullman (Edm)
8. 55 – Anders Hedberg (Win)
   Frank Mahovlich (Tor)
9. 54 – Real Cloutier (Que)
10. 52 – Rejean Houle (Que)
    Danny Lawson (Cal)

Points:
1. 148 – Marc Tardif (Que)
2. 123 – Bobby Hull (Win)
3. 114 – Real Cloutier (Que)
   Ulf Nilsson (Win)
4. 113 – Robbie Ftorek (Phx)
5. 109 – Chris Bordeleau (Que)
6. 105 – Anders Hedberg (Win)
7. 103 – Rejean Houle (Que)
8. 102 – Serge Bernier (Que)
   Gordie Howe (Hou)
9. 101 – Andre Lacroix (SD)
10. 98 – Vaclav Nedomansky (Tor)

1976-77

Goals:
1. 70 – Anders Hedberg (Win)
2. 66 – Real Cloutier (Que)
3. 60 – Mark Napier (Bir)
4. 52 – Rich Leduc (Cin)
   Blaine Stoughton (Cin)
5. 49 – Marc Tardif (Que)
6. 46 – Robbie Ftorek (Phx)
7. 44 – Willy Lindstrom (Win)
8. 43 – Serge Bernier (Que)
9. 42 – Paulin Bordeleau (Que)
10. 41 – Rick Dudley (Cin)
    Tim Sheehy (NE-Bir)

Assists:
1. 85 – Ulf Nilsson (Win)
2. 82 – Andre Lacroix (SD)
3. 75 – Chris Bordeleau (Que)
   Real Cloutier (Que)
4. 71 – Robbie Ftorek (Phx)
5. 63 – Dave Keon (Min-NE)
6. 61 – Anders Hedberg (Win)
7. 60 – Marc Tardif (Que)
8. 58 – Ron Plumb (Cin)
9. 57 – Joe Noris (SD)
   Mike Rogers (NE)
10. 56 – Poul Popiel (Hou)

Points:
1. 141 – Real Cloutier (Que)
2. 131 – Anders Hedberg (Win)
3. 124 – Ulf Nilsson (Win)
4. 117 – Robbie Ftorek (Phx)
5. 114 – Andre Lacroix (SD)
6. 109 – Marc Tardif (Que)
7. 107 – Chris Bordeleau (Que)
   Rich Leduc (Cin)
8. 104 – Blaine Stoughton (Cin)
9. 96 – Serge Bernier (Que)
   Mark Napier (Bir)
   Dennis Sobchuk (Cin)
10. 92 – Joe Noris (SD)

1977-78

Goals:
1. 65 – Marc Tardif (Que)
2. 63 – Anders Hedberg (Win)
3. 59 – Robbie Ftorek (Cin)
4. 56 – Real Cloutier (Que)
5. 46 – Bobby Hull (Win)
6. 42 – Paulin Bordeleau (Que)
   Kent Nilsson (Win)
7. 41 – Bill Flett (Edm)
8. 40 – Morris Lukowich (Hou)
9. 38 – Ken Linseman (Bir)
10. 37 – Paul Henderson (Bir)
    Rich Leduc (Cin)
    Ulf Nilsson (Win)

Assists:
1. 89 – Ulf Nilsson (Win)
   Marc Tardif (Que)
2. 77 – Andre Lacroix (Hou)
3. 73 – Real Cloutier (Que)
4. 71 – Bobby Hull (Win)
5. 65 – Ken Nilsson (Win)
6. 62 – Gordie Howe (NE)
7. 61 – Mark Howe (NE)
8. 59 – Anders Hedberg (Win)
9. 57 – Terry Ruskowski (Hou)
10. 52 – Serge Bernier (Que)
    Ron Chipperfield (Edm)

Points:
1. 154 – Marc Tardif (Que)
2. 129 – Real Cloutier (Que)
3. 126 – Ulf Nilsson (Win)
4. 122 – Anders Hedberg (Win)
5. 117 – Bobby Hull (Win)
6. 113 – Andre Lacroix (Hou)
7. 109 – Robbie Ftorek (Cin)
8. 107 – Kent Nilsson (Win)
9. 96 – Gordie Howe (NE)
10. 91 – Mark Howe (NE)

1978–79

Goals:
1. 75 – Real Cloutier (Que)
2. 65 – Morris Lukowich (Win)
3. 46 – Wayne Gretzky (Ind-Edm)
    Peter Sullivan (Win)
4. 43 – Peter Marsh (Cin)
5. 42 – Mark Howe (NE)
6. 41 – Marc Tardif (Que)
7. 39 – Robbie Ftorek (Cin)
    Kent Nilsson (Win)
8. 36 – Serge Bernier (Que)
9. 35 – Rich Leduc (Ind-Que)
10. 34 – Blair MacDonald (Edm)

Assists:
1. 77 – Robbie Ftorek (Cin)
2. 68 – Kent Nilsson (Win)
3. 66 – Terry Ruskowski (Win)
4. 65 – Mark Howe (NE)
5. 64 – Wayne Gretzky (Ind-Edm)
6. 56 – Andre Lacroix (NE)
7. 55 – Marc Tardif (Que)
8. 54 – Real Cloutier (Que)
9. 51 – Craig Norwich (Cin)
10. 46 – Serge Bernier (Que)
    Gordie Roberts (NE)

Points:
1. 129 – Real Cloutier (Que)
2. 116 – Robbie Ftorek (Cin)
3. 110 – Wayne Gretzky (Ind-Edm)
4. 107 – Mark Howe (NE)
    Kent Nilsson (Win)
5. 99 – Morris Lukowich (Win)
6. 96 – Marc Tardif (Que)
7. 88 – Andre Lacroix (NE)
8. 86 – Terry Ruskowski (Win)
    Peter Sullivan (Win)
9. 82 – Serge Bernier (Que)
10. 76 – Rich Leduc (Ind-Que)

YEAR-BY-YEAR REGULAR-SEASON GOALTENDING LEADERS

1972–73

Games played:
64 – Jack Norris (Alb)
63 – Bernie Parent (Phi)
54 – Jim McLeod (Chi)

Wins:
33 – Bernie Parent (Phi)
32 – Gerry Cheevers (Cle)
31 – Al Smith (NE)

Losses:
29 – Jack Norris (Alb)
28 – Bernie Parent (Phi)
25 – Jim McLeod (Chi)

Ties:
4 – George Gardner (LA)
3 – Gilles Gratton (Ott)
    Jack Norris (Alb)
    Ernie Wakely (Win)
    Bob Whidden (Cle)

Goals-against average:
2.84 – Gerry Cheevers (Cle)
2.90 – Joe Daley (Win)
2.91 – Russ Gillow (LA)

Shutouts:
5 – Gerry Cheevers (Cle)
4 – Mike Curran (Min)
3 – Al Smith (NE)

1973–74

Games played:
59 – Gerry Cheevers (Cle)
57 – Gilles Gratton (Tor)
55 – Al Smith (NE)

Wins:
33 – Don McLeod (Hou)
30 – Gerry Cheevers (Cle)
    Al Smith (NE)

Losses:
25 – Joe Junkin (NY-NJ)
24 – Peter Donnelly (Van)
    Gilles Gratton (Tor)
    Jack Norris (Edm)
23 – George Gardner (LA-Van)

Ties:
6 – Gerry Cheevers (Cle)
4 – Joe Junkin (NY-NJ)
    Ernie Wakely (Win)
3 – Gilles Gratton (Tor)
    Don McLeod (Hou)
    Bob Whidden (Cle)

Goals-against average:
2.56 – Don McLeod (Hou)
3.03 – Gerry Cheevers (Cle)
3.08 – Al Smith (NE)

Shutouts:
4 – Gerry Cheevers (Cle)
3 – Don McLeod (Hou)
    Pete Donnelly (Van)
    Ernie Wakely (Win)

1974–75

Games played:
72 – Don McLeod (Van)
59 – Al Smith (NE)
58 – John Garrett (Min)

Wins:
33 – Ron Grahame (Hou)
    Don McLeod (Van)
    Al Smith (NE)
30 – John Garrett (Min)
    Gilles Gratton (Tor)
29 – Richard Brodeur (Que)

Losses:
35 – Andy Brown (Ind)
    Don McLeod (Van)
28 – Gerry Desjardins (Mich-Bal)
26 – Dave Dryden (chi)

Ties:
4 – Joe Daley (Win)
    Gary Kurt (Phx)
    Jack Norris (Phx)
    Al Smith (NE)
3 – Eddie Dyck (Ind)
    Chris Worthy (Edm)

Goals-against average:
3.03 – Ron Grahame (Hou)
3.23 – Wayne Rutledge (Hou)
    Bob Whidden (Cle)
3.25 – Ernie Wakely (Win-SD)

Shutouts:
4 – Gerry Cheevers (Cle)
    Ron Grahame (Hou)
3 – Ernie Wakely (Win-SD)
2 – Shared by 8 goaltenders

1975-76

Games played:
69 – Richard Brodeur (Que)
67 – Ernie Wakely (SD)
63 – Don McLeod (Cal)

Wins:
44 – Richard Brodeur (Que)
41 – Joe Daley (Win)
39 – Ron Grahame (Hou)

Losses:
34 – Dave Dryden (Edm)
28 – John Garrett (Min-Tor)
27 – Don McLeod (Cal)
    Ernie Wakely (SD)

Ties:
5 – Dave Dryden (Edm)
    Bruce Landon (NE)
4 – John Garrett (Min-Tor)
    Jack Norris (Phx)
    Ernie Wakely (SD)
3 – Leif Holmquist (Ind)
    Don McLeod (Cal)
    Mario Vien (Tor)

Goals-against average:
2.74 – Michel Dion (Ind)
2.84 – Joe Daley (Win)
3.17 – Wayne Rutledge (Hou)

Shutouts:
5 – Joe Daley (Win)
3 – John Garrett (Min-Tor)
    Ron Grahame (Hou)
    Ernie Wakely (SD)
2 – Christer Abrahamsson (NE)
    Richard Brodeur (Que)
    Paul Hoganson (Cin)

1976-77

Games played:
67 – Don McLeod (Cal)
65 – Joe Daley (Win)
    John Garrett (Bir)
56 – Clay Hebenton (Phx)

Wins:
39 – Joe Daley (win)
29 – Richard Brodeur (Que)
27 – Ron Grahame (Hou)

Losses:
34 – John Garrett (Bir)
    Don McLeod (Cal)
29 – Clay Hebenton (Phx)
25 – Norm Lapointe (Cin)

Ties:
5 – Louis Levasseur (Min-Edm)
    Don McLeod (Cal)
4 – Christer Abrahamsson (NE)
    John Garrett (Bir)
    Jim Park (Cin)
    Wayne Rutledge (Hou)

Goals-against average:
2.74 – Ron Grahame (Hou)
3.09 – Ernie Wakely (SD)
3.12 – Cap Raeder (NE)

Shutouts:
4 – Ken Broderick (Edm)
    John Garrett (Bir)
    Ron Grahame (Hou)
3 – Joe Daley (Win)
    Don McLeod (Cal)
    Wayne Rutledge (Hou)
    Ernie Wakely (SD)

1977-78

Games played:
58 – John Garrett (Bir)
57 – Ernie Wakely (Cin-Hou)
55 – Al Smith (NE)

Wins:
30 – Al Smith (NE)
28 – Ernie Wakely (all with Hou)
25 – Gary Bromley (Win)

Losses:
31 – John Garrett (Bir)
30 – Gary Inness (Ind)
23 – Dave Dryden (Edm)
    Ernie Wakely (Cin-Hou)

Goals-against average:
3.22 – Al Smith (NE)
3.30 – Gary Bromley (Win)
    Joe Daley (Win)
    Louis Levasseur (NE)
3.41 – Ernie Wakely (Cin-Hou)

Shutouts:
4 – Michel Dion (Ind)
3 – Louis Levasseur (NE)
2 – Dave Dryden (Edm)
    John Garrett (Bir)
    Don McLeod (both with Edm)
    Al Smith (NE)
    Ernie Wakely (both with Hou)

1978-79

Games played:
63 – Dave Dryden (Edm)
54 – Mike Liut (Cin)
52 – Markus Mattsson (Win)

Wins:
41 – Dave Dryden (Edm)
25 – Richard Brodeur (Que)
    Markus Mattsson (Win)
23 – Mike Liut (Cin)

Losses:
27 – Mike Liut (Cin)
22 – Pat Riggin (Bir)
21 – Markus Mattsson (Win)

Ties:
5 – Pat Riggin (Bir)
    Al Smith (NE)
4 – John Garrett (NE)
    Mike Liut (Cin)
3 – Richard Brodeur (Que)
    Joe Daley (Win)
    Markus Mattsson (Win)

Goals-against average:
2.89 – Dave Dryden (Edm)
3.11 – Richard Brodeur (Que)
3.30 – Jim Corsi (Que)

Shutouts:
3 – Richard Brodeur (Que)
    Jim Corsi (Que)
    Dave Dryden (Edm)
    Mike Liut (Cin)
2 – John Garrett (NE)
    Eddie Mio (Ind-Edm)
1 – Pat Riggin (Bir)
    Al Smith (NE)

YEAR-BY-YEAR REGULAR-SEASON PENALTY MINUTE LEADERS

1972-73

1. 239 – John Schella (Hou)
2. 191 – Tom Gilmore (LA)
3. 189 – Dick Paradise (Min)
4. 188 – John Arbour (Min)
5. 185 – Jim Cardiff (Phi)
6. 169 – Pierre Roy (Que)
   Paul Shmyr (Cle)
7. 159 – Hal Willis (NE)
8. 158 – Poul Popiel (Hou)
9. 157 – Johnny McKenzie (Phi)
   Michel Rouleau (Phi-Que)
10. 155 – Jim Niekamp (LA)

1973-74

1. 223 – Gord Gallant (Min)
2. 214 – Doug Barrie (Edm)
3. 192 – John Arbour (Min)
4. 191 – Colin Campbell (Van)
5. 188 – Jim Cardiff (Van)
6. 182 – Steve Sutherland (LA)
7. 170 – John Schella (Hou)
8. 165 – Paul Shmyr (Cle)
9. 164 – Tom Gilmore (Edm)
10. 157 – Larry Mavety (Chi)

1974-75

1. 203 – Gord Gallant (Min)
2. 201 – John Hughes (Phx)
3. 176 – Ron Busniuk (Min)
   John Schella (Hou))
4. 168 – Cam Connor (Phx)
5. 159 – Rick Jodzio (Van)
6. 153 – Glenn Irwin (Hou)
7. 151 – Ken Baird (Edm)
   Steve Sutherland (Mich-Que)
8. 150 – Larry Mavety (Chi)
9. 144 – Nick Fotiu (NE)
10. 143 – Kevin Morrison (SD)

1975-76

1. 365 – Curt Brackenbury (Min-Que)
2. 351 – Kim Clackson (Ind)
3. 297 – Gord Gallant (Que)
4. 295 – Cam Connor (Phx)
5. 258 – Pierre Roy (Que)
6. 220 – Jack Carlson (Min-Edm)
7. 205 – Ron Busniuk (Min-NE)
8. 204 – John Hughes (Cin)
9. 201 – Paul Baxter (Cle)
10. 197 – Steve Sutherland (Que)

1976-77

1. 274 – Frank Beaton (Edm)
2. 244 – Paul Baxter (Que)
3. 224 – Ron Busniuk (NE-Edm)
   Cam Connor (Hou)
4. 215 – Bill Butters (Min-Edm-NE)
5. 197 – Wally Weir (Que)
6. 186 – Jerry Rollins (Bir-Phx)
7. 176 – Pierre Roy (Que-Cin)
8. 169 – Gordie Roberts (NE)
9. 168 – Kim Clackson (Ind)
   Glenn Irwin (Hou)
10. 166 – Lou Nistico (Bir)

1977-78

1. 284 – Steve Durbano (Bir)
2. 279 – Frank Beaton (Bir)
3. 258 – Gilles Bilodeau (Bir)
4. 241 – Dave Hanson (Bir)
   Paul Stewart (Cin)
5. 240 – Paul Baxter (Que)
6. 217 – Cam Connor (Hou)
7. 203 – Kim Clackson (Win)
8. 192 – Jack Carlson (NE)
9. 170 – Terry Ruskowski (Hou)
10. 158 – Peter Driscoll (Que-Ind)

1978-79

1. 248 – Scott Campbell (Win)
   Rick Vaive (Bir)
2. 240 – Paul Baxter (Que)
3. 222 – Barry Melrose (Cin)
4. 212 – Dave Hanson (Bir)
5. 211 – Terry Ruskowski (Win)
6. 210 – Kim Clackson (Win)
7. 166 – Wally Weir (Que)
8. 165 – Rob Ramage (Bir)
9. 158 – Dave Semenko (Edm)
10. 155 – Curt Brackenbury (Que)

YEAR-BY-YEAR ALL-STAR TEAMS (AS SELECTED BY THE MEDIA)

1972–73	**First team**	**Second team**
Goal	Gerry Cheevers (Cle)	Bernie Parent (Phi)
Defense	J.C. Tremblay (Que)	Jim Dorey (NE)
Defense	Paul Shmyr (Cle)	Larry Hornung (Win)
Centre	Andre Lacroix (Phi)	Ron Ward (NY)
Right Wing	Danny Lawson (Phi)	Tom Webster (NE)
Left Wing	Bobby Hull (Win)	Gary Jarrett (Cle)

1973–74	**First team**	**Second team**
Goal	Don McLeod (Hou)	Gerry Cheevers (Cle)
Defense	Pat Stapleton (Chi)	J.C. Tremblay (Que)
Defense	Paul Shmyr (Cle)	Al Hamilton (Edm)
Centre	Andre Lacroix (NY-NJ)	Wayne Carleton (Tor)
Right Wing	Gordie Howe (Hou)	Mike Walton (Min)
Left Wing	Bobby Hull (Win)	Mark Howe (Hou)

1974–75	**First team**	**Second team**
Goal	Ron Grahame (Hou)	Gerry Cheevers (Cle)
Defense	J.C. Tremblay (Que)	Poul Popiel (Hou)
Defense	Kevin Morrison (SD)	Barry Long (Edm)
Centre	Andre Lacroix (SD)	Serge Bernier (Que)
Right Wing	Gordie Howe (Hou)	Anders Hedberg (Win)
Left Wing	Bobby Hull (Win)	Marc Tardif (Que)

1975–76	**First team**	**Second team**
Goal	Joe Daley (Win)	Ron Grahame (Hou)
Defense	Paul Shmyr (Cle)	Kevin Morrison (SD)
Defense	J.C. Tremblay (Que)	Pat Stapleton (Ind)
Centre	Ulf Nilsson (Win)	Robbie Ftorek (Phx)
Right Wing	Anders Hedberg (Win)	Real Cloutier (Que)
Left Wing	Marc Tardif (Que)	Bobby Hull (Win)

1976–77	**First team**	**Second team**
Goal	John Garrett (Bir)	Joe Daley (Win)
Defense	Darryl Maggs (Ind)	Poul Popiel (Hou)
Defense	Ron Plumb (Cin)	Mark Howe (Hou)
Centre	Robbie Ftorek (Phx)	Ulf Nilsson (Win)
Right Wing	Anders Hedberg (Win)	Real Cloutier (Que)
Left Wing	Marc Tardif (Que)	Rick Dudley (Cin)

1977–78	**First team**	**Second team**
Goal	Al Smith (NE)	Ernie Wakely (Hou)
Defense	Lars-Erik Sjoberg (Win)	Rick Ley (NE)
Defense	Al Hamilton (Edm)	Barry Long (Win)
Centre	Ulf Nilsson (Win)	Robbie Ftorek (Cin)
Right Wing	Anders Hedberg (Win)	Real Cloutier (Que)
Left Wing	Marc Tardif (Que)	Bobby Hull (Win)

1978–79	**First team**	**Second team**
Goal	Dave Dryden (Edm)	Richard Brodeur (Que)
Defense	Rick Ley (NE)	Dave Langevin (Edm)
Defense	Rob Ramage (Bir)	Paul Shmyr (Edm)
Centre	Robbie Ftorek (Cin)	Wayne Gretzky (Edm)
Right Wing	Real Cloutier (Que)	Blair MacDonald (Edm)
Left Wing	Mark Howe (NE)	Morris Lukowich (Win)

YEAR-BY-YEAR ALL-STARS GAME ROSTERS AND SUMMARIES

1973

Date: January 6, 1973
Location: Le Colisee, Quebec City
Attendance: 5,435
Result: East Division 6, West Division 2
Game MVP: Wayne Carleton, Ottawa Nationals

EAST DIVISION ROSTER

Coach: Jack Kelley (NE).
Goaltenders: Gerry Cheevers (Cle), Al Smith (NE), Serge Aubry (Que).
Defensemen: J.C. Tremblay (Que), Rick Ley (NE), Jim Dorey (NE), Ken Block (NY), Paul Shmyr (Cle), John Hanna (Cle).
Forwards: Michel Parizeau (Que), Johnny McKenzie (Phi), Danny Lawson (Phi), Norm Ferguson (NY), Ron Ward (NY), Gerry Pinder (Cle), Gary Jarrett (Cle), Terry Caffery (NE), Larry Pleau (NE), Tom Webster (NE), Wayne Carleton (Ott), Ron Climie (Ott), Guy Trottier (Ott), Bob Charlebois (Ott).

WEST DIVISION ROSTER

Coach: Bobby Hull (Win).
Goaltenders: Ernie Wakely (Win), Jack Norris (Alb), Mike Curran (Min).
Defensemen: Al Hamilton (Alb), Bob Wall (Alb), Ron Anderson (Chi), Bart Crashley (LA), Gerry Odrowski (LA), Mike McMahon (Min), Terry Ball (Min).
Forwards: Bobby Hull (Win), Christian Bordeleau (Win), Norm Beaudin (Win), Gary Veneruzzo (LA), Mike Byers (LA), Jan Popiel (Chi), Jim Harrison (Alb), Ted Hampson (Min), Wayne Connelly (Min), Ted Taylor (Hou), Gord Labossiere (Hou).

SCORING SUMMARY: EAST 6, WEST 2

First period:
1. West, Odrowski (Beaudin) 10:39
2. East, Jarrett (Ward) 10:51

Second period:
3. East, McKenzie (Carleton, Block) 3:37
4. East, Pleau (Webster, Caffery) 12:47
5. East, Dorey (Ward, Lawson) 19:43

Third period:
6. West, Hull (Connelly, Bordeleau) 3:05
7. East, Lawson (Jarrett, Tremblay) 7:29
8. East, Carleton (Charlebois, Dorey) 8:00

Shots on goal: East 47, West 33
Did not play: Bart Crashley, Serge Aubry

1974

Date: January 3, 1974
Location: St. Paul Civic Center, St. Paul, Minnesota
Attendance: 13,196
Result: East Division 8, West Division 4
Game MVP: Mike Walton, Minnesota Fighting Saints

EAST DIVISION ROSTER

Coach: Jack Kelley (NE).
Goaltenders: Gerry Cheevers (Cle), Al Smith (NE), Gilles Gratton (Tor).
Defensemen: Brad Selwood (NE), Rick Ley (NE), Jim Dorey (NE), Pat Stapleton (Chi), Paul Shmyr (Cle), J.C. Tremblay (Que).
Forwards: Bobby Sheehan (NJ), Andre Lacroix (NJ), Wayne Carleton (Tor), Tom Simpson (Tor), Gerry Pinder (Cle), Gary Jarrett (Cle), Hugh Harris (NE), Larry Pleau (NE), Tom Webster (NE), Serge Bernier (Que), Rejean Houle (Que), Ralph Backstrom (Chi), Rosaire Paiement (Chi).

WEST DIVISION ROSTER

Coach: Bobby Hull (Win).
Goaltenders: Ernie Wakely (Win), Jack Norris (Edm), John Garrett (Min).
Defensemen: Al Hamilton (Edm), Rick Smith (Min), Poul Popiel (Hou), Ralph MacSweyn (Van), Larry Hornung (Win), Gerry Odrowski (LA), Bart Crashley (LA).
Forwards: Gordie Howe (Hou), Larry Lund (Hou), Frank Hughes (Hou), Bryan Campbell (Van), Danny Lawson (Van), Wayne Connelly (Min), Mike Walton (Min), Jim Harrison (Edm), Ron Climie (Edm), Marc Tardif (LA), Fran Huck (Win), Bobby Hull (Win).

SCORING SUMMARY: EAST 8, WEST 4

First period:
1. East, Houle (Bernier, Paiement) 2:11
2. East, Backstrom (Carleton, Stapleton) 8:02
3. East, Pleau (unassisted) 10:39
4. West, Walton (Lawson) 14:55
5. East, Pinder (Lacroix, Shmyr) 18:38
6. East, Lacroix (Pinder, Jarrett) 19:12

Second period:
7. West, Walton (Hull, Tardif) 7:27
8. East, Paiement (Backstrom) 9:15
9. West, Walton (Hamilton, Climie) 16:04
10. West, Lund (Hughes, Hamilton) 17:28

Third period:
11. East, Lacroix (Jarrett, Pinder) 9:17
12. East, Pleau (Harris, Webster) 18:59

Shots on goal: East 32, West 30
Did not play: Al Smith, Jim Harrison, Larry Hornung

Overtime 191

1975

Date: January 21, 1975
Location: Northlands Coliseum, Edmonton, Alberta
Attendance: 15,326
Result: West Division 6, East Division 4
Game MVP: Rejean Houle, Quebec Nordiques

EAST DIVISION ROSTER

Coach: Ron Ryan (NE).
Goaltenders: Al Smith (NE), Gerry Cheevers (Cle), Andy Brown (Ind).
Defensemen: Rick Ley (NE), Brad Selwood (NE), J.C. Tremblay (Que), Dale Hoganson (Que), Pat Stapleton (Chi), Paul Shmyr (Cle), Jim Dorey (Tor).
Forwards: Marc Tardif (Que), Rejean Houle (Que), Serge Bernier (Que), Frank Mahovlich (Tor), Paul Henderson (Tor), Tom Simpson (Tor), Gary Veneruzzo (Mich), Pierre Guite (Mich), Ralph Backstrom (Chi), Tom Webster (NE), Larry Pleau (NE).

WEST DIVISION ROSTER

Coach: Bill Dineen (Hou).
Goaltenders: Wayne Rutledge (Hou), Don McLeod (Van), Joe Daley (Win).
Defensemen: Lars-Erik Sjoberg (Win), Gerry Odrowski (Phx), Barry Long (Edm), Al Hamilton (Edm), Doug Barrie (Edm), Poul Popiel (Hou), John Schella (Hou).
Forwards: Bobby Hull (Win), Ulf Nilsson (Win), Gordie Howe (Hou), Mark Howe (Hou), Larry Lund (Hou), Frank Hughes (Hou), Ted Taylor (Hou), Andre Hinse (Hou), Andre Lacroix (SD), Mike Walton (Min), Fran Huck (Min), Danny Lawson (Van).

SCORING SUMMARY: WEST 6, EAST 4

First period:
1. West, Mark Howe (Gordie Howe, Lacroix) 7:08
2. West, Hinse (Lund, Hughes) 8:18
3. East, Tardif (Houle, Selwood) 13:32
4. East, Houle (Pleau, Dorey) 17:37

Second period:
5. West, Hull (Lawson) 4:23
6. West, Hinse (Hughes, Odrowski) 6:35
7. West, Taylor (Lacroix, Schella) 10:07
8. West, Gordie Howe (Lacroix, Mark Howe) 11:53
9. East, Houle (Selwood, Dorey) 14:32

Third period:
10. East, Bernier (Tardif, Houle) 11:20

Shots on goal: West 30, East 28
Did not play: Pierre Guite, Paul Shmyr, Mike Walton

1976

Date: January 13, 1976
Location: Richfield Coliseum, Cleveland, Ohio
Attendance: 15,491
Result: Team Canada 6, Team USA 1
Game MVPs:
Team Canada: Real Cloutier, Quebec Nordiques
Team USA: Paul Shmyr, Cleveland Crusaders

TEAM CANADA ROSTER

Coach: Jean-Guy Gendron (Que).
Goaltenders: Jim Shaw (Tor), Don McLeod (Cal), Joe Daley (Win).
Defensemen: Thommie Bergman (Win), Lars-Erik Sjoberg (Win), Larry Hornung (Win), Paul Terbenche (Cal), John Miszuk (Cal), Barry Long (Edm), J.C. Tremblay (Que).
Forwards: Serge Bernier (Que), Marc Tardif (Que), Rejean Houle (Que), Real Cloutier (Que), Christian Bordeleau (Que), Bobby Hull (Win), Ulf Nilsson (Win), Anders Hedberg (Win), Frank Mahovlich (Tor), Vaclav Nedomansky (Tor), Rusty Patenaude (Edm), Danny Lawson (Cal).

TEAM USA ROSTER

Coach: Bill Dineen (Hou).
Goaltenders: Gerry Cheevers (Cle), Christer Abrahamsson (NE).
Defensemen: Marty Howe (Hou), John Schella (Hou), Paul Shmyr (Cle), Rick Ley (NE), Pat Stapleton (Ind), Kevin Morrison (SD).
Forwards: Gordie Howe (Hou), Mark Howe (Hou), Gene Peacosh (SD), Andre Lacroix (SD), Mike Walton (Min), Dave Keon (Min), Claude Larose (Cin), Wayne Carleton (NE), Tom Webster (NE), Robbie Ftorek (Phx), Don Borgeson (Den-Ott), Ralph Backstrom (Den-Ott).

SCORING SUMMARY: CANADA 6, USA 1

First period:
No scoring.

Second period:
1. Canada, Cloutier (Tardif) 1:45
2. Canada, Mahovlich (Bergman) 11:50
3. Canada, Cloutier (Sjoberg, Bordeleau) 16:44

Third period:
4. Canada, Lawson (unassisted) 3:50
5. USA, Lacroix (Ley) 13:26
6. Canada, Nilsson (Hedberg, Miszuk) 15:33
7. Canada, Cloutier (Bordeleau, Tardif) 18:04

Shots on goal: Team Canada 30, Team USA 25
Did not play: Joe Daley, J.C. Tremblay

1977

Date: January 18, 1977
Location: Hartford Civic Center, Hartford, Connecticut
Attendance: 10,337
Result: East Division 4, West Division 2
Game MVPs:
East Division: Louis Levasseur, Minnesota Fighting Saints
West Division: Willy Lindstrom, Winnipeg Jets

EAST DIVISION ROSTER

Coach: Jacques Demers (Ind).
Goaltenders: Louis Levasseur (Min), John Garrett (Bir).
Defensemen: Pat Stapleton (Ind), Gordie Roberts (NE), Thommie Abrahamsson (NE), John Hughes (Cin), Ron Plumb (Cin), J.C. Tremblay (Que).
Forwards: Marc Tardif (Que), Real Cloutier (Que), Serge Bernier (Que), Mark Napier (Bir), Ralph Backstrom (Ne), George Lyle (NE), Mike Rogers (NE), Rich Leduc (Cin), Dennis Sobchuk (Cin), Michel Parizeau (Ind), Hugh Harris (Ind), Blair MacDonald (Ind).

WEST DIVISION ROSTER

Coach: Bobby Kromm (Win).
Goaltenders: Joe Daley (Win), Wayne Rutledge (Hou).
Defensemen: Thommie Bergman (Win), Paul Terbenche (Cal), Kevin Morrison (SD), Paul Shmyr (SD), Barry Wilkins (Edm), Poul Popiel (Hou).
Forwards: Bobby Hull (Win), Ulf Nilsson (Win), Anders Hedberg (Win), Willy Lindstrom (Win), Danny Lawson (Cal), Gordie Howe (Hou), Cam Connor (Hou), Robbie Ftorek (Phx), Del Hall (Phx), Andre Lacroix (SD), Joe Noris (SD), Norm Ferguson (SD).

SCORING SUMMARY: EAST 4, WEST 2

First period:
1. East, Tremblay (Leduc, Sobchuk) 11:17
2. West, Shmyr (Lindstrom, Lacroix) 11:58
3. East, Tardif (Stapleton, Bernier) 14:56

Second period:
No scoring.

Third period:
4. West, Lindstrom (Wilkins) 4:07
5. East, Cloutier (Tardif, Hughes) 7:57
6. East, Lyle (Rogers, Abrahamsson) 8:35

Shots on goal: West 51, East 27

1978

Date: January 17, 1978
Location: Le Colisee, Quebec City
Attendance: 6,413
Result: (1977 Avco Cup champion) Quebec Nordiques 5, WHA All-Stars 4
Game MVPs:
Quebec: Marc Tardif
WHA All-Stars: Mark Howe, New England Whalers

WHA ALL-STARS ROSTER:

Coach: Bill Dineen (Hou).
Goaltenders: Al Smith (NE), John Garrett (Bir).
Defensemen: Barry Long (Edm), Al Hamilton (Edm), Lars-Erik Sjoberg (Win), Pat Stapleton (Ind), Gordie Roberts (NE), Rick Ley (NE).
Forwards: Bobby Hull (Win), Anders Hedberg (Win), Ulf Nilsson (Win), Mark Napier (Bir), Bill Flett (Edm), Gordie Howe (NE), Mark Howe (NE), Mike Antonovich (NE), Rusty Patenaude (Ind), Robbie Ftorek (Cin), Andre Lacroix (Hou), Morris Lukowich (Hou).

QUEBEC NORDIQUES ROSTER:

Coach: Marc Boileau.
Goaltenders: Ken Broderick, Jim Corsi.
Defensemen: Paul Baxter, Jean Bernier, Garry Lariviere, J.C. Tremblay, Chris Evans, Jim Dorey.
Forwards: Paulin Bordeleau, Andre Boudrias, Marc Tardif, Curt Brackenbury, Warren Miller, Real Cloutier, Norm Dube, Bob Fitchner, Steve Sutherland, Matti Hagman, Serge Bernier, Charles Constantin.

SCORING SUMMARY:
QUEBEC 5, WHA ALL-STARS 4

First period:
1. Quebec, Hagman (Tardif) 12:56
2. WHA All-Stars, Mark Howe (Flett, Sjoberg) 14:50
3. WHA All-Stars, Hedberg (Hull) 18:57
4. WHA All-Stars, Lukowich (Lacroix, Long) 19:10

Second period:
5. WHA All-Stars, Flett (Mark Howe) 7:07
6. Quebec, Miller (Hagman, Tardif) 10:01
7. Quebec, Baxter (Tardif, Fitchner) 12:14
8. Quebec, Tardif (Boudrias) 17:51

Third period:
9. Quebec, Hagman (Tardif, Tremblay) 14:12

Shots on goal: Quebec 32, WHA All-Stars 32

1979

A three-game series between the WHA All-Stars and Moscow Dynamo replaced the league's annual all-star contest.

Dates: January 2, 4 & 5, 1979
Location: Northlands Coliseum, Edmonton, Alberta
Results:
Game 1 – WHA 4, Moscow 2
Game 2 – WHA 4, Moscow 2
Game 3 – WHA 4, Moscow 3
No MVPs selected.

WHA ALL-STARS ROSTER:

GM: John Ferguson (Win).
Coaches: Larry Hillman (Win), Jacques Demers (Que).
Goaltenders: Dave Dryden (Edm), Markus Mattsson (Win).
Defensemen: Rob Ramage (Bir), Paul Shmyr (Edm), Claire Alexander (Edm), John Hughes (Edm), Barry Long (Win), Rick Ley (NE).
Forwards: Gordie Howe (NE), Mark Howe (NE), Dave Keon (NE), Wayne Gretzky (Edm), Blair MacDonald (Edm), Mike Gartner (Cin), Peter Marsh (Cin), Rick Dudley (Cin), Robbie Ftorek (Cin), Serge Bernier (Que), Real Cloutier (Que), Marc Tardif (Que), Peter Sullivan (Win), Morris Lukowich (Win).

MOSCOW DYNAMO ROSTER

Coaches: Vladimir Kiseliov, Pavel Zhiburtovich.
Goaltenders: Vladimir Polupanov, Sergei Babariko.
Defensemen: Vasili Pausov, Vitali Filippov, Aleksandr Filippov, Sergei Gimaev, Alexei Volchenkov, Vladimir Orlov, Mikhail Slipchenko, Viktor Khatulev.
Forwards: Victor Shkurdiuk, Vladimir Vikulov, Aleksandr Lovanov, Alexei Volchkov, Pavel Ezavski, Alexei Frolikov, Mikhail Shostak, Vladimir Devjatov, Evgeni Kotlov, Vladimir Golubovich, Vladimir Semjonov, Sergei Tukmachev, Viacheslav Anisin, Piotr Priordin.

GAME 1 SCORING SUMMARY: WHA 4, MOSCOW 2

First period:
1. WHA, Gretzky (Mark Howe, Shmyr) 1:35
2. Moscow, Frolikov (Tukmachev, Filippov) 14:20
3. Moscow, Semjonov (Khatulev) 18:08

Second period:
4. WHA, Gordie Howe (Mark Howe) 16:29

Third period:
5. WHA, Mark Howe (Gretzky, Gordie Howe) 7:02
6. WHA, Sullivan (unassisted) 19:51

Goaltenders: WHA – Dryden; Moscow – Babariko
Shots on goal: WHA 30; Moscow 21
Attendance: 8,038

GAME 2 SCORING SUMMARY: WHA 4, MOSCOW 2

First period:
1. WHA, Lukowich (Ftorek, Gartner) 2:26
2. Moscow, Shostak (Filippov, Shkurdiuk) 7:38
3. WHA, Mark Howe (Gordie Howe, Gretzky) 9:27
4. WHA, Gartner (Lukowich, Sullivan) 16:51

Second period:
5. Moscow, Shkurdiuk (Lovanov) 19:44

Third period:
6. WHA, Gretzky (Ley) 5:45

Goaltenders: WHA – Mattsson; Moscow – Babariko
Shots on goal: WHA 37; Moscow 22
Attendance: 11,220

GAME 3 SCORING SUMMARY: WHA 4, MOSCOW 3

First period:
1. WHA, Lukowich (Gartner) 1:46
2. WHA, Ramage (Keon, MacDonald) 6:41
3. Moscow, Shkurdiuk (Anisin, Volchenkov) 11:02
4. Moscow, Shostak (Slipchenko, Frolikov) 11:43
5. WHA, Sullivan (unassisted) 18:29

Second period:
6. WHA, Bernier (Ley, Gartner) 14:03

Third period:
7. Moscow, Semjonov (Pausov, Lovanov) 13:12

Goaltenders: WHA – Mattsson; Moscow – Babariko
Shots on goal: WHA 29; Moscow 19
Attendance: 15,590

THE WHA VS. INTERNATIONAL COMPETITION

1974

"Friendship Series"
Team Canada vs. USSR Nationals

Dates: Sept. 17 (Quebec City); Sept. 19 (Toronto); Sept. 21 (Winnipeg); Sept. 23 (Vancouver); Oct. 1, 3, 5, 6 (Moscow).

Results:
Game 1 – Team Canada 3, USSR 3
Game 2 – Team Canada 4, USSR 1
Game 3 – USSR 8, Team Canada 5
Game 4 – Team Canada 5, USSR 5
Game 5 – USSR 3, Team Canada 2
Game 6 – USSR 5, Team Canada 2
Game 7 – Team Canada 4, USSR 4
Game 8 – USSR 3, Team Canada 2

TEAM CANADA ROSTER
GM: Bill Hunter (Edm).
Coaches: Billy Harris (Tor); (assistants) Bobby Hull (Win), Pat Stapleton (Chi).
Goaltenders: Gerry Cheevers (Cle), Don McLeod (Hou), Gilles Gratton (Tor).
Defensemen: Rick Ley (NE), Brad Selwood (NE), J.C. Tremblay (Que), Marty Howe (Hou), Pat Price (Van), Pat Stapleton (Chi), Rick Smith (Min), Paul Shmyr (Cle), Al Hamilton (Edm), Barry Long (Edm).
Forwards: Bobby Hull (Win), Frank Mahovlich (Tor), Paul Henderson (Tor), Gordie Howe (Hou), Mark Howe (Hou), Serge Bernier (Que), Rejean Houle (Que), Marc Tardif (Mich), Jim Harrison (Edm), Bruce MacGregor (Edm), Ralph Backstrom (Chi), Andre Lacroix (SD), Johnny McKenzie (Van), Tom Webster (NE), Mike Walton (Min).
Training camp invitees: Gavin Kirk (Tor), Wayne Dillon (Tor), Dennis Sobchuk (Cin), Ron Chipperfield (Van).

USSR NATIONALS ROSTER
Coach: Boris Kulagin.
Goaltenders: Vladislav Tretiak, Aleksandr Sidelnikov, Vladimir Polupanov.
Defensemen: Aleksandr Gusev, Vladimir Lutchenko, Yuri Liapkin, Valeri Vasilyev, Gennadi Tsygankov, Viktor Kuznetsov, Aleksandr Filippov, Aleksandr Sapelkin, Yuri Shatalov, Juri Fiodorov.
Forwards: Valeri Kharlamov, Aleksandr Yakushev, Sergei Kapustin, Aleksandr Volchkov, Yuri Tiurin, Aleksandr Maltsev, Yuri Lebedev, Boris Mikhailov, Vladimir Popov, Vladimir Petrov, Vladimir Shadrin, Vladimir Vikulov, Viacheslav Anisin, Aleksandr Bodunov, Sergei Kotov, Konstantin Klimov, Viktor Shalimov.

GAME 1 SUMMARY: TEAM CANADA 3, USSR 3

First period:
1. Canada, McKenzie (Lacroix, Hull) 12:13
Penalties: None

Second period:
2. USSR, Lutchenko (Tsygankov, Kapustin) 7:46
3. Canada, Hull (Walton, Gordie Howe) 12:07
4. USSR, Kharlamov (Vasilyev) 14:04
5. USSR, Petrov (Gusev, Kharlamov) 17:10
Penalties: Houle (tripping) 0:24; McKenzie and Liapkin (cross checking) 4:24; Vasilyev (tripping) 11:07; Selwood (tripping) 12:40; Shmyr (tripping) 14:38.

Third period:
6. Canada, Hull (Lacroix, McKenzie) 14:18
Penalties: Kapustin (holding) 6:04; Bodunov (hooking) 15:16.

Goaltenders: Canada – Cheevers; USSR – Tretiak
Shots on goal: Canada 34; USSR 28
Attendance in Quebec City: 10,958

GAME 2 SUMMARY: TEAM CANADA 4, USSR 1

First period:
1. Canada, Backstrom (Mark Howe, Gordie Howe) 4:31
2. Canada, Lacroix (McKenzie, Tremblay) 10:49
Penalties: Smith (elbowing) 1:44; Kapustin (interference) 10:19; Kapustin (tripping) 12:50; Mahovlich (tripping) 16:08.

Second period:
3. Canada, Hull (Lacroix, McKenzie) 2:50
4. USSR, Yakushev (Shadrin, Lebedev) 13:09
Penalties: Mahovlich (slashing) 9:44; Lacroix (high sticking) 15:39.

Third period:
5. Canada, Tremblay (Lacroix, Hull) 17:03
Penalties: Smith (holding) 13:23; Maltsev (high sticking) 16:04; Tremblay (high sticking) 19:00.

Goaltenders: Canada – Cheevers; USSR – Tretiak
Shots on goal: Canada 33; USSR 30
Attendance in Toronto: 16,485

GAME 3 SUMMARY: USSR 8, TEAM CANADA 5

First period:
1. Canada, MacGregor (Henderson) 14:58
2. USSR, Yakushev (Shadrin) 17:25
Penalties: Lacroix (slashing) 5:02; Smith (cross checking) 13:25; Walton (tripping) 19:16.

Second period:
3. USSR, Mikhailov (Petrov) 1:23
4. Canada, Webster (Bernier, Tardif) 12:40
5. USSR, Vasilyev (Mikhailov, Petrov) 15:14
6. USSR, Maltsev (Anisin) 15:31
Penalties: Hamilton (cross checking) 3:26; McKenzie and Kuznetsov (roughing) 5:49; Shadrin (slashing) 8:16; McKenzie and Lebedev (roughing) 13:24.

Third period:
7. USSR, Yakushev (Shadrin) 2:35
8. USSR, Bodunov (unassisted) 8:44
9. USSR, Yakushev (unassisted) 11:27
10. Canada, Henderson (Harrison) 14:31
11. Canada, Henderson (Harrison, MacGregor) 15:04
12. Canada, Bernier (Webster, Hamilton) 16:01
13. USSR, Lebedev (Lutchenko) 18:05
Penalties: Kuznetsov (holding) 12:20; Lutchenko (tripping) 18:56.

Goaltenders: Canada – McLeod; USSR – Tretiak
Shots on goal: Canada 34; USSR 39
Attendance in Winnipeg: 10,100

GAME 4 SUMMARY: TEAM CANADA 5, USSR 5

First period:
1. USSR, Vasilyev (Kharlamov) 3:24
2. Canada, Gordie Howe (Stapleton, Backstrom) 4:20
3. USSR, Mikhailov (Petrov) 5:59
4. Canada, Hull (Mahovlich) 12:45
5. Canada, Hull (Stapleton) 15:11
6. Canada, Mahovlich (Bernier, Houle) 17:10
7. Canada, Hull (Lacroix) 17:45
Penalty: Gusev (slashing) 11:38.

Second period:
8. USSR, Yakushev (Lebedev) 11:04
Penalties: Shmyr (roughing) 4:08; Petrov and Smith (interference) 13:35; Ley (roughing) 17:07.

Third period:
9. USSR, Maltsev (unassisted) 16:08
10. USSR, Gusev (Mikhailov, Petrov) 16:59
Penalties: Shadrin (slashing) 6:45; McKenzie (elbowing) 7:30; McKenzie (hooking) 10:26; Tsygankov (tripping) 17:51.

Goaltenders: Canada – Cheevers; USSR – Tretiak
Shots on goal: Canada 28; USSR 28
Attendance in Vancouver: 15,772

GAME 5 SUMMARY: USSR 3, TEAM CANADA 2

First period:
1. USSR, Maltsev (Vikulov, Anisin) 5:34
Penalties: Mahovlich (holding) 2:32; Petrov (roughing) 6:59; Ley (roughing) 13:52; Bernier (roughing) 15:07.

Second period:
2. Canada, Gordie Howe (Marty Howe, Backstrom) 00:15
3. USSR, Maltsev (Shadrin, Vikulov) 15:04
Penalties: Webster (slashing) 4:14; Lebedev (high sticking) 7:02; McKenzie (hooking) 13:52; Kharlamov and Bernier (roughing) 18:52.

Third period:
4. USSR, Gusev (unassisted) 11:48
5. Canada, Mark Howe (Shmyr) 18:10
Penalties: Lacroix (slashing) 2:46; Backstrom (misconduct) 4:37; Shadrin (elbowing) 5:38; Bodunov (hooking) 16:21.

Goaltenders: Canada – Cheevers; USSR – Tretiak
Shots on goal: Canada 16; USSR 27

GAME 6 SUMMARY: USSR 5, TEAM CANADA 2

First period:
1. USSR, Mikhailov (Kharlamov) 00:34
2. USSR, Vasilyev (Kharlamov) 2:43
3. Canada, Houle (Shmyr) 15:56
Penalties: Mark Howe (cross checking) 00:53; Smith (cross checking) and Tardif (misconduct) 16:58.

Second period:
4. Canada, Gordie Howe (Mark Howe) 6:15
5. USSR, Anisin (Vikulov) 8:22
6. USSR, Shatalov (Tsygankov) 13:57
Penalties: Mark Howe (cross checking) 12:22; MacGregor and Vasilyev (fighting majors) 12:44.

Third period:
7. USSR, Kharlamov (Vikulov) 13:00
Penalties: Smith and Kharlamov (slashing) 10:54; Lebedev (slashing) and Mark Howe (misconduct) 15:04; Ley (game misconduct) 20:00.

Goaltenders: Canada – Cheevers; USSR – Tretiak
Shots on goal: Canada 28; USSR 29

GAME 7 SUMMARY: TEAM CANADA 4, USSR 4

First period:
1. USSR, Anisin (Lutchenko) 3:34
2. USSR, Tiurin (Lebedev, Yakushev) 6:47
3. Canada, Webster (Lacroix) 17:42
Penalties: None.

Second period:
4. Canada, Backstrom (Gordie Howe, Mark Howe) 2:55
5. Canada, Mark Howe (Tremblay, Backstrom) 6:38
6. USSR, Gusev (Petrov, Kharlamov) 7:20
7. USSR, Mikhailov (Petrov, Kharlamov) 7:59
Penalties: Lutchenko (elbowing) 6:11; Stapleton (hooking) 7:06; Maltsev (interference) 9:18.

Third period:
8. Canada, Backstrom (Tremblay) 6:38
Penalties: None.

Goaltenders: Canada – Cheevers; USSR – Tretiak
Shots on goal: Canada 30; USSR 21

GAME 8 SUMMARY: USSR 3, TEAM CANADA 2

First period:
1. Canada, Hull (Backstrom, Tremblay) 13:47
Penalties: Webster (roughing) 7:57; Yakushev (tripping) 13:08; Tiurin (holding) 15:26; Hamilton (elbowing) 18:21.

Second period:
2. USSR, Yakushev (Shadrin) 6:27
Penalties: Popov (interference) and Ley (roughing) 2:18; Harrison (cross checking) 6:12; Harrison (charging) 10:34; Harrison (slashing major) 18:10; Marty Howe (cross checking) 19:03.

Third period:
3. USSR, Shalimov (unassisted) 00:53
4. USSR, Shalimov (Yakushev) 6:59
5. Canada, Backstrom (Gordie Howe, Ley) 12:42
Penalties: Shadrin (high sticking major) and Stapleton (misconduct) 2:15; Tiurin (tripping) 19:20; Team Canada bench minor (served by Webster) 19:58.

Goaltenders: Canada – Cheevers;
USSR – Sidelnikov
Shots on goal: Canada 24; USSR 30

SERIES NOTES:
* Pat Price, Barry Long, Gilles Gratton, Ron Chipperfield, Dennis Sobchuk, Wayne Dillon and Gavin Kirk did not see any game action for Canada.
* Goaltender Vladimir Polupanov did not see any game action for the USSR.
* In deference to Gordie Howe's seniority, Bobby Hull wore sweater Number 16 for Team Canada (the same number he wore in his rookie season in the National Hockey League). Howe wore Number 9.
* Frank Mahovlich, Paul Henderson and Pat Stapleton were the only three members of Team Canada who had also played in the 1972 NHL-Soviet Summit Series.
* The USSR team included 18 players who had seen action in the 1972 Summit Series.

INDIVIDUAL STATISTICS:

CANADA	GP	G	A	PTS	PIM
Hull	8	7	2	9	0
Backstrom	8	3	4	7	10
Lacroix	8	1	6	7	6
Howe (Gordie)	7	3	4	7	2
Howe (Mark)	7	3	3	6	4
Tremblay	8	1	4	5	2
McKenzie	7	1	3	4	12
Webster	4	2	1	3	6
Henderson	7	2	1	3	0
Bernier	8	1	2	3	4
Houle	7	1	1	2	2
Stapleton	8	0	2	2	12
Shmyr	7	0	2	2	4
MacGregor	5	1	1	2	5
Mahovlich	6	1	1	2	6
Harrison	3	0	2	2	9
Ley	7	0	1	1	14
Walton	6	0	1	1	2
Howe (Marty)	4	0	1	1	10
Tardif	5	0	1	1	10
Hamilton	3	0	1	1	4
Selwood	4	0	0	0	2
Smith	7	0	0	0	12

USSR	GP	G	A	PTS	PIM
Yakushev	7	6	2	8	2
Kharlamov	8	2	6	8	4
Petrov	7	1	6	7	4
Mikhailov	7	4	2	6	0
Shadrin	8	0	5	5	11
Maltsev	8	4	0	4	0
Gusev	8	3	1	4	4
Vasilyev	8	3	1	4	7
Anisin	8	2	2	4	0
Lebedev	8	1	3	4	6
Vikulov	4	0	4	4	0
Lutchenko	8	1	2	3	4
Shalimov	4	2	0	2	0
Tsygankov	6	0	2	2	2
Bodunov	7	1	0	1	4
Shatalov	3	1	0	1	0
Tiurin	4	1	0	1	4
Kapustin	5	0	1	1	6
Liapkin	5	0	0	0	2
Volchkov	2	0	0	0	4
Kuznetsov	8	0	0	0	4
Popov	1	0	0	0	0
Filippov	1	0	0	0	0
Sapelkin	1	0	0	0	0
Kotov	5	0	0	0	0
Klimov	1	0	0	0	0
Fiodorov	1	0	0	0	0

1976-77

WHA TEAMS VS. CZECH NATIONALS
(6-game series)

1. Dec. 12: Winnipeg 6, Czechs 5
2. Dec. 13: Edmonton 6, Czechs 4
3. Dec. 15: Czechs 5, Calgary 4
4. Dec. 17: Minnesota 3, Czechs 2
5. Dec. 20: Czechs 4, New England 1
6. Dec. 22: Indianapolis 3, Czechs 2

WHA teams won 4 and lost 2.

CZECH ROSTER:

Coaches: Karel Gut, Jaroslav Volf.
Goaltenders: Vladimir Dzurilla, Miroslav Termer, Miroslav Krasa.
Skaters: Peter Stastny, Marian Stastny, Jaroslav Pouzar, Milan Novy, Joroslav Vins, Otakar Vejvoda, Frantisek Cernik, Lybomi Bauer, Frantisek Pospisil, Frantisek Kaberel, Vaclav Sykora, Miroslav Kravacek, Ladislav Vysusil, Milan Skrebec, Zdenek Muller, Antonin Melc, Eduard Novak.

GAME 1: WINNIPEG JETS 6, CZECHS 5

First period:
No scoring.

Second period:
1. Czechs, Bauer (P. Stastny, Novy) 5:21
2. Czechs, Novak (Novy, P. Stastny) 8:49
3. Czechs, Pouzar (P. Stastny, M. Stastny) 9:31
4. Czechs, Sykora (Vejvoda) 10:42

Third period:
5. Winnipeg, Hedberg (Nilsson, Miller) 4:01
6. Winnipeg, Labraaten (Bergman, Lindstrom) 6:22
7. Winnipeg, Bergman (Nilsson, Hedberg) 8:01
8. Winnipeg, Ruhnke (Hull, Green) 11:47
9. Winnipeg, Lindh (Lesuk) 13:46
10. Czechs, Melc (Pouzar, P. Stastny) 15:41
11. Winnipeg, Sullivan (Lindstrom, Labraaten) 16:02

Goaltenders: Winnipeg – Daley; Czechs – Dzurilla
Shots on goal: Winnipeg 20; Czechs 31
Attendance: 10,023

GAME 2: EDMONTON OILERS 6, CZECHS 4

First period:
1. Edmonton, Kirk (unassisted) 2:35
2. Edmonton, Flett (Campbell, Sather) 4:31
3. Czechs, Bauer (Kaberel) 12:14
4. Czechs, Novak (Novy, Pospisil) 15:19
5. Edmonton, Beaton (Russell, Hamilton) 17:59
6. Edmonton, Morris (Patenaude, Campbell) 19:47

Second period:
7. Edmonton, Flett (Sather, Campbell) 15:28

Third period:
8. Edmonton, Rota (Nevin, Kirk) 2:06
9. Czechs, Pouzar (M. Stastny) 11:48
10. Czechs, Novak (Novy, M. Stastny) 13:38

Goaltenders: Edmonton – Broderick and Dryden; Czechs – Krasa and Termer.
Shots on goal: Edmonton 20; Czechs 38
Attendance: 15,294

GAME 3: CZECHS 5, CALGARY COWBOYS 4

First period:
1. Calgary, Tannahill (Miszuk) 2:43
2. Czechs, Vejvoda (Sykora, Kravacek) 9:36
3. Czechs, Muller (Pouzar) 13:22
4. Czechs, M. Stastny (Pouzar, P. Stastny) 15:59
5. Calgary, Connelly (Morrison, St. Saveur) 18:36

Second period:
6. Calgary, Ford (Miller, Terbench) 1:20
7. Czechs, M. Stastny (Cernik) 3:55
8. Calgary, Ford (Terbenche, Chipperfield) 7:59

Third period:
9. Czechs, Novy (Novak) 19:26

Goaltenders: Calgary – McLeod; Czechs – Dzurilla
Shots on goal: Calgary 28; Czechs 38
Attendance: 7,095

GAME 4:
MINNESOTA FIGHTING SAINTS 3, CZECHS 2

First period:
No scoring.

Second period:
1. Czechs, Pouzar (P. Stastny) 6:07
2. Czechs, Novak (Pospisil, Novy) 18:55

Third period:
3. Minnesota, Adduono (Patrick) 12:34
4. Minnesota, Ward (Adduono, Keon) 19:33

Overtime:
5. Minnesota, Antonovich (Keon, McKenzie) 00:45

Goaltenders: Minnesota – Curran and Levasseur; Czechs – Dzurilla
Shots on goal: Minnesota 31; Czechs 48
Attendance: 4,616

GAME 5: CZECHS 4, NEW ENGLAND WHALERS 1

First period:
1. Czechs, Neliba (Kravacek, Vejvoda) 6:35

Second period:
2. Czechs, M. Stastny (Vins, Dzurilla) 5:50
3. Czechs, M. Stastny (Pouzar) 13:06
4. Czechs, Novak (Novy) 15:06
5. New England, Rogers (Webster, Selwood) 18:40

Third period:
No scoring.

Goaltenders: New England – Raeder and Abrahamsson; Czechs – Dzurilla
Shots on goal: New England 19; Czechs 45
Attendance: 7,322

Big Bucks & Blue Pucks

GAME 6: INDIANAPOLIS RACERS 3, CZECHS 2
First period:
1. Indianapolis, Harris (Clackson, Parizeau) 13:36
2. Czechs, M. Stastny (P. Stastny) 14:20

Second period:
No scoring.

Third period:
3. Indianapolis, Paiement (Sicinski, Maggs) 00:54
4. Indianapolis, Paiement (Sicinski, Peacosh) 16:55
5. Czechs, Kaberel (Novy, Bauer) 19:49

Goaltenders: Indianapolis – Dion; Czechs – Dzurilla
Shots on goal: Indianapolis 29; Czechs 25
Attendance: 4,974

1976–77

WHA teams vs. Soviet Nationals
(8-game series)
1. Dec. 27: New England 5, Soviets 2
2. Dec. 28: Soviets 7, Cincinnati 5
3. Dec. 30: Soviets 10, Houston 1
4. Jan. 1: Soviets 5, Indianapolis 2
5. Jan. 3: Soviets 6, San Diego 3
6. Jan. 5: Soviets 3, Edmonton 2
7. Jan. 6: Soviets 3, Winnipeg 2
8. Jan. 8: Quebec 6, Soviets 1
WHA teams won 2 and lost 6.

SOVIET ROSTER
Goaltenders: Vladislav Tretiak, Aleksandr Sidelnikov.
Skaters: Valeri Kharlamov, Aleksandr Yakushev, Aleksandr Maltsev, Aleksandr Golikov, Aleksandr Biljaletdinov, Sergei Babinov, Viktor Shalimov, Gennadi Tsygankov, Helmut Balderis, Viktor Aleksandrov, Vladimir Vikulov, Vladimir Pervukhin, Vladimir Petrov, Vladimir Lutchenko, Vladimir Shadrin, Viktor Kovin, Viktor Krikunov, Boris Mikhailov, Yuri Liapkin, Valeri Vasilyev, Piotr Prirodin.

GAME 1: NEW ENGLAND WHALERS 5, SOVIETS 2
First period:
1. New England, Swain (D. Roberts, Earl) 4:16
2. New England, Earl (Hangsleben) 15:26
3. Soviets, Maltsev (Golikov, Biljaletdinov) 16:26
4. New England, MacGregor (Bolduc, Backstrom) 17:19

Second period:
No scoring.

Third period:
5. Soviets, Yakushev (Shalimov) 5:22
6. New England, Lyle (Troy, G. Roberts) 7:27
7. New England, Lyle (Rogers, Pleau) 19:07

Goaltenders: New England – Raeder; Soviets – Tretiak
Shots on goal: New England 38; Soviets 33
Attendance: 10,507

GAME 2: SOVIETS 7, CINCINNATI STINGERS 5
First period:
1. Soviets, Aleksandrov (Vikulov, Babinov) 15:48

Second period:
2. Soviets, Pervukhin (Balderis, Kharlamov) 00:33
3. Cincinnati, Stoughton (Carroll, Hughes) 7:12
4. Soviets, Petrov (Kharlamov, Pervukhin) 8:48
5. Cincinnati, Larose (Carroll, Plumb) 11:24

Third period:
6. Cincinnati, Leduc (unassisted) 00:31
7. Soviets, Petrov (unassisted) 3:40
8. Cincinnati, Leduc (Dudley, Abgrall) 7:32
9. Soviets, Shalimov (Biljaletdinov, Yakushev) 8:40
10. Cincinnati, Dudley (Leduc, Angrall) 11:05
11. Soviets, Petrov (Balderis, Tsygankov) 13:36
12. Soviets, Balderis (Petrov) 16:56

Goaltenders: Cincinnati – Hoganson; Soviets – Sidelnikov
Shots on goal: Cincinnati 43; Soviets 31
Attendance: 10,320

GAME 3: SOVIETS 10, HOUSTON AEROS 1
First period:
1. Soviets, Krikunov (unassisted) 5:16
2. Houston, Preston (Gordie Howe) 9:21

Second period:
3. Soviets, Babinov (unassisted) 2:19
4. Soviets, Yakushev (Shadrin, Shalimov) 10:47
5. Soviets, Balderis (unassisted) 13:13
6. Soviets, Kovin (Maltsev) 14:10
7. Soviets, Petrov (Balderis) 16:03
8. Soviets, Shalimov (Lutchenko) 17:26
9. Soviets, Golikov (Kovin, Maltsev) 18:12
10. Soviets, Petrov (Tsygankov) 18:56

Third period:
11. Soviets, Golikov (Petrov) 16:06

Goaltenders: Houston – Grahame and Rutledge; Soviets – Tretiak and Sidelnikov
Shots on goal: Houston 28; Soviets 36
Attendance: 15,302

GAME 4: SOVIETS 5, INDIANAPOLIS RACERS 2
First period: No scoring.

Second period:
1. Soviets, Maltsev (Golikov, Biljaletdinov) 2:33
2. Soviets, Kharlamov (Mikhailov) 3:30
3. Indianapolis, Harris (MacDonald, Block) 8:50
4. Indianapolis, Block (Sicinski, Peacosh) 9:44
5. Soviets, Golikov (Maltsev) 11:40

Third period:
6. Soviets, Liapkin (Pervukhin, Kharlamov) 8:28
7. Soviets, Balderis (Petrov, Lutchenko) 14:27

Goaltenders: Indianapolis – Dion and Park; Soviets – Sidelnikov
Shots on goal: Indianapolis 27; Soviets 40
Attendance: 12,051

GAME 5: SOVIETS 6, SAN DIEGO MARINERS 3

First period:
1. San Diego, Burgess (French) 2:11
2. San Diego, Rivers (Pinder, Hughes) 16:31

Second period:
3. Soviets, Mikhailov (Petrov, Kharlamov) 4:29
4. Soviets, Yakushev (Petrov, Babinov) 17:39
5. Soviets, Petrov (Lutchenko, Babinov) 19:17

Third period:
6. Soviets, Krikunov (Balderis, Pervukhin) 2:05
7. San Diego, Shmyr (Lacroix) 14:13
8. Soviets, Maltsev (Golikov) 15:54
9. Soviets, Mikhailov (Kharlamov, Petrov) 18:14

Goaltenders: San Diego – Lockett and Wakely; Soviets – Tretiak
Shots on goal: San Diego 20; Soviets 33
Attendance: 13,029

GAME 6: SOVIETS 3, EDMONTON OILERS 2

First period:
1. Soviets, Yakushev (Shalimov, Krikunov) 14:27

Second period:
2. Edmonton, Connelly (St. Sauveur, Rota) 3:21
3. Soviets, Prirodin (Biljaletdinov) 18:23

Third period:
4. Soviets, Yakushev (Shadrin, Shalimov) 13:59
5. Edmonton, Connelly (Campbell, Wilkins) 16:22

Goaltenders: Edmonton – Broderick; Soviets – Sidelnikov
Shots on goal: Edmonton 28; Soviets 23
Attendance: 15,571

GAME 7: SOVIETS 3, WINNIPEG JETS 2

First period:
1. Soviets, Yakushev (Shadrin, Shalimov) 9:35

Second period:
2. Winnipeg, Hull (Bergman) 00:20
3. Soviets, Balderis (unassisted) 10:48
4. Soviets, Yakushev (Babinov) 13:23

Third period:
5. Winnipeg, Long (Lindh, Moffatt) 17:21

Goaltenders: Winnipeg – Daley; Soviets – Tretiak
Shots on goal: Winnipeg 30; Soviets 31
Attendance: 10,336

GAME 8: QUEBEC NORDIQUES 6, SOVIETS 1

First period:
1. Quebec, Brackenbury (Fitchner) 6:49
2. Quebec, Bernier (P. Bordeleau, Weir) 9:23
3. Soviets, Mikhailov (Kharlamov, Lutchenko) 12:40
4. Quebec, Tardif (Tremblay, C. Bordeleau) 16:34

Second period:
5. Quebec, Brackenbury (Sutherland, Fitchner) 6:02
6. Quebec, C. Bordeleau (Cloutier, Tremblay) 14:02

Third period:
7. Quebec, Dube (Baxter, Boudrias) 9:20

Goaltenders: Quebec – Humphreys; Soviets – Tretiak and Sidelnikov.
Shots on goal: Quebec 38; Soviets 30
Attendance: 11,119

1976

Izvestia Cup Tournament

The Winnipeg Jets, as defending Avco World Trophy champions, were invited to Moscow to compete in the 1976 Izvestia Cup round-robin tournament against championship club teams from the Soviet Union, Czechoslovakia, Sweden and Finland. The competition was held in December, and the Jets looked lethargic in all four games, losing to the Czechs (3–2) and Soviets (6–4), tying the Swedes 4–4 and wrapping up the tournament with a 2–1 victory over Finland.

1977-78

WHA teams vs. Czechoslovakia Selects (8-game series)

1. Dec. 9: Czechs 5, Indianapolis 3
2. Dec. 11: Quebec 8, Czechs 4
3. Dec. 13: Winnipeg 5, Czechs 1
4. Dec. 14: Edmonton 6, Czechs 1
5. Dec. 16: New England 5, Czechs 3
6. Dec. 18: Houston 3, Czechs 2
7. Dec. 20: Cincinnati 5, Czechs 5 (no overtime)
8. Dec. 21: Birmingham 5, Czechs 0

WHA teams won 6, lost 1 and tied 1.

CZECH ROSTER
Coach: Stanislav Nevesely
Goaltenders: Vladimir Dzurilla, Miroslav Kapoun, Ivan Podesva.
Skaters: Franticek Cernik, Vitezslav Duris, Milan Figala, Vaclav Honc, Jan Klabouch, Jaroslav Kocer, Jindrich Kokrment, Jiri Kolar, Josef Kveton, Jaroslav Lycka, Jaroslav Mec, Milos Novak, Lubomir Ozlizio, Pavel Pazourek, Lubomir Penicka, Ivan Podesva, Pavel Richter, Rudolf Slavic, Milow Tarant, Vladislav Vicek, Frantisek Vyborny, Milan Kraft.

GAME 1: CZECHS 5, INDIANAPOLIS RACERS 3

First period:
1. Czechs, Richter (Vicek, Mec) 1:19
2. Czechs, Richter (Vicek, Mec) 4:30

Second period:
3. Indianapolis, Patenaude (Parizeau, Block) 10:09
4. Indianapolis, St. Sauveur (Goldsworthy, Thomas) 14:54

Third period:
5. Czechs, Richter (Vicek, Mec) 9:07
6. Czechs, Vicek (Penicka, Kolar) 10:59
7. Indianapolis, St. Sauveur (Block, Baltimore) 12:40
8. Czechs, Mec (Richter, Penicka) 14:15

Goaltenders: Indianapolis – Inness; Czechs – Dzurilla
Shots on goal: Indianapolis 25; Czechs 3
Attendance: 5,851

GAME 2: QUEBEC NORDIQUES 8, CZECHS 4

First period:
1. Czechs, Kokrment (Tarant) 5:45
2. Quebec, Miller (S. Bernier) 9:31
3. Czechs, Duris (Penicka, Vicek)
4. Quebec, Cloutier (S. Bernier, Hagman) 15:14
5. Quebec, Hagman (Tardif, Cloutier) 19:18

Second period:
6. Quebec, Baxter (Hagman, Cloutier) 1:03
7. Czechs, Cernik (Kokrment) 13:09

Third period:
8. Quebec, Tardif (Cloutier, Hagman) 00:36
9. Quebec, Cloutier (Hagman, Tardif) 5:28
10. Czechs, Cernik (Kokrment) 11:26
11. Quebec, Hagman (Tardif, Tremblay) 12:12
12. Quebec, P. Bordeleau (S. Bernier) 17:22
Goaltenders: Quebec – Broderick; Czechs – Dzurilla
Shots on goal: Quebec 40; Czechs 44
Attendance: 11,156

GAME 3: WINNIPEG JETS 5, CZECHS 1

First period:
No scoring.

Second period:
1. Winnipeg, Sullivan (Bergman) 00:42
2. Winnipeg, Hedberg (Bergman, Daley) 7:34
3. Winnipeg, Hull (Hedberg, Sjoberg) 12:26
4. Czechs, Vicek (Mec) 13:02
5. Winnipeg, Labraaten (Sullivan, Bergman) 17:13

Third period:
6. Winnipeg, U. Nilsson (unassisted) 11:06.

Goaltenders: Winnipeg – Daley; Czechs – Kapoun
Shots on goal: Winnipeg 39; Czechs 30
Attendance: 10,258

GAME 4: EDMONTON OILERS 6, CZECHS 1

First period:
1. Edmonton, Micheletti (Ferguson, Callighen) 00:29
2. Czechs, Kolar (Vicek, Cernik) 11:45

Second period:
3. Edmonton, Flett (Micheletti, Rota) 16:51

Third period:
4. Edmonton, Flett (Chipperfield, Rota) 1:55
5. Edmonton, Flett (Chipperfield, Rota) 15:50
6. Edmonton, MacDonald (Guite, B. Campbell) 17:59
7. Edmonton, Flett (Chipperfield, Guite) 19:59

Goaltenders: Edmonton – Dryden; Czechs – Kapoun
Shots on goal: Edmonton 36; Czechs 32
Attendance: 15,412

GAME 5: NEW ENGLAND WHALERS 5, CZECHS 3

First period:
1. Czechs, Tarant (Novak, Kveton) 9:32
2. New England, J. Carlson (Pleau, Rogers) 10:55
3. Czechs, Duris (Honc) 18:56

Second period:
4. Czechs, Duris (Cernik, Vyborny) 11:19

Third period:
5. New England, Pleau (Butters, J. Carlson) 7:21
6. New England, G. Howe (Hangsleben, Mark Howe) 13:55
7. New England, J. McKenzie (Keon, Roberts) 16:27
8. New England, Rogers (unassisted) 18:17

Goaltenders: New England – Smith; Czechs – Podesva
Shots on goal: New England 40; Czechs 30
Attendance: 8,940

GAME 6: HOUSTON AEROS 3, CZECHS 2

First period:
1. Czechs, Lycka (unassisted) 10:40

Second period:
2. Houston, A. McLeod (Ruskowski, Hughes) 2:50
3. Houston, Taylor (Lacroix, Schella) 17:17

Third period:
4. Houston, Popiel (unassisted) 2:38
5. Czechs, Duris (Vicek, Cernik) 7:50

Goaltenders: Houston – Wakely; Czechs – Dzurilla
Shots on goal: Houston 15; Czechs 25
Attendance: 6,577

GAME 7: CINCINNATI STINGERS 5, CZECHS 5

First period:
1. Cincinnati, Norwich (Ftorek) 12:36
2. Czechs, Cernik (Mec) 13:50
3. Cincinnati, Hislop (Ftorek, Stapleton) 15:00

Second period:
4. Cincinnati, Marsh (Stoughton) 1:25
5. Czechs, Klabouch (Kolar, Novak) 7:26
6. Czechs, Cernik (Kocer) 8:57
7. Cincinnati, Plumb (Dudley) 17:34
8. Cincinnati, Leduc (Marotte, Marsh) 18:19

Third period:
9. Czechs, Mec (Vicek) 4:15
10. Czechs, Duris (unassisted) 8:34

Goaltenders: Cincinnati – Dion; Czechs – Kapoun and Podesva
Shots on goal: Cincinnati 39; Czechs 34
Attendance: 5,875

GAME 8: BIRMINGHAM BULLS 5, CZECHS 0

First period:
No scoring.

Second period:
1. Birmingham, Linseman (Napier, Roberto) 1:35
2. Birmingham, Henderson (Cassolato, Beaudoin) 5:14
3. Birmingham, Marrin (Turkiewicz, Henderson) 6:20
4. Birmingham, Roberto (Linseman, Beaudoin) 6:55
5. Birmingham, Linseman (Napier) 19:37

Third period:
No scoring.

Goaltenders: Birmingham – Garrett; Czechs – Podesva and Kapoun
Shots on goal: Birmingham 42; Czechs 24
Attendance: 6,559

1977-78

**WHA teams vs. Soviet Stars
(10-game series)**
1. Dec. 14: New England 7, Soviets 2
2. Dec. 17: Soviets 5, Cincinnati 4
3. Dec. 18: Soviets 4, Indianapolis 3
4. Dec. 20: Winnipeg 6, Soviets 4
5. Dec. 21: Edmonton 5, Soviets 2
6. Dec. 23: Soviets 6, Houston 2
7. Dec. 26: Birmingham 6, Soviets 1
8. Dec. 28: Soviets 7, Houston 3
9. Dec. 30: Soviets 4, Indianapolis 2
10. Jan. 3: Quebec 3, Soviets 3 (no overtime)
WHA teams won 4, lost 5 and tied 1.

SOVIET STARS ROSTER:
Coach: Boris Majorov.
Goaltenders: Sergei Babariko, Mikhail Vasilenok.
Skaters: Valeri Bragin, Anatoli Emeljanenko, Jrek Gimaev, Vladimir Golubovich, Sergei Korotkov, Vladimir Lokotko, Nicolai Makarov, Viacheslav Nazarov, Sergei Podgortsev, Vladimir Popov, Mikhail Shostak, Vasili Spiridinov, Victor Tumenev, Alexei Volchenkov, Aleksandr Volchkov, Aleksandr Biljaletdinov, Alexei Kostylev, Viktor Semjonov, Sergei Makarov, Vladimir Romashin, Viktor Lavrentiev.

GAME 1: NEW ENGLAND WHALERS 7, SOVIETS 2

First period:
1. New England, M. Rogers (Pleau, J. Carlson) 3:50
2. Soviets, Biljaletdinov (Semjonov) 9:27
3. New England, Antonovich (Keon, Ley) 13:17
4. New England, Keon (J. McKenzie, G. Roberts) 14:15

Second period:
5. New England, Pleau (M. Rogers, J. Carlson) 3:12
6. New England, Pleau (M. Rogers) 8:56
7. New England, Lyle (Carroll, Mayer) 11:12

Third period:
8. Soviets, Biljaletdinov (Bragin, Semjonov) 4:19
9. New England, Mark Howe (Gordie Howe, Hangsleben) 17:48

Goaltenders: New England – A. Smith; Soviets – Vasilenok
Shots on goal: New England 34; Soviets 34
Attendance: 9,939

GAME 2: SOVIETS 5, CINCINNATI STINGERS 4

First period:
1. Cincinnati, Hislop (Plumb, Stapleton) 3:00
2. Cincinnati, Leduc (Dudley, Stapleton) 9:23
3. Soviets, Volchkov (Emeljanenko, Popov) 16:14

Second period:
4. Soviets, Volchenkov (Nazarov, Volchkov) 4:57
5. Soviets, Popov (Volchenkov) 6:42

Third period:
6. Cincinnati, Stoughton (Marsh) 4:22
7. Soviets, Volchenkov (Nazarov, Emeljanenko) 9:52
8. Soviets, Gimaev (Tumenev) 16:19
9. Cincinnati, Ftorek (Dudley, Abgrall) 16:59

Goaltenders: Cincinnati – Liut and Dion; Soviets – Babariko
Shots on goal: Cincinnati 25; Soviets 28
Attendance: 8,044

GAME 3: SOVIETS 4, INDIANAPOLIS RACERS 3

First period:
1. Indianapolis, Goldsworthy (Block, Fortier) 13:13
2. Indianapolis, Driscoll (Rhiness, Paiement) 15:31

Second period:
3. Indianapolis, Thomas (St. Sauveur, Goldsworthy) 5:41
4. Soviets, Tumenev (Makarov) 8:13
5. Soviets, Emeljanenko (Popov, Volchkov) 9:14

Third period:
6. Soviets, Biljaletdinov (Podgortsev, Shostak) 6:32
7. Soviets, Popov (unassisted) 12:27

Goaltenders: Indianapolis – Inness; Soviets – Babariko
Shots on goal: Indianapolis 20; Soviets 23
Attendance: 6,176

GAME 4: WINNIPEG JETS 6, SOVIETS 4

First period:
1. Soviets, Emeljanenko (Volchkov, Popov) 8:11
2. Winnipeg, K. Nilsson (Hedberg, Sjoberg) 11:09
3. Winnipeg, Hull (K. Nilsson, Green) 15:11

Second period:
4. Winnipeg, Sjoberg (Sullivan, Lindstrom)
5. Winnipeg, Kryskow (K. Nilsson, Hull)
6. Winnipeg, Sullivan (Guindon, Green) 14:24
7. Soviets, Romanshin (Lavrentiev, Biljaletdinov) 16:13

Third period:
8. Winnipeg, Kryskow (Powis) 2:28
9. Soviets, Volchkov (unassisted) 7:34
10. Soviets, Makarov (Romashin, Lavrentiev) 15:43

Goaltenders: Winnipeg – Daley; Soviets – Vasilenok
Shots on goal: Winnipeg 31; Soviets 33
Attendance: 9,111

GAME 5: EDMONTON OILERS 5, SOVIETS 2

First period:
1. Edmonton, DeMarco (Guite) 12:29

Second period:
2. Edmonton, Callighen (Widing, Hamilton) 11:13
3. Soviets, Tumenev (Emeljanenko, Romashin) 12:45
4. Edmonton, Widing (Hamilton) 15:14

Third period:
5. Edmonton, Widing (Shmyr, Ferguson) 14:50
6. Soviets, Semjonov (Bragin, Spiridinov) 16:39
7. Edmonton, Widing (Micheletti) 19:41

Goaltenders: Edmonton – Dryden; Soviets – Babariko
Shots on goal: Edmonton 39, Soviets 14
Attendance: 15,194

GAME 6: SOVIETS 6, HOUSTON AEROS 2
(Summary unavailable)

GAME 7: BIRMINGHAM BULLS 6, SOVIETS 1

First period:
1. Birmingham, Beaudoin (Stevenson) 11:11
2. Birmingham, Durbano (Gorman, Stevenson) 12:08
3. Birmingham, Marrin (Cassolato, Henderson) 15:09

Second period:
4. Birmingham, Marrin (Cassolato, Hughes) 4:00
5. Birmingham, Mahovlich (Gorman) 7:57
6. Soviets, Golubovich (Gimaev, Tumenev) 19:21

Third period:
7. Birmingham, Hughes (Stewart) 9:59

Goaltenders: Birmingham – Wood; Soviets – Vasilenok
Shots on goal: Birmingham 22; Soviets 27
Attendance: 13,173

GAME 8: SOVIETS 7, HOUSTON AEROS 3

First period:
1. Houston, Preston (Lacroix, Gray) 2:15
2. Soviets, Volchkov (Popov) 2:30
3. Soviets, Semjonov (Biljaletdinov, Golubovich) 3:15
4. Soviets, Biljaletdinov (Golubovich, Nazarov) 6:10

Second period:
5. Soviets, Volchkov (Popov, Gimaev) 4:41
6. Houston, Preston (A. McLeod, Lacroix) 16:15

Third period:
7. Soviets, Biljaletdinov (Semjonov, Nazarov) 5:55
8. Soviets, Emeljanenko (Nazarov, Biljaletdinov) 7:51
9. Houston, Tonelli (Lacroix, A. McLeod) 9:27
10. Soviets, Makarov (Biljaletdinov, Romashin) 16:33

Goaltenders: Houston – Zimmerman; Soviets – Babariko
Shots on goal: Houston 13; Soviets 28
Attendance: 6,725

GAME 9: SOVIETS 4, INDIANAPOLIS RACERS 2

First period:
1. Soviets, Volchenkov (Popov) 4:32
2. Soviets, Golubovich (Semjonov, Gimaev) 9:31
3. Soviets, Tumenev (unassisted) 15:22

Second period:
4. Soviets, Tumenev (Spiridinov, Lavrentiev) 3:24
5. Indianapolis, Thomas (Prentice, Paiement) 17:12
6. Indianapolis, French (Stoughton, St. Sauveur) 19:42

Third period:
No scoring.

Goaltenders: Indianapolis – Inness; Soviets – Babariko
Shots on goal: Indianapolis 31; Soviets 30
Attendance: 4,018

GAME 10: QUEBEC NORDIQUES 3, SOVIETS 3

First period:
1. Quebec, Tardif (Cloutier, J. Bernier) 10:56
2. Quebec, Fitchner (Inkpen) 13:55

Second period:
3. Soviets, Romashin (Lavrentiev) 7:43
4. Soviets, Lavrentiev (Romashin) 10:11

Third period:
5. Quebec, Tardif (Hagman) 00:17
6. Soviets, Volchkov (Babariko) 12:31

Goaltenders: Quebec – Broderick; Soviets – Babariko
Shots on goal: Quebec 24; Soviets 21
Attendance: 10,549

Nordiques in Moscow; Jets in Japan:
The Quebec Nordiques, as defending Avco World Trophy champions, were invited to Moscow to compete in the 1977 Izvestia Cup round-robin tournament against championship club teams from the Soviet Union, Czechoslovakia, Sweden and Finland. The competition was held in December, and, like the Winnipeg Jets the previous year, the Nordiques looked tired and weak in losing to the Soviets (5–3), Czechs (6–2) and Swedes (6–2) while managing just a tie (6–6) with Finland. The Jets, meanwhile, squared off against the powerful Soviet National team in a three-game exhibition series in Tokyo, Japan, at the end of December and lost all three games. The Soviet Nationals then travelled to North America for a six-game series against WHA teams.

1978

**WHA teams vs. Soviet Nationals
(6-game series)**
1. Jan. 4: Soviets 7, Edmonton 2
2. Jan. 5: Winnipeg 5, Soviets 3
3. Jan. 7: Soviets 6, Quebec 3
4. Jan. 8: Soviets 9, Cincinnati 2
5. Jan. 10: Soviets 8, Indianapolis 3
6. Jan. 11: Soviets 7, New England 4
WHA teams won 1 and lost 5.

SOVIET NATIONALS ROSTER
Goaltenders: Vladislav Tretiak, Aleksandr Sidelnikov.
Skaters: Valeri Kharlamov, Aleksandr Maltsev, Aleksandr Golikov, Viacheslav Fetisov, Sergei Babinov, Viktor Shalimov, Gennadi Tsygankov, Helmut Balderis, Viktor Aleksandrov, Vladimir Vikulov, Vladimir Pervukhin, Vladimir Petrov, Viktor Kovin, Boris Mikhailov, Valeri Vasilyev, Viktor Kapustin, Aleksandr Fiodorov, Sergei Khatulev, Viacheslav Anisin, Sergei Gusev, Viktor Lobanov, Vladimir Lutchenko.

GAME 1: SOVIETS 7, EDMONTON OILERS 2

First period:
1. Soviets, Golikov (unassisted) 8:19
2. Soviets, Petrov (Vasilyev, Mikhailov) 11:38

Second period:
3. Soviets, Petrov (Tsygankov, Kharlamov) 5:16
4. Edmonton, Holland (Flett) 7:28
5. Soviets, Tsygankov (Vasilyev, Petrov) 9:03
6. Soviets, Balderis (Kapustin, Anisin) 10:59

Third period:
7. Soviets, Anisin (Kapustin, Fiodorov) 2:04
8. Edmonton, Callighen (Widing, Ferguson) 10:22
9. Soviets, Petrov (Mikhailov, Kharlamov) 18:15

Goaltenders: Edmonton – Dryden; Soviets – Tretiak
Shots on goal: Edmonton 38; Soviets 25
Attendance: 15,602

GAME 2: WINNIPEG JETS 5, SOVIETS 3

First period:
1. Winnipeg, Hull (K. Nilsson, Sjoberg) 2:49
2. Winnipeg, Hull (Powis, U. Nilsson) 9:52

Second period:
3. Winnipeg, U. Nilsson (Hedberg, Sjoberg) 5:46
4. Winnipeg, U. Nilsson (Hull, Hedberg) 8:57
5. Soviets, Aleksandrov (Labadov, Fiodorov) 10:59
6. Soviets, Aleksandrov (Vikulov, Fiodorov) 15:40

Third period:
7. Soviets, Pervuhkin (Kapustin, Anisin) 2:43
8. Winnipeg, Hull (Dunn, U. Nilsson) 19:52

Goaltenders: Winnipeg – Daley; Soviets – Sidelnikov
Shots on goal: Winnipeg 31; Soviets 24
Attendance: 10,315

GAME 3: SOVIETS 6, QUEBEC NORDIQUES 3

First period:
1. Soviets, Tsygankov (Fetisov, Kharlamov) 1:12
2. Quebec, Inkpen (Morris) 4:12
3. Soviets, Balderis (Anisin) 6:58
4. Soviets, Kharlamov (Maltsev, Golikov) 8:26
5. Quebec, Dube (P. Bordeleau, Boudrias) 12:22

Second period:
6. Soviets, Kharlamov (Fetisov) 00:32

Third period:
7. Soviets, Maltsev (Pervukhin, Vasilyev) 8:53
8. Quebec, Fitchner (unassisted) 16:39
9. Soviets, Anisin (Kapustin, Pervukhin) 17:27

Goaltenders: Quebec – Corsi; Soviets – Tretiak
Shots on goal: Quebec 32; Soviets 43
Attendance: 11,111

GAME 4: SOVIETS 9, CINCINNATI STINGERS 2

First period:
1. Cincinnati, Ftorek (Lahache, Hislop) 3:04
2. Soviets, Kapustin (Balderis, Pervukhin) 5:41

Second period:
3. Soviets, Mikhailov (Kharlamov, Babinov) 00:46
4. Soviets, Anisin (Kapustin) 1:18
5. Soviets, Gusev (Kharlamov) 6:09
6. Soviets, Maltsev ((Mikhailov, Kharlamov) 6:20
7. Cincinnati, Legge (Hislop, Coates) 8:09

Third period:
8. Soviets, Balderis (Anisin, Aleksandrov) 1:21
9. Soviets, Vikulov (Lobanov) 3:08
10. Soviets, Babinov (Kapustin, Lobanov) 3:58
11. Soviets, Lobanov (Kovin, Golikov) 6:54

Goaltenders: Cincinnati – Dion; Soviets – Tretiak
Shots on goal: Cincinnati 20; Soviets 33
Attendance: 2,571

GAME 5: SOVIETS 8, INDIANAPOLIS RACERS 3

First period:
1. Soviets, Golikov (Vasilyev, Shalimov) 3:58
2. Indianapolis, Maggs (unassisted) 7:12
3. Indianapolis, Patenaude (Driscoll, Marotte) 13:31

Second period:
4. Soviets, Tsygankov (Maltsev, Vikulov) 1:34
5. Soviets, Kapustin (Anisin) 5:30
6. Soviets, Kharlamov (Mikhailov, Maltsev) 12:18
7. Soviets, Kapustin (Anisin, Fetisov) 14:55

Third period:
8. Soviets, Golikov (Fiodorov) 2:41
9. Soviets, Anisin (Aleksandrov, Pervukhin) 4:37
10. Indianapolis, Thomas (St. Sauveur, Wilkins) 7:08
11. Soviets, Fiodorov (Kovin, Lutchenko)

Goaltenders: Indianapolis – McDuffe; Soviets – Sidelnikov
Shots on goal: Indianapolis 20; Soviets 42
Attendance: 4,871

GAME 6: SOVIETS 7, NEW ENGLAND WHALERS 4

First period:
1. New England, Carroll (Rogers) 4:23
2. Soviets, Aleksandrov (Lobanov, Vikulov) 5:42
3. Soviets, Kapustin (Pervukhin) 9:57
4. Soviets, Mikhailov (Maltsev, Khatulev) 12:09
5. Soviets, Anisin (Khatulev, Kapustin) 18:24

Second period:
6. New England, J. McKenzie (Keon) 11:11
7. Soviets, Khatulev (unassisted) 15:50
8. Soviets, Vikulov (Aleksandrov, Lobanov) 18:28
9. New England, Keon (J. McKenzie, Selwood) 19:35

Third period:
10. Soviets, Fetisov (Mikhailov) 00:21
11. New England, G. Howe (Lyle, Selwood) 4:51

Goaltenders: New England – Levasseur; Soviets – Tretiak
Shots on goal: New England 33; Soviets 32
Attendance: 10,338

1978

WHA teams vs. Sweden and Finland:
1. March 18: Finland 3, Birmingham 2
2. March 19: New England 6, Sweden 0
3. March 19: Houston 6, Finland 4
4. March 25: Finland 8, Cincinnati 3
5. March 26: Sweden 5, Cincinnati 4
6. March 26: New England 7, Finland 3
7. March 28: Birmingham 7, Sweden 4

1978-79

WHA teams vs. Soviet All-Stars (6-game series)
1. Dec. 9: Soviets 7, New England 4
2. Dec. 12: Soviets 6, Quebec 3
3. Dec. 14: Soviets 4, Winnipeg 3
4. Dec. 15: Edmonton 5, Soviets 3
5. Dec. 17: Birmingham 2, Soviets 2
6. Dec. 20: Soviets 5, Cincinnati 3

WHA teams won 1, lost 4 and tied 1.

SOVIET ALL-STARS ROSTER:
Goaltenders: Sergei Babariko, Vladimir Myshkin.
Skaters: Aleksandr Andrev, Anatoli Emeljanenko, Jrek Gimaev, Sergei Gimaev, Aleksandr Kabanov, Sergei Kapustin, Vladimir Kovin, Aleksandr Lobanov, Nikolai Makarov, Viacheslav Nazarov, Vasily Pausov, Vladimir Popov, Aleksandr Skvortsov, Mikhail Slipchenko, Victor Tumenev, Alexei Volchenkov, Aleksandr Volchkov, Vladimir Volonkov, Viktor Skvortsov.

GAME 1: SOVIETS 7, NEW ENGLAND WHALERS 4

First period:
1. Soviets, Kovin (Andrev) 1:25
2. Soviets, S. Gimaev (Volchkov, Lobanov) 4:07
3. New England, Selwood (J. McKenzie) 18:19

Second period:
4. New England, Lacroix (Ley, Mark Howe) 00:14
5. Soviets, Volonkov (Lobanov, Emeljankenko) 3:45
6. New England, Mark Howe (Plumb, Keon) 13:31
7. Soviets, S. Gimaev (Lobanov) 14:43

Third period:
8. Soviets, S. Gimaev (Popov) 6:37
9. New England, Rogers (Marty Howe, Miller) 11:31
10. Soviets, Andrev (Skvortsov) 17:17
11. Soviets, Skvortsov (Andrev) 17:55

Goaltenders: New England – Garrett; Soviets – Myshkin
Shots on goal: New England 28; Soviets 30
Attendance: 6,812

GAME 2: SOVIETS 6, QUEBEC NORDIQUES 3
First period:
1. Soviets, Lobanov (unassisted) 8:28
2. Soviets, Skvortsov (Pausov) 12:27
3. Quebec, Cloutier (Hoganson, Bernier) 16:58
4. Soviets, Kabanov (Tumenev) 17:10

Second period:
5. Soviets, Tumenev (S. Gimaev) 3:59
6. Soviets, Tumenev (unassisted) 6:36
7. Quebec, Tardif (unassisted) 7:22

Third period:
8. Quebec, Bernier (Cloutier, Baxter) 4:54
9. Soviets, Kabanov (Nazarov, Tumenev) 8:35

Goaltenders: Quebec – Corsi; Soviets – Myshkin
Shots on goal: Quebec 28; Soviets 35
Attendance: 10,025

GAME 3: SOVIETS 4, WINNIPEG JETS 3

First period:
1. Soviets, Volchkov (Lobanov, S. Gimaev) 1:00
2. Soviets, S. Gimaev (Tumenev) 2:51
3. Soviets, Makarov (S. Gimaev) 5:33
4. Winnipeg, Lukowich (Preston, Ruskowski) 8:43
5. Winnipeg, Preston (Lukowich, Ruskowski) 12:23
6. Soviets, Andrev (Kovin) 15:04

Second period:
7. Winnipeg, Sullivan (Nilsson) 2:14

Third period:
No scoring.

Goaltenders: Winnipeg – Mattson; Soviets – Myshkin and Babariko
Shots on goal: Winnipeg 27; Soviets 35
Attendance: 4,202

GAME 4: EDMONTON OILERS 5, SOVIETS 3

First period:
1. Edmonton, MacDonald (Shmyr, Weir) 1:11
2. Edmonton, Chipperfield (Sobchuk, Neilson) 2:10
3. Soviets, S. Gimaev (unassisted) 7:53
4. Soviets, Nazarov (Tumenev, S. Gimaev) 16:25

Second period:
5. Edmonton, Bailey (Gretzky, Semenko) 3:33

Third period:
6. Edmonton, Sobchuk (Flett, Langevin) 00:13
7. Edmonton, Berry (Shmyr) 7:37
8. Soviets, Kovin (Skvortsov, Andrev) 14:13

Goaltenders: Edmonton – Dryden; Soviets – Myshkin
Shots on goal: Edmonton 19; Soviets 17
Attendance: 13,856

GAME 5: BIRMINGHAM BULLS 2, SOVIETS 2
(Summary unavailable)

GAME 6: SOVIETS 5, CINCINNATI STINGERS 3

First period:
1. Cincinnati, Marsh (Ftorek) 2:32
2. Soviets, Lobanov (S. Gimaev, Volchenkov) 9:27
3. Cincinnati, Debol (Dudley, Melrose) 15:45
4. Soviets, Volchkov (Nazarov, Lobanov) 19:49

Second period:
5. Cincinnati, Dudley (Thomas, Debol) 14:57

6. Soviets, Kapustin (Tumenev, Nazarov) 14:37
7. Soviets, Skvortsov (Kabanov, Pausov) 19:00
8. Soviets, Pausov (unassisted) 19:59

Goaltenders: Cincinnati – Liut; Soviets – Myshkin
Shots on goal: Cincinnati 25; Soviets 34
Attendance: 11,196

**WHA teams vs. Moscow Dynamo
(4-game series)**
1. Dec. 26: New England Whalers 4, Dynamo 1
2. Dec. 27: Quebec Nordiques 5, Dynamo 4
3. Dec. 29: Dynamo 4, Edmonton Oilers 1
4. Dec. 30: Winnipeg Jets 6, Dynamo 4
WHA teams won 3 and lost 1.

Note: The Moscow Dynamo played a three-game series against the WHA All-Stars in Edmonton on Jan. 2, 4 and 5, with the WHA All-Stars winning all three games. For scoring and summaries from that series, please refer to the listings for year-by-year all-star rosters and statistics.

MOSCOW DYNAMO ROSTER
Coaches: Vladimir Kiseliov, Pavel Zhiburtovich.
Goaltenders: Vladimir Polupanov, Sergei Babariko.
Defensemen: Vasili Pausov, Vitali Filippov, Aleksandr Filippov, Sergei Gimaev, Alexei Volchenkov, Vladimir Orlov, Mikhail Slipchenko, Viktor Khatulev.
Forwards: Victor Shkurdiuk, Vladimir Vikulov, Aleksandr Lovanov, Alexei Volchkov, Pavel Ezavski, Alexei Frolikov, Mikhail Shostak, Vladimir Devjatov, Evgeni Kotlov, Vladimir Golubovich, Vladimir Semjonov, Sergei Tukmachev, Viacheslav Anisin, Piotr Priordin.

GAME 1: NEW ENGLAND WHALERS 4, DYNAMO 1

First period:
1. New England, Hangsleben (Selwood, Miller) 10:18

Second period:
2. New England, Hangsleben (Inkpen) 7:49

Third period:
3. New England, Rogers (Hangsleben, Miller) 6:15
4. Dynamo, Devjotov (Golubovich) 14:02
5. New England, Keon (Antonovich, Warner) 17:02

Goaltenders: New England – Garrett; Dynamo – Polupanov
Shots on goal: New England 33; Dynamo 24

GAME 2: QUEBEC NORDIQUES 5, DYNAMO 4

First period:
1. Quebec, Bordeleau (Bernier) 16:19
2. Quebec, Tardif (Tremblay) 19:11

Second period:
3. Dynamo, Vikulov (Anisin) 4:19
4. Dynamo, Semjonov (Filippov) 5:47
5. Quebec, Geoffrion (Tardif, Leduc) 13:37
6. Dynamo, Kotlov (Semjonov) 14:41
7. Quebec, Bernier (Cloutier) 17:48

Third period:
8. Dynamo, Tukmachev (unassisted) 2:33
9. Quebec, Geoffrion (Leduc, Dorey) 18:28

Goaltenders: Quebec – Brodeur and Corsi; Dynamo – Babariko
Shots on goal: Quebec 30; Dynamo 30
Attendance: 6,736

GAME 3: DYNAMO 4, EDMONTON OILERS 1

First period:
1. Edmonton, Sobchuk (unassisted) 10:31

Second period:
2. Dynamo, Semjonov (Kotlov) 10:52
3. Dynamo, Frolikov (Slipchenko, Shostak) 16:07

Third period:
4. Dynamo, Shostak (unassisted) 6:52
5. Dynamo, Volchkov (unassisted) 7:05

Goaltenders: Edmonton – Walsh; Dynamo – Babariko
Shots on goal: Edmonton 21; Dynamo 25
Attendance: 7,954

GAME 4: WINNIPEG JETS 6, DYNAMO 4

First period:
1. Dynamo, Devjatov (Semjonov, Pausov) 14:51
2. Winnipeg, Ruskowski (MacKinnon, K. Nilsson) 15:59
3. Dynamo, Devjatov (Semjonov, Kotlov) 19:53

Second period:
4. Winnipeg, Long (K. Nilsson, Daley) 7:49
5. Winnipeg, Lindstrom (unassisted) 16:22
6. Winnipeg, Moffatt (Gray, MacKinnon) 16:59
7. Dynamo, Semjonov (Kotlov) 18:43

Third period:
8. Winnipeg, Sullivan (Amodeo, Daley) 3:27
9. Winnipeg, Lindstrom (Gray, Sullivan) 4:22
10. Dynamo, Frolikov (Slipchenko, Gimaev) 16:44

Goaltenders: Winnipeg – Daley; Dynamo – Babariko
Shots on goal: Winnipeg 33; Dynamo 28
Attendance: 8,230

**WHA CLUBS VS. CZECHOSLOVAKIA SELECTS
(6-game series)**
1. Dec. 27: New England 10, Czechs 4
2. Dec. 28: Quebec 4, Czechs 0
3. Dec. 30: Edmonton 5, Czechs 1
4. Jan. 1: Winnipeg 3, Czechs 3
5. Jan. 6: Czechs 4, Cincinnati 1
6. Jan. 7: Birmingham 10, Czechs 2
WHA clubs won 4, lost 1 and tied 1.

**WHA CLUBS VS. SWEDEN
(3-game series)**
1. Dec. 15: Winnipeg Jets 4, Sweden 3
2. Dec. 16: Edmonton Oilers 11, Sweden 2
3. Dec. 19: Quebec Nordiques 7, Sweden 3
WHA clubs won 3.

ALL-TIME REGULAR-SEASON PENALTY SHOTS

1972-73:

Oct. 11, Bill Hicke (Alta) vs. Les Binkley (Ott) — SCORE
Nov. 29, Ron Ward (NY) vs. Al Smith (NE) — Save
Jan. 16, Rene Leclerc (Que) vs. Gilles Gratton (Ott) — SCORE
Mar. 22, Bobby Hull (Win) vs. Jack Norris (Alta) — Save
Mar. 25, Rene Leclerc (Que) vs. Jack Norris (Alta) — SCORE

1973-74:

Oct. 11, Andre Lacroix (NY) vs. Cam Newton (Chi) — Save
Oct. 19, Denis Meloche (Van) vs. Jack Norris (Edm) — Save
Oct. 25, Andre Lacroix (NY) vs. Al Smith (NE) — Save
Nov. 3, Ron Buchanan (Cle) vs. Andre Gill (Chi) — Save
Nov. 22, Wayne Connelly (Min) vs. Al Smith (NE) — Save
Nov. 23, Marc Tardif (LA) vs. Jack Norris (Edm) — Save
Dec. 22, Gary Veneruzzo (LA) vs. Don McLeod (Hou) — Save
Dec. 29, Andre Lacroix (NJ) vs. Gerry Cheevers (Cle) — Save
Mar. 1, Brian Carlin (Edm) vs. Don McLeod (Hou) — SCORE
Mar. 10, Ron Garwasiuk (LA) vs. Mike Curran (Min) — Save
Mar. 14, Tom Martin (Tor) vs. Cam Newton (Chi) — Save
Mar. 31, Brian Morenz (NJ) vs. Gerry Cheevers (Cle) — Save
Apr. 1, Frank Hughes (Hou) vs. Al Smith (NE) — Save

1974-75:

Oct. 24, Wayne Connelly (Min) vs. Andy Brown (Ind) — Save
Nov. 12, Gary MacGregor (Chi) vs. Joe Junkin (SD) — Save
Dec. 4, Eddie Joyal (Edm) vs. Don McLeod (Van) — SCORE
Dec. 26, Wayne Connelly (Min) vs. Jacques Plante (Edm) — Save
Jan. 4, Danny Lawson (Cal) vs. Al Smith (NE) — SCORE
Jan. 5, Bob Leduc (Tor) vs. Bob Whidden (Cle) — Save
Jan. 28, Norm Ferguson (SD) vs. Joe Daley (Win) — Save
Feb. 11, Rejean Houle (Que) vs. Ernie Wakely (SD) — SCORE
Mar. 1, Bob Mowat (Phx) vs. Andy Brown (Ind) — SCORE
Mar. 12, Jim Harrison (Cle) vs. Paul Hoganson (Bal) — Save

1975-76:

Oct. 10, Kevin Devine (SD) vs. Gary Kurt (Phx) — Save
Oct. 28, Serge Bernier (Que) vs. Mario Vien (Tor) — SCORE
Feb. 6, Mark Napier (Tor) vs. Joe Daley (Win) — SCORE
Feb. 18, Al McDonough (Cle) vs. Don McLeod (Cal) — Save
Feb. 18, Danny Gruen (Cle) vs. Don McLeod (Cal) — Save
Mar. 2, Rick Morris (Edm) vs. Don McLeod (Cal) — SCORE
Mar. 20, Chris Bordeleau (Que) vs. Don McLeod (Cal) — Save
Mar. 20, Rejean Houle (Que) vs. Don McLeod (Cal) — Save
Mar. 30, Florent Fortier (Que) vs. Chris Worthy (Edm) — Save

NOTE: Don McLeod's sensational performances on Feb. 18 and Mar. 20 made him the only WHA netminder to twice stop two penalty shots in the same period. Against Cleveland the shots came nine minutes apart in the third period of a 4-0 Cowboys' loss. Against Quebec, the shots came two minutes apart in the first period of an 8-7 Cowboys' victory.

1976-77:

Oct. 17, Danny Gruen (Min) vs. Wayne Wood (Bir) — Save
Nov. 11, Danny Lawson (Cal) vs. Curt Larsson (Win) — Save
Dec. 17, Robbie Ftorek (Phx) vs. Ken Broderick (Edm) — Save
Dec. 26, Mark Napier (Bir) vs. Wayne Rutledge (Hou) — SCORE
Jan. 20, Frank Hughes (Phx) vs. Paul Hoganson (Cin) — Save
Feb. 18, Bruce Greig (Cal) vs. Norm LaPointe (Cin) — SCORE

1977-78:

No penalty shots awarded.

1978-79:

Nov. 3, Rich Preston (Win) vs. Eddie Mio (Edm) — Save
Nov. 12, Real Cloutier (Que) vs. Markus Mattson (Win) — Save
Feb. 21, Steve West (Win) vs. Al Smith (NE) — Save
Mar. 7, Dave Debol (Cin) vs. Markus Mattson (Win) — Save

YEAR-BY-YEAR WHA AWARD WINNERS

The annual WHA awards were named for the league's founders and principal backers. In 1974 the Gary Davidson Trophy for the regular-season MVP became the Gordie Howe Trophy, and the Howard Baldwin Trophy for coach of the year was renamed the Robert Schmertz Memorial Trophy in honour of the late New England Whalers' executive.

GARY DAVIDSON TROPHY
(Most Valuable Player)
- **1972–73:** Bobby Hull (Win)
- **1973–74:** Gordie Howe (Hou)

GORDIE HOWE TROPHY
- **1974–75:** Bobby Hull (Win)
- **1975–76:** Marc Tardif (Que)
- **1976–77:** Robbie Ftorek (Phx)
- **1977–78:** Marc Tardif (Que)
- **1978–79:** Dave Dryden (Edm)

LOU KAPLAN TROPHY
(Rookie of the Year)
- **1972–73:** Terry Caffrey (NE)
- **1973–74:** Mark Howe (Hou)
- **1974–75:** Anders Hedberg (Win)
- **1975–76:** Mark Napier (Tor)
- **1976–77:** George Lyle (NE)
- **1977–78:** Kent Nilsson (Win)
- **1978–79:** Wayne Gretzky (Edm)

PLAYOFF MVP
- **1972–73:** No winner
- **1973–74:** No winner
- **1974–75:** Ron Grahame (Hou)
- **1975–76:** Ulf Nilsson (Win)
- **1976–77:** Serge Bernier (Que)
- **1977–78:** Bobby Guindon (Win)
- **1978–79:** Rich Preston (Win)

W.D. (BILL) HUNTER TROPHY
(Leading Scorer)
- **1972–73:** Andre Lacroix (Phi)
- **1973–74:** Mike Walton (Min)
- **1974–75:** Andre Lacroix (SD)
- **1975–76:** Marc Tardif (Que)
- **1976–77:** Real Cloutier (Que)
- **1977–78:** Marc Tardif (Que)
- **1978–79:** Real Cloutier (Que)

BEN HATSKIN TROPHY
(Best Goaltender)
- **1972–73:** Gerry Cheevers (Cle)
- **1973–74:** Don McLeod (Hou)
- **1974–75:** Ron Grahame (Hou)
- **1975–76:** Michel Dion (Ind)
- **1976–77:** Ron Grahame (Hou)
- **1977–78:** Al Smith (NE)
- **1978–79:** Dave Dryden (Edm)

HOWARD BALDWIN TROPHY
(Coach of the Year)
- **1972–73:** Jack Kelley (NE)
- **1973–74:** Billy Harris (Tor)

ROBERT SCHMERTZ MEMORIAL TROPHY
- **1974–75:** Sandy Hucul (Phx)
- **1975–76:** Bobby Kromm (Win)
- **1976–77:** Bill Dineen (Hou)
- **1977–78:** Bill Dineen (Hou)
- **1978–79:** John Brophy (Bir)

DENNIS A. MURPHY TROPHY
(Best Defenseman)
- **1972–73:** J.C. Tremblay (Que)
- **1973–74:** Pat Stapleton (Chi)
- **1974–75:** J.C. Tremblay (Que)
- **1975–76:** Paul Shmyr (Cle)
- **1976–77:** Ron Plumb (Cin)
- **1977–78:** Lars-Erik Sjoberg (Win)
- **1978–79:** Rick Ley (NE)

PAUL DENEAU TROPHY
(Most Gentlemanly Player)
- **1972–73:** Ted Hampson (Min)
- **1973–74:** Ralph Backstrom (Chi)
- **1974–75:** Mike Rogers (Edm)
- **1975–76:** Vaclav Nedomansky (Tor)
- **1976–77:** Dave Keon (NE)
- **1977–78:** Dave Keon (NE)
- **1978–79:** Kent Nilsson (Win)

ALL-STAR GAME MVP:
- **1972–73:** Wayne Carleton (Ott)
- **1973–74:** Mike Walton (Min)
- **1974–75:** Rejean Houle (Que)
- **1975–76:** Real Cloutier (Que, Can)
  Paul Shmyr (Cle, USA)
- **1976–77:** Louis Levasseur (Min)
  Willy Lindstrom (Win)
- **1977–78:** Mark Howe (NE, WHA)
  Marc Tardif (Que)
- **1978–79:** No award (vs. Soviets)

THE WHA VS. THE NHL: EXHIBITION GAME RESULTS

(WHA teams listed first; victories in bold face)

1972 & 1973
No exhibitions scheduled.

1974
(WHA record – 2 wins, 5 losses)

SEPTEMBER
26: **Houston Aeros 5, St. Louis Blues 3**
28: New England Whalers 2, Philadelphia Flyers 4
29: Winnipeg Jets 1, Atlanta Flames 3

OCTOBER
5: **San Diego Mariners 4, California Golden Seals 3**
6: Toronto Toros 3, Minnesota North Stars 5
   Edmonton Oilers 3, Vancouver Canucks 4
   Cleveland Crusaders 3, Pittsburgh Penguins 5

1975
No exhibitions scheduled.

1976
(WHA record – 3 wins, 9 losses, 1 tie)

SEPTEMBER
21: **Birmingham Bulls 7, Atlanta Flames 6**
    Houston Aeros 1, Pittsburgh Penguins 5
23: Calgary Cowboys 3, Pittsburgh Penguins 7
24: **Winnipeg Jets 5, Pittsburgh Penguins 3**
26: Edmonton Oilers 1, Pittsburgh Penguins 3
    Indianapolis Racers 1, Washington Capitals 2
    Winnipeg Jets 6, St. Louis Blues 2
28: Edmonton Oilers 3, Pittsburgh Penguins 7
29: Cincinnati Stingers 2, Washington Capitals 3
    Edmonton Oilers 4, St. Louis Blues 5
30: Houston Aeros 4, Atlanta Flames 8
    Indianapolis Racers 4, Pittsburgh Penguins 6

OCTOBER
1: New England Whalers 2, New York Rangers 2

1977
(WHA record – 12 wins, 6 losses, 2 ties)

SEPTEMBER
25: New England Whalers 2, Chicago Black Hawks 2
28: **New England Whalers 5, Washington Capitals 4**
    Winnipeg Jets 1, Minnesota North Stars 2
30: Birmingham Bulls 0, Atlanta Flames 3
    New England Whalers 7, New York Rangers 4

OCTOBER
1: New England Whalers 0, Boston Bruins 5
   Winnipeg Jets 4, Minnesota North Stars 3
3: **Edmonton Oilers 3, St. Louis Blues 2**
4: **New England Whalers 5, Atlanta Flames 4**
5: Houston Aeros 3, Atlanta Flames 5
   Winnipeg Jets 6, St. Louis Blues 2
6: **Winnipeg Jets 3, St. Louis Blues 0**
7: **New England Whalers 9, Pittsburgh Penguins 0**
   Birmingham Bulls 0, St. Louis Blues 4
8: Quebec Nordiques 5, New York Rangers 5
   Edmonton Oilers 5, Detroit Red Wings 4
9: **New England Whalers 4, Atlanta Flames 3**
   Edmonton Oilers 2, Cleveland Barons 4
   Winnipeg Jets 1, Detroit Red Wings 0
10: **Quebec Nordiques 5, Washington Capitals 1**

1978
(WHA record – 16 wins, 7 losses, 4 ties)

SEPTEMBER
23: **New England Whalers 5, Washington Capitals 2**
24: Winnipeg Jets 2, St. Louis Blues 2
26: Winnipeg Jets 3, Colorado Rockies 5
27: **Quebec Nordiques 3, Colorado Rockies 2**
    New England Whalers 5, New York Islanders 2
28: **Birmingham Bulls 4, Atlanta Flames 2**
    Winnipeg Jets 2, New York Rangers 5
30: Quebec Nordiques 4, Washington Capitals 7

OCTOBER
1: **Quebec Nordiques 5, Minnesota North Stars 2**
   New England Whalers 5, Washington Capitals 1
2: Winnipeg Jets 4, New York Rangers 7
3: New England Whalers 5, Detroit Red Wings 7
   Edmonton Oilers 4, Minnesota North Stars 2
   Quebec Nordiques 3, Pittsburgh Penguins 0
4: **New England Whalers 3, Detroit Red Wings 0**
   Edmonton Oilers 5, Vancouver Canucks 3
5: **Quebec Nordiques 5, Chicago Black Hawks 2**
   Winnipeg Jets 5, Minnesota North Stars 5
   Birmingham Bulls 3, St. Louis Blues 4
6: New England Whalers 4, Chicago Black Hawks 4
   Indianapolis Racers 4, St. Louis Blues 1
7: Edmonton Oilers 3, Minnesota North Stars 9
   Quebec Nordiques 4, New York Rangers 1
   Cincinnati Stingers 6, Pittsburgh Penguins 4
8: **Edmonton Oilers 6, Colorado Rockies 4**
   Winnipeg Jets 6, Minnesota North Stars 5
   New England Whalers 4, New York Rangers 4

The WHA's overall record vs NHL:

Games:	Won:	Lost:	Tied:	GF:	GA:
67	33	27	7	245	239

PRIORITY PICKS AND ROUNDS 1-20
1972 WHA GENERAL PLAYER DRAFT
(Selections in Rounds 1-20 listed alphabetically)

ALBERTA OILERS
Priority selections: Norm Ullman (Toronto, NHL); Bobby Clarke (Philadelphia, NHL); Bruce MacGregor (New York Rangers, NHL); Phil Myre (Montreal, NHL).
Rounds 1-10: Garnet Bailey (Boston, NHL); Doug Barrie (Los Angeles, NHL); Dan Bouchard (Boston, AHL); Willie Brossart (Philadelphia, NHL); Reggie Leach (Boston, NHL); Gilles Marotte (Los Angeles, NHL); Ross Perkins (Fort Worth, CHL); Greg Polis (Pittsburgh, NHL); Pat Quinn (Vancouver, NHL); Randy Wyrozub (Buffalo, NHL).
Rounds 11-20: Ron Anderson (Buffalo, NHL); Tom Bladon (Edmonton, Jr. A); Craig Cameron (Minnesota, NHL); Joe Hardy (Nova Scotia, AHL); Dave Kryskow (Dallas, CHL); Bill Lesuk (Los Angeles, NHL); Len Lunde (retired); Lew Morrison (Philadelphia, NHL); Brian Ogilvie (Edmonton, Jr. A); Bob Stewart (Boston, NHL).
Significant later picks: John Ferguson (retired); Alexander Ragulin (USSR); Henri Richard (Montreal, NHL).

CALGARY BRONCOS:
Priority selections: Barry Gibbs (Minnesota, NHL); Jim Harrison (Toronto, NHL); Dale Hoganson (Montreal, NHL); Jack Norris (Seattle, WHL).
Rounds 1-10: Steve Carlyle (University of Alberta); Ron Homenuke (Calgary, Jr. A); Ross Lonsberry (Philadelphia, NHL); Jim McMasters (Calgary, Jr. A); Morris Mott (Queen's University); Gerry Pinder (California, NHL); Larry Romanchych (Dallas, CHL); Gregg Sheppard (Oklahoma City, CHL); Brian Walker (Calgary, Jr. A); Jim Watson (Calgary, Jr. A).
Rounds 11-20: Ron Boehm (Boston, NHL); Anatoli Firsov (USSR); Josef Golonka (unknown); Lorne Henning (New Westminster, Jr. A); Skip Krake (Salt Lake City, CHL); Bernie Lukowich (New Westminster, Jr. A); Ray Martyniuk (Columbus, IHL); Randy Rota (Nova Scotia, AHL); Dallas Smith (Boston, NHL); Stan Weir (Medicine Hat, Jr. A).
Significant later picks: Valeri Kharlamov (USSR); Darryl Sittler (Toronto, NHL); Vladimir Petrov (USSR).

CHICAGO COUGARS:
Priority selections: Stan Mikita (Chicago, NHL); Jerry Korab (Chicago, NHL); Jim McKenny (Toronto, NHL); Gary Smith (Chicago, NHL).
Rounds 1-10: Ivan Boldirev (California, NHL); Roger Crozier (Buffalo, NHL); Bob Kelly (Philadelphia, NHL); Dan Lodboa (Dallas, CHL); Don Marcotte (Boston, NHL); Pit Martin (Chicago, NHL); Jim McLeod (St. Louis, NHL); Rosaire Paiement (Vancouver, NHL); Jim Pappin (Chicago, NHL); Serge Savard (Montreal, NHL).
Rounds 11-20: Chuck Arnason (Nova Scotia, AHL); Al Blanchard (Kitchener, Jr. A); Tom Cassidy (Kitchener, Jr. A); Bill Clement (Philadelphia, NHL); Chuck Goddard (unknown); John Grisdale (Tulsa, CHL); Pierre Jarry (New York Rangers, NHL); Dick Proceviat (Kansas City, CHL); Don Tannahill (Boston, NHL); Bill Young (Dallas, CHL).
Significant later picks: Jean Ratelle (NY Rangers, NHL); Dale Rolfe (NY Rangers, NHL); Walt Tkaczuk (NY Rangers, NHL).

DAYTON ARROWS:
Priority selections: Guy Trottier (Toronto, NHL); Andre Hinse (Phoenix, WHL); Larry Lund (Phoenix, WHL); Wayne Rutledge (Denver, WHL).
Rounds 1-10: Paul Andrea (Cincinnati, AHL); Mike Corrigan (Los Angeles, NHL); Norm Gratton (Omaha, CHL); Larry Hale (Richmond, AHL); Frank Hughes (Phoenix, WHL); Gordon Labossiere (Cleveland, AHL); Dunc McCallum (San Diego, WHL); John Schella (Vancouver, NHL); Ted Taylor (Vancouver, NHL); Vic Venasky (Denver University).
Rounds 11-20: Gary Dornhoefer (Philadelphia, NHL); Don Grierson (Port Huron, IHL); Murray Hall (Vancouver, NHL); Bill Hogaboam (Omaha, CHL); Gordon Kannegiesser (Denver, WHL); Wayne Lachance (Springfield, AHL); Mike Lampman (Denver University); Ted McAneely (Baltimore, AHL); Don McLeod (Providence, AHL); Jim Shires (St. Louis, NHL).
Significant later picks: Bobby Orr (Boston, NHL); Phil Esposito (Boston, NHL); Frank Mahovlich (Montreal, NHL).

LOS ANGELES SHARKS:
Priority selections: Ken Dryden (Montreal, NHL); Gilbert Perreault (Buffalo, NHL); Matt Ravlich (Detroit, NHL); Steve Sutherland (Port Huron, IHL).
Rounds 1-10: Jean-Paul Bordeleau (Dallas, CHL); Bart Crashley (Dallas, CHL); Norm Dennis (Kansas City, CHL); Reg Fleming (Salt Lake City, CHL); Pete Laframboise (Baltimore, AHL); Ralph MacSweyn (Richmond, AHL); Dan Maloney (Dallas, CHL); Ted McCaskill (Phoenix, WHL); Doug Roberts (Boston, AHL); Bobby Whitlock (Phoenix, WHL).
Rounds 11-20: Christian Bordeleau (Chicago, NHL); Len Fontaine (Port Huron, IHL); Butch Goring (Los Angeles, NHL); John Hanna (Seattle, WHL); Earl Heiskala (San Diego, WHL); J.P. Leblanc (Dallas, CHL); Bob Liddington (Phoenix, WHL); Jim Niekamp (Tidewater, AHL); Noel Price (Nova Scotia, AHL); Marc Tardif (Montreal, NHL).
Signficant later picks: Cesare Maniago (Minnesota, NHL); J.C. Tremblay (Montreal, NHL); Gordie Howe (retired).

MIAMI SCREAMING EAGLES:
Priority selections: Bernie Parent (Toronto, NHL); Jude Drouin (Minnesota, NHL); Derek Sanderson (Boston, NHL); Bill White (Chicago, NHL).
Rounds 1-10: Mike Bloom (St. Catharines, Jr. A); Terry Caffrey (Cleveland, AHL); Neil Komadoski (Springfield, AHL); Yvon Lambert (Nova Scotia, AHL); Brian McSheffrey (Ottawa, Jr. A); Wayne Merrick (Ottawa, Jr. A); Jean Potvin (Philadelphia, NHL); Phil Russell (Edmonton, Jr. A); Carol Vadnais (California, NHL); Rene Villemure (Shawinigan, Jr. A).
Rounds 11-20: Michel Archambault (Dallas, CHL); Rick Dudley (Cincinnati, AHL); Denis Dupere (Toronto, NHL); George Ferguson (Toronto, Jr. A); Rick Foley (Philadelphia, NHL); Don Martineau (New Westminster, Jr. A); Jim Nichols (Cincinnati, AHL); Simon Nolet (Philadelphia, NHL); Paul Shmyr (California, NHL); Claude St. Sauveur (Sherbrooke, Jr. A).
Significant later picks: Boris Mikhailov (USSR); Garry Unger (St. Louis, NHL); Dennis Hull (Chicago, NHL).

MINNESOTA FIGHTING SAINTS:

Priority selections: Pete Mahovlich (Montreal, NHL); Mike Curran (USA Olympic team); Bill Goldsworthy (Minnesota, NHL); Dale Tallon (Vancouver, NHL).

Rounds 1–10: Mike Antonovich (University of Minnesota); Terry Ball (Cincinnati, AHL); Henry Boucha (USA Olympic team); Andre Boudrias (Vancouver, NHL); Brian Glennie (Toronto, NHL); Bill Klatt (Oklahoma City, CHL); Billy MacMillan (Toronto, NHL); Bob Paradise (Seattle, WHL); Tom Peluso (Denver University); Frank Sanders (USA Olympic team).

Rounds 11–20: John Arbour (Minnesota, NHL); Wayne Connelly (Vancouver, NHL); Ray Cullen (retired); Ernie Hicke (California, NHL); Jim Johnson (Los Angeles, NHL); Walt Ledingham (University of Minnesota); Jack McCartan (San Diego, WHL); Bobby MacMillan (St. Catharines, Jr. A); Mike Pelyk (Toronto, NHL); Jim Rutherford (Pittsburgh, NHL).

Significant later picks: Barclay Plager (St. Louis, NHL); Joey Johnston (California, NHL); Wendell Anderson (Governor of Minnesota, former U.S. Olympian).

NEW ENGLAND WHALERS:

Priority selections: Bobby Sheehan (California, NHL); Eddie Johnston (Boston, NHL); Rick Ley (Toronto, NHL); Larry Pleau (Montreal, NHL).

Rounds 1–10: Greg Boddy (Vancouver, NHL); Gerry Cheevers (Boston, NHL); Terry Harper (Montreal, NHL); Rick MacLeish (Philadelphia, NHL); Doug Mohns (Minnesota, NHL); Ron Schock (Pittsburgh, NHL); Wayne Thomas (Nova Scotia, AHL); Steve Vickers (Omaha, CHL); Tom Webster (California, NHL); Ed Westfall (Boston, NHL).

Rounds 11–20: Michel Belhumeur (Richmond, AHL); Curt Bennett (St. Louis, NHL); Gary Doak (New York Rangers, NHL); John French (Baltimore, AHL); Stan Gilbertson (California, NHL); Hilliard Graves (Baltimore, AHL); Paul Hurley (Boston, AHL); Mike Hyndman (Boston, AHL); Dick Sarrazin (Philadelphia, NHL); Tim Sheehy (USA Olympic team).

Significant later picks: Johnny Bucyk (Boston, NHL); Rod Gilbert (NY Rangers, NHL); Richard Martin (Buffalo, NHL).

NEW YORK RAIDERS:

Priority selections: Gerry Desjardins (Chicago, NHL); Dave Gardner (Toronto, Jr. A); Steve Shutt (Toronto, Jr. A); Billy Harris (Toronto, Jr. A).

Rounds 1–10: Don Blackburn (Providence, AHL); Ken Block (Rochester, AHL); Jack Egers (St. Louis, NHL); Garry Peters (Boston, NHL); Larry Sacharuk (Saskatoon, Jr. A); Dave Schultz (Richmond, AHL); Jim Schoenfeld (Niagara Falls, Jr. A); Rogatien Vachon (Los Angeles, NHL); Alton White (Providence, AHL).

Rounds 11–20: Chris Aherns (Kitchener, Jr. A); Lou Angotti (Chicago, NHL); Bill Barber (Kitchener, Jr. A); Norm Ferguson (California, NHL); Ray Fortin (Nova Scotia, AHL); Anthony Gale (unknown); Bert Marshall (California, NHL); Peter McNab (Denver University); Curt Ridley (Oklahoma City, CHL); Mike Usitalo (Michigan Tech.).

Significant later picks: Vladislav Tretiak (USSR); Ulf Sterner (Swedish Nationals); Bill Flett (Philadelphia, NHL).

OTTAWA NATIONALS:

Priority selections: Doug Favell (Philadelphia, NHL); Dave Keon (Toronto, NHL); Brad Park (New York Rangers, NHL); Eddie Shack (Buffalo, NHL).

Rounds 1–10: Mike Amodeo (Oshawa, Jr. A); Bob Berry (Los Angeles, NHL); Dennis Deslauriers (Shawiningan, Jr. A); Buster Harvey (Cleveland, AHL); Chuck Lefley (Nova Scotia, AHL); Don Lever (Niagara Falls, Jr. A); Nick Libbett (Detroit, NHL); Bob Murdoch (Nova Scotia, AHL); Mickey Redmond (Detroit, NHL); Billy Smith (Springfield, AHL).

Rounds 11–20: Syl Apps (Pittsburgh, NHL); Fred Barrett (Cleveland, AHL); Serge Bernier (Los Angeles, NHL); Steve Cardwell (Pittsburgh, NHL); Ron Climie (Kansas City, CHL); Michel Larocque (Ottawa, Jr. A); Wayne Rivers (Springfield, AHL); Larry Robinson (Nova Scotia, AHL); Paul Shakes (St. Catharines, Jr. A); Mike Veisor (Peterborough, Jr. A).

Significant later picks: Marcel Dionne (Detroit, NHL); Bob Baun (Toronto, NHL); Jiri Holocek (Czech Nationals).

QUEBEC NORDIQUES:

Priority selections: Gilles Villemure (New York Rangers, NHL); Guy Lapointe (Montreal, NHL); Jacques Lemaire (Montreal, NHL); Johnny McKenzie (Boston, NHL).

Rounds 1–10: Larry Carriere (Loyola College); Michel Deguise (Nova Scotia, AHL); Gilles Gilbert (Cleveland, AHL); Pierre Guite (University of Pennsylvania); Jean Hamel (Drummondville, Jr. A); Andre Lacroix (Chicago, NHL); Serge Lajeunesse (Fort Worth, CHL); Rich Leduc (Boston, AHL); Jacques Richard (Quebec, Jr. A); Gerry Teeple (Cornwall, Jr. A).

Rounds 11–20: Steve Durbano (Omaha, CHL); Germain Gagnon (Nova Scotia, AHL); Rejean Giroux (Quebec, Jr. A); Don Kozak (Edmonton, Jr. A); Bobby Lalonde (Vancouver, NHL); Alain Langlois (Long Island, EHL); Paul Larose (Syracuse, EHL); Pierre Plante (Philadelphia, NHL); Michel Plasse (Nova Scotia, AHL).

Significant later picks: Guy Lafleur (Montreal, NHL); Red Berenson (Detroit, NHL); Jocelyn Guevremont (Vancouver, NHL).

WINNIPEG JETS:

Priority selections: Bobby Hull (Chicago, NHL); Ted Green (Boston, NHL); Ted Irvine (New York Rangers, NHL); Ernie Wakely (St. Louis, NHL).

Rounds 1–10: Ted Harris (Minnesota, NHL); Billy Heindl (Cleveland, AHL); Bryan Hextall (Pittsburgh, NHL); Dennis Hextall (Minnesota, NHL); Fran Huck (Denver, WHL); John Marks (Dallas, CHL); Rick Newell (Omaha, CHL); Chris Oddleifson (Oklahoma City, CHL); Ron Snell (Hershey, AHL); Bob Woytowich (Los Angeles, NHL).

Rounds 11–20: Wayne Chernicki (Springfield, AHL); Ernest (Butch) Deadmarsh (Cincinnati, AHL); Jim Hargreaves (Rochester, AHL); Bobby Leiter (Pittsburgh, NHL); Brian Spencer (Tulsa, CHL); Pete Stemkowski (New York Rangers, NHL); Wayne Stephenson (St. Louis, NHL); George Surmay (Providence, AHL); Cal Swenson (Tulsa, CHL); Ken Tarnow (Fort Worth, CHL).

Significant later picks: Jacques Laperriere (Montreal, NHL); Dick Duff (retired); Alexei Kosygin (Premier of the Soviet Union).

WHA INTRALEAGUE DRAFTS, 1975–78

1975

1. Denver selected Brian Gibbons from Toronto.
2. Indianapolis selected Bill Prentice from Houston.
3. Cleveland selected Terry Ball from Minnesota.
4. Calgary selected Francois Lacombe from Quebec.
5. Winnipeg selected Larry Hillman from Cleveland.
6. Minnesota selected Gerry Odrowski from Phoenix.
7. San Diego selected Mike McMahon from Minnesota.
8. Indianapolis selected Al Karlander from New England.
9. Cleveland selected Doug Brindley from Indianapolis.
10. Calgary selected Mike Laughton from San Diego.

1976

1. Toronto selected Bill Butters from Houston.
2. Edmonton selected Larry Hornung from Edmonton.
3. Minnesota selected Steve Carlson from New England.
4. Minnesota selected Pat Westrum from Calgary.
5. Calgary selected Jack Carlson from Edmonton.
6. Minnesota selected Jeff Carlson from Edmonton.
7. Calgary selected Michel Deguise from Quebec.
8. Calgary selected Tom Serviss from Quebec.
9. Quebec selected Gord Labossiere from Houston.
10. Edmonton selected Don Borgeson from Calgary.
11. Quebec selected Jerry Zrymiak from Toronto.

1977

Because of the uncertainty of the league's future in the midst of merger talks with the NHL, the WHA did not conduct an intra-league draft in 1977.

1978

1. Indianapolis selected Pierre Jarry from Edmotnon.
2. Indianapolis selected Don McLeod from Edmonton.
3. Cincinnati selected Jim Troy from Edmonton.

WHA EXPANSION DRAFTS, 1974 AND 1975

On May 30, 1974, the Phoenix Roadrunners and the Indianapolis Racers participated in an expansion draft in Toronto to stock their clubs for the 1974–75 season. In May 1975, a dispersal and expansion draft was conducted to disperse players from the defunct Chicago Cougars and Baltimore Blades and to stock the expansion Denver Spurs for the 1975–76 season. The Cincinnati Stingers, who also debuted in 1975–76, had been formed two years earlier and had already signed players that the club had selected in the 1973 and 1974 amateur drafts. Players under contract to the Stingers who were loaned to other WHA teams are listed below.

The 1975 dispersal and expansion draft also eased some of the financial burden the league had incurred by paying the Baltimore and Chicago player contracts after both the Cougars and Blades folded late in the 1974–75 season. Player contracts from the defunct clubs were offered to the highest bidder in the draft, with the league picking up a percentage of the player's salary. Defenseman Jim Watson's $60,000 contract, for example, was claimed by the Quebec Nordiques for $46,000—with the league making up the difference.

1974 Expansion	Selection:	Previous club:
1. Phoenix	Gary Kurt	San Diego
2. Indianapolis	Brian McKenzie	Edmonton
3. Phoenix	Gerry Odrowski	Michigan
4. Indianapolis	Bob Fitchner	Edmonton
5. Phoenix	Ted Hodgson	Michigan
6. Indianapolis	Bob Whitlock	Michigan
7. Phoenix	Bill Young	Michigan
8. Indianapolis	Bob Ash	Winnipeg
9. Phoenix	Rich Pumple	Cleveland
10. Indianapolis	Bob Sicinski	Chicago
11. Phoenix	Robert Jones	San Diego
12. Indianapolis	Richard Campeau	Vancouver
13. Phoenix	Bernie Blanchette	Edmonton
14. Indianapolis	Roger Cote	Edmonton
15. Phoenix	Steve King	Toronto
16. Indianapolis	Steve Cardwell	Minnesota
17. Phoenix	Dick Sarrazin	Chicago
18. Indianapolis	Jim Hargreaves	Winnipeg
19. Phoenix	Terry Ryan	Minnesota
20. Indianapolis	MIchel Archambault	Quebec
21. Phoenix	Ron Anderson	Chicago
22. Indianapolis	Billy Orr	Toronto
23. Phoenix	Jack Gibson	Toronto
24. Indianapolis	Cal Swenson	Winnipeg
25. Phoenix	Jim McMasters	Cleveland
26. Indianapolis	Yves Bergeron	Quebec
27. Phoenix	Michel Plante	Vancouver
28. Indianapolis	Pierre Henry	Vancouver
29. Phoenix	Steve Warr	Toronto
30. Indianapolis	Ken Desjardins	Quebec
31. Indianapolis	Ron Morgan	Cleveland
32. Indianapolis	Tommy Williams	New England

1975 Expansion

DENVER SPURS:

The incoming Denver franchise selected the following players from the roster of the defunct Chicago Cougars:

Ralph Backstrom; Bryon Baltimore; Brian Coates; Chris Grigg (from Cougars' NAHL affiliate in Long Island); Keith Kokkola; Bob Liddington; Mark Lomenda; Gary MacGregor; Darryl Maggs; Peter Mara; Rick Morris; Cam Newton; Rosaire Paiement; Francois Rochon.

CINCINNATI STINGERS:

The incoming Cincinnati franchise had the following players under contract and on loan to the teams listed in brackets:

Dennis Sobchuk (Phoenix); Gene Sobchuk (Phoenix); John Hughes (Phoenix); Mike Pelyk (Vancouver); Ned Yetten (Vancouver); John Kiely (Vancouver); Joe Robertson (Indianapolis); Steve Andrascik (Indianapolis); Ralph Hopiavouri (Indianapolis); Dick Spannbauer (Indianapolis); Jacques Locas (Michigan); Ron Plumb (San Diego); Brad Buetow (not assigned).

WHA DISPERSAL DRAFTS, 1975–79

The WHA's first dispersal draft, involving players whose rights belonged to the defunct Chicago Cougars and Baltimore Blades, was held in conjunction with the Denver Spurs' expansion draft in May 1975. The selections thus included several players (i.e., Gilbert Perreault, Vladimir Petrov and future NHL Players Association executive director Bob Goodenow) who never played a game in the WHA but whose rights belonged to either the Cougars or the Blades.

Subsquent player dispersals following the dissolution of the Ottawa Civics (January 1976), Houston Aeros (July 1978), Birmingham Bulls and Cincinnati Stingers (June 1979) are detailed below.

Following the dissolution of the Minnesota Fighting Saints (February 1976), "new" Minnesota Fighting Saints (January 1977), Phoenix Roadrunners (April 1977), Calgary Cowboys (May 1977), San Diego Mariners (July 1977) and Indianpolis Racers (December 1978), all players under contract to those clubs were declared free agents.

1975 Dispersal Draft

Selecting team: **Player:** **Selected from:**
1. Denver — Barry Legge — Baltimore
2. Indianapolis — Pat Stapleton — Chicago
3. Cleveland — Danny Gruen — Baltimore
4. Edmonton — Dave Dryden — Chicago
5. Calgary — Don Ashby — Baltimore
6. Winnipeg — Randy Legge — Baltimore
7. Cincinnati — Rick Bourbonnais — Baltimore
8. Phoenix — Rick Blight — Baltimore
9. Minnesota — Dennis Owchar — Chicago
10. Toronto — Gord Laxton — Baltimore
11. San Diego — John Raynak — Baltimore
12. New England — Paul Hoganson — Baltimore
13. Quebec — Alain Caron — Baltimore
14. Houston — Ian McKegney — Baltimore
15. Denver — Dale Ross — Baltimore
16. Indianapolis — Michel Dubois — Chicago
17. Cleveland — Gil Perreault — Baltimore
18. Edmonton — Boris Mikhailov — Baltimore
19. Calgary — Duke Harris — Chicago
20. Winnipeg — Gary Sittler — Baltimore
21. Cincinnati — Rich Coutu — Baltimore
22. Phoenix — Aleksandr Gusev — Baltimore
23. Minnesota — Ross Lonsberry — Baltimore
24. Toronto — Denis Herron — Baltimore
25. San Diego — Alton White — Baltimore
26. New England — Dave Birch — Baltimore
27. Quebec — Don Saleski — Baltimore
28. Houston — Dave Forbes — Baltimore
29. Denver — Gilles Villemure — Baltimore
30. Indianapolis — Frank St. Marseille — Baltimore
31. Cleveland — Hilliard Graves — Baltimore
32. Edmonton — Vladimir Petrov — Baltimore
33. Calgary — Paul Nicholson — Baltimore
34. Winnipeg — Scott Garland — Baltimore
35. Cincinnati — Jim Pappin — Baltimore
36. Phoenix — Ken Lockett — Baltimore
37. Minnesota — Gord McDonald — Baltimore
38. Toronto — Doug Towler — Chicago
39. San Diego — Dave Walter — Chicago
40. New England — Bob Goodenow — Baltimore
41. Quebec — Jim Benzelock — Chicago
42. Houston — Lynn Zimmerman — Baltimore

The following players were selected through an auction at the 1975 Dispersal Draft:
From Baltimore: Gary Veneruzzo (Cincinnati); Craig Reichmuth (Minnesota); Tom Serviss (Quebec); John Miszuk (Calgary); Jerry Zrymiak (Minnesota); Bill Evo (Edmonton); Reg Thomas (Indianapolis); Gary Bredin (Denver); Ron Pronchuk (Quebec); Bill Reed (Calgary); Steve Richardson (New England); J.P. Leblanc (Denver).
From Chicago: Jim Watson (Quebec); Rod Zaine (Toronto).

1976 Dispersal
(Ottawa Civics):

All players declared free agents, except for the following:
Ralph Backstrom and Don Borgeson (sold to New England); Gary MacGregor and Barry Legge (sold to Cleveland); Francois Rochon, Darryl Maggs, Bryon Baltimore and Mark Lomenda (sold to Indianapolis).

1978 Dispersal
(Houston Aeros)

Declared free agents: Larry Lund, Poul Popiel, John Schella, Ted Taylor, Ron Hansis, Lynn Zimmerman, Larry Hale.
Purchased by Winnipeg: Andre Lacroix, John Hughes, Al McLeod, Paul Terbenche, Scott Campbell, Cam Connor, Rich Preston, Terry Ruskowski, Don Larway, Morris Lukowich, Steve West, John Gray and Ernie Wakely.

1979 Dispersal
(Birmingham Bulls and Cincinnati Stingers)

From Cincinnati:
Bryon Baltimore, Bryan Watson, Mike Liut, Dave Fortier, Reg Thomas, Dave Forbes, Kelly Davis, Michel Parizeau and Bruce Greig all claimed by Edmonton.
Michel Dion, Dave Dornseif, Barry Melrose, Robbie Ftorek, Bill Gilligan and Paul Stewart all claimed by Quebec.
Barry Legge, Craig Norwich, Peter Marsh and Jamie Hislop all claimed by Winnipeg.
Byron Shutt claimed by Hartford.
From Birmingham:
Paul Henderson, Tony Cassolato, Bob Stephenson and Steve Alley all claimed by Hartford.
Greg Tebbutt, Peter Marrin and John C. Stewart all claimed by Quebec.

WHA'S TOP 20 AMATEUR DRAFT PICKS, 1973-77

1973

	Selection	Last amateur club
1. Chicago Cougars	Bob Neely	Peterborough
2. New England Whalers	Glen Goldup	Toronto
3. Quebec Nordiques	Andre Savard	Quebec
4. Toronto Toros	Paulin Bordeleau	Toronto
5. Vancouver Blazers	Colin Campbell	Peterborough
6. Edmonton Oilers	John Rodgers	Edmonton
7. Minnesota Fighting Saints	Bob Gainey	Peterborough
8. Los Angeles Sharks	Reg Thomas	London
9. Houston Aeros	Darcy Rota	Edmonton
10. Cleveland Crusaders	Lanny McDonald	Medicine Hat
11. Winnipeg Jets	Ron Andruff	Flin Flon
12. New England Whalers	Blake Dunlop	Ottawa
13. Cincinnati Stingers	Dean Talafous	University of Wisconsin
14. Quebec Nordiques	Blaine Stoughton	Flin Flon
15. Chicago Cougars	Larry Goodenough	London
16. New York Golden Blades	Al Sims	Cornwall
17. Quebec Nordiques	Morris Titanic	Sudbury
18. Toronto Toros	Pat Hickey	Hamilton
19. Vancouver Blazers	Brent Leavins	Swift Current
20. Edmonton Oilers	Jim McCrimmon	Medicine Hat

Note:
In response to the National Hockey League's anticipated plan to draft players under the age of 20 for the first time, the WHA conducted its 1974 amateur draft in secret to beat the NHL clubs to signing the best available talent. After announcing that Saskatoon Blades' defenseman Pat Price was the league's first overall draft pick (by the Vancouver Blazers), the WHA later released an "order of selection" of Canadian amateurs taken in the draft. The Top 20 list thus does not include players selected from U.S. or European teams who, after Price, may have been selected higher or lower than the following Canadians:

1974

	Selection	Last amateur club
1. Vancouver Blazers	Pat Price	Saskatoon
2. Indianapolis Racers	Mike Will	Edmonton
3. Cincinnati Stingers	Don Larway	Swift Current
4. Michigan Stags	Bill Reed	Sault Ste. Marie
5. Edmonton Oilers	Clark Gillies	Regina
6. San Diego Mariners	Brad Rhiness	Kingston
7. Phoenix Roadrunners	Cam Connor	Flin Flon
8. Winnipeg Jets	Randy Andrechuk	Kamloops
9. Edmonton Oilers	Doug Soetaert	Edmonton
10. Cleveland Crusaders	Doug Riseborough	Kitchener
11. Quebec Nordiques	Real Cloutier	Quebec
12. Houston Aeros	Pierre Larouche	Sorel
13. Chicago Cougars	Gary MacGregor	Cornwall
14. Indianapolis Racers	Bill Lochead	Oshawa
15. Cleveland Crusaders	Paul Baxter	Winnipeg
16. San Diego Mariners	Rick Chartraw	Kitchener
17. Toronto Toros	Jim Turkiewicz	Peterborough
18. New England Whalers	Tim Young	Ottawa
19. Minnesota Fighting Saints	Bruce Boudreau	Toronto
20. Phoenix Roadrunners	Dave Gorman	St. Catharines

1975

	Selection	Last amateur club
1. Cincinnati Stingers	Claude Larose	Sherbrooke
2. Indianapolis Racers	Bryan Maxwell	Medicine Hat
3. Baltimore Blades	Don Ashby	Calgary
4. Denver Spurs	Mel Bridgman	Victoria
5. Cleveland Crusaders	Ralph Klassen	Saskatoon
6. Edmonton Oilers	Barry Dean	Medicine Hat
7. Calgary Cowboys	Dennis McLean	Calgary
8. Winnipeg Jets	Brad Gassoff	Kamloops
9. Phoenix Roadrunners	Greg Vaydik	Medicine Hat
10. Minnesota Fighting Saints	Greg Hickey	Hamilton
11. Toronto Toros	Rick Lapointe	Victoria
12. San Diego Mariners	Jamie Masters	Ottawa
13. New England Whalers	Terry McDonald	Edmonton
14. Quebec Nordiques	Pierre Mondou	Montreal
15. Houston Aeros	Richard Mulhern	Sherbrooke
16. Cincinnati Stingers	Bob Sauve	Laval
17. Baltimore Blades	Don Cairns	Victoria
18. Baltimore Blades	Robin Sadler	Edmonton
19. Cleveland Crusaders	Mal Zinger	Kamloops
20. Cleveland Crusaders	Kelly Greenbank	Winnipeg

1976	Selection	Last amateur club
1. Edmonton Oilers	Blair Chapman	Saskatoon
2. Cincinnati Stingers	Peter Marsh	Sherbrooke
3. Cleveland Crusaders	Glen Sharpley	Hull
4. Indianapolis Racers	Bob Simpson	Sherbrooke
5. San Diego Mariners	Dave Farrish	Sudbury
6. Edmonton Oilers	Bernie Federko	Saskatoon
7. Cincinnati Stingers	Randy Carlyle	Sudbury
8. Toronto Toros	Bjorn Johanson	Sweden
9. Winnipeg Jets	Thomas Gradin	Sweden
10. Quebec Nordiques	Rick Green	London
11. Toronto Toros	Kent Nilsson	Sweden
12. Cincinnati Stingers	Don Murdoch	Medicine Hat
13. New England Whalers	Mike Fidler	Boston University
14. Cleveland Crusaders	Rod Schutt	Sudbury
15. Indianapolis Racers	Alex McKendry	Sudbury
16. Cincinnati Stingers	Greg Carroll	Medicine Hat
17. Winnipeg Jets	Clayton Pschal	New Westminister
18. Calgary Cowboys	Dave Shand	Peterborough
19. Quebec Nordiques	Bob Manno	St. Catharines
20. Winnipeg Jets	Tom Rowe	London

1977	Selection	Last amateur club
1. Houston Aeros	Scott Campbell	London
2. Calgary Cowboys	Barry Beck	New Westminister
3. Winnipeg Jets	Ron Duguay	Sudbury
4. Edmonton Oilers	Mike Crombeen	Kingston
5. Indianapolis Racers	Doug Wilson	Ottawa
6. Birmingham Bulls	Rod Langway	University of New Hamshire
7. Cincinnati Stingers	Jere Gillis	Sherbrooke
8. Winnipeg Jets	Miles Zaharko	New Westminister
9. Quebec Nordiques	Lucien Deblois	Sorel
10. Houston Aeros	Dwight Foster	Kitchener
11. New England Whalers	Ron Areshenkoff	Medicine Hat
12. Birmingham Bulls	Brad Maxwell	New Westminister
13. Calgary Cowboys	Tom Gorence	University of Minnesota
14. Quebec Nordiques	John Anderson	Toronto
15. New England Whalers	Moe Robinson	Kingston
16. Indianapolis Racers	Wayne Ramsay	Brandon
17. Calgary Cowboys	Doug Berry	Denver University
18. Cincinnati Stingers	Dave Morrow	Calgary
19. New England Whalers	Randy Pierce	Sudbury
20. Quebec Nordiques	Benoit Gosselin	Trois-Rivieres

1978
In response to the National Hockey League's rejection of a merger plan, the WHA chose not to hold an amateur draft for the 1978–79 season. Instead, WHA clubs were given a green light by the league to outbid the NHL to sign junior-aged players, including those who had already been drafted by the rival league.

1979 NHL-WHA RECLAMATION DRAFT

Held in early June 1979, the reclamation draft allowed the 17 established National Hockey League franchises to reclaim players they had lost to the WHA. Some players were later left unprotected and then reselected during the expansion draft that stocked the four incoming WHA clubs, while others were listed as "priority selections" by the WHA teams and therefore were exempt from being returned to the NHL team that held their rights. The NHL clubs were also permitted to reclaim players whose rights they owned from the defunct Cincinnati Stingers and Birmingham Bulls. The remaining players from the defunct teams were made available to the four surviving ex-WHA teams in a special WHA dispersal draft.

RECLAIMED PLAYERS
Atlanta Flames: Kent Nilsson (Winnipeg)
Boston Bruins: Mark Howe (Hartford)
Buffalo Sabres: Dave Dryden (Edmonton)
Chicago Black Hawks: John Garrett (Hartford); Bobby Hull (Winnipeg); Terry Ruskowski (Winnipeg).
Colorado Rockies: Doug Berry (Edmonton).
Detroit Red Wings: Wes George (Edmonton); George Lyle (Hartford); Glenn Hicks (Winnipeg); Barry Long (Winnipeg).
Los Angeles Kings: Steve Carlson (Edmonton).
Minnesota North Stars: Eddie Mio (Edmonton); Paul Shmyr (Edmonton); Cal Sandbeck (Edmonton); Dave Semenko (Edmonton); Greg Tebbutt (Quebec).
Montreal Canadiens: Al Hangsleben (Hartford); Alain Cote (Quebec); Danny Geoffrion (Quebec); Peter Marsh (Winnipeg).
New York Islanders: Dave Langevin (Edmonton); Garry Lariviere (Quebec); Markus Mattson (Winnipeg); Kelly Davis (Edmonton).
New York Rangers: Jim Mayer (Edmonton); Warren Miller (Hartford).
Philadelphia Flyers: Dennis Sobchuk (Edmonton).
Pittsburgh Penguins: Paul Baxter (Quebec); Kim Clackson (Winnipeg); Morris Lukowich (Winnipeg).
St. Louis Blues: Risto Siltanen (Edmonton); Christian Bordeleau (Quebec); Scott Campbell (Winnipeg); Mike Liut (Edmonton).
Toronto Maple Leafs: Stan Weir (Edmonton); Jordy Douglas (Hartford); Rick Ley (Hartford).
Vancouver Canucks: John Hughes (Edmonton).
Washington Capitals: Bengt Gustafsson (Edmonton); Paul MacKinnon (Winnipeg).

1979 NATIONAL HOCKEY LEAGUE ENTRY DRAFT

In an effort to solve the draft problem relating to underage players who were already signed to WHA contracts, the NHL held a closed-door "entry draft" of 19-year-olds on Aug. 9, 1979. The move was seen as a step to head off legal ramifications if the NHL didn't conduct a teenage draft. The NHL also announced it would lower the draft age to 18 in 1980. Edmonton Oilers' star centre Wayne Gretzky, who was 18 in 1979, thus was exempt from the entry draft—but all other 19-year-olds who had played in the WHA in the 1978-79 season were included in the draft pool.

In a related move, two months after the draft the NHL reached a $500,000 settlement with teenagers Pat Riggin, Rob Ramage, Craig Hartsburg, Gaston Gingras and Rick Vaive—all of whom had signed long-term contracts with the WHA's Birmingham Bulls before the league folded. Represented by agent Bill Watters, the five had threatened to take the NHL to court if their contract claims were not settled, thus leaving them free to make their own deals with any NHL team.

The four WHA teams that were absorbed into the NHL were responsible for providing the $500,000 settlement on a pro-rata basis. According to the merger agreement the ex-WHA franchises were required to pay all "clean-up costs" for folding the league, and the matter of the "Baby Bulls" was included in that category. The merger agreement also stipulated the five players would be included in the 1979 entry draft.

First-round selections:	Player:	Former club:
1. Colorado Rockies	Rob Ramage	Birmingham Bulls, WHA
2. St. Louis Blues	Perry Turnbull	Portland
3. Detroit Red Wings	Mike Foligno	Sudbury
4. Washington Capitals	Mike Gartner	Cincinnati Stingers, WHA
5. Vancouver Canucks	Rick Vaive	Birmingham Bulls, WHA
6. Minnesota North Stars	Craig Hartsburg	Birmingham Bulls, WHA
7. Chicago Black Hawks	Keith Brown	Portland
8. Boston Bruins (from L.A.)	Raymond Bourque	Verdun
9. Toronto Maple Leafs	Laurie Boschman	Brandon
10. Minnesota North Stars (from Wash.)	Tom McCarthy	Oshawa
11. Buffalo Sabres	Mike Ramsey	University of Minnesota
12. Atlanta Flames	Paul Reinhart	Kitchener
13. New York Rangers	Doug Sulliman	Kitchener
14. Philadelphia Flyers	Brian Propp	Brandon
15. Boston Bruins	Brad McCrimmon	Brandon
16. Los Angeles Kings (from Mtl)	Jay Wells	Kingston
17. New York Islanders	Duane Sutter	Lethbridge
18. Hartford Whalers	Ray Allison	Brandon
19. Winnipeg Jets	Jimmy Mann	Sherbrooke
20. Quebec Nordiques	Michel Goulet	Birmingham Bulls, WHA
21. Edmonton Oilers	Kevin Lowe	Quebec

Significant later picks:

27. Montreal Canadiens	Gaston Gingras	Birmingham Bulls, WHA
33. Atlanta Flames	Pat Riggin	Birmingham Bulls, WHA
48. Edmonton Oilers	Mark Messier	Cincinnati Stingers, WHA

1979 NATIONAL HOCKEY LEAGUE EXPANSION DRAFT

The expansion draft held on June 13, 1979, stocked the four ex-WHA teams with players left unprotected by the 17 established National Hockey League clubs. Each of the four new teams was allowed to protect up to four "priority selections" from their 1978–79 rosters, while the NHL teams each gave up no more than four players in the draft. The order of selection was: Winnipeg, Edmonton, Hartford, Quebec, followed by the reverse order in each succeeding round. Each club was permitted to draft up to two goaltenders and 15 skaters. Prior to the expansion draft, the four WHA teams were permitted to claim players from the defunct Cincinnati Stingers and Birmingham Bulls who had been made available in a special WHA dispersal draft.

WINNIPEG JETS
Priority selections:
1. Markus Mattson
2. Morris Lukowich
3. Scott Campbell

Expansion draft:
1. Peter Marsh (Mtl)
2. Lindsay Middlebrook (NYR)
3. Bobby Hull (Chi)
4. Al Cameron (Det)
5. Dave Hoyda (Phi)
6. Jim Roberts (Min)
7. Lorne Stamler (Tor)
8. Mark Heaslip (LA)
9. Pierre Hamel (Tor)
10. Gord McTavish (StL)
11. Gord Smith (Was)
12. Clark Hamilton (Det)
13. Jim Cunningham (Phi)
14. Dennis Abgrall (LA)
15. Bill Riley (Was)
16. Gene Carr (Atl)
17. Hilliard Graves (Van)

Pre-draft roster:
Peter Sullivan
Willy Lindstrom
Bill Lesuk
Lyle Moffatt
Robert Guindon
John Gray
Paul Terbenche
Mike Amodeo
Bill Davis
Lars-Erik Sjoberg
Gary Smith
Joe Daley
Jamie Hislop
Ron Wilson
Barry Legge
Craig Norwich
Dale Yakiwchuk
Barry Melrose

EDMONTON OILERS
Priority selections:
1. Dave Dryden
2. Eddie Mio
3. Wayne Gretzky
4. Bengt Gustafsson

Expansion draft:
1. Cam Connor (Mtl)
2. Lee Fogolin (Buf)
3. Pat Price (NYI)
4. Colin Campbell (Pit)
5. Larry Brown (LA)
6. Pete LoPresti (Min)
7. Ron Areshenkoff (Buf)
8. Inge Hammarstrom (StL)
9. John Gould (Atl)
10. Doug Hicks (Chi)
11. Tom Edur (Pit)
12. Wayne Bianchin (Pit)
13. Mike Forbes (Bos)
14. Doug Favell (Col)
15. Doug Patey (Was)
16. Bob Kelly (Chi)

Pre-draft roster:
Blair MacDonald
Brett Callighen
Ron Chipperfield
Stan Weir
Peter Driscoll
Joe Micheletti
Al Hamilton
Dave Hunter
Dan Newman
Dave Lumley
Pierre Guite
Kari Makkonen
Mark Miller
Hannu Kampurri
Ed Walsh
Cal Sandbeck
Byron Baltimore
Reg Thomas
Bryan Watson
Dave Forbes
Michel Parizeau

HARTFORD WHALERS
Priority selections:
1. John Garrett
2. Jordy Douglas
3. Mark Howe

Expansion draft:
1. Alan Hangsleben (Mtl)
2. Nick Fotiu (NYR)
3. Rick Ley (Tor)
4. Al Sims (Bos)
5. Jean Savard (Chi)
6. Ralph Klassen (Col)
7. Rick Hodgson (Atl)
8. Kevin Kemp (Tor)
9. Bill Bennett (Bos)
10. Bernie Johnston (Phi)
11. Brian Hill (Atl)
12. Dave Given (Buf)
13. Maynard Schurman (Phi)
14. Nick Beverley (Col)
15. Norm Lapointe (Van)
16. Don Kozak (Van)

Pre-draft roster:
Andre Lacroix
Mike Rogers
Dave Keon
Gordie Roberts
Mike Antonovich
Johnny McKenzie
Blaine Stoughton
Marty Howe
Ron Plumb
Dave Inkpen
Larry Pleau
Al Smith
Jeff Brubaker
Byron Shutt
Bob Stephenson
Steve Alley
Tony Cassolato
Al McLeod
Steve Richardson

QUEBEC NORDIQUES
Priority selections:
1. Richard Brodeur
2. Paul Baxter
3. Garry Lariviere

Expansion draft:
1. Dave Farrish (NYR)
2. Gerry Hart (NYI)
3. Ron Low (Det)
4. Pierre Plante (NYR)
5. Blair Stewart (Was)
6. John Baby (Min)
7. John Smrke (StL)
8. Dave Parro (Bos)
9. Ken Kuzyk (Min)
10. Roland Cloutier (Det)
11. Terry Martin (Buf)
12. Jamie Masters (StL)
13. Hartland Monahan (LA)
14. Ron Andruff (Col)
15. Alain Cote (Mtl)
16. Lars Zetterstrom (Van)

Pre-draft roster:
Real Cloutier
Marc Tardif
Serge Bernier
Rich Leduc
Bob Fitchner
Paulin Bordeleau
Curt Brackenbury
Francois Lacombe
Dale Hoganson
Norm Dube
Rene Leclerc
Gilles Bilodeau
Kevin Morrison
Wally Weir
Richard David
Jim Corsi
Louis Levasseur
Pierre Lagace
Robbie Ftorek
Bill Gilligan
Paul Stewart
Michel Dion
Dave Dornseif
Peter Marrin

Part 5

MINUTIAE FROM THE WHA

A League and Its Trivia

Famous Names, Obscure Facts
"Putting on the Foil, Coach"
From Brawler to Zebra
Birmingham Bullies
Czech Out that Trench Coat!
One Hull of a Mistake
Joe Hardy: Superstar
Jumping in Reverse
Roadrunners Rally
Crusaders "Band" Together
Shootouts and Shooting Stars
Howe About That!
Streaky . . . and Freaky
Maxwell Was Smart
Avco Trophy in Triplicate
First Games, First Goals
All-Time Franchise Leaders
Beer League to Big League
The Pheenom
These Guys Could be Travel Agents

FAMOUS NAMES, OBSCURE FACTS

When **Wayne Gretzky** played his first game with the WHA Edmonton Oilers on November 3, 1978, he wore sweater Number 20 because the Oilers' didn't yet have a jersey bearing his trademark Number 99. That game marked the only time in Gretzky's professional career that he didn't wear his signature number ... Speaking of trademarks, defenseman **Roger Cote**, an original Alberta Oiler who went on to appear in 153 WHA games, routinely played with a toothpick clenched between his teeth—a forerunner to Kansas City Royals' shortstop U.L. Washington, who was featured in *Sports Illustrated* several years later for doing the same thing. Cote's toothpick was such a common sight that many fans got the impression it was somehow surgically attached to his lips ... **Brian Morenz**, an original New York Raider who tallied 110 points in 223 WHA games, was a distant cousin of Hall of Fame immortal Howie Morenz ... **Robbie Ftorek** and **Claude Larose** both wore sweater Number Eight for the Cincinnati Stingers in 1977–78 after being granted special permission by the league (for an explanation, see Ftorek's profile in "Gallery of Stars") ... Quebec Nordiques' coach **Jacques Demers** signed himself to a five-game tryout contract and actually dressed for a game against the Oilers on March 18, 1979. The unusual move became necessary after several Quebec players fell ill with the flu, leaving the club with only 14 skaters. A league rule mandated that 15 skaters had to be dressed or the game would be forfeited, so Demers, who hadn't played for real in years, suited up but wisely didn't give himself any ice time ... The Nords' very first coach in the WHA was none other than **Maurice (Rocket) Richard**, the legendary scoring star of the Montreal Canadiens. But after just two games (a win and a loss), Richard asked for a one-week leave of absence to reassess his position. A few days later he quit, citing health reasons. Said Nordiques' GM **Marius Fortier**: "We can't ask Maurice Richard to die behind the bench. And it is obvious that this has become a superhuman task, beyond his powers." ... **Derek Sanderson**, the WHA's highest-profile signing after **Bobby Hull** in 1972, played only eight games before the Philadelphia Blazers bought out his contract for a reported $1 million and sent him back to the NHL. "I never should have gone to the WHA in the first place; Philadelphia was the stupidest mistake I ever made," Sanderson recalled years later. "Everything went downhill from there. I drove around in a Rolls Royce. American Express Gold—that was my favorite colour." ... **Blake Ball**, whose entire WHA career consisted of two playoff games for the Cleveland Crusaders in 1973, had previously played six seasons as a defensive end in the Canadian Football League. He was promoted to the Crusaders after a long career in the Eastern Hockey League ... Motorcycle daredevil **Evel Knievel**, who once played semipro hockey in Montana, was the featured intermission attraction during the Toronto Toros' 8–4 home victory over the Vancouver Blazers on March 25, 1975. Decked out in a star-spangled helmet and wearing sweater Number 13, Knievel put on a penalty shot demonstration, scoring a nifty goal against Toros' netminder **Les Binkley**. Toronto owner **Johnny Bassett** was reportedly so impressed with Knievel's puck prowess that he considered signing him to a five-game tryout ... The very first player selected in the WHA's 1972 general

Minutiae from the WHA

One of the Toronto Toro's biggest crowds of the 1975–75 season turned out to watch motorcycle daredevil Evel Knievel test his shooting eye against goaltender Les Binkley in a penalty shot exhibition. Knievel, who once played semipro hockey in Montana, made a nifty move to beat Brinkley at close range. (CANADA WIDE PHOTOS)

player draft was **Henry Boucha,** by the Minnesota Fighting Saints. The last player chosen was **Gordie Howe,** by the Los Angeles Sharks. In between Boucha and Howe, the 1,079 other selections included Green Bay Packers' football star **Jim Carter** and Minnesota governor **Wendell Anderson** (an ex-Olympian), both by the Fighting Saints, and Soviet Premier **Alexei Kosygin,** by the Winnipeg Jets ... Tough guy **Dave Semenko,** who debuted with the WHA Oilers in 1977 and later played nine seasons in the NHL with Edmonton, Hartford and Toronto, was the last opponent to face former world heavyweight champion **Muhammad Ali** in a "real" exhibition boxing match. The three-round bout, which Ali won easily, took place at Northlands Coliseum in 1983 … **Bobby Kromm** notched the middle milestone in a unique coaching hat trick when he won the Robert Schmertz Memorial Trophy as the WHA's coach of the year with Winnipeg in 1975–76. In 1961 Kromm was the playing coach of the world amateur champion Trail Smoke Eaters, and in 1977–78 he won the Jack Adams Trophy as the NHL coach of the year in Detroit. Kromm is the only man to be voted top bench boss in both major leagues.

"PUTTING ON THE FOIL, COACH"

In 1977 Paul Newman starred as an aging minor league player in the big-screen cult comedy *Slap Shot*. The story revolves around a lameduck team called the Charlestown Chiefs, which is suddenly transformed into a contender with the arrival of three goofy-looking goons called the Hanson Brothers. The boys all wear thick horn-rimmed corrective lenses, bring a suitcase full of toys on their first road trip, and delight in taping foil to their knuckles in order to deliver harder punches. After finally getting into the lineup, they loudly exhort their teammates to play "old-time hockey … you know, like Eddie Shore!"

Hilarious as it is, *Slap Shot* was actually based on a real-life incident that took place in the North American Hockey League in 1975. Three players from the Johnstown Jets—Steve Carlson, his brother Jeff and Guido Tenesi—charged up into the stands in Utica, New York to challenge a group of overly abusive fans. The players were arrested, but the fight jolted the Jets out of their season-long lethargy and ignited a long winning streak that saw them come from far back in the standings to sneak into the playoffs and eventually defeat the Syracuse Blazers for the NAHL championship.

In *Slap Shot* the Hanson Brothers were portrayed by Steve and Jeff Carlson, who made their WHA debut with the Minnesota Fighting Saints in 1975–76, along with Dave Hanson, who also played briefly for the Saints before the Minnesota franchise folded midway through the following season. After the Saints' demise, Hanson and Steve Carlson moved on to the New England Whalers for the balance of the 1976–77 season, where they were joined by the third real-life Carlson brother, Jack. He had originally been penciled in for a role in the movie but was summoned by the Edmonton Oilers just before filming began and his part was given to Hanson.

Jack Carlson, nicknamed "The Big Bopper," joined the NHL's Minnesota North Stars in 1978–79 and went on to play 170 NHL games with the Stars and St. Louis Blues. Steve, easily the most talented of the trio, joined the Edmonton Oilers in 1978–79 and wrapped up his career with the NHL's Los Angeles Kings in 1979–80. Jeff Carlson's entire major league career consisted of seven games with the Fighting Saints, while Hanson played 33 games in the NHL with Detroit and Minnesota and 103 in the WHA—most notably as one of the leading hitmen on the 1978–79 Birmingham Bulls.

A footnote to the WHA's *Slap Shot* connection is that the movie character of Ogie Oglethorpe was based on a wild minor leaguer named Billy Goldthorpe, who logged a total of 33 WHA games with four teams: Minnesota, Baltimore, San Diego and Denver. Known for his huge blonde afro and a helter-skelter skating style reminiscent of an egg-beater gone berserk, Goldthorpe was once suspended in the Southern Hockey League for biting an official during a fight.

FROM BRAWLER TO ZEBRA

Chuckling at the antics of the Carlsons and Dave Hanson as real-life hockey players portraying Hollywood caricatures is understandable. But how do we explain the metamorphosis of Paul Stewart, who went from being a real-life thug in the WHA to becoming one of the National Hockey League's most respected referees?

Stewart's strange odyssey began on December 14, 1975—the day he completed his degree at the University of Pennsylvania. Perusing the sports page of a local paper, he noticed that the Binghampton Dusters were buried in the cellar of the North American Hockey League, 25 points back of their nearest rival. He called the Dusters' office, asked for a tryout, and within a week had established himself as the NAHL's new heavyweight champion. Two years later he was the designated enforcer on the Cincinnati Stingers, riding shotgun for little guys like Robbie Ftorek and Rich Leduc while accumulating 286 penalty minutes in 63 WHA games.

Stewart joined the Quebec Nordiques for one season after the merger, then retired in 1980 with 360 penalty minutes in just 84 major league appearances. He became a full-time NHL referee in 1987 and quickly earned a reputation as a "no nonsense" guy who didn't tolerate goons. Go figure.

BIRMINGHAM BULLIES

Nicknames are an unappreciated art form. Over the years, the monikers we ascribe to our sporting heroes—whether affectionate or villainous—take on a life of their own. The best ones become a part of the sport's mythos, acquiring a recognition factor that often transcends the athlete's actual accomplishments (or lack of same).

Some nicknames are perfectly precise. Nobody but Muhammad Ali could be "The Greatest." Baseball's Stan Musial was simply "The Man." And for the better part of a decade, hockey's most meteoric star was "The Rocket," Maurice Richard. Other handles evoke the darker side. "The Michigan Assassin" fit boxer Stanley Ketchel like a six-ounce glove, as did "The Hammer" for Dave Shultz, the most notorious of Philadelphia's ferocious Flyers in the mid-1970s.

Lying somewhere in between, in the no-man's land bracketed by fan adulation and well-founded infamy, were two of the World Hockey Association's all-time single season penalty leaders: Frank "Seldom" Beaton, and Gilles "Bad News" Bilodeau.

Beaton was a genuine WHA legend. The native of Antigonish, Nova Scotia, first attracted notice as a 22-year-old rookie with the Hampton Gulls of the Southern Hockey League. In 1976 he shattered the league record for penalty minutes for an entire season in just 38 games, then took his act to the Cincinnati Stingers, where he picked up a relatively angelic 61 minutes in 29 games. He spent the 1976–77 season with the Edmonton Oilers and led the league with 274 minutes. But the real fun started in 1977–78 when Beaton and Bilodeau became teammates with the

Birmingham Bulls and brawled their way to a combined total of 537 minutes. Along with Steve Durbano's 284 minutes and Dave Hanson's 241, the quartet of Birmingham Bullies combined for 17.7 hours in the sin bin.

On Thanksgiving night 1977, Birmingham coach Glen Sonmor started Beaton, Bilodeau, Durbano, Bob Stephenson and Serge Beaudoin against the visiting Stingers. One newspaper account described it as "like the German Army invading Poland … it took all of 24 seconds for all hell to break loose, with more than 200 penalty minutes handed out before order was finally restored. There were wounded Stingers everywhere, bloodied and battered." Added Cincinnati forward Rich Leduc: "It was a total butcher job; it was a struggle just to stay alive out there."

It wasn't long afterward that the "Birmingham flu" became the all-encompassing excuse for visiting players who suddenly came down with a mysterious ailment rather than face the prospect of squaring off against "Seldom" Beaton, "Bad News" Bilodeau et al.

Beaton's reputation for fistic ferocity quickly spread to all corners of the WHA. A few months later, in what looked like a rejected script from *Barney Miller*, he was arrested at Cincinnati's Riverfront Coliseum on a two-year-old warrant charging him with assault in an altercation with a local gas station attendant. Frank had dodged the warrant-servers for nearly two years while playing for Edmonton and Birmingham, but on the afternoon of February 19 his luck ran out.

Late in the first period, with the Bulls leading 1–0, a phalanx of Cincinnati police officers appeared at the Coliseum. Spotting them as the teams filed off the ice for intermission, Beaton sneaked off with the Stingers rather than going with his teammates. He was smuggled into the Cincinnati dressing room, where he took refuge in the stick closet. Meanwhile, six policemen forced their way into the Bulls' room with drawn billy clubs. Unable to locate Beaton, they ordered each player to show some identification.

Beaton surrendered a few minutes later when the cops discovered him calmly planing down a stick in the Stingers' dressing room, and he was allowed to shower before being handcuffed and escorted to the slammer. The Bulls continued on their road trip while Frank cooled his heels behind bars.

"It turned out to be not very funny," Beaton said on his arrival back in Birmingham. "They had me surrounded. I was treated well, though, and [Stingers' captain] Rick Dudley brought me some food. The next day he and [Cincinnati coach] Jacques Demers posted my bail. It was very nice of them … "

Beaton said farewell to Dixie after the 1977–78 season and jumped to the NHL, where he played 25 games for the New York Rangers over the next two years and tallied just 43 minutes in penalties.

CZECH OUT THAT TRENCH COAT!

World Hockey Association teams were the first in North America to hold training camps in Europe. The Toronto Toros and Winnipeg Jets trained in Sweden in 1975, and the Jets returned in 1977. The Phoenix Roadrunners held their camp in Finland in 1976, while the Cincinnati Stingers trained in Prague, Czechoslovakia in 1977. Remember now, this was before the collapse of

Communism and the Czechs were still very sensitive about snoopy Westerners. Stingers' winger Dennis Abgrall found that out when he was arrested and jailed for three hours for taking a photograph of a police station.

Of course, the fact that the fun-loving Abgrall was doing his best impersonation of Maxwell Smart at the time, including wearing a long white trench coat and wrap-around shades, might have had something to do with it …

ONE HULL OF A MISTAKE
Bobby Hull was the most famous athlete in North America when he signed his historic contract with the Winnipeg Jets and gave the WHA instant credibility in 1972. What's not as well known is that the Ottawa Nationals tried to cash in on the Golden Jet's enormous popularity by signing his younger brother, Garry Hull, to a tryout contract before the league's debut season.

As former Nats' owner Doug Michel related in his superb book *Left Wing and a Prayer*: "Garry was the in-between brother of Bobby and Dennis, but unlike his spectacular brothers he had never made it in hockey. He operated a farm in Millbrook, Ontario, and in fact, few hockey fans had ever been aware there even was a third Hull brother. With Dennis acting as his agent, Garry walked into our office one day. He wanted to play. Any hockey sense I had told me that if a third Hull brother existed, it was inconceivable he could have arrived at 27 years of age without having been thoroughly scouted by every hockey man in the business. Nevertheless, we were desperate for bodies whose presence in the fold we could announce, and when Garry was agreeable to a contract conditional to his making the team, I thought 'Why not?' The name at least had some magic and would be worth some publicity … "

The signing turned out to be a public relations nightmare that made the Nats look like total morons. The club's gushing press release announced that "Garry is considered by many knowledgeable hockey people as the best Hull of them all. His brothers claim he is stronger than they are and given the chance will be the best Hull to lace on skates … " An Ottawa television commentator summed up the media's reaction with a single line: "Don't insult our intelligence."

Hull's tryout was over almost before it began, and he was soon back tending to his cattle.

JOE HARDY: SUPERSTAR
Garry Hull wasn't the only "famous unknown" to test the WHA waters. Alain "Boom Boom" Caron, the first professional hockey player to score 70-plus goals in a season (77 with the Central League's St. Louis Braves in 1963–64) was an original Quebec Nordique and notched 132 points in 193 WHA games. Even more impressive was Joe Hardy, a hard-shooting centre who was cut by the Chicago Cougars, Indianapolis Racers and San Diego Mariners before becoming the first pro in history to top 200 points in a season when he finished with 207 for the North American Hockey League's Beauce Jaros in 1975–76.

Hardy's linemates in his record-setting year were none other than Boom Boom Caron and Luc Simard. Hardy tallied 60 goals and an electrifying 147 assists in 72 games, while Caron was 78–59–137 and Simard 65–71–136. The line's combined total of 481 scoring points for the season established an all-time record for professional hockey that still stands.

JUMPING IN REVERSE

By the fall of 1973 it wasn't unusual for a player to defect from the National Hockey League to the fledgling WHA. By that time a few had even jumped from the WHA back to the NHL. But veteran defenseman Jean Gauthier executed an unusual "first" when he jumped from the WHA to the American Hockey League, leaving the lucrative paycheques he'd been cashing from the New York Raiders for slightly more than half as much from the Rochester Americans.

"It's a tough thing to try to explain," Gauthier said at the time. "I'm 36 years old and I've played pro hockey for quite a while. I have some pride, but the New York people have treated me as though I am nothing. There never was a problem with the money—it was always there, despite the problems the team had with different owners and everything. But when I signed with the Raiders it was under the understanding I'd just come in and get the same thing this fall. But with the management change I haven't even had an offer. I was told to go to camp, but there was no guarantee of a contract or a job. They just didn't seem to care about me."

Gauthier had gone the same route with the Montreal Canadiens in the six-team NHL. He wasn't good enough to crack the Habs' blue line corps, but he was too good to let go to one of Montreal's rivals. For six straight seasons he was called up for a few games, until the Canadiens finally let him go to Philadelphia in the 1967 expansion draft. With the Raiders in 1972–73 he broke a shoulder and only saw action in 31 games.

Gauthier's "reverse jump" to the AHL was the last move of his long career. He never played major league hockey again.

ROADRUNNERS RALLY

In early 1976 the WHA ordered the cash-strapped Phoenix Roadrunners to cough up $80,000 to cover expenses for a game that had to be postponed when all the team's equipment was "lost" on a flight to Indianapolis. The missing gear was later located at the Phoenix airport, still sitting on a baggage ramp in a torrential downpour.

Six months after the equipment debacle, the Roadrunner players shelled out $110,000 of their own money to purchase 528 season tickets in a last-ditch effort to keep the franchise afloat.

"The city and the people have been so good to us, we just want to remain in business," defenseman Jim Niekamp said at the time. Added captain Al McLeod: "When you get older and start raising a family, you can really appreciate a place like this. We just want to do something to help make hockey viable here. If I was still playing in Detroit, I doubt I'd do something like this because I felt no attachment to that city. But Phoenix is different."

Unfortunately, the Roadrunners' ticket rally proved to be too little, too late. The franchise suspended operations the following April.

CRUSADERS "BAND" TOGETHER

On March 10, 1976, the Cleveland Crusaders skated onto the ice at Richfield Coliseum wearing black armbands to protest on-going talks between club owner Jay Moore and the ownership group of the National Hockey League's Kansas City Scouts. According to

Crusaders' captain Paul Shmyr, Moore and GM Jack Vivian "were trying to undermine our efforts to win first place and keep the team in Cleveland."

Apparently worried that Moore was attempting to buy the Scouts and move them to Cleveland, the players unanimously agreed to a public display of their concern in front of the 12,286 hometown fans who turned out to watch a 5–2 win over Cincinnati. It was enough to cause Vivian to resign his position the next day, but the long-term effect of the protest was negligible. The Crusaders transferred to Minnesota as the new incarnation of the Fighting Saints just five months later.

SHOOTOUTS AND SHOOTING STARS

Long before it became fashionable in the minor leagues and international competition, the tie-breaking shootout was tried in some of the WHA's initial exhibition games before being abandoned.

The most bizarre shootout experiment took place the very first time it was tested, on October 3, 1972, in a pre-season game that saw the Houston Aeros edge the Minnesota Fighting Saints 7–6. Don Grierson, a journeyman minor leaguer, emerged as the hero when he scored the deciding goal after an incredible 18 penalty shots! The teams were tied 4–4 after regulation time, and when they failed to break the deadlock in a ten-minute overtime, the shootout began. Jim Johnson and Ted Hampson each scored for the Saints in the first five-shot round, while Larry Lund and Murray Hall tallied for the Aeros to keep the game tied 6–6. The Saints then missed on four consecutive shots and the Aeros muffed three before Grierson buried the winner.

Speaking of shots, the San Diego Mariners established the WHA's all-time records for shots on goal in a period (32) and a game (64) when they bombed the Quebec Nordiques 10–4 on December 23, 1975. The league record for most shots in a game by both teams is 107, set November 29, 1974, when the Winnipeg Jets outshot the Michigan Stags 54–53 and then won the game 7–6. That mark was tied on March 14, 1975, when the Toronto Toros outshot the Mariners 59–48 but lost the game 6–4.

The Indianapolis Racers and Edmonton Oilers share the WHA record for fewest shots on goal by one team in one game with 11, while the New England Whalers set a record for accuracy by scoring five times on just 13 shots in a 5–2 victory over the Los Angeles Sharks on November 18, 1973.

In the strangest shooting feat in the league's seven-year history, on March 1, 1973 Alton White of the Sharks was credited with a hat trick in a 4–1 victory over Minnesota—yet he only had two official shots on goal! He scored on both of his "official" shots and was awarded his third goal of the game after a Minnesota player threw his stick to thwart White's breakaway after the Saints had pulled their goaltender in the dying seconds.

HOWE ABOUT THAT!

After 28 seasons and 2,012 games in major league hockey, Gordie Howe achieved a long-overdue career milestone on February 27, 1976, when he scored in overtime to lift the Houston Aeros to a 7–6 victory over the Toronto Toros. It was the first OT goal of Howe's professional career and capped a come-from-behind win that also featured a hat trick by Mark Howe. Gordie, incidentally, also scored on his very first WHA shot—beating New England netminder Bill Berglund after just 21 seconds of Houston's exhibition victory over the Whalers at Madison Square Garden on September 26, 1974.

STREAKY... AND FREAKY

Don McLeod was one of the steadiest goaltenders in the history of the WHA, but you'd never know it by checking his stats from the 1976–77 season with the Calgary Cowboys. McLeod posted a superb 24–11–2 record in the friendly confines of the Calgary Corral that season, but was a brutal 1–24–3 on the road. McLeod also assisted on a record 43 goals in six seasons with Houston, Vancouver, Calgary, Edmonton and Quebec, and owns the WHA's most impressive streak in stopping penalty shots. His sensational performances on February 18 and March 20, 1976, made him the only netminder to twice stop two penalty shots in the same period.

Andre Lacroix of the San Diego Mariners posted a record 32-game point scoring streak, potting 17 goals and 53 assists from January 4 through March 19, 1975. Quebec's Serge Bernier had the WHA's longest goal-scoring streak when he fired 16 goals in 11 consecutive games in December 1974, while Winnipeg's Ulf Nilsson set the consecutive assist mark by notching 27 in 18 games from October 13 to November 27, 1977.

The single-game points record is held by Edmonton's Jim Harrison, who collected three goals and seven assists for a ten-point night in an 11–3 wipeout of the New York Raiders on January 30, 1973. Harrison had another seven-assist night with the Cleveland Crusaders in 1975.

MAXWELL WAS SMART

Quick thinking by Cleveland defenseman Bryan Maxwell was credited with ensuring that Phoenix Roadrunners' rookie Barry Dean wasn't more seriously injured when he had a tendon, a radial artery and a minor nerve in his right forearm slashed by an errant skate during a game against the Crusaders on March 19, 1976. The nerve, which supplies sensation to the web of the thumb, and the radial artery were repaired. The tendon, cut 80 percent through, was resewn.

"I dumped Barry in the corner, but when he came up shaking his gloves off I didn't think he wanted to fight me," the six-foot-three, 210-pound Maxwell told *The Hockey News*. "Then I realized he was saying 'Maxie, get me to a doctor.' I just grabbed Dino's arm, pushed the two sides of the gash together and ran to the dressing room with him."

Ironically, Dean and Maxwell had been junior teammates in Medicine Hat for three years, and Dean had been best man at Maxwell's wedding the previous summer.

Dr. Eli Krigsten, who performed emergency surgery on Dean's arm at a Phoenix hospital, credited Maxwell's quick action for saving his friend from permanent damage. "Dean lost a unit of blood right out there on the ice and he would have lost a whole lot more if Maxwell hadn't had the presence of mind to put some pressure on it," Krigsten said.

Both players later went to the NHL. Maxwell spent eight seasons with Minnesota, St. Louis, Winnipeg and Pittsburgh, while Dean played three years with the Colorado Rockies and Philadelphia Flyers.

AVCO TROPHY IN TRIPLICATE

The Avco World Trophy had its share of bumps, bruises and bad luck during the WHA's seven-year lifetime.

Commissioned and donated by Avco Financial Services as the symbol of playoff supremacy, the $13,000 trophy was not completed in time for the league's first championship. A substitute was hastily made available for presentation to the New England Whalers on May 6, 1973, but CBS, which was televising the game, cut away with a few minutes left and the presentation never made it to the airwaves.

"It was kind of funny," former Whalers' co-owner Howard Baldwin recalled in 1995. "It was a Sunday, so we had to get somebody to open a sporting goods store in Boston and buy the biggest trophy they had. The league never paid me back, so I kept it."

In 1974 there was, finally, an Avco World Trophy. It had been formally presented to the Whalers during the off-season but was lost in transit between Boston and Houston, site of the 1974 final between the Aeros and Chicago Cougars. It turned up in a storage room at the Houston airport just a few hours before game time, but all was still not well. The one-piece trophy that had been sent from Boston was found in three pieces, so a silversmith had to be hired to put it back in presentable shape.

The following year, when the Aeros repeated as WHA champs, Houston captain Ted Taylor fumbled and dropped the Avco Trophy as he was bringing it off the plane from Quebec. The base broke and the hardware received several new dents, but nothing too serious. In 1976, fearing that the NHL might try to create a border delay that would prevent the Avco Trophy from crossing into the United States, the WHA had a duplicate made so that one could be kept in Canada and one in the U.S. Today, one of those trophies is on display at the Hockey Hall of Fame in Toronto, and the other is at the Winnipeg Arena, where the Jets became the last team to be crowned WHA champions in 1979.

A third Avco World Trophy is on display at the Nova Scotia Sports Hall of Fame in Halifax. Though never presented, the third trophy was apparently made for a former president of Avco International who was a resident of Kentville, Nova Scotia. He donated the trophy after his retirement.

FIRST GAMES, FIRST GOALS

The first WHA games were all-rookie exhibition contests played on September 23, 1972. The New England Whalers defeated the Philadelphia Blazers 5–3 and the Minnesota Fighting Saints blasted the Chicago Cougars 10–7. When the regular season schedule opened two weeks later, the following players scored and assisted on the first franchise goals:

Alberta Oilers: Ron Anderson (Jim Harrison, Steve Carlyle); October, 11, 1972, at 6:19 of the first period.

Chicago Cougars: Reggie Fleming (unassisted); October 12, 1972, at 15:55 of the second period.

Cleveland Crusaders: Bob Dillabough (Grant Erickson, Paul Shmyr); October 11, 1972, at 10:30 of the second period.

Houston Aeros: Larry Lund (Poul Popiel); October 12, 1972, at 1:52 of the first period.

Los Angeles Sharks: Steve Sutherland (Mike Byers, J.P. LeBlanc); October 13, 1972, at 2:33 of the second period.

Minnesota Fighting Saints: Wayne Connelly (Mel Pearson, John Arbour); October 13, 1972, at 13:00 of the first period.

New England Whalers: Tom Williams (Tom Earl, John Cunniff); October 12, 1972, at 13:42 of the first period.

New York Raiders: Ron Ward (Ken Block, Brian Bradley); October 12, 1972, at 17:20 of the first period.

Ottawa Nationals: Bob Charlebois (Chris Meloff); October 11, 1972, at 11:06 of the first period.

Philadelphia Blazers: Derek Sanderson (Dan O'Donoghue, Jim Cardiff); October 12, 1972, at 6:52 of the first period.

Quebec Nordiques: Francois Lacombe (Mike Harvey, Ray Larose); October 13, 1972, at 3:51 of the first period.

Winnipeg Jets: Ab McDonald (Joe Zanussi, Norm Gratton); October 12, 1972, at 8:14 of the first period.

The WHA's first season opened on October 11, with the Alberta Oilers defeating the Nationals 7–4 in Ottawa and the Cleveland Crusaders blanking the visiting Quebec Nordiques 2–0. The next night the visiting Winnipeg Jets topped the New York Raiders 6–4; the Houston Aeros were at home for a 3–2 triumph over the Chicago Cougars, and the visiting Philadelphia Blazers were nipped 4–3 by the New England Whalers. On October 13, Quebec blanked Alberta 6–0, Houston edged the Los Angeles Sharks 3–2, and Winnipeg topped the Minnesota Fighting Saints 4–3.

ALL-TIME FRANCHISE LEADERS

Alberta Oilers / Edmonton Oilers: Goals – Rusty Patenaude, 136. Assists – Al Hamilton, 258. Points – Al Hamilton, 311. Penalty minutes – Doug Barrie, 620. Goaltending wins – Dave Dryden, 94.

Chicago Cougars: Goals – Rosaire Paiement, 89. Assists – Rosaire Paiement, 119. Points – Rosaire Paiement, 208. Penalty minutes – Larry Mavety, 356. Goaltending wins – Cam Newton, 37.

Cincinnati Stingers: Goals – Rick Dudley, 131. Assists – Rick Dudley, 146. Points – Rick Dudley, 278. Penalty minutes – Rick Dudley, 516. Goaltending wins: Mike Liut and Michel Dion, both with 31.

Cleveland Crusaders: Goals – Gary Jarrett, 104. Assists – Gary Jarrett, 119. Points – Gary Jarrett, 223. Penalty minutes – Paul Shmyr, 538. Goaltending wins – Gerry Cheevers, 99.

Denver Spurs / Ottawa Civics: Goals – Ralph Backstrom and Don Borgeson, each with 21. Assists – Ralph Backstrom, 29. Points – Ralph Backstrom, 50. Penalty minutes – Rick Morris, 58. Goaltending wins – Bob Johnson, 8.

Houston Aeros: Goals – Larry Lund, 149. Assists – Larry Lund, 277. Points – Larry Lund, 426. Penalty minutes – John Schella, 844. Goaltending wins: Ron Grahame, 102.

Indianapolis Racers: Goals – Reg Thomas, 63. Assists – Michel Parizeau, 88. Points – Michel Parizeau, 136. Penalty minutes – Kim Clackson, 519. Goaltending wins – Michel Dion, 31.

Los Angeles Sharks / Michigan Stags / Baltimore Blades: Goals – Gary Veneruzzo, 105. Assists – J.P. LeBlanc, 129. Points – Gary Veneruzzo, 201. Penalty minutes – Steve Sutherland, 317. Goaltending wins – Russ Gillow, 21.

Minnesota Fighting Saints: Goals – Mike Walton, 136. Assists – Mike Walton, 145. Points – Mike Walton, 281. Penalty minutes – John Arbour, 461. Goaltending wins: John Garrett, 77.

New England Whalers: Goals – Tom Webster, 220. Assists – Rick Ley, 210. Points – Tom Webster, 425. Penalty minutes – Rick Ley, 716. Goaltending wins – Al Smith, 141.

New York Raiders / New York Golden Blades / New Jersey Knights / San Diego Mariners: Goals – Wayne Rivers, 158. Assists – Andre Lacroix, 340. Points – Andre Lacroix, 473. Penalty minutes – Kevin Morrison, 399. Goaltending wins – Ernie Wakely, 77.

Ottawa Nationals / Toronto Toros / Birmingham Bulls: Goals – Paul Henderson, 140. Assists – Gavin Kirk, 202. Points – Gavin Kirk, 303. Penalty minutes – Dave Hanson, 453. Goaltending wins – Gilles Gratton, 81.

Philadelphia Blazers / Vancouver Blazers / Calgary Cowboys: Goals – Danny Lawson, 212. Assists – Danny Lawson, 197. Points – Danny Lawson, 409. Penalty minutes – Butch Deadmarsh, 401. Goaltending wins – Don McLeod, 88.

Phoenix Roadrunners: Goals – Robbie Ftorek, 118. Assists – Robbie Ftorek, 180. Points – Robbie Ftorek, 298. Penalty minutes – Cam Connor, 463. Goaltending wins – Gary Kurt, 54.

Quebec Nordiques: Goals – Real Cloutier, 281. Assists – J.C. Tremblay, 358. Points – Marc Tardif, 579. Penalty minutes – Paul Baxter, 724. Goaltending wins – Richard Brodeur, 165.

Winnipeg Jets: Goals – Bobby Hull, 303. Assists – Ulf Nilsson, 344. Points – Bobby Hull, 638. Penalty minutes – Kim Clackson, 413. Goaltending wins – Joe Daley, 167.

BEER LEAGUE TO BIG LEAGUE

Scoring the winning goal in his first professional hockey game was a big thrill for Derek Haas. The fact that it was also the winning goal in the very first victory posted by the Calgary Cowboys was an even bigger thrill—especially considering that Haas was only a few months removed from playing beer league hockey in his hometown of Trail, British Columbia.

"I played all my minor hockey in Trail and then tried out for the Junior 'A' Kamloops Chiefs in the Western Canada Hockey League when I was 16," Haas recalled in a telephone interview from France, where he coaches a First Division team. "Kamloops sent me to the Calgary Centennials, but they said I was too young. They wanted me to play somewhere up in northern B.C., but I decided to go back to Trail. The next year I went to Blairmore in the Alberta Junior League and scored over 100 points. I figured I'd have a good shot at making the Centennials, but I wound up being drafted by the Victoria Cougars.

"I had a good rookie year in Victoria and made the all-star team, but the next season I had a lot of personal problems. I couldn't get along with the coach and everything seemed to be going wrong. I just wanted to forget hockey because it wasn't fun anymore. So I packed up my stuff, went back to Trail and played with a bunch of my friends in a commercial league. It was great. We played late at night, then all the guys would sit around and have a couple of beers. No pressure. Not too serious.

"In 1975 both the Philadelphia Flyers and the Calgary Cowboys invited me to their tryout camps, even though I hadn't been drafted. I thought I'd have a better shot at making the WHA, so I went to Calgary, had a good camp and started the season playing on a line with Danny Lawson and Larry Israelson. We got our first win by beating Houston 4–3 in an exhibition game, and I scored the winning goal. It was quite an experience, especially playing against Gordie Howe. I remember he elbowed Ron Chipperfield in the mouth right at the opening face-off. He did it so quick that nobody really saw it happen, and then all of a sudden Chipper had blood all over him. After I saw that, it really hit me that I wasn't playing beer league hockey anymore."

Haas remained with the Cowboys until Christmas, then was sent to the minors for more experience. He was recalled by Calgary for the playoffs but only saw action in one game. His entire WHA career consisted of 30 games, in which he scored five goals and 14 points. He kicked around the minors for another couple of years, then went to Europe. He played one season in Switzerland and another in Germany before moving to France in the summer of 1982. Six years later, along with ex-WHA star Paulin Bordeleau, Haas was a key member of the French national team that competed at the 1988 Winter Olympics in Calgary.

"That was the biggest thrill of my career—playing in the Olympics in the city where I first played pro hockey," he says. "It was kind of strange being a Canadian playing in the Olympics for another country, but it was an experience I wouldn't trade for anything."

Haas retired from playing in 1995, but remains active in French hockey as a highly respected First Division coach.

"The game is growing over here and more kids are getting involved every year, but they've still got a long way to go before it achieves widespread popularity. The key is getting some of the games televised. If we can do that on a regular basis, I think hockey will really catch on all over France."

THE PHEENOM

It was the summer of 1974. The New York Yankees were four months away from making Catfish Hunter the wealthiest player in baseball history, and Muhammad Ali was preparing to challenge George Foreman in one of the greatest heavyweight title fights of all time.

In the midst of those two epoch-shaping benchmarks in sports history, Pat Price, an 18-year-old pheenom from Nelson, British Columbia, briefly became one of the highest-paid team sport athletes on the planet when he inked a five-year personal services contact with Vancouver Blazers' owner Jimmy Pattison.

Pattison, always the gambler, was prepared to invest $1.3 million plus a $200,000 signing bonus in Price, a hulking defenseman who notched 27 goals and 95 points with the junior Saskatoon Blades in 1973–74. It was more money than the Winnipeg Jets were paying Bobby Hull. It was considerably more cash than the Boston Bruins were paying Bobby Orr. But after the initial furor over the contract died down, it didn't take long before Price and the Blazers were looking to go their separate ways.

Price got a sports car as a signing bonus, but shortly afterwards he totalled it. Selected to try out for Team Canada '74, he was injured at training camp and was out of shape when the season opened. A Vancouver columnist labelled Price "the biggest bust since Dolly Parton," while his teammates dubbed him "Pat the Brat." Unable to trade the high-priced teenager, the Blazers let it be known they wouldn't stop him from jumping to the NHL. After 69 games and 34 points in a Vancouver uniform, Price bolted to the New York Islanders the following season.

Today, more than two decades removed from the hype and hoopla that heralded his baptism into the big leagues, Price is uniquely qualified to comment on the money woes plaguing big-league hockey.

"The fact that I was one of the very first players to get the big dollars and experienced first-hand the ramifications of that contract perhaps gives me a different perspective on what's now happening to hockey," says the personable Price.

"Like every other fan, I was extremely disappointed with the whole situation a few years ago. The NHL was positioned to take a large-market share of pro sports in North America, but all the good that a guy like Wayne Gretzky had done in popularizing the game south of the border pretty much went down the toilet. The strike or lockout or whatever you choose to call it did a lot of damage to the game ... damage that might take years to rectify."

Price is no stranger to the machinations of NHL collective bargaining. After four years with the Islanders, he later played for Edmonton, Quebec, Pittsburgh, the New York Rangers and Minnesota. He retired in 1988, with 261 points in 726 NHL games.

"Too many players have bought into the agent's line that it's somehow their right to play in the National Hockey League. That's bull. To be the one percent of one percent fortunate enough to play at that level is a privilege, not a right. The agents only reinforced the players' greed by convincing them that they're bigger than the game.

"When I came up we played out of love for the game and loyalty to the club and our teammates. We thought of ourselves as being very, very lucky. Today that kind of attitude is ancient history."

Price says his own experiences in the pro ranks put him in a unique position to see both sides.

"I was once a young kid out to prove myself to the world, and I stumbled a few times along the way ... especially in the WHA," he says. "But I never use myself as an example. The kids I coach today are walking their own path in life, so there are no failures so long as they adhere to the standards set by the team. Failure only occurs if I as their coach fail to bring out the best in each individual.

"I use my own career and experiences as sort of a reference gauge, not as an example. I try to treat these young kids the way I always wanted to be treated and, above all, to instill in them a sense of pride in how special it is to play hockey at an elite level."

THESE GUYS COULD BE TRAVEL AGENTS
Brent Ashton had nothing on Ron Ward, Gary MacGregor and Barry Legge.

Ashton, the most traded player in NHL history, showcased his talents for nine different teams in 14 seasons, starting in 1979–80 when he was drafted by the Vancouver Canucks. Ward, MacGregor and Legge all played for seven different WHA teams—an accomplishment that takes on even greater significance when you consider the league itself only lasted seven years.

Ward was the WHA's second-highest scorer in 1972–73 when he notched 118 points for the New York Raiders. During the off-season he was shipped to Vancouver as compensation for Andre Lacroix, who joined the New York franchise after refusing to go to Vancouver with the rest of the transplanted Philadelphia Blazers. Two weeks later Ward was traded to the Los Angeles Sharks for George Gardner and Ralph MacSweyn. The Sharks subsequently swapped him to Cleveland for Bill Young and Ted Hodgson, and he was an important cog in the Crusaders' attack for the next two seasons. When the Cleveland franchise transferred to Minnesota in 1976, Ward went along. He was signed by the Winnipeg Jets when the Fighting Saints folded, and the Jets traded him to Calgary, along with Veli Pekka Ketola, for Danny Lawson and Mike Ford in March, 1977. Ward retired three months later.

MacGregor, the Chicago Cougars' number one pick in the 1974 amateur draft, played for the Denver Spurs and Ottawa Civics after the Cougars suspended operations, then moved on to Cleveland, New England, Indianapolis and Edmonton before retiring in 1978. Legge broke into the WHA with the Michigan Stags in 1975, then spent the next three seasons watching franchises disintegrate around him. He also saw action with the Baltimore Blades, Denver Spurs, Ottawa Civics, Cleveland Crusaders, Minnesota Fighting Saints and Cincinnati Stingers. After the merger he played 107 games in the NHL with Winnipeg and Quebec.

Andre Lacroix, the WHA's all-time leading scorer, had the distinction of playing for six different teams without ever officially being traded. Lacroix started out as a Philadelphia Blazer, then became a New York Golden Blade when he refused to move to Vancouver. He also toiled for the New Jersey Knights, San Diego Mariners, Houston Aeros and New England Whalers, and his contract was owned, briefly, by the Winnipeg Jets. Hugh Harris, Claude St. Sauveur, Paul Hoganson, Gary Veneruzzo and Larry Mavety also each played for six different clubs during their tenure in the WHA.